ŚRĪ CAITANYA-CARITĀMṚTA

BOOKS by
His Divine Grace A.C. Bhaktivedanta Swami Prabhupāda

Bhagavad-gītā As It Is
Śrīmad-Bhāgavatam, Cantos 1-5 (15 Vols.)
Śrī Caitanya-caritāmṛta (17 Vols.)
Teachings of Lord Caitanya
The Nectar of Devotion
Śrī Īśopaniṣad
Easy Journey to Other Planets
Kṛṣṇa Consciousness: The Topmost Yoga System
Kṛṣṇa, The Supreme Personality of Godhead (3 Vols.)
Transcendental Teachings of Prahlād Mahārāja
Kṛṣṇa, the Reservoir of Pleasure
The Perfection of Yoga
Beyond Birth and Death
On the Way to Kṛṣṇa
Rāja-vidyā: The King of Knowledge
Elevation to Kṛṣṇa Consciousness
Kṛṣṇa Consciousness: The Matchless Gift
Back to Godhead Magazine (Founder)

A complete catalogue is available upon request

International Society for Krishna Consciousness
3764 Watseka Avenue
Los Angeles, California 90034

All Glory to Śrī Guru and Gaurāṅga

Krshnadāsa Kaviraja, b. 1518 or 19.

ŚRĪ CAITANYA-CARITĀMṚTA

of Kṛṣṇadāsa Kavirāja Gosvāmī

Madhya-līlā
Volume Five

"The Pastimes of the Lord at Ratha-yātrā and the Guṇḍicā Temple"

with the original Bengali text, Roman transliterations, synonyms, translation and elaborate purports

by

HIS DIVINE GRACE

A.C. Bhaktivedanta Swami Prabhupāda

Founder-Ācārya of the International Society for Krishna Consciousness

THE BHAKTIVEDANTA BOOK TRUST
New York · Los Angeles · London · Bombay

Readers interested in the subject matter of this book
are invited by the International Society for Krishna Consciousness
to correspond with its Secretary.

International Society for Krishna Consciousness
3764 Watseka Avenue
Los Angeles, California 90034

Library of Congress Catalogue Card Number: 73-93206
International Standard Book Number: 0-912776-67-6

First printing, 1975: 20,000 copies

Printed in the United States of America

Contents

Introduction

Śrī Caitanya-caritāmṛta is the principal work on the life and teachings of Śrī Kṛṣṇa Caitanya. Śrī Caitanya is the pioneer of a great social and religious movement which began in India a little less than five hundred years ago and which has directly and indirectly influenced the subsequent course of religious and philosophical thinking not only in India but in the recent West as well.

Caitanya Mahāprabhu is regarded as a figure of great historical significance. However, our conventional method of historical analysis—that of seeing a man as a product of his times—fails here. Śrī Caitanya is a personality who transcends the limited scope of historical settings.

At a time when, in the West, man was directing his explorative spirit toward studying the structure of the physical universe and circumnavigating the world in search of new oceans and continents, Śrī Kṛṣṇa Caitanya, in the East, was inaugurating and masterminding a revolution directed inward, toward a scientific understanding of the highest knowledge of man's spiritual nature.

The chief historical sources for the life of Śrī Kṛṣṇa Caitanya are the *kaḍacās* (diaries) kept by Murāri Gupta and Svarūpa Dāmodara Gosvāmī. Murāri Gupta, a physician and close associate of Śrī Caitanya's, recorded extensive notes on the first twenty-four years of Śrī Caitanya's life, culminating in his initiation into the renounced order, *sannyāsa*. The events of the rest of Caitanya Mahāprabhu's forty-eight years are recorded in the diary of Svarūpa Dāmodora Gosvāmī, another of Caitanya Mahāprabhu's intimate associates.

Śrī Caitanya-caritāmṛta is divided into three sections called *līlās,* which literally means "pastimes"—*Ādi-līlā* (the early period), *Madhya-līlā* (the middle period) and *Antya-līlā* (the final period). The notes of Murāri Gupta form the basis of the *Ādi-līlā,* and Svarūpa Dāmodara's diary provides the details for the *Madhya-* and *Antya-līlās.*

The first twelve of the seventeen chapters of *Ādi-līlā* constitute the preface for the entire work. By referring to Vedic scriptural evidence, this preface establishes Śrī Caitanya as the *avatāra* (incarnation) of Kṛṣṇa (God) for the age of Kali—the current epoch, beginning five thousand years ago and characterized by materialism, hypocrisy and dissension. In these descriptions, Caitanya Mahāprabhu, who is identical with Lord Kṛṣṇa, descends to liberally grant pure love of God to the fallen souls of this degraded age by propagating *saṅkīrtana*—literally, "congregational glorification of God"—especially by organizing massive public chanting of the *mahā-mantra* (Great Chant for Deliverance). The esoteric purpose of Lord Caitanya's appearance in the world is revealed, his co-*avatāras* and principal devotees are described and his teachings are summarized. The remaining portion of *Ādi-līlā,* chapters thirteen through seventeen, briefly recounts his divine birth and his life until he accepted the renounced order. This includes his childhood miracles, schooling, marriage and early philosophical confrontations, as well as his organization of a widespread *saṅkīrtana* movement and his civil disobedience against the repression of the Mohammedan government.

The subject of *Madhya-līlā,* the longest of the three divisions, is a detailed narration of Lord Caitanya's extensive and eventful travels throughout India as a renounced mendicant, teacher, philosopher, spiritual preceptor and mystic. During this period of six years, Śrī Caitanya transmits his teachings to his principal disciples. He debates and converts many of the most renowned philosophers and theologians of his time, including Śaṅkarites, Buddhists and Muslims, and incorporates their many thousands of followers and disciples into his own burgeoning numbers. A dramatic account of Caitanya Mahāprabhu's miraculous activities at the giant Jagannātha Cart Festival in Orissa is also included in this section.

Antya-līlā concerns the last eighteen years of Śrī Caitanya's manifest presence, spent in semiseclusion near the famous Jagannātha temple at Jagannātha Purī in Orissa. During these final years, Śrī Caitanya drifted deeper and deeper into trances of spiritual ecstasy unparalleled in all of religious and literary history, Eastern or Western. Śrī Caitanya's perpetual and ever-increasing religious beatitude, graphically described in the eyewitness accounts of Svarūpa Dāmodara Gosvāmī, his constant companion during this period, clearly defy the investigative and descriptive abilities of modern psychologists and phenomenologists of religious experience.

The author of this great classic, Kṛṣṇadāsa Kavirāja Gosvāmī, born in the year 1507, was a disciple of Raghunātha dāsa Gosvāmī, a confidential follower of Caitanya Mahāprabhu. Raghunātha dāsa, a renowned ascetic saint, heard and memorized all the activities of Caitanya Mahāprabhu told to him by Svarūpa Dāmodara. After the passing away of Śrī Caitanya and Svarūpa Dāmodara, Raghunātha dāsa, unable to bear the pain of separation from these objects of his complete devotion, traveled to Vṛndāvana, intending to commit suicide by jumping from Govardhana Hill. In Vṛndāvana, however, he encountered Rūpa Gosvāmī and Sanātana Gosvāmī, the most confidential disciples of Caitanya Mahāprabhu. They convinced him to give up his plan of suicide and impelled him to reveal to them the spiritually inspiring events of Lord Caitanya's later life. Kṛṣṇadāsa Kavirāja Gosvāmī was also residing in Vṛndāvana at this time, and Raghunātha dāsa Gosvāmī endowed him with a full comprehension of the transcendental life of Śrī Caitanya.

By this time, several biographical works had already been written on the life of Śrī Caitanya by contemporary and near-contemporary scholars and devotees. These included *Śrī Caitanya-carita* by Murāri Gupta, *Caitanya-maṅgala* by Locana dāsa Ṭhākura and *Caitanya-bhāgavata.* This latter text, a work by Vṛndāvana dāsa Ṭhākura, who was then considered the principal authority on Śrī Caitanya's life, was highly revered. While composing his important work, Vṛndāvana dāsa, fearing that it would become too voluminous, avoided elaborately describing many of the events of Śrī Caitanya's life, particulary the later ones. Anxious to hear of these later pastimes, the devotees of Vṛndāvana requested Kṛṣṇadāsa Kavirāja Gosvāmī, whom they respected as a great saint, to compose a book to narrate these episodes in detail. Upon this request, and with the permission and blessings of the Madana-mohana Deity of Vṛndāvana, he began compiling *Śrī Caitanya-caritāmṛta,* which, due to its biographical excellence and thorough exposition of Lord Caitanya's profound philosophy and teachings, is regarded as the most significant of biographical works on Śrī Caitanya.

He commenced work on the text while in his late nineties and in failing health, as he vividly describes in the text itself: "I have now become too old and disturbed in invalidity. While writing, my hands tremble. I cannot remember anything, nor can I see or hear properly. Still I write, and this is a great wonder." That he nevertheless completed, under such debilitating conditions, the greatest literary gem of medieval India is surely one of the wonders of literary history.

This English translation and commentary is the work of His Divine Grace A. C. Bhaktivedanta Swami Prabhupāda, the world's most distinguished teacher of Indian religious and philosophical thought. His commentary is based upon two Bengali commentaries, one by his teacher Śrīla Bhaktisiddhānta Sarasvatī Gosvāmī, the eminent Vedic scholar who predicted, "The time will come when the people of the world will learn Bengali to read *Śrī Caitanya-caritāmṛta,*" and the other by Śrīla Bhaktisiddhānta's father, Bhaktivinoda Ṭhākura.

His Divine Grace A. C. Bhaktivedanta Swami Prabhupāda is himself a disciplic descendant of Śrī Caitanya Mahāprabhu, and he is the first scholar to execute systematic English translations of the major works of Śrī Caitanya's followers. His consummate Bengali and Sanskrit scholarship and intimate familiarity with the precepts of Śrī Kṛṣṇa Caitanya are a fitting combination that eminently qualifies him to present this important classic to the English-speaking world. The ease and clarity with which he expounds upon difficult philosophical concepts lures even a reader totally unfamiliar with Indian religious tradition into a genuine understanding and appreciation of this profound and monumental work.

The entire text, with commentary, presented in seventeen lavishly illustrated volumes by the Bhaktivedanta Book Trust, represents a contribution of major importance to the intellectual, cultural and spiritual life of contemporary man.

—The Publishers

His Divine Grace
A. C. Bhaktivedanta Swami Prabhupāda
Founder-Ācārya of the International Society for Krishna Consciousness

The Guṇḍicā temple, situated two miles northeast of the Jagannātha Purī temple, where Lord Jagannātha stays for one week at the time of the Ratha-yātrā festival.

The great annual Ratha-yātrā festival at Jagannātha Purī in Orissa, unchanged since the time of Śrī Caitanya Mahāprabhu.

The same Ratha-yātrā festival observed by Caitanya Mahāprabhu has been introduced to cities all over the Western world by His Divine Grace A. C. Bhaktivedanta Swami Prabhupāda, the founder-*ācārya* of the International Society for Krishna Consciousness.

One of the many gardens near the Guṇḍicā temple where Śrī Caitanya Mahāprabhu used to perform the pastimes of Vṛndāvana.

PLATE ONE

"One day, Lord Śrī Kṛṣṇa and His cowherd boys and flocks of animals were present on the pasturing grounds near Mathurā. At that time the cowherd boys, being a little hungry, requested food, and Lord Kṛṣṇa asked them to go to the *brāhmaṇas* who were engaged nearby in performing *yajña,* or sacrifice, and to get some food from that *yajña.* Being so ordered by the Lord, the cowherd boys went to the *brāhmaṇas* and asked them for food, but they were denied. After this, the cowherd boys begged food from the wives of the *brāhmaṇas.* All these wives were very much devoted to Lord Kṛṣṇa in spontaneous love, and as soon as they heard the request of the cowherd boys and understood that Kṛṣṇa wanted some food, they immediately left the place of sacrifice. They were very much chastised for this by their husbands, and they were ready to give up their lives. It is the nature of a pure devotee to sacrifice his life for the transcendental loving service of the Lord." (*pp.16-17*)

PLATE TWO

"After Śrī Caitanya Mahāprabhu and all the Vaiṣṇavas cleansed the temple for the second time, the Lord was very happy to see the cleansing work. While the temple was being swept, about a hundred men stood ready with filled waterpots, and they simply awaited the Lord's order to throw them. As soon as Śrī Caitanya Mahāprabhu called for water, all the men immediately brought the hundred waterpots, which were completely filled, and delivered them before the Lord. In this way, Śrī Caitanya Mahāprabhu first washed the main temple and then thoroughly washed the ceiling, the walls, the floor, the sitting place (*siṁhāsana*) and everything else within the room. Śrī Caitanya Mahāprabhu Himself and His devotees began to throw water onto the ceiling. When this water fell, it washed the walls and the floor. Then Śrī Caitanya Mahāprabhu began to wash the sitting place of Lord Jagannātha with His own hands, and all the devotees began to bring water to the Lord. In this way all the rooms were cleansed with a hundred waterpots. After the rooms had been cleansed, the minds of the devotees were as clean as the rooms. When the temple was cleansed, it was purified, cool and pleasing, just as if the Lord's own mind had appeared." (*pp.46-51*)

PLATE THREE

"The very strongly built *dayitās* (carriers of the Jagannātha Deity) were as powerful as drunken elephants. They manually carried Lord Jagannātha from the throne to the car. While carrying the Deity of Lord Jagannātha, some of the *dayitās* took hold of the shoulders of the Lord, and some caught His lotus feet. The Lord Jagannātha Deity was bound at the waist by a strong, thick rope made of silk. From two sides the *dayitās* caught hold of this rope and raised the Deity. While the Lord was being carried from the throne to the car, King Pratāparudra personally engaged in the Lord's service by cleansing the road with a broom that had a golden handle. The King sprinkled the road with sandalwood-scented water. Although he was the owner of the royal throne, he engaged in menial service for the sake of Lord Jagannātha. Although the King was the most exalted, respectable person, still he accepted menial service for the Lord; he therefore became a suitable candidate for receiving the Lord's mercy." (*pp.117-121*)

PLATE FOUR

"When Śrī Caitanya Mahāprabhu danced and jumped high, roaring like thunder and moving in a circle like a wheel, He appeared like a circling firebrand. Wherever Śrī Caitanya Mahāprabhu stepped while dancing, the whole earth, with its hills and seas, appeared to tilt. When Caitanya Mahāprabhu danced, He displayed various, blissful transcendental changes in His body. Sometimes He appeared as though stunned. Sometimes the hairs of His body stood on end. Sometimes He perspired, cried, trembled and changed color, and sometimes He exhibited symptoms of helplessness, pride, exuberance and humility. Nityānanda Prabhu would stretch out His two hands and try to catch the Lord when He was running here and there. Advaita Ācārya would walk behind the Lord and loudly chant, 'Hari bol! Hari bol!' again and again." (*pp.155-157*)

PLATE FIVE

"All the inhabitants of Vṛndāvana-dhāma—My mother, father, cowherd boy friends and everything else—are like My life and soul. And among all the inhabitants of Vṛndāvana, the *gopīs* are My very life and soul." (*p.193*)

PLATE SIX

"Mahārāja Pratāparudra was so humble that with folded hands he first took permission from all the devotees. Then, with great courage, he fell down and touched the lotus feet of the Lord. Śrī Caitanya Mahāprabhu was lying on the ground with His eyes closed in ecstatic love and emotion, and the King very expertly began to massage His legs. The King began to recite verses about the *rāsa-līlā* from *Śrīmad-Bhāgavatam.* He recited the chapter beginning with the words *'jayati te 'dhikam.'* When Śrī Caitanya Mahāprabhu heard these verses, He was pleased beyond limits, and He said again and again, 'Go on reciting, go on reciting.' " (*pp.226-228*)

PLATE SEVEN

"Outside the garden, when it was time to pull Jagannātha's car, all the workers called *gauḍas* tried to pull it, but it would not move forward. When the *gauḍas* saw that they could not budge the car, they abandoned the attempt. Then the King arrived in great anxiety, and he was accompanied by his officers and friends. The King then arranged for big wrestlers to try to pull the car, and even the King himself joined in, but the car could not be moved. Becoming even more eager to move the car, the King had very strong elephants brought forth and harnessed to it. The strong elephants pulled with all their strength, but still the car remained at a standstill, not budging an inch. As soon as Śrī Caitanya Mahāprabhu heard this news, He went there with all His personal associates. They then stood there and watched the elephants try to pull the car. The elephants, being beaten by the elephant goad, were crying, but still the car would not move. The assembled people cried out, 'Alas!' At that time, Śrī Caitanya Mahāprabhu let all the elephants go free and placed the car's ropes in the hands of His own men. Śrī Caitanya Mahāprabhu then went to the back of the car and began to push with His head. It was then that the car began to move and ramble along, making a rattling sound. Indeed, the car began to move automatically, and the devotees simply carried the rope in their hands. Since it was moving effortlessly, they did not need to pull it. When the car moved forward, everyone began to chant with great pleasure, 'All glories! All glories!' and 'All glories to Lord Jagannātha!' No one could hear anything else." *(pp.248-252)*

PLATE EIGHT

"There were many gardens near the Guṇḍicā temple, and Śrī Caitanya Mahāprabhu and His devotees used to perform the pastimes of Vṛndāvana in each of them. In the lake named Indradyumna, He sported in the water. The Lord personally splashed all the devotees with water, and the devotees, surrounding Him on all sides, also splashed the Lord. Sometimes two would pair off to fight in the water. One would emerge victorious and the other defeated, and the Lord would watch all this fun. The first sporting took place between Advaita Ācārya and Nityānanda Prabhu, who threw water upon one another. Advaita Ācārya was defeated, and He later began to rebuke Nityānanda Prabhu, calling Him bad names. Svarūpa Dāmodara and Vidyānidhi also threw water upon one another, and Murāri Gupta and Vāsudeva Datta also sported in that way. Another duel took place between Śrīvāsa Ṭhākura and Gadādhara Paṇḍita, and yet another between Rāghava Paṇḍita and Vakreśvara Paṇḍita. Thus they all engaged in throwing water. Indeed, Sārvabhauma Bhaṭṭācārya engaged in water sports with Śrī Rāmānanda Rāya, and they both lost their gravity and became like children." (*pp.260-263*)

PLATE NINE

"Whenever Śrīmatī Rādhārāṇī leaves Her house, She is always well-dressed and attractive. It is Her womanly nature to attract Śrī Kṛṣṇa's attention, and upon seeing Her so attractively dressed, Śrī Kṛṣṇa desires to touch Her body. The Lord then finds some fault in Her and prohibits Her from going to a river crossing and stops Her from picking flowers. Such are the pastimes between Śrīmatī Rādhārāṇī and Śrī Kṛṣṇa. Being a cowherd girl, Śrīmatī Rādhārāṇī regularly carries a container of milk and often goes to sell it on the other side of the Yamunā. To cross the river, She has to pay the boatman, and the spot where the boatman collects his fares is called the *dāna-ghāṭi*. Lord Śrī Kṛṣṇa stops Her from going, telling Her, 'First You have to pay the fee; then You will be allowed to go.' This pastime is called *dāna-keli-līlā*." (*pp.305-306*)

CHAPTER 12

The Cleansing of the Guṇḍicā Temple

In his *Amṛta-pravāha-bhāṣya,* Śrīla Bhaktivinoda Ṭhākura summarizes this chapter as follows. The King of Orissa, Mahārāja Pratāparudra, tried his best to see Lord Caitanya Mahāprabhu. Śrīla Nityānanda Prabhu and the other devotees informed the Lord about the King's desire, but Śrī Caitanya Mahāprabhu would not agree to see him. At that time Śrī Nityānanda Prabhu devised a plan, and He sent a piece of the Lord's outward garment to the King. The next day, when Rāmānanda Rāya again entreated Śrī Caitanya Mahāprabhu to see the King, the Lord, denying the request, asked Rāmānanda Rāya to bring the King's son before Him. The prince visited the Lord dressed like a Vaiṣṇava, and this awakened remembrance of Kṛṣṇa. Thus Śrī Caitanya Mahāprabhu delivered the son of Mahārāja Pratāparudra.

After this, Śrī Caitanya Mahāprabhu washed the Guṇḍicā house before the Ratha-yātrā took place. He then took His bath at Indradyumna and partook of *prasāda* in the garden nearby. While Śrī Caitanya Mahāprabhu washed the temple of Guṇḍicā, some Gauḍīya Vaiṣṇava washed the lotus feet of the Lord and drank the water. This incident is very significant, for it awoke within the devotee ecstatic love. Then again, the son of Advaita Prabhu named Gopāla fainted during *kīrtana,* and when he did not come to his senses, Śrī Caitanya Mahāprabhu favored him by awakening him. There was also some humorous talk between Nityānanda Prabhu and Advaita Prabhu during *prasāda.* Advaita Prabhu said that Nityānanda Prabhu was unknown to anyone and that it was not the duty of a householder *brāhmaṇa* to accept dinner with a person unknown in society. In answer to this humorous statement, Śrī Nityānanda Prabhu replied that Advaita Ācārya was a monist and that one could not know how his mind could be turned by eating with such an impersonal monist. The conversation of these two *prabhus*—Nityānanda Prabhu and Advaita Prabhu—carried a deep meaning that only an intelligent man can understand. After all the Vaiṣṇavas finished their luncheon, Svarūpa Dāmodara and others took their *prasāda* within the room. Śrī Caitanya Mahāprabhu took great pleasure when He saw the Jagannātha Deity after the Deity's retirement. At that time He was accompanied by all the devotees, and all of them were very pleased.

TEXT 1

শ্রীগুণ্ডিচা-মন্দিরমাত্মবৃন্দৈঃ
সংমার্জয়ন্ ক্ষালনতঃ স গৌরঃ ।

স্বচিত্তবচ্ছীতলমুজ্জ্বলঞ্চ
কৃষ্ণোপবেশৌপয়িকং চকার ॥ ১ ॥

śrī-guṇḍicā-mandiram ātma-vṛndaiḥ
sammārjayan kṣālanataḥ sa gauraḥ
sva-cittavac chītalam ujjvalaṁ ca
kṛṣṇopaveśaupayikaṁ cakāra

SYNONYMS

śrī-guṇḍicā—known as Guṇḍicā; *mandiram*—the temple; *ātma-vṛndaiḥ*—with His associates; *sammārjayan*—washing; *kṣālanataḥ*—by cleansing; *saḥ*—that; *gauraḥ*—Śrī Caitanya Mahāprabhu; *sva-citta-vat*—like His own heart; *śītalam*—cool and calm; *ujjvalam*—bright and clean; *ca*—and; *kṛṣṇa*—of Lord Śrī Kṛṣṇa; *upaveśa*—for the sitting; *aupayikam*—befitting; *cakāra*—made.

TRANSLATION

Śrī Caitanya Mahāprabhu washed and cleansed the Guṇḍicā temple with His devotees and associates. In this way He made the temple as cool and bright as His own heart, and thus He made the place befitting for Lord Śrī Kṛṣṇa to sit.

TEXT 2

জয় জয় গৌরচন্দ্র জয় নিত্যানন্দ ।
জয়াদ্বৈতচন্দ্র জয় গৌরভক্তবৃন্দ ॥ ২ ॥

jaya jaya gauracandra jaya nityānanda
jayādvaita-candra jaya gaura-bhakta-vṛnda

SYNONYMS

jaya jaya—all glories; *gauracandra*—to Gauracandra, Lord Śrī Caitanya Mahāprabhu; *jaya*—all glories; *nityānanda*—to Nityānanda Prabhu; *jaya*—all glories; *advaita-candra*—to Advaita Prabhu; *jaya*—all glories; *gaura-bhakta-vṛnda*—to the devotees of Lord Caitanya Mahāprabhu.

TRANSLATION

All glories to Gauracandra! All glories to Nityānanda! All glories to Advaita-candra! And all glories to the devotees of Lord Śrī Caitanya Mahāprabhu!

TEXT 3

জয় জয় শ্রীবাসাদি গৌরভক্তগণ ।
শক্তি দেহ,—করি যেন চৈতন্য বর্ণন ॥ ৩॥

jaya jaya śrīvāsādi gaura-bhakta-gaṇa
śakti deha,——kari yena caitanya varṇana

SYNONYMS

jaya jaya—all glories; *śrīvāsa-ādi*—headed by Śrīvāsa Ṭhākura; *gaura-bhakta-gaṇa*—to the devotees of Śrī Caitanya Mahāprabhu; *śakti deha*—please give me power; *kari yena*—so that I may do; *caitanya*—of Śrī Caitanya Mahāprabhu; *varṇana*—description.

TRANSLATION

All glories to the devotees of Lord Śrī Caitanya Mahāprabhu, headed by Śrīvāsa Ṭhākura! I beg their power so that I can properly describe Śrī Caitanya Mahāprabhu.

TEXT 4

পূর্বে দক্ষিণ হৈতে প্রভু যবে আইলা।
তাঁরে মিলিতে গজপতি উৎকণ্ঠিত হৈলা ॥ ৪ ॥

pūrve dakṣiṇa haite prabhu yabe āilā
tāṅre milite gajapati utkaṇṭhita hailā

SYNONYMS

pūrve—formerly; *dakṣiṇa haite*—from South India; *prabhu*—Lord Śrī Caitanya Mahāprabhu; *yabe*—when; *āilā*—returned; *tāṅre*—Him; *milite*—to meet; *gajapati*—the King of Orissa; *utkaṇṭhita*—full of anxieties; *hailā*—became.

TRANSLATION

When Śrī Caitanya Mahāprabhu returned from His South Indian tour, Mahārāja Pratāparudra, the King of Orissa, became very anxious to meet Him.

TEXT 5

কটক হৈতে পত্রী দিল সার্বভৌম-ঠাঞি।
প্রভুর আজ্ঞা হয় যদি, দেখিবারে যাই ॥ ৫ ॥

kaṭaka haite patrī dila sārvabhauma-ṭhāñi
prabhura ājñā haya yadi, dekhibāre yāi

SYNONYMS

kaṭaka haite—from Kaṭaka, the capital of Orissa; *patrī*—a letter; *dila*—sent; *sārvabhauma*—of Sārvabhauma Bhaṭṭācārya; *ṭhāñi*—to the place; *prabhura*—of Śrī

Caitanya Mahāprabhu; *ājñā*—order; *haya*—there is; *yadi*—if; *dekhibāre yāi*—I can go and see.

TRANSLATION

The King sent a letter from his capital, Kaṭaka, to Sārvabhauma Bhaṭṭācārya, entreating him to obtain the Lord's permission so that he could go and see Him.

TEXT 6

ভট্টাচার্য লিখিল,—প্রভুর আজ্ঞা না হৈল ।
পুনরপি রাজা তাঁরে পত্রী পাঠাইল ॥ ৬ ॥

bhaṭṭācārya likhila,——prabhura ājñā nā haila
punarapi rājā tāṅre patrī pāṭhāila

SYNONYMS

bhaṭṭācārya likhila—Sārvabhauma Bhaṭṭācārya replied; *prabhura*—of Śrī Caitanya Mahāprabhu; *ājñā*—order; *nā*—not; *haila*—there is; *punarapi*—again; *rājā*—the King; *tāṅre*—unto him; *patrī*—a letter; *pāṭhāila*—dispatched.

TRANSLATION

Replying to the King's letter, Bhaṭṭācārya wrote that Śrī Caitanya Mahāprabhu had not given His permission. After this, the King wrote him another letter.

TEXT 7

প্রভুর নিকটে আছে যত ভক্তগণ ।
মোর লাগি' তাঁ-সবারে করিহ নিবেদন ॥ ৭ ॥

prabhura nikaṭe āche yata bhakta-gaṇa
mora lāgi' tāṅ-sabāre kariha nivedana

SYNONYMS

prabhura nikaṭe—in the place of Śrī Caitanya Mahāprabhu; *āche*—there are; *yata*—all; *bhakta-gaṇa*—devotees; *mora lāgi'*—for me; *tāṅ-sabāre*—unto all of them; *kariha*—please submit; *nivedana*—petition.

TRANSLATION

In this letter the King requested Sārvabhauma Bhaṭṭācārya, "Please appeal to all the devotees associated with Śrī Caitanya Mahāprabhu and submit this petition to them on my behalf.

TEXT 8

সেই সব দয়ালু মোরে হঞা সদয়।
মোর লাগি' প্রভুপদে করিবে বিনয়॥ ৮॥

sei saba dayālu more hañā sadaya
mora lāgi' prabhu-pade karibe vinaya

SYNONYMS

sei saba—all of them; *dayālu*—merciful; *more*—unto me; *hañā*—becoming; *sa-daya*—favorably disposed; *mora lāgi'*—for me; *prabhu-pade*—at the lotus feet of Lord Śrī Caitanya Mahāprabhu; *karibe*—will do; *vinaya*—humble submission.

TRANSLATION

"If all the devotees associated with the Lord are favorably disposed toward me, they can submit my petition at the lotus feet of the Lord.

TEXT 9

তাঁ-সবার প্রসাদে মিলে শ্রীপ্রভুর পায়।
প্রভুকৃপা বিনা মোর রাজ্য নাহি ভায়॥ ৯॥

tāṅ-sabāra prasāde mile śrī-prabhura pāya
prabhu-kṛpā vinā mora rājya nāhi bhāya

SYNONYMS

tāṅ-sabāra prasāde—by the mercy of all of them; *mile*—one gets; *śrī-prabhura pāya*—the lotus feet of Śrī Caitanya Mahāprabhu; *prabhu-kṛpā*—the mercy of the Lord; *vinā*—without; *mora*—my; *rājya*—kingdom; *nāhi*—does not; *bhāya*—appeal to me.

TRANSLATION

"By the mercy of all the devotees, one can attain the shelter of the lotus feet of the Lord. Without His mercy, my kingdom does not appeal to me.

TEXT 10

যদি মোরে কৃপা না করিবে গৌরহরি।
রাজ্য ছাড়ি' যোগী হই' হইব ভিখারী॥ ১০॥

yadi more kṛpā nā karibe gaurahari
rājya chāḍi' yogī ha-i' ha-iba bhikhārī

SYNONYMS

yadi—if; *more*—unto me; *kṛpā*—mercy; *nā*—not; *karibe*—will do; *gaurahari*—Śrī Caitanya Mahāprabhu; *rājya chāḍi'*—giving up the kingdom; *yogī*—mendicant; *ha-i'*—becoming; *ha-iba*—I shall become; *bhikhārī*—a beggar.

TRANSLATION

"If Gaurahari, Lord Śrī Caitanya Mahāprabhu, will not show mercy to me, I shall give up my kingdom, become a mendicant and beg from door to door."

TEXT 11

ভট্টাচার্য পত্রী দেখি' চিন্তিত হঞা ।
ভক্তগণ-পাশ গেলা সেই পত্রী লঞা ॥ ১১ ॥

bhaṭṭācārya patrī dekhi' cintita hañā
bhakta-gaṇa-pāśa gelā sei patrī lañā

SYNONYMS

bhaṭṭācārya—Sārvabhauma Bhaṭṭācārya; *patrī*—the letter; *dekhi'*—seeing; *cintita hañā*—becoming very anxious; *bhakta-gaṇa*—all the devotees; *pāśa*—near; *gelā*—went; *sei*—that; *patrī*—letter; *lañā*—taking.

TRANSLATION

When Bhaṭṭācārya received this letter, he became very anxious. He then took the letter and went to the devotees of the Lord.

TEXT 12

সবারে মিলিয়া কহিল রাজ-বিবরণ ।
পিছে সেই পত্রী সবারে করাইল দরশন ॥ ১২ ॥

sabāre miliyā kahila rāja-vivaraṇa
piche sei patrī sabāre karāila daraśana

SYNONYMS

sabāre—everyone; *miliyā*—meeting; *kahila*—said; *rāja-vivaraṇa*—description of the King's desire; *piche*—later; *sei patrī*—that letter; *sabāre*—unto everyone; *karāila daraśana*—showed.

TRANSLATION

Sārvabhauma Bhaṭṭācārya met with all the devotees and described the King's wishes. Then he presented the letter to all of them for inspection.

TEXT 13

পত্রী দেখি' সবার মনে হইল বিস্ময়।
প্রভুপদে গজপতির এত ভক্তি হয়!! ১৩ ॥

patrī dekhi' sabāra mane ha-ila vismaya
prabhu-pade gajapatira eta bhakti haya!!

SYNONYMS

patrī—the letter; *dekhi'*—seeing; *sabāra*—of everyone; *mane*—in the mind; *ha-ila*—there was; *vismaya*—astonishment; *prabhu-pade*—unto the lotus feet of Śrī Caitanya Mahāprabhu; *gajapatira*—of the King of Orissa; *eta*—so much; *bhakti*—devotion; *haya*—there is.

TRANSLATION

Upon reading the letter, everyone was astonished to see that King Pratāparudra had so much devotion for the lotus feet of Śrī Caitanya Mahāprabhu.

TEXT 14

সবে কহে,—প্রভু তাঁরে কভু না মিলিবে।
আমি-সব কহি যদি, দুঃখ সে মানিবে ॥ ১৪ ॥

sabe kahe,——prabhu tāṅre kabhu nā milibe
āmi-saba kahi yadi, duḥkha se mānibe

SYNONYMS

sabe kahe—everyone said; *prabhu*—Lord Śrī Caitanya Mahāprabhu; *tāṅre*—unto him; *kabhu*—at any time; *nā*—not; *milibe*—would see; *āmi-saba*—all of us; *kahi*—say; *yadi*—if; *duḥkha*—unhappiness; *se*—Lord Śrī Caitanya Mahāprabhu; *mānibe*—will feel.

TRANSLATION

The devotees gave their opinion and said, "The Lord would never meet the King, and if we requested Him to do so, the Lord would surely feel very unhappy."

TEXT 15

সার্বভৌম কহে,—সবে চল' একবার ।
মিলিতে না কহিব, কহিব রাজ-ব্যবহার ॥ ১৫ ॥

sārvabhauma kahe,——sabe cala' eka-bāra
milite nā kahiba, kahiba rāja-vyavahāra

SYNONYMS

sārvabhauma kahe—Sārvabhauma Bhaṭṭācārya said; *sabe cala'*—let all of us go; *eka-bāra*—once; *milite*—to meet; *nā kahiba*—we shall not request; *kahiba*—we shall simply describe; *rāja-vyavahāra*—the behavior of the King.

TRANSLATION

Sārvabhauma Bhaṭṭācārya then said, "We shall go once again to the Lord, but we shall not request Him to meet the King. Rather, we shall simply describe the good behavior of the King."

TEXT 16

এত বলি' সবে গেলা মহাপ্রভুর স্থানে ।
কহিতে উন্মুখ সবে, না কহে বচনে ॥ ১৬ ॥

eta bali' sabe gelā mahāprabhura sthāne
kahite unmukha sabe, nā kahe vacane

SYNONYMS

eta bali'—deciding like this; *sabe*—all of them; *gelā*—went; *mahāprabhura*—of Śrī Caitanya Mahāprabhu; *sthāne*—to the place; *kahite*—to speak; *unmukha*—ready; *sabe*—all; *nā*—do not; *kahe*—say; *vacane*—any word.

TRANSLATION

Having thus reached a decision, they all went to the place of Śrī Caitanya Mahāprabhu. There, although ready to speak, they could not even utter a word.

TEXT 17

প্রভু কহে,—কি কহিতে সবার আগমন ।
দেখিয়ে কহিতে চাহ,—না কহ, কি কারণ ? ১৭ ॥

prabhu kahe,——ki kahite sabāra āgamana
dekhiye kahite cāha,——nā kaha, ki kāraṇa?

SYNONYMS

prabhu kahe—Śrī Caitanya Mahāprabhu said; *ki*—what; *kahite*—to speak; *sabāra*—of all of you; *āgamana*—there is the presence here; *dekhiye*—I see; *kahite cāha*—you want to speak; *nā kaha*—but do not speak; *ki kāraṇa*—what is the reason.

TRANSLATION

After they arrived at Śrī Caitanya Mahāprabhu's place, the Lord, seeing them, said, "What have you all come here to say? I see that you want to say something, but you do not speak. What is the reason?"

TEXT 18

নিত্যানন্দ কহে,—তোমায় চাহি নিবেদিতে ।
না কহিলে রহিতে নারি, কহিতে ভয় চিত্তে ॥ ১৮ ॥

nityānanda kahe,——tomāya cāhi nivedite
nā kahile rahite nāri, kahite bhaya citte

SYNONYMS

nityānanda kahe—Lord Nityānanda said; *tomāya*—unto You; *cāhi*—we want; *nivedite*—to submit; *nā kahile*—if we do not speak; *rahite nāri*—we cannot stay; *kahite*—but to speak; *bhaya citte*—we are very fearful.

TRANSLATION

Nityānanda Prabhu then said, "We want to tell You something. Although we cannot stay without speaking, we are still very much afraid to speak.

TEXT 19

যোগ্যাযোগ্য তোমায় সব চাহি নিবেদিতে ।
তোমা না মিলিলে রাজা চাহে যোগী হৈতে ॥ ১৯ ॥

yogyāyogya tomāya saba cāhi nivedite
tomā nā milile rājā cāhe yogī haite

SYNONYMS

yogya—befitting; *ayogya*—not befitting; *tomāya*—unto You; *saba*—we all; *cāhi*—want; *nivedite*—to submit; *tomā*—You; *nā milile*—if he does not meet; *rājā*—the King; *cāhe*—wants; *yogī haite*—to become a mendicant.

TRANSLATION

"We want to submit before You something that may or may not be befitting. The matter is this: unless he sees You, the King of Orissa will become a mendicant."

TEXT 20

কাণে মুদ্রা লই' মুঞি হইব ভিখারী ।
রাজ্যভোগ নহে চিত্তে বিনা গৌরহরি ॥ ২০ ॥

kāṇe mudrā la-i' muñi ha-iba bhikhārī
rājya-bhoga nahe citte vinā gaurahari

SYNONYMS

kāṇe mudrā—a kind of earring; *la-i'*—taking; *muñi*—I; *ha-iba*—shall become; *bhikhārī*—a beggar; *rājya-bhoga*—enjoyment of the kingdom; *nahe*—not; *citte*—in the mind; *vinā*—without; *gaurahari*—Śrī Caitanya Mahāprabhu.

TRANSLATION

Nityānanda Prabhu continued, "The King has decided to become a mendicant and accept the sign of a mendicant by wearing an ivory earring. He does not want to enjoy his kingdom without seeing the lotus feet of Śrī Caitanya Mahāprabhu."

PURPORT

In India there is still a class of professional mendicants who are very much like the gypsies of Western countries. They know some magical art and mystical processes, and their business is to beg from door to door, sometimes pleading and sometimes threatening. Such mendicants are sometimes called *yogīs* and sometimes *kāṇaphāṭā yogīs.* The word *kāṇaphāṭā* refers to one who has put a hole in his ear to wear an earring made of ivory. Mahārāja Pratāparudra was so depressed by not getting to see Śrī Caitanya Mahāprabhu that he decided to become such a *yogī.* Ordinary men think that a *yogī* must have an ivory earring in his ear, but this is not the sign of a real *yogī.* Mahārāja Pratāparudra also thought that to become a mendicant *yogī,* one must wear such an earring.

TEXT 21

দেখিব সে মুখচন্দ্র নয়ন ভরিয়া।
ধরিব সে পাদপদ্ম হৃদয়ে তুলিয়া ॥ ২১ ॥

dekhiba se mukha-candra nayana bhariyā
dhariba se pāda-padma hṛdaye tuliyā

SYNONYMS

dekhiba—I shall see; *se*—that; *mukha-candra*—moonlike face; *nayana bhariyā*—to the fulfillment of the eyes; *dhariba*—I shall catch; *se*—those; *pāda-padma*—lotus feet; *hṛdaye*—on my heart; *tuliyā*—raising.

TRANSLATION

Nityānanda Prabhu continued, "The King also expressed his desire to see the moonlike face of Śrī Caitanya Mahāprabhu to his eye's full satisfaction. He would like to raise the lotus feet of the Lord to his heart."

TEXT 22

যদ্যপি শুনিয়া প্রভুর কোমল হয় মন।
তথাপি বাহিরে কহে নিষ্ঠুর বচন ॥ ২২ ॥

yadyapi śuniyā prabhura komala haya mana
tathāpi bāhire kahe niṣṭhura vacana

SYNONYMS

yadyapi—although; *śuniyā*—hearing; *prabhura*—of Lord Śrī Caitanya Mahāprabhu; *komala*—softened; *haya*—becomes; *mana*—mind; *tathāpi*—still; *bāhire*—externally; *kahe*—He says; *niṣṭhura vacana*—hard words.

TRANSLATION

Hearing all these statements, Śrī Caitanya Mahāprabhu's mind was certainly softened, but externally He wished to speak some harsh words.

TEXT 23

তোমা-সবার ইচ্ছা,—এই আমারে লঞা।
রাজাকে মিলহ ইহঁ কটকেতে গিয়া ॥ ২৩ ॥

tomā-sabāra icchā,——ei āmāre lañā
rājāke milaha ihaṅ kaṭakete giyā

SYNONYMS

tomā-sabāra—of all of you; *icchā*—the desire; *ei*—is; *āmāre lañā*—taking Me; *rājāke*—the King; *milaha*—meet; *ihaṅ*—here; *kaṭakete giyā*—by going to Kaṭaka.

TRANSLATION

Śrī Caitanya Mahāprabhu said, "I can understand that you all desire to take Me to Kaṭaka to see the King."

PURPORT

Śrī Caitanya Mahāprabhu is naturally the reservoir of all kindness, and as soon as He heard the statement made by the King, His heart immediately softened. Thus the Lord was ready to go see the King even at Kaṭaka. He did not even consider allowing the King to come from Kaṭaka to Jagannātha Purī to see Him. It is significant that Śrī Caitanya Mahāprabhu was so kind that He was ready to go see the King at Kaṭaka. Apparently it was never expected that the King wanted to see the Lord at His place, but by way of being externally harsh, the Lord indicated that if all the devotees so desired, He would go to Kaṭaka to see the King.

TEXT 24

পরমার্থ থাকুক —লোকে করিবে নিন্দন ।
লোকে রহু —দামোদর করিবে ভর্ৎসন ॥ ২৪ ॥

paramārtha thākuka——loke karibe nindana
loke rahu——dāmodara karibe bhartsana

SYNONYMS

parama-artha thākuka—what to speak of spiritual advancement; *loke*—people in general; *karibe nindana*—will blaspheme; *loke rahu*—what to speak of people in general; *dāmodara*—Dāmodara Paṇḍita; *karibe*—will do; *bhartsana*—chastisement.

TRANSLATION

Śrī Caitanya Mahāprabhu continued, "What to speak of spiritual advancement—all the people will blaspheme Me. And what to speak of all the people—Dāmodara would chastise Me.

TEXT 25

তোমা-সবার আজ্ঞায় আমি না মিলি রাজারে ।
দামোদর কহে যবে, মিলি তবে তাঁরে ॥ ২৫ ॥

tomā-sabāra ājñāya āmi nā mili rājāre
dāmodara kahe yabe, mili tabe tāṅre

SYNONYMS

tomā-sabāra—of all of you; *ājñāya*—by the order; *āmi*—I; *nā*—not; *mili*—shall meet; *rājāre*—the King; *dāmodara*—Dāmodara Paṇḍita; *kahe*—says; *yabe*—when; *mili*—I shall meet; *tabe*—then; *tāṅre*—him.

TRANSLATION

"I shall not meet the King at the request of all the devotees, but I shall do so if Dāmodara will give his permission."

PURPORT

From the spiritual point of view, a *sannyāsī* is strictly forbidden to see materialistic people, especially a king who is always engaged in counting pounds, shillings and pence. Indeed, the meeting between a *sannyāsī* and a king is always considered abominable. A *sannyāsī* is always subjected to public criticism, and a small fault on his part is taken seriously by the public. People actually expect a *sannyāsī* to preach and not take part in any social or political matters. If a *sannyāsī* is subject to public criticism, his preaching will not be fruitful. Śrī Caitanya Mahāprabhu specifically wanted to avoid such criticism so that His preaching work would not be hampered. It so happened that while the Lord was talking to His disciples at that time, the devotee Dāmodara Paṇḍita was present. This Dāmodara Paṇḍita was a very faithful devotee and a staunch lover of Śrī Caitanya Mahāprabhu. Whenever there was anything that might touch or taint the character of the Lord, Dāmodara Paṇḍita would immediately point it out, not even considering the exalted position of the Lord. It is sometimes said that fools rush in where angels dare not, and Śrī Caitanya Mahāprabhu wanted to point out Dāmodara Paṇḍita's foolishness in coming forward to criticize the Lord. Thus the Lord indirectly hinted that if Dāmodara Paṇḍita would give Him permission, He would go to see the King. There was deep meaning in this statement, for it is a warning that Dāmodara should not dare criticize the Lord any more, for it was not befitting his position as a devotee. Śrī Caitanya Mahāprabhu was considered the guide and spiritual master of all the devotees living with Him. Dāmodara Paṇḍita was one of them, and the Lord rendered Dāmodara Paṇḍita a special favor by warning him to avoid criticizing Him any further. A devotee or a disciple should never attempt to criticize the Lord or His representative, the spiritual master.

TEXT 26

দামোদর কহে,—তুমি স্বতন্ত্র ঈশ্বর ।
কর্তব্যাকর্তব্য সব তোমার গোচর ॥ ২৬ ॥

dāmodara kahe,——tumi svatantra īśvara
kartavyākartavya saba tomāra gocara

SYNONYMS

dāmodara kahe—Paṇḍita Dāmodara said; *tumi*—You; *svatantra*—fully independent; *īśvara*—the Supreme Personality of Godhead; *kartavya*—duty which is permissible; *akartavya*—duty which is not permissible; *saba*—all; *tomāra*—of You; *gocara*—within knowledge.

TRANSLATION

Dāmodara immediately replied, "My Lord, You are the fully independent Supreme Personality of Godhead. Since everything is known to You, You know what is permissible and what is not permissible.

TEXT 27

আমি কোন্ ক্ষুদ্রজীব, তোমাকে বিধি দিব ?
আপনি মিলিবে তাঁরে, তাহাও দেখিব ॥ ২৭ ॥

āmi kon kṣudra-jīva, tomāke vidhi diba?
āpani milibe tāṅre, tāhāo dekhiba

SYNONYMS

āmi kon—I am just some; *kṣudra-jīva*—insignificant living entity; *tomāke*—unto You; *vidhi*—injunction; *diba*—I shall give; *āpani*—You; *milibe*—will meet; *tāṅre*—the King; *tāhāo dekhiba*—I shall see it.

TRANSLATION

"I am merely an insignificant jīva, so what power do I have to give directions to You? By Your own personal choice You will meet with the King. I shall see it.

TEXT 28

রাজা তোমারে স্নেহ করে, তুমি—স্নেহবশ ।
তাঁর স্নেহে করাবে তাঁরে তোমার পরশ ॥ ২৮ ॥

rājā tomāre sneha kare, tumi——sneha-vaśa
tāṅra snehe karābe tāṅre tomāra paraśa

SYNONYMS

rājā—the King; *tomāre*—You; *sneha kare*—loves; *tumi*—You; *sneha-vaśa*—controlled by love and affection; *tāṅra*—his; *snehe*—by love; *karābe*—will do; *tāṅre*—unto him; *tomāra*—Your; *paraśa*—touching.

TRANSLATION

"The King is very much attached to You, and You are feeling affection and love toward him. Thus I can understand that by virtue of the King's affection for You, You will touch him.

TEXT 29

যদ্যপি ঈশ্বর তুমি পরম স্বতন্ত্র ।
তথাপি স্বভাবে হও প্রেম-পরতন্ত্র ॥ ২৯ ॥

yadyapi īśvara tumi parama svatantra
tathāpi svabhāve hao prema-paratantra

SYNONYMS

yadyapi—although; *īśvara*—the Supreme Personality of Godhead; *tumi*—You; *parama*—supremely; *svatantra*—independent; *tathāpi*—still; *sva-bhāve*—by Your nature; *hao*—You become; *prema-paratantra*—subordinate to love.

TRANSLATION

"Although You are the Supreme Personality of Godhead and are completely independent, still You are dependent on the love and affection of Your devotees. That is Your nature."

TEXT 30

নিত্যানন্দ কহে—ঐছে হয় কোন্ জন ।
যে তোমারে কহে, 'কর রাজদরশন' ॥ ৩০ ॥

nityānanda kahe——aiche haya kon jana
ye tomāre kahe, 'kara rāja-daraśana'

SYNONYMS

nityānanda kahe—Nityānanda Prabhu said; *aiche*—such; *haya*—there is; *kon jana*—any person; *ye*—who; *tomāre*—unto You; *kahe*—orders; *kara*—do; *rāja-daraśana*—meeting the King.

TRANSLATION

Nityānanda Prabhu then said, "Who is there in the three worlds who can ask You to see the King?

TEXT 31

কিন্তু অনুরাগী লোকের স্বভাব এক হয়।
ইষ্ট না পাইলে নিজ প্রাণ সে ছাড়য় ॥ ৩১ ॥

kintu anurāgī lokera svabhāva eka haya
iṣṭa nā pāile nija prāṇa se chāḍaya

SYNONYMS

kintu—still; *anurāgī*—affectionate; *lokera*—of the people; *sva-bhāva*—nature; *eka*—one; *haya*—there is; *iṣṭa*—desirable; *nā pāile*—without getting; *nija*—own; *prāṇa*—life; *se*—he; *chāḍaya*—gives up.

TRANSLATION

"Still, isn't it the nature of an attached man to give up his life if he does not attain his desired object?

TEXT 32

যাজ্ঞিক-ব্রাহ্মণী সব তাহাতে প্রমাণ।
কৃষ্ণ লাগি' পতি-আগে ছাড়িলেক প্রাণ ॥ ৩২ ॥

yājñika-brāhmaṇī saba tāhāte pramāṇa
kṛṣṇa lāgi' pati-āge chāḍileka prāṇa

SYNONYMS

yājñika-brāhmaṇī—the wives of the *brāhmaṇas* who were engaged in performing great sacrifices; *saba*—all; *tāhāte*—in that connection; *pramāṇa*—evidence; *kṛṣṇa lāgi'*—for the matter of Kṛṣṇa; *pati-āge*—in front of their husbands; *chāḍileka prāṇa*—gave up their lives.

TRANSLATION

"For instance, some of the wives of the brāhmaṇas who were performing sacrifices gave up their lives in the presence of their husbands for the sake of Kṛṣṇa."

PURPORT

This refers to the day Lord Śrī Kṛṣṇa and His cowherd boys and flocks of animals were present on the pasturing grounds near Mathurā. At that time the cowherd boys, being a little hungry, requested food, and Lord Kṛṣṇa asked them to go to the *brāhmaṇas* who were engaged nearby in performing *yajña*, or sacrifice, and to get some food from that *yajña*. Being so ordered by the Lord, all the cowherd boys went to the *brāhmaṇas* and asked them for food, but they were denied. After this, the cowherd boys begged food from the wives of the *brāhmaṇas*. All these wives were very much devoted to Lord Kṛṣṇa in spontaneous love, and as soon as they heard the request of the cowherd boys and understood that Kṛṣṇa wanted some food, they immediately left the place of sacrifice. They were very much chastised for this by their husbands, and they were ready to give up their lives. It is the nature of a pure devotee to sacrifice his life for the transcendental loving service of the Lord.

TEXT 33

এক যুক্তি আছে, যদি কর অবধান ।
তুমি না মিলিলেহ তাঁরে, রহে তাঁর প্রাণ ॥ ৩৩ ॥

eka yukti āche, yadi kara avadhāna
tumi nā milileha tāṅre, rahe tāṅra prāṇa

SYNONYMS

eka yukti—one plan; *āche*—there is; *yadi*—if; *kara avadhāna*—You consider it; *tumi*—You; *nā milileha*—may not meet; *tāṅre*—with him; *rahe*—remains; *tāṅra*—his; *prāṇa*—life.

TRANSLATION

Nityānanda Prabhu then submitted one suggestion for the Lord's consideration. "There is a way," He suggested, "by which You need not meet the King but which would enable the King to continue living.

TEXT 34

এক বহির্বাস যদি দেহ' কৃপা করি' ।
তাহা পাঞা প্রাণ রাখে তোমার আশা ধরি' ॥ ৩৪ ॥

eka bahirvāsa yadi deha' kṛpā kari'
tāhā pāñā prāṇa rākhe tomāra āśā dhari'

SYNONYMS

eka bahirvāsa—one outward covering; *yadi*—if; *deha'*—You give; *kṛpā kari'*—by Your mercy; *tāhā pāñā*—getting that; *prāṇa rākhe*—he would live; *tomāra āśā dhari'*—hoping to meet You some time in the future.

TRANSLATION

"If You, out of Your mercy, send one of Your outward garments to the King, the King would live hoping to see You some time in the future."

PURPORT

Śrī Nityānanda Prabhu was thus very tactfully suggesting that Caitanya Mahāprabhu give a piece of His old clothing to the King. Even though the King was not fit to meet the Lord, the King would then be pacified by receiving such a cloth. The King was very much anxious to see the Lord, yet it was not possible for the Lord to see him. Just to resolve the situation, Nityānanda Prabhu suggested that the Lord send an old piece of clothing. Thus the King would understand that the Lord was showing mercy to him. The King would then not do anything drastic like giving up his life or becoming a mendicant.

TEXT 35

প্রভু কহে,—তুমি-সব পরম বিদ্বান্ ।
যেই ভাল হয়, সেই কর সমাধান ॥ ৩৫ ॥

prabhu kahe,——tumi-saba parama vidvān
yei bhāla haya, sei kara samādhāna

SYNONYMS

prabhu kahe—the Lord replied; *tumi-saba*—all of you; *parama vidvān*—greatly learned personalities; *yei*—whatever; *bhāla haya*—is right; *sei*—that; *kara samādhāna*—execute.

TRANSLATION

The Lord said, "Since you are all very learned personalities, whatever you decide I shall accept."

TEXT 36

তবে নিত্যানন্দ-গোসাঞি গোবিন্দের পাশ ।
মাগিয়া লইল প্রভুর এক বহির্বাস ॥ ৩৬ ॥

tabe nityānanda-gosāñi govindera pāśa
māgiyā la-ila prabhura eka bahirvāsa

SYNONYMS

tabe—at that time; *nityānanda-gosāñi*—Lord Nityānanda Prabhu; *govindera pāśa*—from Govinda, the personal servant of Śrī Caitanya Mahāprabhu; *māgiyā*—requesting; *la-ila*—took; *prabhura*—of the Lord; *eka*—one; *bahirvāsa*—outer garment.

TRANSLATION

Lord Nityānanda Prabhu then obtained an external garment used by the Lord by requesting it from Govinda.

TEXT 37

সেই বহির্বাস সার্বভৌমপাশ দিল ।
সার্বভৌম সেই বস্ত্র রাজারে পাঠা'ল ॥ ৩৭ ॥

sei bahirvāsa sārvabhauma-pāśa dila
sārvabhauma sei vastra rājāre pāṭhā'la

SYNONYMS

sei—that; *bahirvāsa*—garment; *sārvabhauma-pāśa*—in the care of Sārvabhauma Bhaṭṭācārya; *dila*—delivered; *sārvabhauma*—Sārvabhauma Bhaṭṭācārya; *sei*—that; *vastra*—cloth; *rājāre*—unto the King; *pāṭhā'la*—sent.

TRANSLATION

Thus Nityānanda Prabhu delivered the old cloth to the care of Sārvabhauma Bhaṭṭācārya, and Sārvabhauma Bhaṭṭācārya sent it to the King.

TEXT 38

বস্ত্র পাঞা রাজার হৈল আনন্দিত মন ।
প্রভুরূপ করি' করে বস্ত্রের পূজন ॥ ৩৮ ॥

vastra pāñā rājāra haila ānandita mana
prabhu-rūpa kari' kare vastrera pūjana

SYNONYMS

vastra pāñā—getting that cloth; *rājāra*—of the King; *haila*—there was; *ānandita mana*—very happy mind; *prabhu-rūpa kari'*—accepting as Śrī Caitanya Mahāprabhu Himself; *kare*—executes; *vastrera*—of the cloth; *pūjana*—worship.

TRANSLATION

When the King received the old cloth, he began to worship it exactly as he would worship the Lord personally.

PURPORT

This is also the conclusion of the Vedic injunctions. Since the Supreme Personality of Godhead is the Absolute Truth, everything in relation to Him is also on the same platform. The King had great affection for Śrī Caitanya Mahāprabhu, and although he did not see the Lord, he had nonetheless already attained the conclusion of devotional service. Immediately upon receiving the cloth from Sārvabhauma Bhaṭṭācārya, the King began to worship it, accepting it as Śrī Caitanya Mahāprabhu. The Lord's clothing, bedding, slippers and everything required as an ordinary necessity are all transformations of Śeṣa, Viṣṇu, the expansion of Śrī Baladeva. Thus the cloth and other paraphernalia of the Supreme Personality of Godhead are but other forms of the Supreme Personality of Godhead. Everything connected to the Lord is worshipable. Śrī Caitanya Mahāprabhu instructs us that just as Kṛṣṇa is worshipable, Kṛṣṇa's place, Vṛndāvana, is also worshipable. And as Vṛndāvana is worshipable, similarly the paraphernalia in Vṛndāvana—the trees, roads, river, everything—is worshipable. A pure devotee thus sings, *jaya jaya vṛndāvana-vāsī yata jana:* "All glories to the residents of Vṛndāvana." If a devotee has a staunch devotional attitude, all these conclusions will be awakened or revealed within the heart.

yasya deve parā bhaktir
yathā deve tathā gurau
tasyaite kathitā hy arthāḥ
prakāśante mahātmanaḥ

"Only unto those great souls who have implicit faith in both the Lord and the spiritual master are all the imports of Vedic knowledge automatically revealed." (*Śvetāśvatara Upaniṣad,* 6.23)

Thus following in the footsteps of Mahārāja Pratāparudra and other devotees, we should learn to worship everything belonging to the Supreme Personality of Godhead. This is referred to by Lord Śiva as *tadīyānām*. In the *Padma Purāṇa* it is said:

ārādhanānāṁ sarveṣāṁ
viṣṇor ārādhanaṁ param
tasmāt parataraṁ devi
tadīyānāṁ samarcanam

"O Devī, the most exalted system of worship is the worship of Lord Viṣṇu. Greater than that is the worship of *tadīya,* or anything belonging to Viṣṇu." Śrī Viṣṇu is *sac-cid-ānanda-vigraha.* Similarly, the most confidential servant of Kṛṣṇa, the spiritual master, and all devotees of Viṣṇu are *tadīya.* The *sac-cid-ānanda-vigraha, guru,* Vaiṣṇavas, and things used by them must be considered *tadīya* and without a doubt worshipable by all living beings.

TEXT 39

রামানন্দ রায় যবে 'দক্ষিণ' হৈতে আইলা ।
প্রভুসঙ্গে রহিতে রাজাকে নিবেদিলা ॥ ৩৯ ॥

rāmānanda rāya yabe 'dakṣiṇa' haite āilā
prabhu-saṅge rahite rājāke nivedilā

SYNONYMS

rāmānanda rāya—Rāmānanda Rāya; *yabe*—when; *dakṣiṇa*—South India; *haite*—from; *āilā*—returned; *prabhu-saṅge*—with Lord Śrī Caitanya Mahāprabhu; *rahite*—to stay; *rājāke*—unto the King; *nivedilā*—requested.

TRANSLATION

After returning from his service in South India, Rāmānanda Rāya requested the King to allow him to remain with Śrī Caitanya Mahāprabhu.

TEXT 40

তবে রাজা সন্তোষে তাঁহারে আজ্ঞা দিলা ।
আপনি মিলন লাগি' সাধিতে লাগিলা ॥ ৪০ ॥

tabe rājā santoṣe tāṅhāre ājñā dilā
āpani milana lāgi' sādhite lāgilā

SYNONYMS

tabe—at that time; *rājā*—the King; *santoṣe*—in great satisfaction; *tāṅhāre*—unto Rāmānanda Rāya; *ājñā dilā*—gave the order; *āpani*—personally; *milana lāgi'*—to meet; *sādhite lāgilā*—began to solicit.

TRANSLATION

When Rāmānanda Rāya requested the King to allow him to stay with the Lord, the King immediately gave him permission with great satisfaction. As for

the King himself, he began to solicit Rāmānanda Rāya to make a meeting arrangement.

TEXT 41

মহাপ্রভু মহাকৃপা করেন তোমারে ।
মোরে মিলিবারে অবশ্য সাধিবে তাঁহারে ॥ ৪১ ॥

mahāprabhu mahā-kṛpā karena tomāre
more milibāre avaśya sādhibe tāṅhāre

SYNONYMS

mahāprabhu—Śrī Caitanya Mahāprabhu; *mahā-kṛpā*—great mercy; *karena*—does; *tomāre*—unto you; *more*—me; *milibāre*—for meeting; *avaśya*—certainly; *sādhibe*—you must solicit; *tāṅhāre*—Him.

TRANSLATION

The King told Rāmānanda Rāya, "Śrī Caitanya Mahāprabhu is very, very merciful to you. Therefore please solicit my meeting with Him without fail."

TEXT 42

একসঙ্গে দুই জন ক্ষেত্রে যবে আইলা ।
রামানন্দ রায় তবে প্রভুরে মিলিলা ॥ ৪২ ॥

eka-saṅge dui jana kṣetre yabe āilā
rāmānanda rāya tabe prabhure mililā

SYNONYMS

eka-saṅge—together; *dui jana*—these two persons; *kṣetre*—at Jagannātha-kṣetra (Jagannātha Purī); *yabe*—when; *āilā*—came back; *rāmānanda rāya*—Rāmānanda Rāya; *tabe*—at that time; *prabhure*—Śrī Caitanya Mahāprabhu; *mililā*—met.

TRANSLATION

The King and Rāmānanda Rāya returned together to Jagannātha-kṣetra [Purī], and Śrī Rāmānanda Rāya met Śrī Caitanya Mahāprabhu.

TEXT 43

প্রভুপদে প্রেমভক্তি জানাইল রাজার ।
প্রসঙ্গ পাঞা ঐছে কহে বারবার ॥ ৪৩ ॥

prabhu-pade prema-bhakti jānāila rājāra
prasaṅga pāñā aiche kahe bāra-bāra

SYNONYMS

prabhu-pade—unto the lotus feet of the Lord; *prema-bhakti*—ecstatic love; *jānāila*—informed; *rājāra*—of the King; *prasaṅga*—discussion; *pāñā*—getting; *aiche*—thus; *kahe*—says; *bāra-bāra*—again and again.

TRANSLATION

At that time, Rāmānanda Rāya informed Śrī Caitanya Mahāprabhu about the ecstatic love of the King. Indeed, as soon as there was some opportunity, he repeatedly informed the Lord about the King.

TEXT 44

রাজমন্ত্রী রামানন্দ—ব্যবহারে নিপুণ ।
রাজপ্রীতি কহি' দ্রবাইল প্রভুর মন ॥ ৪৪ ॥

rāja-mantrī rāmānanda——vyavahāre nipuṇa
rāja-prīti kahi' dravāila prabhura mana

SYNONYMS

rāja-mantrī—diplomatic minister; *rāmānanda*—Śrī Rāmānanda Rāya; *vyavahāre*—in general behavior; *nipuṇa*—very expert; *rāja-prīti*—the love of the King for Śrī Caitanya Mahāprabhu; *kahi'*—describing; *dravāila*—softened; *prabhura*—of Lord Śrī Caitanya Mahāprabhu; *mana*—the mind.

TRANSLATION

Śrī Rāmānanda Rāya was indeed a diplomatic minister for the King. His general behavior was very expert, and simply by describing the King's love for Śrī Caitanya Mahāprabhu, he gradually softened the Lord's mind.

PURPORT

A diplomat in the material world knows how to deal with people, especially in political affairs. Some of the great devotees of the Lord—like Rāmānanda Rāya, Raghunātha dāsa Gosvāmī, Sanātana Gosvāmī and Rūpa Gosvāmī—were government officers and had a background of very opulent householder life. Consequently they knew how to deal with people. In many instances we have seen the diplomacy of Rūpa Gosvāmī, Raghunātha dāsa Gosvāmī and Rāmānanda Rāya employed in the service of the Lord. When Raghunātha dāsa Gosvāmī's father and uncle were to be arrested by government officials, Raghunātha dāsa Gosvāmī hid them and personally met the government officers and settled the affair diplomatically. This is but one instance. Similarly, Sanātana Gosvāmī, after resigning his ministership, was thrown in jail, and he bribed the attendant of the jail so he could leave the clutches of the Nawab and live with Śrī Caitanya Mahāprabhu. Now we see Rāmānanda Rāya, a most confidential devotee of the Lord, diplomatically soften the heart of Śrī Caitanya Mahāprabhu, despite the fact that the Lord definitely decided not to meet the King. The diplomacy of Rāmānanda Rāya and entreaties of Sārvabhauma Bhaṭṭācārya and all the other great devotees succeeded. The conclusion is that diplomacy used for the service of the Lord is a form of devotional service.

TEXT 45

উৎকণ্ঠাতে প্রতাপরুদ্র নারে রহিবারে ।
রামানন্দ সাধিলেন প্রভুরে মিলিবারে ॥ ৪৫ ॥

utkaṇṭhāte pratāparudra nāre rahibāre
rāmānanda sādhilena prabhure milibāre

SYNONYMS

utkaṇṭhāte—in great anxiety; *pratāparudra*—King Pratāparudra; *nāre rahibāre*—could not stay; *rāmānanda*—Śrī Rāmānanda Rāya; *sādhilena*—solicited; *prabhure*—unto Śrī Caitanya Mahāprabhu; *milibāre*—to meet.

TRANSLATION

Mahārāja Pratāparudra, in great anxiety, could not endure not seeing the Lord; therefore Śrī Rāmānanda Rāya, by his diplomacy, arranged a meeting with the Lord for the King.

TEXT 46

রামানন্দ প্রভু-পায় কৈল নিবেদন ।
একবার প্রতাপরুদ্রে দেখাহ চরণ ॥ ৪৬ ॥

rāmānanda prabhu-pāya kaila nivedana
eka-bāra pratāparudre dekhāha caraṇa

SYNONYMS

rāmānanda—Rāmānanda; *prabhu-pāya*—at the lotus feet of Śrī Caitanya Mahāprabhu; *kaila*—did; *nivedana*—submission; *eka-bāra*—once only; *pratāparudre*—unto Mahārāja Pratāparudra; *dekhāha*—show; *caraṇa*—Your lotus feet.

TRANSLATION

Śrī Rāmānanda Rāya frankly requested Śrī Caitanya Mahāprabhu, "Please show Your lotus feet to the King at least once."

TEXT 47

প্রভু কহে,—রামানন্দ, কহ বিচারিয়া।
রাজাকে মিলিতে যুয়ায় সন্ন্যাসী হঞা ? ৪৭ ॥

prabhu kahe,——rāmānanda, kaha vicāriyā
rājāke milite yuyāya sannyāsī hañā?

SYNONYMS

prabhu kahe—Śrī Caitanya Mahāprabhu said; *rāmānanda*—My dear Rāmānanda; *kaha*—please ask Me; *vicāriyā*—after due consideration; *rājāke*—the King; *milite*—to meet; *yuyāya*—is it befitting; *sannyāsī*—in the renounced order of life; *hañā*—being.

TRANSLATION

Śrī Caitanya Mahāprabhu replied, "My dear Rāmānanda, you should make this request after duly considering whether it is befitting for a sannyāsī to meet a king.

TEXT 48

রাজার মিলনে ভিক্ষুকের দুই লোক নাশ।
পরলোক রহু, লোকে করে উপহাস ॥ ৪৮ ॥

rājāra milane bhikṣukera dui loka nāśa
paraloka rahu, loke kare upahāsa

SYNONYMS

rājāra milane—by meeting with a king; *bhikṣukera*—of the mendicant; *dui loka*—in two worlds; *nāśa*—destruction; *para-loka*—spiritual world; *rahu*—let alone; *loke*—in this material world; *kare*—do; *upahāsa*—joking.

TRANSLATION

"If a mendicant meets a king, this world and the next world are both destroyed for the mendicant. Indeed, what is there to say of the next world? In this world, people will joke if a sannyāsī meets a king."

TEXT 49

রামানন্দ কহে,—তুমি ঈশ্বর স্বতন্ত্র ।
কারে তোমার ভয়, তুমি নহ পরতন্ত্র ॥ ৪৯ ॥

rāmānanda kahe,——tumi īśvara svatantra
kāre tomāra bhaya, tumi naha paratantra

SYNONYMS

rāmānanda kahe—Rāmānanda said; *tumi*—You; *īśvara*—the Supreme Lord; *svatantra*—independent; *kāre tomāra bhaya*—why should You be afraid of anyone; *tumi naha*—You are not; *para-tantra*—dependent.

TRANSLATION

Rāmānanda Rāya replied, "My Lord, You are the supreme independent personality. You have nothing to fear from anyone because You are not dependent on anyone."

TEXT 50

প্রভু কহে,—আমি মনুষ্য আশ্রমে সন্ন্যাসী ।
কায়মনোবাক্যে ব্যবহারে ভয় বাসি ॥ ৫০ ॥

prabhu kahe,——āmi manuṣya āśrame sannyāsī
kāya-mano-vākye vyavahāre bhaya vāsi

SYNONYMS

prabhu kahe—the Lord said; *āmi manuṣya*—I am a human being; *āśrame*—in the social order; *sannyāsī*—a renounced person; *kāya-manaḥ-vākye*—with My body, mind and words; *vyavahāre*—in general dealings; *bhaya*—fear; *vāsi*—I do.

TRANSLATION

When Rāmānanda Rāya addressed Śrī Caitanya Mahāprabhu as the Supreme Personality of Godhead, Caitanya Mahāprabhu objected, saying, "I am not the Supreme Personality of Godhead but an ordinary human being. Therefore I must fear public opinion in three ways—with My body, mind and words.

TEXT 51

শুক্লবস্ত্রে মসি-বিন্দু যৈছে না লুকায় ।
সন্ন্যাসীর অল্প ছিদ্র সর্বলোকে গায় ॥ ৫১ ॥

śukla-vastre masi-bindu yaiche nā lukāya
sannyāsīra alpa chidra sarva-loke gāya

SYNONYMS

śukla-vastre—on white cloth; *masi-bindu*—a spot of ink; *yaiche*—as much as; *nā*—does not; *lukāya*—become hidden; *sannyāsīra*—of a *sannyāsī*; *alpa*—a very little; *chidra*—fault; *sarva-loke*—the general public; *gāya*—advertise.

TRANSLATION

"As soon as the general public finds a little fault in the behavior of a sannyāsī, they advertise it like wildfire. A black spot of ink cannot be hidden on a white cloth. It is always very prominent."

TEXT 52

রায় কহে,—কত পাপীর করিয়াছ অব্যাহতি ।
ঈশ্বর-সেবক তোমার ভক্ত গজপতি ॥ ৫২ ॥

rāya kahe,——kata pāpīra kariyācha avyāhati
īśvara-sevaka tomāra bhakta gajapati

SYNONYMS

rāya kahe—Rāmānanda Rāya replied; *kata pāpīra*—of numberless sinful persons; *kariyācha*—You have done; *avyāhati*—deliverance; *īśvara-sevaka*—a servitor of the Lord; *tomāra*—Your; *bhakta*—devotee; *gajapati*—the King.

TRANSLATION

Rāmānanda Rāya replied, "My dear Lord, You have delivered so many sinful people. This King Pratāparudra, the King of Orissa, is actually a servitor of the Lord and Your devotee."

TEXT 53

প্রভু কহে,—পূর্ণ যৈছে দুগ্ধের কলস ।
সুরাবিন্দু-পাতে কেহ না করে পরশ ॥ ৫৩ ॥

prabhu kahe,——pūrṇa yaiche dugdhera kalasa
surā-bindu-pāte keha nā kare paraśa

SYNONYMS

prabhu kahe—the Lord replied; *pūrṇa*—completely filled; *yaiche*—just as; *dugdhera*—of milk; *kalasa*—container; *surā-bindu-pāte*—with simply a drop of liquor; *keha*—anyone; *nā kare*—does not; *paraśa*—touch.

TRANSLATION

Śrī Caitanya Mahāprabhu then said, "There may be much milk in a big pot, but if it is contaminated by a drop of liquor, it is untouchable.

TEXT 54

যদ্যপি প্রতাপরুদ্র—সর্বগুণবান্ ।
তাঁহারে মলিন কৈল এক 'রাজা'-নাম ॥ ৫৪ ॥

yadyapi pratāparudra——sarva-guṇavān
tāṅhāre malina kaila eka 'rājā'-nāma

SYNONYMS

yadyapi—although; *pratāparudra*—the King; *sarva-guṇa-vān*—qualified in every respect; *tāṅhāre*—unto him; *malina kaila*—makes impure; *eka*—one; *rājā-nāma*—the name "king."

TRANSLATION

"The King certainly possesses all good qualities, but simply by taking up the name 'king,' he has infected everything.

TEXT 55

তথাপি তোমার যদি মহাগ্রহ হয় ।
তবে আনি' মিলাহ তুমি তাঁহার তনয় ॥ ৫৫ ॥

tathāpi tomāra yadi mahāgraha haya
tabe āni' milāha tumi tāṅhāra tanaya

SYNONYMS

tathāpi—still; *tomāra*—your; *yadi*—if; *mahā-āgraha*—great eagerness; *haya*—there is; *tabe*—then; *āni'*—bringing; *milāha*—cause to meet; *tumi*—you; *tāṅhāra*—his; *tanaya*—son.

TRANSLATION

"But if you are still very eager for the King to meet with Me, please first bring his son to meet Me.

TEXT 56

"আত্মা বৈ জায়তে পুত্রঃ"—এই শাস্ত্রবাণী ।
পুত্রের মিলনে যেন মিলিবে আপনি ॥ ৫৬ ॥

"ātmā vai jāyate putraḥ"——ei śāstra-vāṇī
putrera milane yena milibe āpani

SYNONYMS

ātmā vai jāyate putraḥ—his self appears as the son; *ei*—this; *śāstra-vāṇī*—the indication of revealed scriptures; *putrera milane*—by meeting the son; *yena*—as if; *milibe*—he will meet; *āpani*—personally.

TRANSLATION

"It is indicated in the revealed scriptures that the son represents the father; therefore the son's meeting with Me would be just as good as the King's meeting with Me."

PURPORT

In *Śrīmad-Bhāgavatam* (10.78.36) it is said: *ātmā vai putra utpanna iti vedānuśāsanam.* The *Vedas* enjoin that one is born as his own son. The son is non-different from the father, and this is admitted in every revealed scripture. In Christian theology it is believed that Christ, the son of God, is also God. Both of them are identical.

TEXT 57

তবে রায় যাই' সব রাজারে কহিলা ।
প্রভুর আজ্ঞায় তাঁর পুত্র লঞা আইলা ॥ ৫৭ ॥

tabe rāya yāi' saba rājāre kahilā
prabhura ājñāya tāṅra putra lañā āilā

SYNONYMS

tabe—thereafter; *rāya*—Rāmānanda Rāya; *yāi'*—going; *saba*—everything; *rājāre*—unto the King; *kahilā*—described; *prabhura ājñāya*—under the order of the Lord; *tāṅra putra*—his son; *lañā āilā*—he brought with him.

TRANSLATION

Rāmānanda Rāya then went to inform the King about his talks with Śrī Caitanya Mahāprabhu, and, following the Lord's orders, brought the King's son to see Him.

TEXT 58

সুন্দর, রাজার পুত্র—শ্যামল-বরণ ।
কিশোর বয়স, দীর্ঘ কমলনয়ন ॥ ৫৮ ॥

sundara, rājāra putra——śyāmala-varaṇa
kiśora vayasa, dīrgha kamala-nayana

SYNONYMS

sundara—beautiful; *rājāra putra*—the son of the King; *śyāmala-varaṇa*—blackish complexion; *kiśora vayasa*—the age just before youth; *dīrgha*—long; *kamala-nayana*—lotus eyes.

TRANSLATION

The prince, just entering upon his youth, was very beautiful. He was blackish in complexion and had large lotus eyes.

TEXT 59

পীতাম্বর, ধরে অঙ্গে রত্ন-আভরণ ।
শ্রীকৃষ্ণ-স্মরণে তেঁহ হৈলা 'উদ্দীপন' ॥ ৫৯ ॥

pītāmbara, dhare aṅge ratna-ābharaṇa
śrī-kṛṣṇa-smaraṇe teṅha hailā 'uddīpana'

SYNONYMS

pīta-ambara—dressed in yellow cloth; *dhare*—carries; *aṅge*—on the body; *ratna-ābharaṇa*—ornaments of jewels; *śrī-kṛṣṇa-smaraṇe*—for remembering Śrī Kṛṣṇa; *teṅha*—he; *hailā*—was; *uddīpana*—stimulation.

TRANSLATION

The prince was dressed in yellow cloth, and there were jeweled ornaments decorating his body. Therefore anyone who saw him would remember Lord Kṛṣṇa.

TEXT 60

তাঁরে দেখি, মহাপ্রভুর কৃষ্ণস্মৃতি হৈল ।
প্রেমাবেশে তাঁরে মিলি' কহিতে লাগিল ॥ ৬০ ॥

tāṅre dekhi, mahāprabhura kṛṣṇa-smṛti haila
premāveśe tāṅre mili' kahite lāgila

SYNONYMS

tāṅre dekhi—seeing him; *mahāprabhura*—of Lord Śrī Caitanya Mahāprabhu; *kṛṣṇa-smṛti*—remembrance of Kṛṣṇa; *haila*—there was; *prema-āveśe*—in ecstatic love; *tāṅre*—him; *mili'*—meeting; *kahite lāgila*—began to say.

TRANSLATION

Seeing the boy, Śrī Caitanya Mahāprabhu immediately remembered Kṛṣṇa. Meeting the boy in ecstatic love, the Lord began to speak.

TEXT 61

এই—মহাভাগবত, যাঁহার দর্শনে।
ব্রজেন্দ্রনন্দন-স্মৃতি হয় সর্বজনে ॥ ৬১ ॥

ei——mahā-bhāgavata, yāṅhāra darśane
vrajendra-nandana-smṛti haya sarva-jane

SYNONYMS

ei—here is; *mahā-bhāgavata*—a first-class devotee; *yāṅhāra darśane*—by the sight of whom; *vrajendra-nandana*—of the son of the King of Vraja; *smṛti*—remembrance; *haya*—becomes; *sarva-jane*—for everyone.

TRANSLATION

"Here is a great devotee," Śrī Caitanya Mahāprabhu said. "Upon seeing him, everyone can remember the Supreme Personality of Godhead, Kṛṣṇa, son of Mahārāja Nanda."

PURPORT

In his *Anubhāṣya,* Śrīla Bhaktisiddhānta Sarasvatī Ṭhākura states that a materialist mistakenly accepts the body and mind as the source of material enjoyment. In other words, a materialist accepts the bodily conception of life. Śrī Caitanya Mahāprabhu did not regard the son of Mahārāja Pratāparudra with the idea that he was a materialist, being the son of a materialist. Nor did He consider Himself the enjoyer. Māyāvādī philosophers make a great mistake by assuming that the *sac-cid-ānanda-vigraha,* the transcendental form of the Lord, is like a material body. However, there is no material contamination in transcendence, nor is there any possibility of imagining a spirituality in matter. One cannot accept matter as spirit. As indicated by the technical words *bhauma ijya-dhīḥ* (*Bhāg.* 10.84.13), materialistic Māyāvādīs imagine the form of God in matter, although according to their imagination, God is unlimitedly formless. This is simply mental speculation. Even though Śrī Caitanya Mahāprabhu is the Supreme Personality of Godhead, He placed Himself in the position of a *gopī.* He also accepted the King's son directly as the son of Mahārāja Nanda, Vrajendra-nandana Hari. This is perfect vision according to the direction of the Vedic culture, as confirmed in *Śrīmad Bhagavad-gītā* (*paṇḍitāḥ sama-darśinaḥ*). Such acceptance of the Absolute Truth according to Vaiṣṇava philosophy is explained in both the *Muṇḍaka Upaniṣad* (3.2.3) and the *Kaṭha Upaniṣad* (1.2.23) in the following words:

nāyam ātmā pravacanena labhyo
na medhayā na bahunā śrutena
yam evaiṣa vṛṇute tena labhyas
tasyaiṣa ātmā vivṛṇute tanūṁ svām

"The Supreme Lord is not obtained by expert explanations, by vast intelligence, nor even by much hearing. He is obtained only by one whom He Himself chooses. To such a person He manifests His own form."

The living entity is entangled in material existence due to his lack of such spiritual vision. Śrīla Bhaktivinoda Ṭhākura has sung in his *Kalyāṇa-kalpataru: saṁsāre āsiyā prakṛti bhajiyā 'puruṣa' abhimāne mari.* When the living entity comes to the material world, he thinks himself the enjoyer. Thus he becomes more and more entangled.

TEXT 62

কৃতার্থ হইলাঙ আমি ইঁহার দরশনে।
এত বলি' পুনঃ তারে কৈল আলিঙ্গনে ॥ ৬২ ॥

kṛtārtha ha-ilāṅa āmi iṅhāra daraśane
eta bali' punaḥ tāre kaila āliṅgane

SYNONYMS

kṛta-artha ha-ilāṅa—have become very much obligated; *āmi*—I; *iṅhāra*—of this boy; *daraśane*—by seeing; *eta bali'*—saying this; *punaḥ*—again; *tāre*—him; *kaila*—did; *āliṅgane*—embrace.

TRANSLATION

Śrī Caitanya Mahāprabhu continued, "I have become very much obligated just by seeing this boy." After saying this, the Lord again embraced the prince.

TEXT 63

প্রভুস্পর্শে রাজপুত্রের হৈল প্রেমাবেশ।
স্বেদ, কম্প, অশ্রু, স্তম্ভ, পুলক বিশেষ ॥ ৬৩ ॥

prabhu-sparśe rāja-putrera haila premāveśa
sveda, kampa, aśru, stambha, pulaka viśeṣa

SYNONYMS

prabhu-sparśe—because of being touched by the Lord; *rāja-putrera*—of the King's son; *haila*—there was; *prema-āveśa*—ecstatic love; *sveda*—perspiration;

kampa—trembling; *aśru*—tears; *stambha*—being stunned; *pulaka*—jubilation; *viśeṣa*—specifically.

TRANSLATION

As soon as the prince was touched by Lord Śrī Caitanya Mahāprabhu, symptoms of ecstatic love immediately manifested themselves in his body. These symptoms included perspiration, trembling, tears, being stunned and jubilation.

TEXT 64

'কৃষ্ণ' 'কৃষ্ণ' কহে, নাচে, করয়ে রোদন।
তাঁর ভাগ্য দেখি' শ্লাঘা করে ভক্তগণ॥ ৬৪ ॥

'kṛṣṇa' 'kṛṣṇa' kahe, nāce, karaye rodana
tāṅra bhāgya dekhi' ślāghā kare bhakta-gaṇa

SYNONYMS

kṛṣṇa kṛṣṇa—O Kṛṣṇa, O Kṛṣṇa; *kahe*—chants; *nāce*—dances; *karaye*—does; *rodana*—crying; *tāṅra*—his; *bhāgya*—fortune; *dekhi'*—seeing; *ślāghā*—praise; *kare*—do; *bhakta-gaṇa*—all the devotees.

TRANSLATION

The boy began to cry and dance, and he chanted, "Kṛṣṇa! Kṛṣṇa!" Upon seeing his bodily symptoms and his chanting and dancing, all the devotees praised him for his great spiritual fortune.

TEXT 65

তবে মহাপ্রভু তাঁরে ধৈর্য করাইল।
নিত্য আসি' আমায় মিলিহ—এই আজ্ঞা দিল ॥৬৫॥

tabe mahāprabhu tāṅre dhairya karāila
nitya āsi' āmāya miliha——ei ājñā dila

SYNONYMS

tabe—at that time; *mahāprabhu*—Śrī Caitanya Mahāprabhu; *tāṅre*—the boy; *dhairya*—patient; *karāila*—caused to be; *nitya*—daily; *āsi'*—coming; *āmāya*—Me; *miliha*—meet; *ei ājñā*—this order; *dila*—gave.

TRANSLATION

At that time, Śrī Caitanya Mahāprabhu calmed the youth and ordered him to come there daily to meet Him.

TEXT 66

বিদায় হঞা রায় আইল রাজপুত্রে লঞা ।
রাজা সুখ পাইল পুত্রের চেষ্টা দেখিয়া ॥ ৬৬ ॥

vidāya hañā rāya āila rāja-putre lañā
rājā sukha pāila putrera ceṣṭā dekhiyā

SYNONYMS

vidāya hañā—taking leave; *rāya*—Rāmānanda Rāya; *āila*—came back; *rāja-putre lañā*—taking the King's son; *rājā*—the King; *sukha pāila*—felt great happiness; *putrera*—of his son; *ceṣṭā*—activities; *dekhiyā*—seeing.

TRANSLATION

They then departed from Śrī Caitanya Mahāprabhu, and Rāmānanda Rāya took the boy back to the King's palace. The King was very happy when he heard of his son's activities.

TEXT 67

পুত্রে আলিঙ্গন করি' প্রেমাবিষ্ট হৈলা ।
সাক্ষাৎ পরশ যেন মহাপ্রভুর পাইলা ॥ ৬৭ ॥

putre āliṅgana kari' premāviṣṭa hailā
sākṣāt paraśa yena mahāprabhura pāilā

SYNONYMS

putre—his son; *āliṅgana*—embracing; *kari'*—doing; *prema-āviṣṭa hailā*—he became ecstatic; *sākṣāt*—directly; *paraśa*—touch; *yena*—as if; *mahāprabhura*—of Lord Śrī Caitanya Mahāprabhu; *pāilā*—he got.

TRANSLATION

Just by embracing his son, the King was filled with ecstatic love, just as if he had touched Śrī Caitanya Mahāprabhu directly.

TEXT 68

সেই হৈতে ভাগ্যবান্ রাজার নন্দন ।
প্রভুভক্তগণ-মধ্যে হৈলা একজন ॥ ৬৮ ॥

sei haite bhāgyavān rājāra nandana
prabhu-bhakta-gaṇa-madhye hailā eka-jana

SYNONYMS

sei haite—from that day; *bhāgyavān*—the most fortunate; *rājāra nandana*—the son of the King; *prabhu-bhakta-gaṇa-madhye*—among the intimate devotees of the Lord; *hailā*—became; *eka-jana*—one of them.

TRANSLATION

Since then, the fortunate prince was one of the most intimate devotees of the Lord.

PURPORT

In this regard, Śrīla Prabodhānanda Sarasvatī wrote: *yat-kāruṇya-kaṭākṣa-vaibhava-vatām.* If Śrī Caitanya Mahāprabhu simply glanced at someone for a moment, that person immediately turned into one of the most confidential devotees of the Lord. The prince came to see the Lord for the first time, but by the Lord's mercy the boy immediately became a topmost devotee. This was not in theory but in practice. We cannot apply the *nagna-mātṛkā-nyāya* formula. This states that if one's mother was naked in her childhood, she should continue to remain naked, even though she has become a mother of so many children. If a person is actually benedicted by the mercy of the Lord, he can immediately become a topmost devotee of the Lord. The logic of *nagna-mātṛkā* states that if a person is not elevated on such and such a date, he cannot become an exalted devotee overnight, as it were. This particular instance offers evidence to contradict that theory. On the previous day, the boy was simply an ordinary prince, and the next day he was counted as one of the topmost devotees of the Lord. This was all made possible by the causeless mercy of the Lord. The Lord is omnipotent, all-powerful and almighty, and He can act as He likes.

TEXT 69

এইমত মহাপ্রভু ভক্তগণ-সঙ্গে ।
নিরন্তর ক্রীড়া করে সংকীর্তন-রঙ্গে ॥ ৬৯ ॥

ei-mata mahāprabhu bhakta-gaṇa-saṅge
nirantara krīḍā kare saṅkīrtana-raṅge

SYNONYMS

ei-mata—in this way; *mahāprabhu*—Śrī Caitanya Mahāprabhu; *bhakta-gaṇa-saṅge*—in the society of His pure devotees; *nirantara*—constantly; *krīḍā kare*—performs pastimes; *saṅkīrtana-raṅge*—in the course of His *saṅkīrtana* movement.

TRANSLATION

Thus Śrī Caitanya Mahāprabhu acts in the society of His pure devotees, performing His pastimes and spreading the saṅkīrtana movement.

TEXT 70

আচার্যাদি ভক্ত করে প্রভুরে নিমন্ত্রণ।
তাহাঁ তাহাঁ ভিক্ষা করে লঞা ভক্তগণ ॥ ৭০ ॥

ācāryādi bhakta kare prabhure nimantraṇa
tāhāṅ tāhāṅ bhikṣā kare lañā bhakta-gaṇa

SYNONYMS

ācārya-ādi—headed by Advaita Ācārya; *bhakta*—devotees; *kare*—do; *prabhure*—unto Śrī Caitanya Mahāprabhu; *nimantraṇa*—invitation; *tāhāṅ tāhāṅ*—here and there; *bhikṣā kare*—takes His lunch; *lañā*—taking; *bhakta-gaṇa*—all the devotees.

TRANSLATION

Some of the prominent devotees like Advaita Ācārya used to invite Śrī Caitanya Mahāprabhu to take His meals at their homes. The Lord accepted such invitations accompanied by His devotees.

TEXT 71

এইমত নানা রঙ্গে দিন কত গেল।
জগন্নাথের রথযাত্রা নিকট হইল ॥ ৭১ ॥

ei-mata nānā raṅge dina kata gela
jagannāthera ratha-yātrā nikaṭa ha-ila

SYNONYMS

ei-mata—in this way; *nānā raṅge*—in great jubilation; *dina kata*—some days; *gela*—passed; *jagannāthera*—of Lord Śrī Jagannātha; *ratha-yātrā*—the car festival; *nikaṭa ha-ila*—became nearer.

TRANSLATION

In this way, the Lord passed some days in great jubilation. Then the car festival of Lord Jagannātha approached.

TEXT 72

প্রথমেই কাশীমিশ্রে প্রভু বোলাইল।
পড়িছা-পাত্র, সার্বভৌমে বোলাঞা আনিল ॥ ৭২ ॥

prathamei kāśī-miśre prabhu bolāila
paḍichā-pātra, sārvabhaume bolāñā ānila

SYNONYMS

prathamei—in the beginning; *kāśī-miśre*—Kāśī Miśra; *prabhu*—Śrī Caitanya Mahāprabhu; *bolāila*—called for; *paḍichā-pātra*—the superintendent of the temple; *sārvabhaume*—of the name; *bolāñā*—calling; *ānila*—brought.

TRANSLATION

Śrī Caitanya Mahāprabhu first of all called for Kāśī Miśra, then for the superintendent of the temple, then for Sārvabhauma Bhaṭṭācārya.

TEXT 73

তিনজন-পাশে প্রভু হাসিয়া কহিল ।
গুণ্ডিচা-মন্দির-মার্জন-সেবা মাগি' নিল ॥ ৭৩ ॥

tina-jana-pāśe prabhu hāsiyā kahila
guṇḍicā-mandira-mārjana-sevā māgi' nila

SYNONYMS

tina-jana-pāśe—in the presence of the three persons; *prabhu*—the Lord; *hāsiyā*—smiling; *kahila*—said; *guṇḍicā-mandira-mārjana*—of washing the temple known as Guṇḍicā; *sevā*—service; *māgi' nila*—obtained by begging.

TRANSLATION

When these three people came before the Lord, He begged them to wash the temple known as Guṇḍicā.

PURPORT

This Guṇḍicā temple is situated two miles northeast of the Jagannātha temple. At the time of the Ratha-yātrā festival, Lord Jagannātha goes to the Guṇḍicā temple from His original temple and stays there for one week. After one week, He returns to His original temple. It is understood by hearsay that the wife of Indradyumna, the King who established the Jagannātha temple, was known as Guṇḍicā. There is also mention of the name of the Guṇḍicā temple in authoritative scripture. The area of the Guṇḍicā temple is estimated to be 288 cubits by 215 cubits. The main temple inside is about 36 cubits by 30 cubits, and the meeting hall is thirty-two cubits by thirty cubits.

TEXT 74

পড়িছা কহে,—আমি-সব সেবক তোমার ।
যে তোমার ইচ্ছা সেই কর্তব্য আমার ॥ ৭৪ ॥

paḍichā kahe,——āmi-saba sevaka tomāra
ye tomāra icchā sei kartavya āmāra

SYNONYMS

paḍichā kahe—the superintendent said; *āmi-saba*—we are all; *sevaka tomāra*—Your servants; *ye tomāra*—whatever Your; *icchā*—desire; *sei*—that; *kartavya āmāra*—our duty.

TRANSLATION

Upon hearing the Lord's request for them to wash the Guṇḍicā temple, the paḍichā, the superintendent of the temple, said, "My dear sir, we are all Your servants. Whatever You desire is our duty to perform.

TEXT 75

বিশেষে রাজার আজ্ঞা হঞাছে আমারে ।
প্রভুর আজ্ঞা যেই, সেই শীঘ্র করিবারে ॥ ৭৫ ॥

viśeṣe rājāra ājñā hañāche āmāre
prabhura ājñā yei, sei śīghra karibāre

SYNONYMS

viśeṣe—specifically; *rājāra*—of the King; *ājñā*—order; *hañāche*—there is; *āmāre*—upon me; *prabhura*—of Your Lordship; *ājñā*—order; *yei*—whatever; *sei*—that; *śīghra karibāre*—to execute without delay.

TRANSLATION

"The King gave a special order for me to do without delay whatever Your Lordship orders.

TEXT 76

তোমার যোগ্য সেবা নহে মন্দির-মার্জন ।
এই এক লীলা কর, যে তোমার মন ॥ ৭৬ ॥

tomāra yogya sevā nahe mandira-mārjana
ei eka līlā kara, ye tomāra mana

SYNONYMS

tomāra—of You; *yogya*—befitting; *sevā*—service; *nahe*—not; *mandira-mārjana*—washing the temple; *ei*—this; *eka*—one; *līlā*—pastime; *kara*—You perform; *ye tomāra mana*—as You like.

TRANSLATION

"My dear Lord, washing the temple is not service befitting You. Nonetheless, if You wish to do so, it is to be accepted as one of Your pastimes.

TEXT 77

কিন্তু ঘট, সংমার্জনী বহুত চাহিয়ে ।
আজ্ঞা দেহ—আজি সব ইহাঁ আনি দিয়ে ॥ ৭৭ ॥

kintu ghaṭa, sammārjanī bahuta cāhiye
ājñā deha——āji saba ihāṅ āni diye

SYNONYMS

kintu—but; *ghaṭa*—waterpots; *sammārjanī*—brooms; *bahuta*—many; *cāhiye*—You require; *ājñā deha*—just order; *āji*—immediately today; *saba*—everything; *ihāṅ*—here; *āni diye*—I shall bring and deliver.

TRANSLATION

"To wash the temple, You need many waterpots and brooms. Therefore order me. I can immediately bring all these things to You."

TEXT 78

নূতন একশত ঘট, শত সংমার্জনী ।
পড়িছা আনিয়া দিল প্রভুর ইচ্ছা জানি' ॥ ৭৮ ॥

nūtana eka-śata ghaṭa, śata sammārjanī
paḍichā āniyā dila prabhura icchā jāni'

SYNONYMS

nūtana—new; *eka-śata*—one hundred; *ghaṭa*—waterpots; *śata*—hundred; *sammārjanī*—brooms; *paḍichā*—the superintendent; *āniyā*—bringing; *dila*—delivered; *prabhura*—of the Lord; *icchā*—the desire; *jāni'*—knowing.

TRANSLATION

As soon as the superintendent understood the desire of the Lord, he immediately delivered a hundred new waterpots and a hundred brooms for sweeping the temple.

TEXT 79

আর দিনে প্রভাতে লঞা নিজগণ ।
শ্রীহস্তে সবার অঙ্গে লেপিলা চন্দন ॥ ৭৯ ॥

āra dine prabhāte lañā nija-gaṇa
śrī-haste sabāra aṅge lepilā candana

SYNONYMS

āra dine—on the next day; *prabhāte*—in the morning; *lañā*—taking; *nija-gaṇa*—His personal devotees; *śrī-haste*—by His own hand; *sabāra aṅge*—on everyone's body; *lepilā candana*—smeared pulp of sandalwood.

TRANSLATION

The next day, early in the morning, the Lord took His personal associates with Him and, with His own hand, smeared sandalwood pulp on their bodies.

TEXT 80

শ্রীহস্তে দিল সবারে এক এক মার্জনী ।
সবগণ লঞা প্রভু চলিলা আপনি ॥ ৮০ ॥

śrī-haste dila sabāre eka eka mārjanī
saba-gaṇa lañā prabhu calilā āpani

SYNONYMS

śrī-haste—by His own hand; *dila*—delivered; *sabāre*—unto every one of them; *eka eka*—one by one; *mārjanī*—a broom; *saba-gaṇa*—all the associates; *lañā*—taking; *prabhu*—Śrī Caitanya Mahāprabhu; *calilā*—went; *āpani*—personally.

TRANSLATION

He then gave each devotee a broom with His own hand, and, taking all of them personally with Him, the Lord went to Guṇḍicā.

TEXT 81

গুণ্ডিচা-মন্দিরে গেলা করিতে মার্জন ।
প্রথমে মার্জনী লঞা করিল শোধন ॥ ৮১ ॥

guṇḍicā-mandire gelā karite mārjana
prathame mārjanī lañā karila śodhana

SYNONYMS

guṇḍicā-mandire—to the temple known as Guṇḍicā; *gelā*—went; *karite*—to do; *mārjana*—washing; *prathame*—in the first instance; *mārjanī*—the brooms; *lañā*—taking; *karila*—did; *śodhana*—cleansing.

TRANSLATION

In this way the Lord and His associates went to cleanse the Guṇḍicā temple. At first they cleansed the temple with the brooms.

TEXT 82

ভিতর মন্দির উপর,—সকল মাজিল ।
সিংহাসন মাজি' পুনঃ স্থাপন করিল ॥ ৮২ ॥

bhitara mandira upara,——sakala mājila
siṁhāsana māji' punaḥ sthāpana karila

SYNONYMS

bhitara mandira—of the interior of the temple; *upara*—the ceiling; *sakala mājila*—cleansed everything; *siṁhāsana*—the sitting place of the Lord; *māji'*—cleansing; *punaḥ*—again; *sthāpana*—setting down; *karila*—did.

TRANSLATION

The Lord cleansed everything inside the temple very nicely, including the ceiling. He then took up the sitting place [siṁhāsana], cleansed it and again put it in its original place.

TEXT 83

ছোট-বড়-মন্দির কৈল মার্জন-শোধন ।
পাছে তৈছে শোধিল শ্রীজগমোহন ॥ ৮৩ ॥

choṭa-baḍa-mandira kaila mārjana-śodhana
pāche taiche śodhila śrī-jagamohana

SYNONYMS

choṭa-baḍa-mandira—all the small and big temples; *kaila*—did; *mārjana-śodhana*—proper cleansing; *pāche*—thereafter; *taiche*—in the similar way; *śodhila*—cleansed; *śrī-jagamohana*—the place between the original temple and the meeting hall.

TRANSLATION

Thus the Lord and His companions cleansed and swept all the temple's buildings, big and small, and finally cleansed the area between the temple and the meeting place.

TEXT 84

চারিদিকে শত ভক্ত সংমার্জনী-করে ।
আপনি শোধেন প্রভু, শিখা'ন সবারে ॥ ৮৪ ॥

cāri-dike śata bhakta sammārjanī-kare
āpani śodhena prabhu, śikhā'na sabāre

SYNONYMS

cāri-dike—all around; *śata*—hundreds of; *bhakta*—devotees; *sammārjanī-kare*—do the cleansing work; *āpani*—personally; *śodhena*—cleanses; *prabhu*—the Lord; *śikhā'na sabāre*—teaches all others.

TRANSLATION

Indeed, hundreds of devotees were engaged in cleansing all around the temple, and Śrī Caitanya Mahāprabhu was personally carrying out the operation just to instruct others.

TEXT 85

প্রেমোল্লাসে শোধেন, লয়েন কৃষ্ণনাম ।
ভক্তগণ 'কৃষ্ণ' কহে, করে নিজ-কাম ॥ ৮৫ ॥

premollāse śodhena, layena kṛṣṇa-nāma
bhakta-gaṇa 'kṛṣṇa' kahe, kare nija-kāma

SYNONYMS

prema-ullāse—in great jubilation; *śodhena*—cleanses; *layena*—chants; *kṛṣṇa*—Hare Kṛṣṇa; *nāma*—name; *bhakta-gaṇa*—the devotees; *kṛṣṇa kahe*—chant Kṛṣṇa; *kare*—do; *nija-kāma*—their own duty.

TRANSLATION

Śrī Caitanya Mahāprabhu washed and cleansed the temple in great jubilation, chanting the holy name of Lord Kṛṣṇa all the time. Similarly, all the devotees were also chanting and at the same time performing their respective duties.

TEXT 86

ধূলি-ধূসর তনু দেখিতে শোভন।
কাহাঁ কাহাঁ অশ্রুজলে করে সংমার্জন ॥ ৮৬ ॥

dhūli-dhūsara tanu dekhite śobhana
kāhāṅ kāhāṅ aśru-jale kare sammārjana

SYNONYMS

dhūli—dust; *dhūsara*—dirt; *tanu*—body; *dekhite*—to see; *śobhana*—very beautiful; *kāhāṅ kāhāṅ*—somewhere; *aśru-jale*—with tears; *kare*—does; *sammārjana*—washing.

TRANSLATION

The entire beautiful body of the Lord was covered with dust and dirt. In this way it became transcendentally beautiful. At times, when cleansing the temple, the Lord shed tears, and in some places He even cleansed with those tears.

TEXT 87

ভোগমন্দির শোধন করি' শোধিল প্রাঙ্গণ।
সকল আবাস ক্রমে করিল শোধন ॥ ৮৭ ॥

bhoga-mandira śodhana kari' śodhila prāṅgaṇa
sakala āvāsa krame karila śodhana

SYNONYMS

bhoga-mandira—the place where food is placed; *śodhana kari'*—cleansing; *śodhila prāṅgaṇa*—cleansed the yard; *sakala*—all; *āvāsa*—residential places; *krame*—one after another; *karila śodhana*—cleansed.

TRANSLATION

After this, the place where the Deity's food was kept [bhoga-mandira] was cleansed. Then the yard was cleansed, and then all the residential quarters, one after the other.

TEXT 88

তৃণ, ধূলি, ঝিঁকুর, সব একত্র করিয়া।
বহির্বাসে লঞা ফেলায় বাহির করিয়া ॥ ৮৮ ॥

tṛṇa, dhūli, jhiṅkura, saba ekatra kariyā
bahirvāse lañā phelāya bāhira kariyā

SYNONYMS

tṛṇa—straws; *dhūli*—dust; *jhiṅkura*—grains of sand; *saba*—all; *ekatra*—in one place; *kariyā*—combining; *bahirvāse lañā*—taking on His personal cloth; *phelāya*—throws; *bāhira kariyā*—outside.

TRANSLATION

After Śrī Caitanya Mahāprabhu collected all the straw, dust and grains of sand in one place, He gathered it all in His cloth and threw it outside.

TEXT 89

এইমত ভক্তগণ করি' নিজ-বাসে ।
তৃণ, ধূলি বাহিরে ফেলায় পরম হরিষে ॥ ৮৯ ॥

ei-mata bhakta-gaṇa kari' nija-vāse
tṛṇa, dhūli bāhire phelāya parama hariṣe

SYNONYMS

ei-mata—similarly; *bhakta-gaṇa*—all the devotees; *kari'*—doing; *nija-vāse*—in their own cloths; *tṛṇa*—straw; *dhūli*—dust; *bāhire phelāya*—throw outside; *parama hariṣe*—with great jubilation.

TRANSLATION

Following the example of Śrī Caitanya Mahāprabhu, all the devotees, in great jubilation, began to gather straws and dust with their own cloths and throw them outside the temple.

TEXT 90

প্রভু কহে,—কে কত করিয়াছ সংমার্জন ।
তৃণ, ধূলি দেখিলেই জানিব পরিশ্রম ॥ ৯০ ॥

prabhu kahe,——ke kata kariyācha sammārjana
tṛṇa, dhūli dekhilei jāniba pariśrama

SYNONYMS

prabhu kahe—the Lord said; *ke*—every one of you; *kata*—how much; *kariyācha*—have done; *sammārjana*—cleansing; *tṛṇa*—straw; *dhūli*—dust;

dekhilei—when I see; *jāniba*—I can understand; *pariśrama*—how much you have labored.

TRANSLATION

The Lord then told the devotees, "I can tell how much you have labored and how well you have cleansed the temple simply by seeing all the straw and dust you have collected outside."

TEXT 91

সবার ঝাঁটান বোঝা একত্র করিল ।
সবা হৈতে প্রভুর বোঝা অধিক হইল ॥ ৯১ ॥

sabāra jhyāṅṭāna bojhā ekatra karila
sabā haite prabhura bojhā adhika ha-ila

SYNONYMS

sabāra—of all; *jhyāṅṭāna*—the dirt collected; *bojhā*—load; *ekatra*—combined in one place; *karila*—made; *sabā haite*—than all of them; *prabhura bojhā*—the pile of dirt collected by Śrī Caitanya Mahāprabhu; *adhika ha-ila*—was greater.

TRANSLATION

Even though all the devotees collected dirt in one pile, the dirt collected by Śrī Caitanya Mahāprabhu was much greater.

TEXT 92

এইমত অভ্যন্তর করিল মার্জন ।
পুনঃ সবাকারে দিল করিয়া বণ্টন ॥ ৯২ ॥

ei-mata abhyantara karila mārjana
punaḥ sabākāre dila kariyā vaṇṭana

SYNONYMS

ei-mata—in this way; *abhyantara*—inside; *karila*—did; *mārjana*—cleansing; *punaḥ*—again; *sabākāre*—to all of them; *dila*—gave; *kariyā vaṇṭana*—allotting areas.

TRANSLATION

After the inside of the temple was cleansed, the Lord again allotted areas for the devotees to cleanse.

TEXT 93

সূক্ষ্ম ধূলি, তৃণ, কাঁকর, সব করহ দূর ।
ভালমতে শোধন করহ প্রভুর অন্তঃপুর ॥ ৯৩ ॥

sūkṣma dhūli, tṛṇa, kāṅkara, saba karaha dūra
bhāla-mate śodhana karaha prabhura antaḥpura

SYNONYMS

sūkṣma dhūli—fine dust; *tṛṇa*—straw; *kāṅkara*—grains of sand; *saba*—all; *karaha*—do; *dūra*—away; *bhāla-mate*—very well; *śodhana*—cleansing; *karaha*—do; *prabhura*—of the Lord; *antaḥpura*—inside.

TRANSLATION

The Lord then ordered everyone to cleanse the inside of the temple very perfectly by taking finer dust, straws and grains of sand and throwing them outside.

TEXT 94

সব বৈষ্ণব লঞা যবে দুইবার শোধিল ।
দেখি' মহাপ্রভুর মনে সন্তোষ হইল ॥ ৯৪ ॥

saba vaiṣṇava lañā yabe dui-bāra śodhila
dekhi' mahāprabhura mane santoṣa ha-ila

SYNONYMS

saba—all; *vaiṣṇava*—devotees; *lañā*—taking; *yabe*—when; *dui-bāra*—for the second time; *śodhila*—cleansed; *dekhi'*—seeing; *mahāprabhura*—of Śrī Caitanya Mahāprabhu; *mane*—in the mind; *santoṣa*—satisfaction; *ha-ila*—there was.

TRANSLATION

After Śrī Caitanya Mahāprabhu and all the Vaiṣṇavas cleansed the temple for the second time, Śrī Caitanya Mahāprabhu was very happy to see the cleansing work.

TEXT 95

আর শত জন শত ঘটে জল ভরি' ।
প্রথমেই লঞা আছে কাল অপেক্ষা করি' ॥ ৯৫ ॥

āra śata jana śata ghaṭe jala bhari'
prathamei lañā āche kāla apekṣā kari'

SYNONYMS

āra—other; *śata jana*—about one hundred men; *śata ghaṭe*—in a hundred waterpots; *jala*—water; *bhari'*—filling; *prathamei*—in the first instance; *lañā*—taking; *āche*—were; *kāla*—the time; *apekṣā kari'*—awaiting.

TRANSLATION

While the temple was being swept, about a hundred men stood ready with filled waterpots, and they simply awaited the Lord's order to throw them.

TEXT 96

'জল আন' বলি' যবে মহাপ্রভু কহিল ।
তবে শত ঘট আনি' প্রভু-আগে দিল ॥ ৯৬ ॥

'jala āna' bali' yabe mahāprabhu kahila
tabe śata ghaṭa āni' prabhu-āge dila

SYNONYMS

jala āna—bring water; *bali'*—saying; *yabe*—when; *mahāprabhu*—Śrī Caitanya Mahāprabhu; *kahila*—ordered; *tabe*—at that time; *śata ghaṭa*—one hundred pots; *āni'*—bringing; *prabhu-āge*—before the Lord; *dila*—delivered.

TRANSLATION

As soon as Śrī Caitanya Mahāprabhu called for water, all the men immediately brought the hundred waterpots, which were completely filled, and delivered them before the Lord.

TEXT 97

প্রথমে করিল প্রভু মন্দির প্রক্ষালন ।
ঊর্ধ্ব-অধো ভিত্তি, গৃহ-মধ্য, সিংহাসন ॥ ৯৭ ॥

prathame karila prabhu mandira prakṣālana
ūrdhva-adho bhitti, gṛha-madhya, siṁhāsana

SYNONYMS

prathame—in the first instance; *karila*—did; *prabhu*—Śrī Caitanya Mahāprabhu; *mandira prakṣālana*—washing of the temple; *ūrdhva*—on the ceiling; *adhaḥ*—on the floor; *bhitti*—walls; *gṛha-madhya*—within the home; *siṁhāsana*—the sitting place of the Lord.

TRANSLATION

In this way, Śrī Caitanya Mahāprabhu first washed the main temple and then thoroughly washed the ceiling, the walls, the floor, the sitting place [siṁhāsana] and everything else within the room.

TEXT 98

খাপরা ভরিয়া জল ঊর্ধ্বে চালাইল ।
সেই জলে ঊর্ধ্ব শোধি ভিত্তি প্রক্ষালিল ॥ ৯৮ ॥

khāparā bhariyā jala ūrdhve cālāila
sei jale ūrdhva śodhi bhitti prakṣālila

SYNONYMS

khāparā—basin; *bhariyā*—filling; *jala*—water; *ūrdhve*—on the ceiling; *cālāila*—began to throw; *sei jale*—with that water; *ūrdhva śodhi*—washing the ceiling; *bhitti*—walls and floor; *prakṣālila*—washed.

TRANSLATION

Śrī Caitanya Mahāprabhu Himself and His devotees began to throw water onto the ceiling. When this water fell, it washed the walls and floor.

TEXT 99

শ্রীহস্তে করেন সিংহাসনের মার্জন ।
প্রভু আগে জল আনি' দেয় ভক্তগণ ॥ ৯৯ ॥

śrī-haste karena siṁhāsanera mārjana
prabhu āge jala āni' deya bhakta-gaṇa

SYNONYMS

śrī-haste—with his own hand; *karena*—does; *siṁhāsanera mārjana*—washing of the sitting place of the Lord; *prabhu āge*—before the Lord; *jala*—water; *āni'*—bringing; *deya*—deliver; *bhakta-gaṇa*—all devotees.

TRANSLATION

Then Śrī Caitanya Mahāprabhu began to wash the sitting place of Lord Jagannātha with His own hands, and all the devotees began to bring water to the Lord.

TEXT 100

ভক্তগণ করে গৃহ-মধ্য প্রক্ষালন ।
নিজ নিজ হস্তে করে মন্দির মার্জন ॥ ১০০ ॥

bhakta-gaṇa kare gṛha-madhya prakṣālana
nija nija haste kare mandira mārjana

SYNONYMS

bhakta-gaṇa—devotees; *kare*—do; *gṛha-madhya*—within the room; *prakṣālana*—washing; *nija nija*—each one of them; *haste*—in the hand; *kare*—does; *mandira mārjana*—cleansing of the temple.

TRANSLATION

All the devotees within the temple began to wash. Each one had a broom in his hand, and in this way they cleansed the temple of the Lord.

TEXT 101

কেহ জল আনি' দেয় মহাপ্রভুর করে ।
কেহ জল দেয় তাঁর চরণ-উপরে ॥ ১০১ ॥

keha jala āni' deya mahāprabhura kare
keha jala deya tāṅra caraṇa-upare

SYNONYMS

keha—someone; *jala āni'*—bringing water; *deya*—delivers; *mahāprabhura kare*—to the hand of Śrī Caitanya Mahāprabhu; *keha*—someone; *jala deya*—pours water; *tāṅra*—His; *caraṇa-upare*—on the lotus feet.

TRANSLATION

Someone brought water to pour into the hands of Śrī Caitanya Mahāprabhu, and someone poured water on His lotus feet.

TEXT 102

কেহ লুকাঞা করে সেই জল পান ।
কেহ মাগি' লয়, কেহ অন্যে করে দান ॥ ১০২ ॥

keha lukāñā kare sei jala pāna
keha māgi' laya, keha anye kare dāna

SYNONYMS

keha—someone; *lukāñā*—concealing himself; *kare*—does; *sei jala*—of that water; *pāna*—drinking; *keha*—someone; *māgi' laya*—begging, takes; *keha*—another; *anye*—to another; *kare*—gives; *dāna*—in charity.

TRANSLATION

The water that fell from the lotus feet of Śrī Caitanya Mahāprabhu was drunk by someone who hid himself. Someone else begged for that water, and another person was giving that water in charity.

TEXT 103

ঘর ধুই' প্রণালিকায় জল ছাড়ি' দিল ।
সেই জলে প্রাঙ্গণ সব ভরিয়া রহিল ॥ ১০৩ ॥

ghara dhui' praṇālikāya jala chāḍi' dila
sei jale prāṅgaṇa saba bhariyā rahila

SYNONYMS

ghara dhui'—washing the room; *praṇālikāya*—unto the outlet; *jala*—water; *chāḍi' dila*—let go; *sei jale*—by that water; *prāṅgaṇa*—the yard; *saba*—all; *bhariyā*—filled; *rahila*—remained.

TRANSLATION

After the room was washed, the water was let out through an outlet, and it then flowed and filled the yard outside.

TEXT 104

নিজ-বস্ত্রে কৈল প্রভু গৃহ সংমার্জন ।
মহাপ্রভু নিজ-বস্ত্রে মাজিল সিংহাসন ॥ ১০৪ ॥

nija-vastre kaila prabhu gṛha sammārjana
mahāprabhu nija-vastre mājila siṁhāsana

SYNONYMS

nija-vastre—by His own garment; *kaila*—did; *prabhu*—Śrī Caitanya Mahāprabhu; *gṛha*—room; *sammārjana*—mopping; *mahāprabhu*—Śrī Caitanya Mahāprabhu; *nija-vastre*—by His own garment; *mājila*—polished; *siṁhāsana*—throne.

TRANSLATION

The Lord mopped the rooms with His own clothes, and He polished the throne with them also.

TEXT 105

শত ঘট জলে হৈল মন্দির মার্জন।
মন্দির শোধিয়া কৈল—যেন নিজ মন॥ ১০৫॥

śata ghaṭa jale haila mandira mārjana
mandira śodhiyā kaila——yena nija mana

SYNONYMS

śata—one hundred; *ghaṭa*—of waterpots; *jale*—by the water; *haila*—became; *mandira*—the temple; *mārjana*—cleansed; *mandira*—the temple; *śodhiyā*—cleansing; *kaila*—did; *yena*—as if; *nija mana*—his own mind.

TRANSLATION

In this way all the rooms were cleansed with a hundred waterpots. After the rooms had been cleansed, the minds of the devotees were as clean as the rooms.

TEXT 106

নির্মল, শীতল, স্নিগ্ধ করিল মন্দিরে।
আপন-হৃদয় যেন ধরিল বাহিরে॥ ১০৬॥

nirmala, śītala, snigdha karila mandire
āpana-hṛdaya yena dharila bāhire

SYNONYMS

nirmala—purified; *śītala*—cool; *snigdha*—pleasing; *karila*—made; *mandire*—the temple; *āpana-hṛdaya*—own heart; *yena*—as if; *dharila*—kept; *bāhire*—outside.

TRANSLATION

When the temple was cleansed, it was purified, cool and pleasing, just as if the Lord's own pure mind had appeared.

TEXT 107

শত শত জন জল ভরে সরোবরে।
ঘাটে স্থান নাহি, কেহ কূপে জল ভরে॥ ১০৭॥

śata śata jana jala bhare sarovare
ghāṭe sthāna nāhi, keha kūpe jala bhare

SYNONYMS

śata śata jana—hundreds of men; *jala bhare*—draw water; *sarovare*—from the lake; *ghāṭe*—on the bank; *sthāna*—place; *nāhi*—there is not; *keha*—someone; *kūpe*—from the well; *jala bhare*—draws the water.

TRANSLATION

Since hundreds of men were engaged in bringing water from the lake, there was no place to stand on the banks. Consequently someone began to draw water from a well.

TEXT 108

পূর্ণ কুম্ভ লঞা আইসে শত ভক্তগণ ।
শূন্য ঘট লঞা যায় আর শত জন ॥ ১০৮ ॥

pūrṇa kumbha lañā āise śata bhakta-gaṇa
śūnya ghaṭa lañā yāya āra śata jana

SYNONYMS

pūrṇa kumbha—a filled waterpot; *lañā*—taking; *āise*—come; *śata bhakta-gaṇa*—hundreds of devotees; *śūnya ghaṭa*—an empty waterpot; *lañā*—taking back; *yāya*—go; *āra*—another; *śata jana*—hundreds of men.

TRANSLATION

Hundreds of devotees brought water in the pots, and hundreds took the empty pots away to fill them up again.

TEXT 109

নিত্যানন্দ, অদ্বৈত, স্বরূপ, ভারতী, পুরী ।
ইঁহা বিনু আর সব আনে জল ভরি' ॥ ১০৯ ॥

nityānanda, advaita, svarūpa, bhāratī, purī
iṅhā vinu āra saba āne jala bhari'

SYNONYMS

nityānanda—Nityānanda Prabhu; *advaita*—Advaita Ācārya; *svarūpa*—Svarūpa Dāmodara; *bhāratī*—Brahmānanda Bhāratī; *purī*—Paramānanda Purī; *iṅhā*—

these; *vinu*—except; *āra*—others; *saba*—all; *āne*—bring; *jala*—water; *bhari'*—filling up.

TRANSLATION

With the exception of Nityānanda Prabhu, Advaita Ācārya, Svarūpa Dāmodara, Brahmānanda Bhāratī and Paramānanda Purī, everyone was engaged in filling the waterpots and bringing them there.

TEXT 110

ঘটে ঘটে ঠেকি' কত ঘট ভাঙ্গি' গেল।
শত শত ঘট লোক তাহাঁ লঞা আইল ॥১১০ ॥

ghaṭe ghaṭe ṭheki' kata ghaṭa bhāṅgi' gela
śata śata ghaṭa loka tāhāṅ lañā āila

SYNONYMS

ghaṭe ghaṭe ṭheki'—when there was a collision between one pot and another; *kata*—so many; *ghaṭa*—pots; *bhāṅgi' gelā*—became broken; *śata śata*—hundreds of; *ghaṭa*—pots; *loka*—people; *tāhāṅ*—there; *lañā*—bringing; *āila*—came.

TRANSLATION

Many of the waterpots were broken when people collided with one another, and hundreds of men had to bring new waterpots to fill.

TEXT 111

জল ভরে, ঘর ধোয়, করে হরিধ্বনি।
'কৃষ্ণ' 'হরি' ধ্বনি বিনা আর নাহি শুনি ॥ ১১১ ॥

jala bhare, ghara dhoya, kare hari-dhvani
'kṛṣṇa' 'hari' dhvani vinā āra nāhi śuni

SYNONYMS

jala bhare—they were drawing water; *ghara dhoya*—washing the rooms; *kare hari-dhvani*—chanting the holy name of Hari; *kṛṣṇa*—Lord Kṛṣṇa; *hari*—the holy name of Hari; *dhvani*—vibration; *vinā*—except; *āra*—anything else; *nāhi*—there was not; *śuni*—hearing.

TRANSLATION

Some people were filling the pots, and others were washing the rooms, but everyone was engaged in chanting the holy name of Kṛṣṇa and Hari.

TEXT 112

'কৃষ্ণ' 'কৃষ্ণ' কহি' করে ঘটের প্রার্থন।
'কৃষ্ণ' 'কৃষ্ণ' কহি' করে ঘট সমর্পণ ॥ ১১২ ॥

'kṛṣṇa' 'kṛṣṇa' kahi' kare ghaṭera prārthana
'kṛṣṇa' 'kṛṣṇa' kahi' kare ghaṭa samarpaṇa

SYNONYMS

kṛṣṇa kṛṣṇa kahi'—while chanting Kṛṣṇa Kṛṣṇa; *kare*—do; *ghaṭera*—for the waterpots; *prārthana*—begging; *kṛṣṇa kṛṣṇa*—the holy name of Lord Kṛṣṇa; *kahi'*—chanting; *kare*—does; *ghaṭa*—of the waterpots; *samarpaṇa*—delivery.

TRANSLATION

One person begged for a waterpot by chanting the holy names Kṛṣṇa, Kṛṣṇa, and another delivered a pot while chanting Kṛṣṇa, Kṛṣṇa.

TEXT 113

যেই যেই কহে, সেই কহে কৃষ্ণনামে।
কৃষ্ণনাম হইল সঙ্কেত সব-কামে ॥ ১১৩ ॥

yei yei kahe, sei kahe kṛṣṇa-nāme
kṛṣṇa-nāma ha-ila saṅketa saba-kāme

SYNONYMS

yei yei kahe—anyone who was speaking; *sei*—he; *kahe*—says; *kṛṣṇa-nāme*—by uttering the holy name of Kṛṣṇa; *kṛṣṇa-nāma ha-ila*—the holy name of Kṛṣṇa became; *saṅketa*—indication; *saba-kāme*—for everyone who wanted something.

TRANSLATION

Whenever anyone had to speak, he did so by uttering the holy name of Kṛṣṇa. Consequently, the holy name of Kṛṣṇa became an indication for everyone who wanted something.

TEXT 114

প্রেমাবেশে প্রভু কহে 'কৃষ্ণ' 'কৃষ্ণ'-নাম।
একলে প্রেমাবেশে করে শতজনের কাম ॥ ১১৪ ॥

premāveśe prabhu kahe 'kṛṣṇa' 'kṛṣṇa'-nāma
ekale premāveśe kare śata-janera kāma

SYNONYMS

prema-āveśe—in ecstatic love; *prabhu*—Lord Śrī Caitanya Mahāprabhu; *kahe*—says; *kṛṣṇa kṛṣṇa-nāma*—the holy name of Lord Kṛṣṇa; *ekale*—alone; *prema-āveśe*—in ecstatic love; *kare*—does; *śata-janera kāma*—the work of hundreds of men.

TRANSLATION

As Śrī Caitanya Mahāprabhu was vibrating the holy name of Kṛṣṇa in ecstatic love, He Himself was performing the work of hundreds of men.

TEXT 115

শত-হস্তে করেন যেন ক্ষালন-মার্জন ।
প্রতিজন-পাশে যাই' করান শিক্ষণ ॥ ১১৫ ॥

śata-haste karena yena kṣālana-mārjana
pratijana-pāśe yāi' karāna śikṣaṇa

SYNONYMS

śata-haste—with one hundred hands; *karena*—He does; *yena*—as if; *kṣālana-mārjana*—rinsing and washing; *pratijana-pāśe yāi'*—going to the side of everyone; *karāna śikṣaṇa*—He was teaching them.

TRANSLATION

It appeared as though Śrī Caitanya Mahāprabhu were cleansing and washing with a hundred hands. He approached everyone just to teach them how to work.

TEXT 116

ভাল কর্ম দেখি' তারে করে প্রসংশন ।
মনে না মিলিলে করে পবিত্র ভৎর্সন ॥ ১১৬ ॥

bhāla karma dekhi' tāre kare prasaṁśana
mane nā milile kare pavitra bhartsana

SYNONYMS

bhāla—good; *karma*—work; *dekhi'*—seeing; *tāre*—to him; *kare*—does; *prasaṁśana*—praising; *mane*—in His mind; *nā*—not; *milile*—being approved; *kare*—He does; *pavitra*—purified, ungrudgingly; *bhartsana*—chastisement.

TRANSLATION

When He saw someone doing nicely, the Lord praised him, but if He saw that someone was not working to His satisfaction, He immediately chastised that person, not bearing him any grudge.

TEXT 117

তুমি ভাল করিয়াছ, শিখাহ অন্যেরে ।
এইমত ভাল কর্ম সেহো যেন করে ॥ ১১৭ ॥

tumi bhāla kariyācha, śikhāha anyere
ei-mata bhāla karma seho yena kare

SYNONYMS

tumi—you; *bhāla kariyācha*—have done well; *śikhāha anyere*—teach others; *ei-mata*—in this way; *bhāla karma*—good work; *seho*—he also; *yena*—so that; *kare*—performs.

TRANSLATION

The Lord would say, "You have done well. Please teach this to others so that they may act in the same way."

TEXT 118

এ-কথা শুনিয়া সবে সঙ্কুচিত হঞা ।
ভাল-মতে কর্ম করে সবে মন দিয়া ॥ ১১৮ ॥

e-kathā śuniyā sabe saṅkucita hañā
bhāla-mate karma kare sabe mana diyā

SYNONYMS

e-kathā śuniyā—hearing these words; *sabe*—all; *saṅkucita hañā*—being ashamed; *bhāla-mate*—very well; *karma kare*—do work; *sabe*—all; *mana diyā*—with attention.

TRANSLATION

As soon as they heard Śrī Caitanya Mahāprabhu say this, everyone became ashamed. Thus they began to work with great attention.

TEXT 119

তবে প্রক্ষালন কৈল শ্রীজগমোহন ।
ভোগমন্দির-আদি তবে কৈল প্রক্ষালন ॥ ১১৯ ॥

tabe prakṣālana kaila śrī-jagamohana
bhoga-mandira-ādi tabe kaila prakṣālana

SYNONYMS

tabe—thereafter; *prakṣālana*—washing; *kaila*—performed; *śrī-jagamohana*—in front of the temple; *bhoga-mandira*—the place where food is offered; *ādi*—all such places; *tabe*—then; *kaila prakṣālana*—washed.

TRANSLATION

They washed the Jagamohana area and then the place where food was kept. All other places were also washed.

TEXT 120

নাটশালা ধুই' ধুইল চত্বর-প্রাঙ্গণ ।
পাকশালা-আদি করি' করিল প্রক্ষালন ॥ ১২০ ॥

nāṭaśālā dhui' dhuila catvara-prāṅgaṇa
pākaśālā-ādi kari' karila prakṣālana

SYNONYMS

nāṭa-śālā—the meeting place; *dhui'*—washing; *dhuila*—washed; *catvara-prāṅgaṇa*—the yard and the raised sitting place; *pāka-śālā*—the kitchen; *ādi*—and so on; *kari'*—making; *karila prakṣālana*—washed.

TRANSLATION

In this way the meeting place was washed, the entire yard, the raised sitting places, the kitchen and every other room.

TEXT 121

মন্দিরের চতুর্দিক্ প্রক্ষালন কৈল ।
সব অন্তঃপুর ভালমতে ধোয়াইল ॥ ১২১ ॥

mandirera catur-dik prakṣālana kaila
saba antaḥpura bhāla-mate dhoyāila

SYNONYMS

mandirera—the temple; *catuḥ-dik*—all around; *prakṣālana kaila*—washed; *saba*—all; *antaḥpura*—inside the rooms; *bhāla-mate*—with great care; *dhoyāila*—washed.

TRANSLATION

Thus all places around the temple were thoroughly washed within and without.

TEXT 122

হেনকালে গৌড়ীয়া এক সুবুদ্ধি সরল ।
প্রভুর চরণ-যুগে দিল ঘট-জল ॥ ১২২ ॥

hena-kāle gauḍīyā eka subuddhi sarala
prabhura caraṇa-yuge dila ghaṭa-jala

SYNONYMS

hena-kāle—at this time; *gauḍīyā*—Vaiṣṇava from Bengal; *eka*—one; *su-buddhi*—very intelligent; *sarala*—simple; *prabhura caraṇa-yuge*—on the lotus feet of the Lord; *dila*—poured; *ghaṭa-jala*—one potful of water.

TRANSLATION

After everything was thoroughly washed, a Vaiṣṇava from Bengal, who was very intelligent and simple, came and poured water on the lotus feet of the Lord.

TEXT 123

সেই জল লঞা আপনে পান কৈল ।
তাহা দেখি' প্রভুর মনে দুঃখ রোষ হৈল ॥ ১২৩ ॥

sei jala lañā āpane pāna kaila
tāhā dekhi' prabhura mane duḥkha roṣa haila

SYNONYMS

sei jala—that water; *lañā*—taking; *āpane*—personally; *pāna kaila*—drank; *tāhā dekhi'*—seeing that; *prabhura*—of the Lord; *mane*—in the mind; *duḥkha*—unhappiness; *roṣa*—anger; *haila*—there was.

TRANSLATION

The Gauḍīya Vaiṣṇava then took that water and drank it himself. Seeing that, Śrī Caitanya Mahāprabhu felt a little unhappy and was also outwardly angry.

TEXT 124

যদ্যপি গোসাঞি তারে হঞাছে সন্তোষ ।
ধর্মসংস্থাপন লাগি' বাহিরে মহারোষ ॥ ১২৪ ॥

yadyapi gosāñi tāre hañāche santoṣa
dharma-saṁsthāpana lāgi' bāhire mahā-roṣa

SYNONYMS

yadyapi—although; *gosāñi*—the Lord; *tāre*—with him; *hañāche*—became; *santoṣa*—satisfied; *dharma-saṁsthāpana lāgi'*—for establishing the etiquette of religious principles; *bāhire*—externally; *mahā-roṣa*—very angry.

TRANSLATION

Although the Lord was certainly satisfied with him, He became angry externally in order to establish the etiquette of religious principles.

TEXT 125

শিক্ষা লাগি' স্বরূপে ডাকি' কহিল তাঁহারে ।
এই দেখ তোমার 'গৌড়ীয়া'র ব্যবহারে ॥ ১২৫ ॥

śikṣā lāgi' svarūpe ḍāki' kahila tāṅhāre
ei dekha tomāra 'gauḍīyā'ra vyavahāre

SYNONYMS

śikṣā lāgi'—for instruction; *svarūpe*—unto Svarūpa Dāmodara; *ḍāki'*—calling; *kahila*—said; *tāṅhāre*—unto him; *ei dekha*—just see here; *tomāra*—your; *gauḍīyāra*—of this Vaiṣṇava from Bengal; *vyavahāre*—behavior.

TRANSLATION

The Lord then called for Svarūpa Dāmodara and told him, "Just see the behavior of your Bengali Vaiṣṇava.

TEXT 126

ঈশ্বরমন্দিরে মোর পদ ধোয়াইল ।
সেই জল আপনি লঞা পান কৈল ॥ ১২৬ ॥

īśvara-mandire mora pada dhoyāila
sei jala āpani lañā pāna kaila

SYNONYMS

īśvara-mandire—in the temple of the Lord; *mora*—My; *pada*—feet; *dhoyāila*—washed; *sei jala*—that water; *āpani*—personally; *lañā*—taking; *pāna kaila*—drank.

TRANSLATION

"This person from Bengal has washed My feet within the temple of the Personality of Godhead. Not only that, but he has drunk the water himself.

TEXT 127

এই অপরাধে মোর কাহাঁ হবে গতি ।
তোমার 'গৌড়ীয়া' করে এতেক ফৈজতি ! ১২৭ ॥

ei aparādhe mora kāhāṅ habe gati
tomāra 'gauḍīyā' kare eteka phaijati!

SYNONYMS

ei aparādhe—by such an offense; *mora*—of Me; *kāhāṅ*—where; *habe*—will be; *gati*—destination; *tomāra gauḍīyā*—your Bengali Vaiṣṇava; *kare*—does; *eteka*—such; *phaijati*—implication.

TRANSLATION

"I now do not know what My destination is because of this offense. Indeed, your Bengali Vaiṣṇava has greatly implicated Me."

PURPORT

It is significant that Śrī Caitanya Mahāprabhu told Svarūpa Dāmodara Gosvāmī that the Bengali Vaiṣṇava was "your Gauḍīya Vaiṣṇava." This means that all Gauḍīya Vaiṣṇavas who are followers of the Caitanya cult are subordinate to Svarūpa Dāmodara Gosvāmī. The *paramparā* system is very strictly observed by Gauḍīya Vaiṣṇavas. Śrī Caitanya Mahāprabhu's personal secretary was Svarūpa Dāmodara Gosvāmī. The next group of devotees was the six Gosvāmīs, then Kavirāja Gosvāmī. It is necessary to observe the *paramparā* system of the Caitanya cult. There are many offenses one can commit while serving the Lord, and these are described in the *Bhakti-rasāmṛta-sindhu, Hari-bhakti-vilāsa* and other books. According to the rules and regulations, no one should accept obeisances in the temple of the Lord before the Deity. Nor is it proper for a devotee to offer obeisances and touch the feet of the spiritual master before the Deity. This is considered an offense. Śrī Caitanya Mahāprabhu Himself was personally the Supreme

Personality of Godhead; therefore it was not actually offensive to wash His lotus feet in the temple. However, because He was playing the part of an *ācārya,* the Lord considered Himself an ordinary human being. He also wanted to give instructions to ordinary human beings. The point is that even though one plays the part of a spiritual master, he should not accept obeisances or permit a disciple to wash his feet before the Deity. This is a matter of etiquette.

TEXT 128

তবে স্বরূপ গোসাঞি তার ঘাড়ে হাত দিয়া ।
ঢেকা মারি' পুরীর বাহির রাখিলেন লঞা ॥ ১২৮ ॥

tabe svarūpa gosāñi tāra ghāḍe hāta diyā
ḍhekā māri' purīra bāhira rākhilena lañā

SYNONYMS

tabe—thereafter; *svarūpa gosāñi*—Svarūpa Dāmodara Gosāñi; *tāra*—of him; *ghāḍe*—on the neck; *hāta diyā*—touching with the hand; *ḍhekā māri'*—pushing a little; *purīra bāhira*—out of the temple of Guṇḍicā Purī; *rākhilena*—kept; *lañā*—taking.

TRANSLATION

At this point Svarūpa Dāmodara Gosvāmī caught the Gauḍīya Vaiṣṇava by the neck and, giving him a little push, ejected him from the Guṇḍicā Purī temple and made him stay outside.

TEXT 129

পুনঃ আসি' প্রভু পায় করিল বিনয় ।
'অজ্ঞ-অপরাধ' ক্ষমা করিতে যুয়ায় ॥ ১২৯ ॥

punaḥ āsi' prabhu pāya karila vinaya
'ajña-aparādha' kṣamā karite yuyāya

SYNONYMS

punaḥ āsi'—again coming back; *prabhu pāya*—at the lotus feet of the Lord; *karila vinaya*—made a submission; *ajña-aparādha*—offense by innocent person; *kṣamā karite*—to be excused; *yuyāya*—deserves.

TRANSLATION

After Svarūpa Dāmodara Gosvāmī returned within the temple, he requested Śrī Caitanya Mahāprabhu to excuse that innocent person.

TEXT 130

তবে মহাপ্রভুর মনে সন্তোষ হইলা।
সারি করি' দুই পাশে সবারে বসাইলা॥ ১৩০ ॥

tabe mahāprabhura mane santoṣa ha-ilā
sāri kari' dui pāśe sabāre vasāilā

SYNONYMS

tabe—thereafter; *mahāprabhura*—of Śrī Caitanya Mahāprabhu; *mane*—in the mind; *santoṣa ha-ilā*—there was satisfaction; *sāri kari'*—making a line; *dui pāśe*—on two sides; *sabāre*—all of them; *vasāilā*—made to sit.

TRANSLATION

After this incident, Śrī Caitanya Mahāprabhu was very satisfied. He then asked all of the devotees to sit down in two lines on both sides.

TEXT 131

আপনে বসিয়া মাঝে, আপনার হাতে।
তৃণ, কাঁকর, কুটা লাগিলা কুড়াইতে॥ ১৩১ ॥

āpane vasiyā mājhe, āpanāra hāte
tṛṇa, kāṅkara, kuṭā lāgilā kuḍāite

SYNONYMS

āpane—personally; *vasiyā mājhe*—sitting in the middle; *āpanāra hāte*—with His own hand; *tṛṇa*—straw; *kāṅkara*—grains of sand; *kuṭā*—dirt; *lāgilā*—began; *kuḍāite*—to pick up.

TRANSLATION

The Lord then personally sat down in the middle and picked up all kinds of straw, grains of sand and dirty things.

TEXT 132

কে কত কুড়ায়, সব একত্র করিব।
যার অল্প, তার ঠাঞি পিঠা-পানা লইব॥ ১৩২ ॥

ke kata kuḍāya, saba ekatra kariba
yāra alpa, tāra ṭhāñi piṭhā-pānā la-iba

SYNONYMS

ke kata kuḍāya—how much one has collected; *saba*—all; *ekatra*—in one place; *kariba*—I shall gather; *yāra*—of whom; *alpa*—small; *tāra ṭhāñi*—from him; *piṭhā-pānā la-iba*—I will ask for cakes and sweet rice as a fine.

TRANSLATION

While Śrī Caitanya Mahāprabhu was picking up the straws and grains of sand, He said, "I shall gather everyone's collections, and I shall ask whoever has collected less than all the others to pay a fine of sweet cakes and sweet rice."

TEXT 133

এই মত সব পুরী করিল শোধন ।
শীতল, নির্মল কৈল—যেন নিজ-মন ॥ ১৩৩ ॥

ei mata saba purī karila śodhana
śītala, nirmala kaila——yena nija-mana

SYNONYMS

ei mata—in this way; *saba purī*—all of Guṇḍicā Purī; *karila śodhana*—they cleansed; *śītala*—cool; *nirmala*—clean; *kaila*—made; *yena*—as; *nija-mana*—his own mind.

TRANSLATION

In this way all the quarters of the Guṇḍicā temple were completely cleansed and cleared. All quarters were cool and spotless, like one's cleansed and pacified mind.

TEXT 134

প্রণালিকা ছাড়ি' যদি পানি বহাইল ।
নূতন নদী যেন সমুদ্রে মিলিল ॥ ১৩৪ ॥

praṇālikā chāḍi' yadi pāni vahāila
nūtana nadī yena samudre milila

SYNONYMS

praṇālikā—water from the outlets; *chāḍi'*—releasing; *yadi*—when; *pāni*—water; *vahāila*—flowed; *nūtana*—new; *nadī*—river; *yena*—as if; *samudre*—in the ocean; *milila*—met.

TRANSLATION

When the water from the different rooms was finally let out through the halls, it appeared as if new rivers were rushing out to meet the waters of the ocean.

TEXT 135

এইমত পুরদ্বার-আগে পথ যত ।
সকল শোধিল, তাহা কে বর্ণিবে কত ॥ ১৩৫ ॥

ei-mata puradvāra-āge patha yata
sakala śodhila, tāhā ke varṇibe kata

SYNONYMS

ei-mata—in this way; *pura-dvāra*—of the gateway of the temple; *āge*—in front; *patha yata*—as many avenues; *sakala*—all; *śodhila*—were cleansed; *tāhā*—that; *ke varṇibe*—who can describe; *kata*—how much.

TRANSLATION

Outside the gateway of the temple, all the roads were also cleansed, and no one could tell exactly how this was done.

PURPORT

In commenting on the cleansing of the Guṇḍicā temple, Śrīla Bhaktisiddhānta Sarasvatī Ṭhākura says that Śrī Caitanya Mahāprabhu was personally giving instructions on how one should receive Lord Kṛṣṇa, the Supreme Personality of Godhead, within one's cleansed and pacified heart. If one wants to see Kṛṣṇa seated in his heart, he must first cleanse the heart, as prescribed by Śrī Caitanya Mahāprabhu in His *Śikṣāṣṭaka* (*ceto-darpaṇa-mārjanam*). In this age, everyone's heart is unclean, as confirmed in *Śrīmad-Bhāgavatam* (*hṛdy antaḥ-stho hy abhadrāṇi*). To wash all dirty things accumulated within the heart, Śrī Caitanya Mahāprabhu advised everyone to chant the Hare Kṛṣṇa *mantra*. The first result will be that the heart is cleansed (*ceto-darpaṇa-mārjanam*). Similarly, *Śrīmad-Bhāgavatam* (1.2.17) also confirms this statement:

śṛṇvatāṁ sva-kathāḥ kṛṣṇaḥ
puṇya-śravaṇa-kīrtanaḥ
hṛdy antaḥ-stho hy abhadrāṇi
vidhunoti suhṛt-satām

"Śrī Kṛṣṇa, the Personality of Godhead, who is the Paramātmā [Supersoul] in everyone's heart and the benefactor of the truthful devotee, cleanses desire for material enjoyment from the heart of the devotee who relishes His messages, which are in themselves virtuous when properly heard and chanted."

If the devotee at all wants to cleanse his heart, he must chant and hear the glories of the Lord, Śrī Kṛṣṇa (*śṛṇvatāṁ sva-kathāḥ kṛṣṇaḥ*). This is a simple process. Kṛṣṇa Himself will help cleanse the heart because He is already seated there. Kṛṣṇa wants to continue living within the heart, and the Lord wants to give directions, but one has to keep his heart as clean as Lord Caitanya Mahāprabhu kept the Guṇḍicā temple. The devotee therefore has to cleanse his heart just as the Lord cleansed the Guṇḍicā temple. In this way one can be pacified and enriched in devotional service. If the heart is filled with straw, grains of sand, weeds or dust (in other words, *anyābhilāṣa-pūrṇa*), one cannot enthrone the Supreme Personality of Godhead there. The heart must be cleansed of all material motives brought about through fruitive work, speculative knowledge, the mystic *yoga* system and so many other forms of so-called meditation. The heart must be cleansed without ulterior motive. As Śrīla Rūpa Gosvāmī says: *anyābhilāṣitā-śūnyaṁ jñāna-karmādy-anāvṛtam.* In other words, there should not be any external motive. One should not attempt material upliftment, understanding the Supreme by speculative knowledge, fruitive activity, severe austerity and penance, and so on. All these activities are against the natural growth of spontaneous love of Godhead. As soon as these are present within the heart, the heart should be understood to be unclean and therefore unfit to serve as Kṛṣṇa's sitting place. We cannot perceive the Lord's presence in our hearts unless our hearts are cleansed.

A material desire is explained as a desire to enjoy the material world to its fullest extent. In modern language, this is called economic development. An inordinate desire for economic development is considered to be like straws and grains of sand within the heart. If one is overly engaged in material activity, the heart will always remain disturbed. As stated by Narottama dāsa Ṭhākura:

saṁsāra viṣānale, divā-niśi hiyā jvale,
juḍāite nā kainu upāya

In other words, endeavor for material opulence is against the principle of devotional service. Material enjoyment includes activities such as great sacrifices for auspicious activity, charity, austerity, elevation to the higher planetary system, and even living happily within the material world.

Modernized material benefits are like the dust of material contamination. When this dust is agitated by the whirlwind of fruitive activity, it overcomes the heart. Thus the mirror of the heart is covered with dust. There are many desires to perform auspicious and inauspicious activities, but people do not know how life after life they are keeping their hearts unclean. One who cannot give up the desire for fruitive activity is understood to be covered by the dust of material contamination. *Karmīs* generally think that the interaction of fruitive activities can be counteracted by another *karma,* or fruitive activity. This is certainly a mistaken conception. If one is deluded by such a conception, he is cheated by his own activity. Such activities have been compared to an elephant's bathing. An elephant may bathe very thoroughly, but as soon as it comes out of the river, it immediately takes some sand from the land and throws it all over its body. If one suffers due to his past fruitive activities, he cannot counteract his suffering by performing auspicious activities. The sufferings of human society cannot be counteracted by material plans. The only way suffering can be mitigated is by Kṛṣṇa consciousness. When one takes to Kṛṣṇa consciousness and engages himself in the devotional service of the Lord—beginning with chanting and hearing the glories of the Lord—the cleansing of the heart begins.

Impersonal speculation, monism (merging into the existence of the Supreme), speculative knowledge, mystical *yoga* and meditation are all compared to grains of sand. They simply cause irritation to the heart. No one can satisfy the Supreme Personality of Godhead by such activities, nor do we give the Lord a chance to sit in our hearts peacefully. Rather, the Lord is simply disturbed by them. Sometimes *yogīs* and *jñānīs* in the beginning take to the chanting of the Hare Kṛṣṇa *mahā-mantra* as a way to begin their various practices. However, when they falsely think that they have attained release from the bondage of material existence, they give up chanting. They do not consider that the ultimate goal is the form of the Lord or the name of the Lord. Such unfortunate creatures are never favored by the Supreme Personality of Godhead, for they do not know what devotional service is. They are described in *Bhagavad-gītā* in this way:

tān ahaṁ dviṣataḥ krūrān
saṁsāreṣu narādhamān
kṣipāmy ajasram aśubhān
āsurīṣv eva yoniṣu

"Those who are envious and mischievous, who are the lowest among men, are cast by Me into the ocean of material existence, into various demoniac species of life." (Bg. 16.19)

The demons are always envious of the Lord and are therefore most mischievous. By His practical example, Śrī Caitanya Mahāprabhu has shown us that all the grains of sand must be picked up thoroughly and thrown outside. Śrī Caitanya Mahāprabhu also cleansed the outside of the temple, fearing that the grains of sand would again come within.

Śrīla Bhaktisiddhānta Sarasvatī Ṭhākura explains that even though one may become free from the desire for fruitive activity, sometimes the subtle desire for fruitive activity comes into being within the heart. One often thinks of conducting business to improve devotional activity. However, the contamination is so strong that it may later develop into misunderstanding, described as *kuṭi-nāṭi* (faultfinding) and *pratiṣṭhāśā* (the desire for name and fame and for high position), *jīva-hiṁsā* (envy of other living entities), *niṣiddhācāra* (accepting things forbidden in the *śāstra*), *kāma* (desire for material gain) and *pūjā* (hankering for popularity). The word *kuṭi-nāṭi* means duplicity. As an example, one may attempt to imitate Śrīla Haridāsa Ṭhākura by living in a solitary place. One's real desire may be for name and fame—in other words, one thinks that fools will accept one to be as good as Haridāsa Ṭhākura just because one lives in a solitary place. These are all material desires. A neophyte devotee is certain to be attacked by other material desires as well—women and money. In this way the heart is again filled with dirty things and becomes harder and harder, like that of a materialist. Gradually one desires to become a reputed devotee or an *avatāra* (incarnation).

The word *jīva-hiṁsā* (envy of other living entities) actually means stopping the preaching of Kṛṣṇa consciousness. Preaching work is described as *paropakāra,* welfare activity for others. Those who are ignorant of the benefits of devotional service must be educated by preaching. If one stops preaching and simply sits down in a solitary place, he is engaging in material activity. If one desires to make a compromise with the Māyāvādīs, he is also engaged in material activity. A devotee should never make compromises with nondevotees. By acting as a professional *guru,* mystic *yogī* or miracle man, one may cheat and bluff the general public and gain fame as a wonderful mystic, but all this is considered to be dust, straw and grains of sand within the heart. In addition, one should follow the regulative principles and not desire illicit sex, gambling, intoxicants and meat.

To give us practical instructions, Lord Śrī Caitanya Mahāprabhu cleansed the temple twice. His second cleansing was more thorough. The idea was to throw away all the stumbling blocks on the path of devotional service. He cleansed the temple with firm conviction, as is evident from His using His own personal garments for cleaning. Śrī Caitanya Mahāprabhu wanted to see personally that the temple was thoroughly cleansed as clean as marble. Clean marble gives a cooling effect. Devotional service means attaining peace from all disturbances caused by material contamination. In other words, it is the process by which the mind is cooled. The mind can be peaceful and thoroughly cleansed when one no longer desires anything but devotional service.

Even though all dirty things may be cleansed away, sometimes subtle desires remain in the mind for impersonalism, monism, success and the four principles of religious activity (*dharma, artha, kāma* and *mokṣa*). All these are like spots on clean cloth. Śrī Caitanya Mahāprabhu also wanted to cleanse all these away.

By His practical activity, Śrī Caitanya Mahāprabhu informed us how to cleanse our hearts. Once the heart is cleansed, we should invite Lord Śrī Kṛṣṇa to sit down, and we should observe the festival by distributing *prasāda* and chanting the Hare Kṛṣṇa *mahā-mantra.* Śrī Caitanya Mahāprabhu used to teach every devotee by His personal behavior. Everyone who spreads the cult of Śrī Caitanya Mahāprabhu accepts a similar responsibility. The Lord was personally chastising and praising individuals in the course of the cleaning, and those who are engaged as *ācāryas* must learn from Śrī Caitanya Mahāprabhu how to train devotees by personal example. The Lord was very pleased with those who could cleanse the temple by taking out undesirable things accumulated within. This is called *anartha-nivṛtti,* cleansing the heart of all unwanted things. Thus the cleansing of the Guṇḍicā-mandira was conducted by Śrī Caitanya Mahāprabhu to let us know how the heart should be cleansed and soothed to receive Lord Śrī Kṛṣṇa and enable Him to sit within the heart without disturbance.

TEXT 136

নৃসিংহমন্দির-ভিতর-বাহির শোধিল ।
ক্ষণেক বিশ্রাম করি' নৃত্য আরম্ভিল ॥ ১৩৬ ॥

nṛsiṁha-mandira-bhitara-bāhira śodhila
kṣaṇeka viśrāma kari' nṛtya ārambhila

SYNONYMS

nṛsiṁha-mandira—the temple of Nṛsiṁhadeva; *bhitara*—inside; *bāhira*—outside; *śodhila*—cleansed; *kṣaṇeka*—for a few moments; *viśrāma*—rest; *kari'*—after taking; *nṛtya*—dancing; *ārambhila*—began.

TRANSLATION

Śrī Caitanya Mahāprabhu also cleansed the Nṛsiṁha temple inside and outside. Finally, He rested a few minutes and then began dancing.

PURPORT

The Nṛsiṁha temple is a nice temple, just outside the Guṇḍicā temple. In this temple there is a great festival on the day of Nṛsiṁha-caturdaśī. There is also a Nṛsiṁha temple at Navadvīpa where the same festival is observed, as described by Murāri Gupta in his book *Caitanya-carita.*

TEXT 137

চারিদিকে ভক্তগণ করেন কীর্তন ।
মধ্যে নৃত্য করেন প্রভু মত্তসিংহ-সম ॥ ১৩৭ ॥

cāri-dike bhakta-gaṇa karena kīrtana
madhye nṛtya karena prabhu matta-siṁha-sama

SYNONYMS

cāri-dike—all around; *bhakta-gaṇa*—devotees; *karena*—performed; *kīrtana*—congregational chanting; *madhye*—in the middle; *nṛtya*—dancing; *karena*—does; *prabhu*—Śrī Caitanya Mahāprabhu; *matta-siṁha-sama*—just like a maddened lion.

TRANSLATION

All around Śrī Caitanya Mahāprabhu all the devotees performed congregational chanting. The Lord, just like a maddened lion, danced in the middle.

TEXT 138

স্বেদ, কম্প, বৈবর্ণ্যাশ্রু পুলক, হুঙ্কার ।
নিজ-অঙ্গ ধুই' আগে চলে অশ্রুধার ॥ ১৩৮ ॥

sveda, kampa, vaivarṇyāśru pulaka, huṅkāra
nija-aṅga dhui' āge cale aśru-dhāra

SYNONYMS

sveda—perspiration; *kampa*—trembling; *vaivarṇya*—fading; *aśru*—tears; *pulaka*—jubilation; *huṅkāra*—roaring; *nija-aṅga*—personal body; *dhui'*—washing; *āge*—forward; *cale*—goes; *aśru-dhāra*—a flow of tears.

TRANSLATION

As usual, when Caitanya Mahāprabhu danced, there were perspiration, trembling, fading, tears, jubilation and roaring. Indeed, the tears from His eyes washed His body and those before Him.

TEXT 139

চারিদিকে ভক্ত-অঙ্গ কৈল প্রক্ষালন ।
শ্রাবণের মেঘ যেন করে বরিষণ ॥ ১৩৯ ॥

cāri-dike bhakta-aṅga kaila prakṣālana
śrāvaṇera megha yena kare variṣaṇa

SYNONYMS

cāri-dike—all around; *bhakta-aṅga*—the bodies of the devotees; *kaila*—did; *prakṣālana*—washing; *śrāvaṇera megha*—exactly like a cloud in the month of Śrāvaṇa (July-August); *yena*—as if; *kare variṣaṇa*—pour.

TRANSLATION

In this way Śrī Caitanya Mahāprabhu washed the bodies of all the devotees with the tears from His eyes. The tears poured like rains in the month of Śrāvaṇa.

TEXT 140

মহা-উচ্চসংকীর্তনে আকাশ ভরিল।
প্রভুর উদ্দণ্ড-নৃত্যে ভূমিকম্প হৈল ॥ ১৪০ ॥

mahā-ucca-saṅkīrtane ākāśa bharila
prabhura uddaṇḍa-nṛtye bhūmi-kampa haila

SYNONYMS

mahā-ucca-saṅkīrtane—by a great and loud performance of chanting; *ākāśa*—the sky; *bharila*—became filled; *prabhura*—of Lord Śrī Caitanya Mahāprabhu; *uddaṇḍa-nṛtye*—by dancing and jumping high; *bhūmi-kampa*—earthquake; *haila*—there was.

TRANSLATION

The sky was filled with the great and loud chanting of saṅkīrtana, and the earth shook from the jumping and dancing of Lord Caitanya Mahāprabhu.

TEXT 141

স্বরূপের উচ্চ-গান প্রভুরে সদা ভায়।
আনন্দে উদ্দণ্ড নৃত্য করে গৌররায়॥ ১৪১ ॥

svarūpera ucca-gāna prabhure sadā bhāya
ānande uddaṇḍa nṛtya kare gaurarāya

SYNONYMS

svarūpera—of Svarūpa Dāmodara Gosvāmī; *ucca-gāna*—loud singing; *prabhure*—to Śrī Caitanya Mahāprabhu; *sadā bhāya*—always very pleasing; *ānande*—in jubilation; *uddaṇḍa nṛtya*—jumping high and dancing; *kare*—performs; *gaurarāya*—Śrī Caitanya Mahāprabhu.

TRANSLATION

Śrī Caitanya Mahāprabhu always liked the loud chanting of Svarūpa Dāmodara. Therefore when Svarūpa Dāmodara sang, Śrī Caitanya Mahāprabhu danced and jumped high in jubilation.

TEXT 142

এইমত কতক্ষণ নৃত্য যে করিয়া ।
বিশ্রাম করিলা প্রভু সময় বুঝিয়া ॥ ১৪২ ॥

ei-mata kata-kṣaṇa nṛtya ye kariyā
viśrāma karilā prabhu samaya bujhiyā

SYNONYMS

ei-mata—in this way; *kata-kṣaṇa*—for some time; *nṛtya*—dancing; *ye*—that; *kariyā*—after performing; *viśrāma karilā*—rested; *prabhu*—Śrī Caitanya Mahāprabhu; *samaya bujhiyā*—understanding the time.

TRANSLATION

The Lord thus chanted and danced for some time. Finally, understanding the circumstances, He stopped.

TEXT 143

আচার্য-গোসাঞির পুত্র শ্রীগোপাল-নাম ।
নৃত্য করিতে তাঁরে আজ্ঞা দিল গৌরধাম ॥ ১৪৩ ॥

ācārya-gosāñira putra śrī-gopāla-nāma
nṛtya karite tāṅre ājñā dila gauradhāma

SYNONYMS

ācārya-gosāñira—of Śrī Advaita Ācārya; *putra*—son; *śrī-gopāla-nāma*—named Śrī Gopāla; *nṛtya karite*—to dance; *tāṅre*—unto him; *ājñā*—order; *dila*—gave; *gauradhāma*—Śrī Caitanya Mahāprabhu.

TRANSLATION

Śrī Caitanya Mahāprabhu then ordered Śrī Gopāla, the son of Advaita Ācārya, to dance.

TEXT 144

প্রেমাবেশে নৃত্য করি' হইলা মূর্চ্ছিতে ।
অচেতন হঞা তেঁহ পড়িলা ভূমিতে ॥ ১৪৪ ॥

premāveśe nṛtya kari' ha-ilā mūrcchite
acetana hañā teṅha paḍilā bhūmite

SYNONYMS

prema-āveśe—in ecstatic love; *nṛtya kari'*—dancing; *ha-ilā mūrcchite*—fainted; *acetana hañā*—being unconscious; *teṅha*—he; *paḍilā*—fell; *bhūmite*—on the ground.

TRANSLATION

While dancing in ecstatic love, Śrī Gopāla fainted and fell to the ground unconscious.

TEXT 145

আস্তে-ব্যস্তে আচার্য তাঁরে কৈল কোলে।
শ্বাস-রহিত দেখি' আচার্য হৈলা বিকলে॥ ১৪৫ ॥

āste-vyaste ācārya tāṅre kaila kole
śvāsa-rahita dekhi' ācārya hailā vikale

SYNONYMS

āste-vyaste—with great haste; *ācārya*—Advaita Ācārya; *tāṅre*—him; *kaila*—took; *kole*—on His lap; *śvāsa-rahita*—without breathing; *dekhi'*—seeing; *ācārya*—Advaita Ācārya; *hailā*—became; *vikale*—agitated.

TRANSLATION

When Śrī Gopāla fainted, Advaita Ācārya hastily took him upon His lap. Seeing that he was not breathing, He became very agitated.

TEXT 146

নৃসিংহের মন্ত্র পড়ি' মারে জল-ছাঁটি।
হুঙ্কারের শব্দে ব্রহ্মাণ্ড যায় ফাটি'॥ ১৪৬ ॥

nṛsiṁhera mantra paḍi' māre jala-chāṅṭi
huṅkārera śabde brahmāṇḍa yāya phāṭi'

SYNONYMS

nṛsiṁhera mantra—prayers to Nṛsiṁhadeva; *paḍi'*—chanting; *māre*—throws; *jala-chāṅṭi*—sprinkling of water; *huṅkārera śabde*—by the sound of roaring; *brahmāṇḍa*—the whole universe; *yāya*—becomes; *phāṭi'*—cracking.

TRANSLATION

Advaita Ācārya and others began to chant the holy name of Lord Nṛsiṁha and sprinkle water. The roaring of the chant was so great that it seemed to shake the entire universe.

TEXT 147

অনেক করিল, তবু না হয় চেতন ।
আচার্য কান্দেন, কান্দে সব ভক্তগণ ॥ ১৪৭ ॥

aneka karila, tabu nā haya cetana
ācārya kāndena, kānde saba bhakta-gaṇa

SYNONYMS

aneka karila—much endeavor was done; *tabu*—still; *nā haya*—there was not; *cetana*—consciousness; *ācārya kāndena*—Advaita Ācārya began to cry; *kānde*—cried; *saba bhakta-gaṇa*—all the other devotees.

TRANSLATION

When the boy did not regain consciousness after some time, Advaita Ācārya and the other devotees began to cry.

TEXT 148

তবে মহাপ্রভু তাঁর বুকে হস্ত দিল ।
'উঠহ গোপাল' বলি' উচ্চৈঃস্বরে কহিল ॥ ১৪৮ ॥

tabe mahāprabhu tāṅra buke hasta dila
'uṭhaha gopāla' bali' uccaiḥsvare kahila

SYNONYMS

tabe—at that time; *mahāprabhu*—Śrī Caitanya Mahāprabhu; *tāṅra buke*—on his chest; *hasta*—hand; *dila*—placed; *uṭhaha gopāla*—stand up, Gopāla; *bali'*—saying; *uccaiḥ-svare*—very loudly; *kahila*—said.

TRANSLATION

Then Śrī Caitanya Mahāprabhu placed His hand on the chest of Śrī Gopāla and said loudly, "Gopāla, stand up."

TEXT 149

শুনিতেই গোপালের হইল চেতন ।
'হরি' বলি' নৃত্য করে সর্বভক্তগণ ॥ ১৪৯ ॥

śunitei gopālera ha-ila cetana
'hari' bali' nṛtya kare sarva-bhakta-gaṇa

SYNONYMS

śunitei—upon hearing; *gopālera*—of Śrī Gopāla; *ha-ila*—there was; *cetana*—consciousness; *hari bali'*—chanting the holy name of Hari; *nṛtya kare*—danced; *sarva-bhakta-gaṇa*—all the devotees.

TRANSLATION

As soon as Gopāla heard the voice of Śrī Caitanya Mahāprabhu, he immediately came to his senses. All the devotees then began to dance, chanting the holy name of Hari.

TEXT 150

এই লীলা বর্ণিয়াছেন দাস বৃন্দাবন ।
অতএব সংক্ষেপ করি' করিলুঁ বর্ণন ॥ ১৫০ ॥

ei līlā varṇiyāchena dāsa vṛndāvana
ataeva saṅkṣepa kari' kariluṅ varṇana

SYNONYMS

ei līlā—this pastime; *varṇiyāchena*—has described; *dāsa vṛndāvana*—Vṛndāvana dāsa Ṭhākura; *ataeva*—therefore; *saṅkṣepa*—briefly; *kari'*—doing; *kariluṅ varṇana*—I have described.

TRANSLATION

This incident has been described in detail by Vṛndāvana dāsa Ṭhākura. Therefore I have described it only in brief.

PURPORT

This is a matter of etiquette. If a previous *ācārya* has already written about something, there is no need to repeat it for personal sense gratification or to outdo the previous *ācārya*. Unless there is some definite improvement, one should not repeat.

TEXT 151

তবে মহাপ্রভু ক্ষণেক বিশ্রাম করিয়া ।
স্নান করিবারে গেলা ভক্তগণ লঞা ॥ ১৫১ ॥

tabe mahāprabhu kṣaṇeka viśrāma kariyā
snāna karibāre gelā bhakta-gaṇa lañā

SYNONYMS

tabe—thereafter; *mahāprabhu*—Śrī Caitanya Mahāprabhu; *kṣaṇeka*—for some time; *viśrāma kariyā*—taking rest; *snāna karibāre*—for bathing; *gelā*—went; *bhakta-gaṇa lañā*—taking all the devotees.

TRANSLATION

After taking rest, Śrī Caitanya Mahāprabhu and all the devotees departed to take their baths.

TEXT 152

তীরে উঠি' পরেন প্রভু শুষ্ক বসন ।
নৃসিংহ-দেবে নমস্করি' গেলা উপবন ॥ ১৫২ ॥

tīre uṭhi' parena prabhu śuṣka vasana
nṛsiṁha-deve namaskari' gelā upavana

SYNONYMS

tīre uṭhi'—getting on the bank; *parena*—puts on; *prabhu*—Śrī Caitanya Mahāprabhu; *śuṣka vasana*—dry garments; *nṛsiṁha-deve*—unto Lord Nṛsiṁhadeva; *namaskari'*—offering obeisances; *gelā upavana*—entered a garden.

TRANSLATION

After bathing, the Lord stood on the bank of the lake and put on dry garments. After offering obeisances to Lord Nṛsiṁhadeva, whose temple was nearby, the Lord entered a garden.

TEXT 153

উদ্যানে বসিলা প্রভু ভক্তগণ লঞা ।
তবে বাণীনাথ আইলা মহাপ্রসাদ লঞা ॥ ১৫৩ ॥

udyāne vasilā prabhu bhakta-gaṇa lañā
tabe vāṇīnātha āilā mahā-prasāda lañā

SYNONYMS

udyāne—in the garden; *vasilā*—sat down; *prabhu*—Śrī Caitanya Mahāprabhu; *bhakta-gaṇa lañā*—with the devotees; *tabe*—at that time; *vāṇīnātha*—Vāṇīnātha Rāya; *āilā*—came; *mahā-prasāda lañā*—bringing all kinds of *mahā-prasāda.*

TRANSLATION

In the garden, Śrī Caitanya Mahāprabhu sat down with the other devotees. Vāṇīnātha Rāya then came and brought all kinds of mahā-prasāda.

TEXTS 154-155

কাশীমিশ্র, তুলসী-পড়িছা—তুই জন ।
পঞ্চশত লোক যত করয়ে ভোজন ॥ ১৫৪ ॥
তত অন্ন-পিঠা-পানা সব পাঠাইল ।
দেখি' মহাপ্রভুর মনে সন্তোষ হইল ॥ ১৫৫ ॥

kāśī-miśra, tulasī-paḍichā——dui jana
pañca-śata loka yata karaye bhojana

tata anna-piṭhā-pānā saba pāṭhāila
dekhi' mahāprabhura mane santoṣa ha-ila

SYNONYMS

kāśī-miśra—Kāśī Miśra; *tulasī-paḍichā*—Tulasī, the superintendent of the temple; *dui jana*—two persons; *pañca-śata loka*—five hundred men; *yata*—as much; *karaye bhojana*—eat; *tata*—so; *anna-piṭhā-pānā*—rice, cakes and sweet rice; *saba*—all; *pāṭhāila*—sent; *dekhi'*—seeing; *mahāprabhura*—of Śrī Caitanya Mahāprabhu; *mane*—in the mind; *santoṣa*—satisfaction; *ha-ila*—there was.

TRANSLATION

Both Kāśī Miśra and Tulasī, the superintendent of the temple, brought as much prasāda as five hundred men could eat. Seeing the large quantity of prasāda, which consisted of rice, cakes, sweet rice and a variety of vegetables, Śrī Caitanya Mahāprabhu was very satisfied.

TEXT 156

পুরী-গোসাঞি, মহাপ্রভু, ভারতী ব্রহ্মানন্দ ।
অদ্বৈত-আচার্য, আর প্রভু-নিত্যানন্দ ॥ ১৫৬ ॥

purī-gosāñi, mahāprabhu, bhāratī brahmānanda
advaita-ācārya, āra prabhu-nityānanda

SYNONYMS

purī-gosāñi—Paramānanda Purī; *mahāprabhu*—Śrī Caitanya Mahāprabhu; *bhāratī brahmānanda*—Brahmānanda Bhāratī; *advaita-ācārya*—Advaita Ācārya; *āra*—and; *prabhu-nityānanda*—Nityānanda Prabhu.

TRANSLATION

Among the devotees present with Śrī Caitanya Mahāprabhu were Paramānanda Purī, Brahmānanda Bhāratī, Advaita Ācārya and Nityānanda Prabhu.

TEXT 157

আচার্যরত্ন, আচার্যনিধি, শ্রীবাস, গদাধর ।
শঙ্কর, নন্দনাচার্য, আর রাঘব, বক্রেশ্বর ॥ ১৫৭ ॥

ācāryaratna, ācāryanidhi, śrīvāsa, gadādhara
śaṅkara, nandanācārya, āra rāghava, vakreśvara

SYNONYMS

ācāryaratna—Candraśekhara; *ācāryanidhi*—Ācāryanidhi; *śrīvāsa*—Śrīvāsa Ṭhākura; *gadādhara*—Gadādhara Paṇḍita; *śaṅkara*—Śaṅkara; *nandana-ācārya*—Nandanācārya; *āra*—and; *rāghava*—Rāghava Paṇḍita; *vakreśvara*—Vakreśvara.

TRANSLATION

Ācāryaratna, Ācāryanidhi, Śrīvāsa Ṭhākura, Gadādhara Paṇḍita, Śaṅkara, Nandanācārya, Rāghava Paṇḍita and Vakreśvara were also present.

TEXT 158

প্রভু-আজ্ঞা পাঞা বৈসে আপনে সার্বভৌম ।
পিণ্ডার উপরে প্রভু বৈসে লঞা ভক্তগণ ॥ ১৫৮ ॥

prabhu-ājñā pāñā vaise āpane sārvabhauma
piṇḍāra upare prabhu vaise lañā bhakta-gaṇa

SYNONYMS

prabhu-ājñā—the order of the Lord; *pāñā*—getting; *vaise*—sits down; *āpane*—personally; *sārvabhauma*—Sārvabhauma Bhaṭṭācārya; *piṇḍāra upare*—on raised platforms; *prabhu*—Śrī Caitanya Mahāprabhu; *vaise*—sits; *lañā*—along with; *bhakta-gaṇa*—all the devotees.

TRANSLATION

Receiving the permission of the Lord, Sārvabhauma Bhaṭṭācārya sat down. Śrī Caitanya Mahāprabhu and all His devotees sat on raised wooden seats.

TEXT 159

তার তলে, তার তলে করি' অনুক্রম ।
উদ্যান ভরি' বৈসে ভক্ত করিতে ভোজন ॥ ১৫৯ ॥

tāra tale, tāra tale kari' anukrama
udyāna bhari' vaise bhakta karite bhojana

SYNONYMS

tāra tale—below them; *tāra tale*—below them; *kari'*—in this way; *anukrama*—consecutively; *udyāna bhari'*—filling the entire garden; *vaise*—sit; *bhakta*—all the devotees; *karite bhojana*—to take lunch.

TRANSLATION

In this way all the devotees sat down to take their lunch in consecutive lines, one beside the other.

TEXT 160

'হরিদাস' বলি' প্রভু ডাকে ঘনে ঘন ।
দূরে রহি' হরিদাস করে নিবেদন ॥ ১৬০ ॥

'haridāsa' bali' prabhu ḍāke ghane ghana
dūre rahi' haridāsa kare nivedana

SYNONYMS

haridāsa bali'—calling Haridāsa; *prabhu*—Śrī Caitanya Mahāprabhu; *ḍāke*—calls; *ghane ghana*—repeatedly; *dūre rahi'*—standing at a distance; *haridāsa*—Ṭhākura Haridāsa; *kare nivedana*—submitted.

TRANSLATION

Śrī Caitanya Mahāprabhu was repeatedly calling, "Haridāsa, Haridāsa," and at that time Haridāsa, standing at a distance, spoke as follows.

TEXT 161

ভক্ত-সঙ্গে প্রভু করুন প্রসাদ অঙ্গীকার।
এ-সঙ্গে বসিতে যোগ্য নহি মুঞি ছার ॥ ১৬১ ॥

bhakta-saṅge prabhu karuna prasāda aṅgīkāra
e-saṅge vasite yogya nahi muñi chāra

SYNONYMS

bhakta-saṅge prabhu—let Śrī Caitanya Mahāprabhu sit down with the devotees; *karuna*—let Him do; *prasāda*—of remnants of food; *aṅgīkāra*—accepting; *e-saṅge*—with this batch; *vasite*—to sit down; *yogya*—befitting; *nahi*—am not; *muñi*—I; *chāra*—most abominable.

TRANSLATION

Haridāsa Ṭhākura said, "Let Lord Śrī Caitanya Mahāprabhu take His lunch with the devotees. Since I am abominable, I cannot sit down among you.

TEXT 162

পাছে মোরে প্রসাদ গোবিন্দ দিবে বহির্দ্বারে।
মন জানি' প্রভু পুনঃ না বলিল তাঁরে ॥ ১৬২ ॥

pāche more prasāda govinda dibe bahirdvāre
mana jāni' prabhu punaḥ nā balila tāṅre

SYNONYMS

pāche—at last; *more*—unto me; *prasāda*—remnants of food; *govinda*—the personal servant of Śrī Caitanya Mahāprabhu; *dibe*—will deliver; *bahirdvāre*—outside the door; *mana jāni'*—understanding the mind; *prabhu*—Śrī Caitanya Mahāprabhu; *punaḥ*—again; *nā*—not; *balila*—called; *tāṅre*—him.

TRANSLATION

"Govinda will give me prasāda later, outside the door." Understanding his mind, Śrī Caitanya Mahāprabhu did not call him again.

TEXTS 163-164

স্বরূপ-গোসাঞি, জগদানন্দ, দামোদর।
কাশীশ্বর, গোপীনাথ, বাণীনাথ, শঙ্কর ॥ ১৬৩ ॥

পরিবেশন করে তাহাঁ এই সাতজন।
মধ্যে মধ্যে হরিধ্বনি করে ভক্তগণ ॥ ১৬৪ ॥

svarūpa-gosāñi, jagadānanda, dāmodara
kāśīśvara, gopīnātha, vāṇīnātha, śaṅkara

pariveśana kare tāhāṅ ei sāta-jana
madhye madhye hari-dhvani kare bhakta-gaṇa

SYNONYMS

svarūpa-gosāñi—Svarūpa Dāmodara Gosvāmī; *jagadānanda*—Jagadānanda; *dāmodara*—Dāmodara Paṇḍita; *kāśīśvara*—Kāśīśvara; *gopīnātha, vāṇīnātha, śaṅkara*—Gopīnātha, Vāṇīnātha and Śaṅkara; *pariveśana kare*—distribute; *tāhāṅ*—there; *ei*—these; *sāta-jana*—seven persons; *madhye madhye*—at intervals; *hari-dhvani*—resounding of the holy name of Hari; *kare*—do; *bhakta-gaṇa*—all the devotees.

TRANSLATION

Svarūpa Dāmodara Gosvāmī, Jagadānanda, Dāmodara Paṇḍita, Kāśīśvara, Gopīnātha, Vāṇīnātha and Śaṅkara distributed prasāda, and the devotees chanted the holy names at intervals.

TEXT 165

পুলিন-ভোজন কৃষ্ণ পূর্বে যৈছে কৈল।
সেই লীলা মহাপ্রভুর মনে স্মৃতি হৈল ॥ ১৬৫ ॥

pulina-bhojana kṛṣṇa pūrve yaiche kaila
sei līlā mahāprabhura mane smṛti haila

SYNONYMS

pulina—in the forest; *bhojana*—eating; *kṛṣṇa*—Lord Kṛṣṇa; *pūrve*—formerly; *yaiche*—as; *kaila*—performed; *sei līlā*—the same pastime; *mahāprabhura*—of Śrī Caitanya Mahāprabhu; *mane*—in the mind; *smṛti haila*—there was remembrance.

TRANSLATION

Lord Śrī Kṛṣṇa had previously taken His lunch in the forest, and that very pastime was remembered by Śrī Caitanya Mahāprabhu.

TEXT 166

যদ্যপি প্রেমাবেশে প্রভু হৈলা অস্থির ।
সময় বুঝিয়া প্রভু হৈলা কিছু ধীর ॥ ১৬৬ ॥

yadyapi premāveśe prabhu hailā asthira
samaya bujhiyā prabhu hailā kichu dhīra

SYNONYMS

yadyapi—although; *prema-āveśe*—in ecstatic love; *prabhu*—Śrī Caitanya Mahāprabhu; *hailā*—became; *asthira*—agitated; *samaya bujhiyā*—understanding the time and circumstances; *prabhu*—Śrī Caitanya Mahāprabhu; *hailā*—became; *kichu*—somewhat; *dhīra*—patient.

TRANSLATION

Just by remembering the pastimes of Lord Śrī Kṛṣṇa, Śrī Caitanya Mahāprabhu was agitated by ecstatic love. However, considering the time and circumstance, He remained somewhat patient.

TEXT 167

প্রভু কহে,—মোরে দেহ' লাফ্রা-ব্যঞ্জনে ।
পিঠা-পানা, অমৃত-গুটিকা দেহ' ভক্তগণে ॥ ১৬৭ ॥

prabhu kahe, —more deha' lāphrā-vyañjane
piṭhā-pānā, amṛta-guṭikā deha' bhakta-gaṇe

SYNONYMS

prabhu kahe—the Lord said; *more*—unto Me; *deha'*—give; *lāphrā-vyañjane*—ordinary vegetable; *piṭhā-pānā*—cakes and sweet rice; *amṛta-guṭikā*—and the preparation named *amṛta-guṭikā; deha'*—deliver; *bhakta-gaṇe*—to the devotees.

TRANSLATION

Śrī Caitanya Mahāprabhu said, "You can give me the ordinary vegetable known as lāphrā-vyañjana, and you may deliver to all the devotees better preparations like cakes, sweet rice and amṛta-guṭikā."

PURPORT

This *lāphrā-vyañjana* is a combination of several green vegetables all mixed together. It is often mixed with rice and delivered to poor men. *Amṛta-guṭikā* is a preparation of thick *purī* mixed with condensed milk. It is also known as *amṛta-rasāvalī.*

TEXT 168

সর্বজ্ঞ প্রভু জানেন যাঁরে যেই ভায়।
তাঁরে তাঁরে সেই দেওয়ায় স্বরূপ-দ্বারায়॥ ১৬৮॥

sarvajña prabhu jānena yāṅre yei bhāya
tāṅre tāṅre sei deoyāya svarūpa-dvārāya

SYNONYMS

sarva-jña prabhu—the omniscient Lord Śrī Caitanya Mahāprabhu; *jānena*—knows; *yāṅre*—to whom; *yei*—whatever; *bhāya*—appeals; *tāṅre tāṅre*—unto each person; *sei*—that; *deoyāya*—orders to administer; *svarūpa-dvārāya*—by Svarūpa Dāmodara.

TRANSLATION

Since Lord Śrī Caitanya Mahāprabhu is omniscient, He knew what type of preparation each person liked. He therefore had Svarūpa Dāmodara deliver these preparations to their full satisfaction.

TEXT 169

জগদানন্দ বেড়ায় পরিবেশন করিতে।
প্রভুর পাতে ভাল-দ্রব্য দেন আচম্বিতে॥ ১৬৯॥

jagadānanda beḍāya pariveśana karite
prabhura pāte bhāla-dravya dena ācambite

SYNONYMS

jagadānanda—Jagadānanda; *beḍāya*—walks; *pariveśana*—distribution of *prasāda; karite*—to do; *prabhura pāte*—on the plate of Śrī Caitanya Mahāprabhu; *bhāla-dravya*—the first-class preparations; *dena*—puts; *ācambite*—suddenly.

TRANSLATION

Jagadānanda went to distribute prasāda, and suddenly he placed all the first-class preparations on the plate of Śrī Caitanya Mahāprabhu.

TEXT 170

যদ্যপি দিলে প্রভু তাঁরে করেন রোষ।
বলে-ছলে তবু দেন, দিলে সে সন্তোষ॥ ১৭০॥

yadyapi dile prabhu tāṅre karena roṣa
bale-chale tabu dena, dile se santoṣa

SYNONYMS

yadyapi—although; *dile*—by such deliverance; *prabhu*—Śrī Caitanya Mahāprabhu; *tāṅre*—unto him; *karena*—does; *roṣa*—anger; *bale-chale*—somehow or other (sometimes by tricks, sometimes by force); *tabu*—still; *dena*—delivers; *dile*—when he delivers; *se santoṣa*—Śrī Caitanya Mahāprabhu was very pleased.

TRANSLATION

When such nice prasāda was put on the plate of Śrī Caitanya Mahāprabhu, the Lord was outwardly very angry. Nonetheless, when the preparations were placed on His plate sometimes by tricks and sometimes by force, the Lord was satisfied.

TEXT 171

পুনরপি সেই দ্রব্য করে নিরীক্ষণ ।
তাঁর ভয়ে প্রভু কিছু করেন ভক্ষণ ॥ ১৭১ ॥

punarapi sei dravya kare nirīkṣaṇa
tāṅra bhaye prabhu kichu karena bhakṣaṇa

SYNONYMS

punarapi—again; *sei dravya*—that very thing; *kare nirīkṣaṇa*—sees carefully; *tāṅra bhaye*—out of fear of Jagadānanda; *prabhu*—Śrī Caitanya Mahāprabhu; *kichu*—something; *karena*—does; *bhakṣaṇa*—eating.

TRANSLATION

When the food was thus delivered, Śrī Caitanya Mahāprabhu looked at it for some time. Being afraid of Jagadānanda, He finally ate something.

TEXT 172

না খাইলে জগদানন্দ করিবে উপবাস ।
তাঁর আগে কিছু খা'ন—মনে ঐ ত্রাস ॥ ১৭২ ॥

nā khāile jagadānanda karibe upavāsa
tāṅra āge kichu khā'na——mane ai trāsa

SYNONYMS

nā khāile—if He did not eat; *jagadānanda*—Jagadānanda; *karibe*—will observe; *upavāsa*—fasting; *tāṅra āge*—before him; *kichu khā'na*—eats something; *mane*—within the mind; *ai*—that; *trāsa*—fear.

TRANSLATION

The Lord knew that if He did not eat the food offered by Jagadānanda, Jagadānanda would certainly fast. Being afraid of this, Lord Śrī Caitanya Mahāprabhu ate some of the prasāda he offered.

TEXT 173

স্বরূপ-গোসাঞি ভাল মিষ্টপ্রসাদ লঞা ।
প্রভুকে নিবেদন করে আগে দাণ্ডাঞা ॥ ১৭৩ ॥

svarūpa-gosāñi bhāla miṣṭa-prasāda lañā
prabhuke nivedana kare āge dāṇḍāñā

SYNONYMS

svarūpa-gosāñi—Svarūpa Dāmodara; *bhāla*—first-class; *miṣṭa-prasāda*—sweetmeats; *lañā*—taking; *prabhuke*—unto Lord Caitanya Mahāprabhu; *nivedana kare*—offered; *āge*—in front of Him; *dāṇḍāñā*—standing.

TRANSLATION

Svarūpa Dāmodara Gosvāmī then brought some excellent sweetmeats, and, standing before the Lord, offered them to Him.

TEXT 174

এই মহাপ্রসাদ অল্প করহ আস্বাদন ।
দেখ, জগন্নাথ কৈছে কর্যাছেন ভোজন ॥ ১৭৪ ॥

ei mahā-prasāda alpa karaha āsvādana
dekha, jagannātha kaiche karyāchena bhojana

SYNONYMS

ei mahā-prasāda—this *mahā-prasāda; alpa*—a little; *karaha āsvādana*—You must taste; *dekha*—just see; *jagannātha*—Lord Jagannātha; *kaiche*—how; *karyāchena*—has done; *bhojana*—eating.

TRANSLATION

Svarūpa Dāmodara Gosvāmī then said, "Just take a little of this mahā-prasāda, and see how it is that Lord Jagannātha has accepted it."

TEXT 175

এত বলি' আগে কিছু করে সমর্পণ ।
তাঁর স্নেহে প্রভু কিছু করেন ভোজন ॥ ১৭৫ ॥

eta bali' āge kichu kare samarpaṇa
tāṅra snehe prabhu kichu karena bhojana

SYNONYMS

eta bali'—saying this; *āge*—in front; *kichu*—something; *kare samarpaṇa*—offers; *tāṅra*—of him; *snehe*—out of affection; *prabhu*—Lord Śrī Caitanya Mahāprabhu; *kichu*—some; *karena bhojana*—eats.

TRANSLATION

Upon saying this, Svarūpa Dāmodara Gosvāmī placed some food before the Lord, and the Lord, out of affection, ate it.

TEXT 176

এই মত দুইজন করে বারবার ।
বিচিত্র এই দুই ভক্তের স্নেহ-ব্যবহার ॥ ১৭৬ ॥

ei mata dui-jana kare bāra-bāra
vicitra ei dui bhaktera sneha-vyavahāra

SYNONYMS

ei mata—in this way; *dui-jana*—both persons (Svarūpa Dāmodara and Jagadānanda); *kare*—do; *bāra-bāra*—again and again; *vicitra*—uncommon; *ei*—these; *dui*—two; *bhaktera*—of devotees; *sneha-vyavahāra*—affectionate behavior.

TRANSLATION

Svarūpa Dāmodara and Jagadānanda again and again offered the Lord some food. Thus they behaved affectionately with the Lord. This was very, very uncommon.

TEXT 177

সার্বভৌমে প্রভু বসাঞাছেন বাম-পাশে ।
দুই ভক্তের স্নেহ দেখি' সার্বভৌম হাসে ॥ ১৭৭ ॥

sārvabhaume prabhu vasāñāchena vāma-pāśe
dui bhaktera sneha dekhi' sārvabhauma hāse

SYNONYMS

sārvabhaume—Sārvabhauma Bhaṭṭācārya; *prabhu*—the Lord; *vasāñāchena*—made to sit; *vāma-pāśe*—on His left side; *dui bhaktera*—of the two devotees; *sneha*—the affection; *dekhi'*—seeing; *sārvabhauma*—Sārvabhauma Bhaṭṭācārya; *hāse*—smiles.

TRANSLATION

The Lord made Sārvabhauma Bhaṭṭācārya sit on His left side, and when Sārvabhauma saw the behavior of Svarūpa Dāmodara and Jagadānanda, he smiled.

TEXT 178

সার্বভৌমে দেয়ান প্রভু প্রসাদ উত্তম ।
স্নেহ করি' বারবার করান ভোজন ॥ ১৭৮ ॥

sārvabhaume deyāna prabhu prasāda uttama
sneha kari' bāra-bāra karāna bhojana

SYNONYMS

sārvabhaume—unto Sārvabhauma Bhaṭṭācārya; *deyāna*—causes others to deliver; *prabhu*—Śrī Caitanya Mahāprabhu; *prasāda*—remnants of food; *uttama*—first-class; *sneha kari'*—out of affection; *bāra-bāra*—again and again; *karāna*—causes; *bhojana*—his eating.

TRANSLATION

Lord Śrī Caitanya Mahāprabhu also wanted to offer Sārvabhauma Bhaṭṭācārya first-class food; therefore, out of affection, He had the servers put first-class food on his plate again and again.

TEXT 179

গোপীনাথাচার্য উত্তম মহাপ্রসাদ আনি' ।
সার্বভৌমে দিয়া কহে সুমধুর বাণী ॥ ১৭৯ ॥

gopīnāthācārya uttama mahā-prasāda āni'
sārvabhaume diyā kahe sumadhura vāṇī

SYNONYMS

gopīnātha-ācārya—Gopīnātha Ācārya; *uttama*—first-class; *mahā-prasāda*—remnants of food; *āni'*—bringing; *sārvabhaume*—to Sārvabhauma Bhaṭṭācārya; *diyā*—delivering; *kahe*—says; *su-madhura*—very sweet; *vāṇī*—words.

TRANSLATION

Gopīnātha Ācārya also brought first-class food and offered it to Sārvabhauma Bhaṭṭācārya while speaking sweet words.

TEXT 180

কাহাঁ ভট্টাচার্যের পূর্ব জড়-ব্যবহার ।
কাহাঁ এই পরমানন্দ,—করহ বিচার ॥ ১৮০ ॥

kāhāṅ bhaṭṭācāryera pūrva jaḍa-vyavahāra
kāhāṅ ei paramānanda,——karaha vicāra

SYNONYMS

kāhāṅ—where; *bhaṭṭācāryera*—of Sārvabhauma Bhaṭṭācārya; *pūrva*—previous; *jaḍa-vyavahāra*—material behavior; *kāhāṅ*—where; *ei*—this; *parama-ānanda*—transcendental bliss; *karaha vicāra*—just try to consider.

TRANSLATION

After serving Bhaṭṭācārya with first-class prasāda, Gopīnātha Ācārya said, "Just imagine what Bhaṭṭācārya's previous mundane behavior must have been! Just consider how at present he is enjoying transcendental bliss."

PURPORT

Sārvabhauma Bhaṭṭācārya was previously a *smārta-brāhmaṇa*—that is, one who strictly follows the Vedic principles on the mundane platform. On the mundane platform, one cannot believe that *prasāda* is transcendental, that Govinda is the original form of the Supreme Personality of Godhead, or that a Vaiṣṇava is a liberated person. These transcendental considerations are out of the ordinary Vedic scholar's jurisdiction. Most scholars are called Vedāntists. So-called followers of Vedānta philosophy consider the Absolute Truth to be impersonal. They also believe that a person born in a particular caste cannot change his caste until he dies and takes rebirth. The *smārta-brāhmaṇas* also reject the fact that *mahā-prasāda* (food offered to the Deity) is transcendental and materially uncontaminated. Originally, Sārvabhauma Bhaṭṭācārya was subjected to all the rules and regulations of the Vedic principles on the mundane platform. Now Gopīnātha Ācārya pointed out how Sārvabhauma Bhaṭṭācārya had been converted by the causeless mercy of Śrī Caitanya Mahāprabhu. Being converted, Sārvabhauma partook of *prasāda* with the Vaiṣṇavas. Indeed, he sat by the side of Śrī Caitanya Mahāprabhu.

TEXT 181

সার্বভৌম কহে,—আমি তার্কিক কুবুদ্ধি।
তোমার প্রসাদে মোর এ সম্পৎ-সিদ্ধি ॥ ১৮১ ॥

sārvabhauma kahe,——āmi tārkika kubuddhi
tomāra prasāde mora e sampat-siddhi

SYNONYMS

sārvabhauma kahe—Sārvabhauma Bhaṭṭācārya replied; *āmi*—I; *tārkika*—a mundane logician; *ku-buddhi*—less intelligent; *tomāra prasāde*—by your mercy; *mora*—my; *e*—this; *sampat*—opulence; *siddhi*—perfection.

TRANSLATION

Sārvabhauma Bhaṭṭācārya replied, "I was simply a less intelligent logician. However, by Your grace, I have received this opulence of perfection.

TEXT 182

মহাপ্রভু বিনা কেহ নাহি দয়াময়।
কাকেরে গরুড় করে,—ঐছে কোন্ হয় ॥ ১৮২ ॥

mahāprabhu vinā keha nāhi dayāmaya
kākere garuḍa kare,——aiche kon haya

SYNONYMS

mahāprabhu—Lord Śrī Caitanya Mahāprabhu; *vinā*—except; *keha*—anybody; *nāhi*—there is not; *dayā-maya*—so merciful; *kākere*—unto a crow; *garuḍa*—the biggest eagle; *kare*—transformed; *aiche*—such; *kon haya*—who is another.

TRANSLATION

"But for Śrī Caitanya Mahāprabhu," Sārvabhauma Bhaṭṭācārya continued, "who is so merciful? He has converted a crow into a Garuḍa. Who could be so merciful?

TEXT 183

তার্কিক-শৃগাল-সঙ্গে ভেউ-ভেউ করি ।
সেই মুখে এবে সদা কহি 'কৃষ্ণ' 'হরি' ॥ ১৮৩ ॥

tārkika-śṛgāla-saṅge bheu-bheu kari
sei mukhe ebe sadā kahi 'kṛṣṇa' 'hari'

SYNONYMS

tārkika—logician; *śṛgāla*—jackals; *saṅge*—in the association of; *bheu-bheu kari*—barking; *sei mukhe*—in that very mouth; *ebe*—now; *sadā*—always; *kahi*—speak; *kṛṣṇa*—the holy name of Lord Kṛṣṇa; *hari*—Hari.

TRANSLATION

"In the association of the jackals of logic, I simply continued to bark a resounding bheu bheu. Now, from the same mouth I am chanting the holy names Kṛṣṇa and Hari.

TEXT 184

কাহাঁ বহির্মুখ তার্কিক-শিষ্যগণ-সঙ্গে ।
কাহাঁ এই সঙ্গসুধা-সমুদ্র-তরঙ্গে ॥ ১৮৪ ॥

kāhāṅ bahirmukha tārkika-śiṣyagaṇa-saṅge
kāhāṅ ei saṅga-sudhā-samudra-taraṅge

SYNONYMS

kāhāṅ—whereas; *bahiḥ-mukha*—nondevotees; *tārkika*—of logic; *śiṣya-gaṇa*—disciples; *saṅge*—with; *kāhāṅ*—now; *ei*—this; *saṅga*—association; *sudhā*—of nectar; *samudra*—of the ocean; *taraṅge*—in the waves.

TRANSLATION

"Whereas I associated with the disciples of logic, all nondevotees, I am now merged in the waves of the nectarean ocean of the association of devotees."

PURPORT

As Śrīla Bhaktisiddhānta Sarasvatī Ṭhākura explains, the word *bahirmukha* refers to a person who is very busy tasting material enjoyment. Such a person always poses himself as an enjoyer of the external energy of the Supreme Personality of

Godhead. Being attracted by external opulence, the nondevotee always forgets his intimate relationship with Kṛṣṇa. Such a person does not like the idea of becoming Kṛṣṇa conscious. This is explained by Śrīla Prahlāda Mahārāja in *Śrīmad-Bhāgavatam* (7.5.30):

matir na kṛṣṇe parataḥ svato vā
mitho 'bhipadyeta gṛha-vratānām
adānta-gobhir viśatāṁ tamisraṁ
punaḥ punaś carvita-carvaṇānām

Materialists who are overly attracted to the material body, material world and material enjoyment, who cannot control their material senses, are carried to the darkest regions of material existence. Such people cannot become Kṛṣṇa conscious, neither by themselves nor by congregational effort. Such people do not understand that the goal of life for a human being is to understand the Supreme Personality of Godhead, Viṣṇu. A human life is especially meant for this purpose, and one has to go through all kinds of penances and austerities and set aside the propensity for sense gratification. Materialists always remain blind because they are always guided by blind rascals. A materialistic person considers himself free to act as he likes. He does not know that he is rigidly controlled by the stringent laws of nature, nor does he know that he has to transmigrate from one body to another and perpetually rot in material existence. Such rascals and foolish people are lured by the prayers of their foolish leaders for sense gratification, and they cannot understand what is meant by Kṛṣṇa consciousness. The material world exists outside the spiritual sky, and a foolish materialist cannot estimate the extent of this material sky. What, then, can he know of the spiritual sky? Materialists simply believe their imperfect senses and do not take instructions from the revealed scriptures. According to Vedic civilization, one has to see through the authority of the revealed scriptures. *Śāstra-cakṣuḥ:* one should see everything through the medium of the Vedic literature. In this way, one can distinguish between the spiritual world and material world. If one ignores such instructions, he cannot be convinced of the existence of the spiritual world. Because they have forgotten their spiritual identity, materialists take this material world as the all in all. They are therefore called *bahirmukha.*

TEXT 185

প্রভু কহে,—পূর্বে সিদ্ধ কৃষ্ণে তোমার প্রীতি ।
তোমা-সঙ্গে আমা-সবার হৈল কৃষ্ণে মতি ॥ ১৮৫ ॥

prabhu kahe,——pūrve siddha kṛṣṇe tomāra prīti
tomā-saṅge āmā-sabāra haila kṛṣṇe mati

SYNONYMS

prabhu kahe—the Lord said; *pūrve*—previously; *siddha*—perfected; *kṛṣṇe*—in Kṛṣṇa consciousness; *tomāra*—your; *prīti*—love for Kṛṣṇa; *tomā-saṅge*—by your association; *āmā-sabāra*—of all of us; *haila*—there was; *kṛṣṇe*—unto Kṛṣṇa; *mati*—consciousness.

TRANSLATION

Śrī Caitanya Mahāprabhu replied, "From your previous birth you have been in Kṛṣṇa consciousness. Thus you love Kṛṣṇa so much that simply by your association we are all developing Kṛṣṇa consciousness."

TEXT 186

ভক্ত-মহিমা বাড়াইতে, ভক্তে সুখ দিতে ।
মহাপ্রভু বিনা অন্য নাহি ত্রিজগতে ॥ ১৮৬ ॥

bhakta-mahimā bāḍāite, bhakte sukha dite
mahāprabhu vinā anya nāhi trijagate

SYNONYMS

bhakta-mahimā—the glories of the devotees; *bāḍāite*—to increase; *bhakte*—unto the devotees; *sukha dite*—to give pleasure; *mahāprabhu*—Śrī Caitanya Mahāprahbu; *vinā*—except; *anya*—anyone else; *nāhi*—there is no one; *trijagate*—within these three worlds.

TRANSLATION

Thus there is no one within these three worlds—save for Śrī Caitanya Mahāprabhu—who is always so willing to increase the glories of the devotees and give them satisfaction.

PURPORT

In this regard, one should consult the discussion between Kapiladeva and Devahūti on the subject matter of devotional service. This is found in *Śrīmad-Bhāgavatam,*Third Canto.

TEXT 187

তবে প্রভু প্রত্যেকে, সব ভক্তের নাম লঞা ।
পিঠা-পানা দেওয়াইল প্রসাদ করিয়া ॥ ১৮৭ ॥

tabe prabhu pratyeke, saba bhaktera nāma lañā
piṭhā-pānā deoyāila prasāda kariyā

SYNONYMS

tabe—thereafter; *prabhu*—Śrī Caitanya Mahāprabhu; *pratyeke*—individually; *saba bhaktera*—of all the devotees; *nāma*—the names; *lañā*—calling; *piṭhā-pānā*—cakes and sweet rice; *deoyāila*—administered; *prasāda*—remnants of food; *kariyā*—making.

TRANSLATION

Śrī Caitanya Mahāprabhu then took all the remnants of food offered to Jagannātha, such as cakes and sweet rice, and distributed them to all the other devotees, calling them individually.

TEXT 188

অদ্বৈত-নিত্যানন্দ বসিয়াছেন এক ঠাঞি ।
দুইজনে ক্রীড়া-কলহ লাগিল তথাই ॥ ১৮৮ ॥

advaita-nityānanda vasiyāchena eka ṭhāñi
dui-jane krīḍā-kalaha lāgila tathāi

SYNONYMS

advaita-nityānanda—Advaita Ācārya and Nityānanda Prabhu; *vasiyāchena*—sat; *eka ṭhāñi*—in one place; *dui-jane*—those two persons; *krīḍā-kalaha*—mock fighting; *lāgila*—began; *tathāi*—there.

TRANSLATION

Śrī Advaita Ācārya and Nityānanda Prabhu sat side by side, and when prasāda was being distributed, They both engaged in a type of mock fighting.

TEXT 189

অদ্বৈত কহে, –অবধূতের সঙ্গে এক পংক্তি ।
ভোজন করিলুঁ, না জানি হবে কোন্ গতি ॥ ১৮৯ ॥

advaita kahe,——avadhūtera saṅge eka paṅkti
bhojana kariluṅ, nā jāni habe kon gati

SYNONYMS

advaita kahe—Advaita Ācārya said; *avadhūtera saṅge*—with a mendicant; *eka paṅkti*—in one line; *bhojana kariluṅ*—I am taking My food; *nā jāni*—I do not know; *habe*—will be; *kon*—what; *gati*—destination.

TRANSLATION

First Advaita Ācārya said, "I am sitting in line with an unknown mendicant, and because I am eating with Him, I do not know what kind of destination is awaiting Me.

TEXT 190

প্রভু ত' সন্ন্যাসী, উঁহার নাহি অপচয়।
অন্ন-দোষে সন্ন্যাসীর দোষ নাহি হয় ॥ ১৯০ ॥

prabhu ta' sannyāsī, uṅhāra nāhi apacaya
anna-doṣe sannyāsīra doṣa nāhi haya

SYNONYMS

prabhu—Lord Śrī Caitanya Mahāprabhu; *ta'*—indeed; *sannyāsī*—in the renounced order of life; *uṅhāra*—for Him; *nāhi*—there is not; *apacaya*—any discrepancy; *anna-doṣe*—by contamination of food; *sannyāsīra*—of a person in the renounced order; *doṣa*—fault; *nāhi*—not; *haya*—there is.

TRANSLATION

"Śrī Caitanya Mahāprabhu is in the renounced order of life. Consequently He does not recognize discrepancies. As a matter of fact, a sannyāsī is not affected by eating food from anywhere and everywhere.

TEXT 191

"নান্নদোষেণ মস্করী"—এই শাস্ত্র-প্রমাণ।
আমি ত' গৃহস্থ-ব্রাহ্মণ, আমার দোষ-স্থান ॥ ১৯১ ॥

"nānna-doṣeṇa maskarī"——ei śāstra-pramāṇa
āmi ta' gṛhastha-brāhmaṇa, āmāra doṣa-sthāna

SYNONYMS

na anna-doṣeṇa maskarī—a *sannyāsī* does not become affected by faulty acceptance of food; *ei*—this; *śāstra-pramāṇa*—evidence of revealed scriptures; *āmi*—I; *ta'*—indeed; *gṛhastha-brāhmaṇa*—a householder *brāhmaṇa; āmāra*—My; *doṣa*—faulty; *sthāna*—situation.

TRANSLATION

"According to śāstras, there is no discrepancy in a sannyāsī's eating at another's house. However, for a householder brāhmaṇa, this kind of eating is faulty.

TEXT 192

জন্মকুলশীলাচার না জানি যাহার ।
তার সঙ্গে এক পংক্তি—বড় অনাচার ॥ ১৯২ ॥

janma-kula-śīlācāra nā jāni yāhāra
tāra saṅge eka paṅkti——baḍa anācāra

SYNONYMS

janma—birth; *kula*—family; *śīla*—character; *ācāra*—behavior; *nā*—not; *jāni*—I know; *yāhāra*—of whom; *tāra saṅge*—with him; *eka paṅkti*—in one line; *baḍa anācāra*—a great discrepancy.

TRANSLATION

"It is not proper for householders to dine with those whose previous birth, family, character and behavior are unknown."

TEXT 193

নিত্যানন্দ কহে,—তুমি অদ্বৈত-আচার্য ।
'অদ্বৈত-সিদ্ধান্তে' বাধে শুদ্ধভক্তিকার্য ॥ ১৯৩ ॥

nityānanda kahe——tumi advaita-ācārya
'advaita-siddhānte' bādhe śuddha-bhakti-kārya

SYNONYMS

nityānanda kahe—Śrīla Nityānanda Prabhu said; *tumi*—You; *advaita-ācārya*—Advaita Ācārya, or a teacher of impersonal monism; *advaita-siddhānte*—in that monistic conclusion; *bādhe*—is greatly hindered; *śuddha-bhakti-kārya*—the matter of pure devotional service.

TRANSLATION

Nityānanda Prabhu immediately refuted Śrīla Advaita Ācārya, saying, "You are a teacher of impersonal monism, and the monistic conclusion is a great hindrance to progressive, pure devotional service.

TEXT 194

তোমার সিদ্ধান্ত-সঙ্গ করে যেই জনে ।
'এক' বস্তু বিনা সেই 'দ্বিতীয়' নাহি মানে ॥ ১৯৪ ॥

tomāra siddhānta-saṅga kare yei jane
'eka' vastu vinā sei 'dvitīya' nāhi māne

SYNONYMS

tomāra—Your; *siddhānta-saṅga*—acceptance of the conclusion; *kare*—does; *yei jane*—the person who; *eka*—one; *vastu*—substance; *vinā*—except; *sei*—such a person; *dvitīya*—a second thing; *nāhi māne*—does not accept.

TRANSLATION

"One who participates in Your impersonal monistic philosophy does not accept anything but the one Brahman."

PURPORT

The impersonal monist does not believe that God is the only object of worship and that the living entities are His eternal servants. According to the monists, God and the devotee may be separate in the material state, but when they are spiritually situated, there is no difference between them. This is called *advaita-siddhānta,* the conclusion of the monists. Monists consider devotional service of the Lord to be material activity; therefore they consider such devotional activities to be the same as *karma,* or fruitive activity. This monistic mistake is a great stumbling block on the road to devotional service.

Actually this discussion between Advaita Ācārya and Nityānanda was a mock fight to serve as a great instruction for all devotees. Śrī Nityānanda Prabhu wanted to point out that Advaita Ācārya, a pure devotee, did not agree with the monistic conclusion. The conclusion of devotional service is:

vadanti tat tattva-vidas
tattvaṁ yaj jñānam advayam
brahmeti paramātmeti
bhagavān iti śabdyate

"Learned transcendentalists who know the Absolute Truth call this nondual substance Brahman, Paramātmā or Bhagavān." (*Bhāg.* 1.2.11)

Absolute knowledge consists of Brahman, Paramātmā and Bhagavān. This conclusion is not the same as that of the monists. Śrīla Advaita Ācārya was given the title of *ācārya* because He spread the *bhakti* cult, not the philosophy of monism. The true conclusion of *advaita-siddhānta* is not the same as the philosophy of the monists. Here *advaita-siddhānta* means *advaya-jñāna,* or oneness in variety. Actually Śrīla Nityānanda Prabhu was praising Śrīla Advaita Ācārya through friendly mock fighting. He was giving the Vaiṣṇava conclusion in terms of the *Bhāgavatam's* conclusive words, *vadanti tat tattva-vidas.* This is also the conclusion of a *mantra* in the *Chāndogya Upaniṣad, ekam evādvitīyam.*

A devotee knows that there is oneness in diversity. The *mantras* of the *śāstras* do not support the monistic conclusions of the impersonalists, nor does Vaiṣṇava philosophy accept impersonalism without variety. Brahman is the greatest, He who includes everything, and that is oneness. As Kṛṣṇa says in *Bhagavad-gīta* (7.7), *mattaḥ parataraṁ nānyat:* there is no one superior to Kṛṣṇa Himself. He is the original substance because every category emanates from Him. Thus He is simultaneously one with and different from all other categories. The Lord is always engaged in a variety of spiritual activities, but the monist cannot understand spiritual variety. The conclusion is that although the powerful and the power are one and the same, within the energy of the powerful there are varieties. In those varieties there is a difference between one's personal self, between types of the same category and between types of different categories. In other words, there is always variety in the categories, which are understood as knowledge, the knower and the knowable. Due to the eternal existence of knowledge, the knower and the knowable, devotees everywhere know about the eternal existence of the form, name, qualities, pastimes and entourage of the Supreme Personality of Godhead. Devotees never agree with the monist's preaching of oneness. Unless one adheres to the conceptions of the knower, the knowable and knowledge, there is no possibility of understanding spiritual variety, nor can one taste the transcendental bliss of spiritual variety.

The philosophy of monism is an adjustment of the Buddhist philosophy of voidism. In a mock fight with Śrī Advaita Ācārya, Śrī Nityānanda Prabhu was refuting this type of monistic philosophy. Vaiṣṇavas certainly accept Lord Śrī Kṛṣṇa as the ultimate one, and that which is without Kṛṣṇa is called *māyā,* or that which has no existence. External *māyā* is exhibited in two phases—*jīva-māyā,* the living entities, and *guṇa-māyā,* the material world. In the material world there is *prakṛti* (material nature) and *pradhāna* (the ingredients of material nature). However, when one becomes Kṛṣṇa conscious, material and spiritual variety do not exist. An advanced devotee like Prahlāda Mahārāja sees everything as one—Kṛṣṇa. As stated in *Śrīmad-Bhāgavatam: kṛṣṇa-graha-gṛhītātmā na veda jagad īdṛśam* (*Bhāg.* 7.4.37). One who is in full Kṛṣṇa consciousness does not distinguish between things material and spiritual. He takes everything to be related to Kṛṣṇa and therefore spiritual. By *advaya-jñāna-darśana,* Śrīla Advaita Ācārya has glorified pure devotional service. Śrīla Nityānanda Prabhu herein sarcastically condemns the philosophy of the impersonal monists and praises the correct nondual philosophy of Śrī Advaita Prabhu.

TEXT 195

হেন তোমার সঙ্গে মোর একত্রে ভোজন।
না জানি, তোমার সঙ্গে কৈছে হয় মন ॥ ১৯৫ ॥

hena tomāra saṅge mora ekatre bhojana
nā jāni, tomāra saṅge kaiche haya mana

SYNONYMS

hena—thus; *tomāra*—Your; *saṅge*—in association; *mora*—My; *ekatre*—together; *bhojana*—eating; *nā jāni*—I do not know; *tomāra saṅge*—by Your association; *kaiche*—how; *haya mana*—My mind will turn.

TRANSLATION

Nityānanda Prabhu continued: "You are such a monist! And now I am eating beside You. I do not know how My mind will be affected in this way."

PURPORT

Saṅgāt sañjāyate kāmaḥ (Bg. 2.62). One develops his consciousness according to society and association. As Śrīla Nityānanda Prabhu admits, a devotee should be very careful when associating with those who are not devotees. When asked by a householder devotee what the behavior of a devotee should be, Śrī Caitanya Mahāprabhu immediately replied:

asat-saṅga-tyāga,——ei vaiṣṇava-ācāra
'strī-saṅgī'——eka asādhu, 'kṛṣṇābhakta' āra

(Cc. *Madhya* 22.87)

A Vaiṣṇava, a devotee, should simply discard intimate association with nondevotees. In his *Upadeśāmṛta,* Śrīla Rūpa Gosvāmī has described the symptoms of intimate relationships in this way:

dadāti pratigṛhṇāti
guhyam ākhyāti pṛcchati
bhuṅkte bhojayate caiva
ṣaḍ-vidhaṁ prīti-lakṣaṇam

The words *bhuṅkte bhojayate* indicate that one should eat with devotees. One should carefully avoid eating food offered by nondevotees. Indeed, a devotee should be very strict in not accepting food from a nondevotee, especially food prepared in restaurants or hotels or on airplanes. Śrīla Nityānanda Prabhu's reference in this connection is meant to emphasize that one should avoid eating with Māyāvādīs and covert Māyāvādīs like the *sahijiyā* Vaiṣṇavas, who are materially affected.

TEXT 196

এইমত দুইজনে করে বলাবলি।
ব্যাজ-স্তুতি করে দুঁহে, যেন গালাগালি ॥ ১৯৬ ॥

ei-mata dui-jane kare balābali
vyāja-stuti kare duṅhe, yena gālāgāli

SYNONYMS

ei-mata—in this way; *dui-jane*—two persons; *kare*—do; *balābali*—accusing and counter-accusing; *vyāja-stuti*—praise in the form of accusations; *kare*—do; *duṅhe*—both of Them; *yena*—as if; *gālāgāli*—exchanges of ill names.

TRANSLATION

Thus They both went on talking and praising one another, although Their praise appeared negative, for it appeared as if They exchanged ill names.

TEXT 197

তবে প্রভু সর্ব-বৈষ্ণবের নাম লঞা।
মহাপ্রসাদ দেন মহা-অমৃত সিঞ্চিয়া॥ ১৯৭ ॥

tabe prabhu sarva-vaiṣṇavera nāma lañā
mahā-prasāda dena mahā-amṛta siñciyā

SYNONYMS

tabe—thereafter; *prabhu*—Śrī Caitanya Mahāprabhu; *sarva-vaiṣṇavera*—of all the Vaiṣṇavas; *nāma*—names; *lañā*—calling; *mahā-prasāda*—the remnants of the food of Lord Jagannātha; *dena*—delivers; *mahā-amṛta*—transcendental nectar; *siñciyā*—sprinkling.

TRANSLATION

Thereafter, calling all the Vaiṣṇavas, Śrī Caitanya Mahāprabhu distributed mahā-prasāda as if sprinkling nectar. At that time the mock fight between Advaita Ācārya and Nityānanda Prabhu became more and more delicious.

TEXT 198

ভোজন করি' উঠে সবে হরিধ্বনি করি'।
হরিধ্বনি উঠিল সব স্বর্গমর্ত্য ভরি'॥ ১৯৮ ॥

bhojana kari' uṭhe sabe hari-dhvani kari'
hari-dhvani uṭhila saba svarga-martya bhari'

SYNONYMS

bhojana kari'—after eating; *uṭhe*—stood up; *sabe*—all; *hari-dhvani*—the sound of Hari; *kari'*—making; *hari-dhvani*—the sound of Hari; *uṭhila*—rose; *saba*—all; *svarga-martya*—the upper and lower planetary systems; *bhari'*—filling.

TRANSLATION

After taking their lunch, all the Vaiṣṇavas stood up and chanted the holy name of Hari, and the resounding noise filled all the upper and lower planetary systems.

TEXT 199

তবে মহাপ্রভু সব নিজ-ভক্তগণে ।
সবাকারে শ্রীহস্তে দিলা মাল্য-চন্দনে ॥ ১৯৯ ॥

tabe mahāprabhu saba nija-bhakta-gaṇe
sabākāre śrī-haste dilā mālya-candane

SYNONYMS

tabe—thereafter; *mahāprabhu*—Śrī Caitanya Mahāprabhu; *saba*—all; *nija-bhakta-gaṇe*—personal devotees; *sabākāre*—unto all of them; *śrī-haste*—with His own hand; *dilā*—delivered; *mālya-candane*—flower garlands and sandalwood pulp.

TRANSLATION

After this, Śrī Caitanya Mahāprabhu offered flower garlands and sandalwood pulp to all His devoted personal associates.

TEXT 200

তবে পরিবেশক স্বরূপাদি সাত জন।
গৃহের ভিতরে কৈল প্রসাদ ভোজন ॥ ২০০ ॥

tabe pariveśaka svarūpādi sāta jana
gṛhera bhitare kaila prasāda bhojana

SYNONYMS

tabe—thereafter; *pariveśaka*—the distributers of *prasāda; svarūpa-ādi*—headed by Svarūpa Dāmodara; *sāta jana*—seven men; *gṛhera bhitare*—within the room; *kaila*—did; *prasāda bhojana*—eating of *prasāda.*

TRANSLATION

The seven persons headed by Svarūpa Dāmodara who were engaged in distributing prasāda to others then took their meals within the room.

TEXT 201

প্রভুর অবশেষ গোবিন্দ রাখিল ধরিয়া ।
সেই অন্ন হরিদাসে কিছু দিল লঞা ॥ ২০১ ॥

prabhura avaśeṣa govinda rākhila dhariyā
sei anna haridāse kichu dila lañā

SYNONYMS

prabhura—of Lord Śrī Caitanya Mahāprabhu; *avaśeṣa*—remnants; *govinda*—Govinda; *rākhila*—saved; *dhariyā*—keeping; *sei anna*—that *prasāda; haridāse*—unto Haridāsa Ṭhākura; *kichu*—some; *dila*—delivered; *lañā*—taking.

TRANSLATION

Govinda saved some remnants of food left by Śrī Caitanya Mahāprabhu and kept them carefully. Later, one portion of these remnants was delivered to Haridāsa Ṭhākura.

TEXT 202

ভক্তগণ গোবিন্দ-পাশ কিছু মাগি' নিল ।
সেই প্রসাদান্ন গোবিন্দ আপনি পাইল ॥ ২০২ ॥

bhakta-gaṇa govinda-pāśa kichu māgi' nila
sei prasādānna govinda āpani pāila

SYNONYMS

bhakta-gaṇa—all the other devotees; *govinda-pāśa*—from Govinda; *kichu*—a little; *māgi'*—begging; *nila*—took; *sei*—those; *prasāda-anna*—remnants of food; *govinda*—Govinda; *āpani*—personally; *pāila*—partook.

TRANSLATION

The remnants of food left by Śrī Caitanya Mahāprabhu were later distributed among devotees who begged for them, and finally Govinda personally took the last remnants.

TEXT 203

স্বতন্ত্র ঈশ্বর প্রভু করে নানা খেলা ।
'ধোয়াপাখলা' নাম কৈল এই এক লীলা ॥ ২০৩ ॥

svatantra īśvara prabhu kare nānā khelā
'dhoyā-pākhalā' nāma kaila ei eka līlā

SYNONYMS

svatantra īśvara—the independent Personality of Godhead; *prabhu*—Śrī Caitanya Mahāprabhu; *kare*—performs; *nānā*—various; *khelā*—pastimes; *dhoyā-pākhalā*—washing and cleansing; *nāma*—named; *kaila*—performed; *ei*—this; *eka*—one; *līlā*—pastime.

TRANSLATION

The fully independent Supreme Personality of Godhead performs various types of pastimes. The pastime of washing and cleansing the Guṇḍicā temple is but one of them.

TEXT 204

আর দিনে জগন্নাথের 'নেত্রোৎসব' নাম ।
মহোৎসব হৈল ভক্তের প্রাণ-সমান ॥ ২০৪ ॥

āra dine jagannāthera 'netrotsava' nāma
mahotsava haila bhaktera prāṇa-samāna

SYNONYMS

āra dine—the next day; *jagannāthera*—of Lord Jagannātha; *netra-utsava*—the festival of seeing the eyes; *nāma*—named; *mahotsava*—great festival; *haila*—performed; *bhaktera*—of the devotees; *prāṇa-samāna*—the life and soul.

TRANSLATION

The next day marked the performance of the festival of Netrotsava. This great festival was the life and soul of the devotees.

PURPORT

After the bathing ceremony of Lord Jagannātha, during the fortnight before the Ratha-yātrā ceremony, the body of Lord Jagannātha, having been washed, needs repainting. This is known as *aṅga-rāga*. The Netrotsava festival performed gorgeously in the early morning of the Nava-yauvana day, constitutes the life and soul of the devotees.

TEXT 205

পক্ষদিন দুঃখী লোক প্রভুর অদর্শনে।
দর্শন করিয়া লোক সুখ পাইল মনে॥ ২০৫ ॥

pakṣa-dina duḥkhī loka prabhura adarśane
darśana kariyā loka sukha pāila mane

SYNONYMS

pakṣa-dina—for a fortnight; *duḥkhī*—unhappy; *loka*—devotees; *prabhura*—of Lord Jagannātha; *adarśane*—without the sight; *darśana kariyā*—by seeing; *loka*—all the devotees; *sukha*—happiness; *pāila*—got; *mane*—in the mind.

TRANSLATION

Everyone was unhappy for a fortnight because they could not see the Deity of Lord Jagannātha. Upon seeing the Lord at the festival, the devotees were very happy.

TEXT 206

মহাপ্রভু সুখে লঞা সব ভক্তগণ।
জগন্নাথ-দরশনে করিলা গমন ॥ ২০৬ ॥

mahāprabhu sukhe lañā saba bhakta-gaṇa
jagannātha-daraśane karilā gamana

SYNONYMS

mahāprabhu—Śrī Caitanya Mahāprabhu; *sukhe*—in great happiness; *lañā*—taking; *saba*—all; *bhakta-gaṇa*—devotees; *jagannātha-daraśane*—for visiting Lord Jagannātha; *karilā gamana*—went.

TRANSLATION

On this occasion, greatly happy, Śrī Caitanya Mahāprabhu took all the devotees with Him and visited the Lord in the temple.

TEXT 207

আগে কাশীশ্বর যায় লোক নিবারিয়া।
পাছে গোবিন্দ যায় জল-করঙ্গ লঞা ॥ ২০৭ ॥

āge kāśīśvara yāya loka nivāriyā
pāche govinda yāya jala-karaṅga lañā

SYNONYMS

āge—in front; *kāśīśvara*—Kāśīśvara; *yāya*—goes; *loka*—the crowd; *nivāriyā*—checking; *pāche*—at the end; *govinda*—Govinda; *yāya*—goes; *jala*—of water; *karaṅga*—a pitcher carried by saintly persons; *lañā*—taking.

TRANSLATION

When Śrī Caitanya Mahāprabhu went to visit the temple, Kāśīśvara walked in front, checking the crowds of people, and Govinda walked in the rear, bringing the sannyāsīs pitchers filled with water.

PURPORT

The *karaṅga* is a kind of waterpot especially carried by Māyāvādī *sannyāsīs* and generally carried by all other *sannyāsīs.*

TEXT 208

প্রভুর আগে পুরী, ভারতী,—দুঁহার গমন ।
স্বরূপ, অদ্বৈত,—দুঁহের পার্শ্বে দুইজন ॥ ২০৮ ॥

prabhura āge purī, bhāratī,——duṅhāra gamana
svarūpa, advaita,——duṅhera pārśve dui-jana

SYNONYMS

prabhura āge—in front of Lord Śrī Caitanya Mahāprabhu; *purī*—Paramānanda Purī; *bhāratī*—Brahmānanda Bhāratī; *duṅhāra gamana*—first they went; *svarūpa*—Svarūpa Dāmodara; *advaita*—Advaita Ācārya; *duṅhera*—of both; *pārśve*—on the two sides; *dui-jana*—two persons.

TRANSLATION

When Śrī Caitanya Mahāprabhu went toward the temple, Paramānanda Purī and Brahmānanda Bhāratī walked in front of Him, and at His two sides walked Svarūpa Dāmodara and Advaita Ācārya.

TEXT 209

পাছে পাছে চলি' যায় আর ভক্তগণ ।
উৎকণ্ঠাতে গেলা সব জগন্নাথ-ভবন ॥ ২০৯ ॥

pāche pāche cali' yāya āra bhakta-gaṇa
utkaṇṭhāte gelā saba jagannātha-bhavana

SYNONYMS

pāche pāche—following; *cali' yāya*—walk; *āra*—other; *bhakta-gaṇa*—devotees; *utkaṇṭhāte*—in great anxiety; *gelā*—they went; *saba*—all; *jagannātha-bhavana*—in the temple of Lord Jagannātha.

TRANSLATION

With great anxiety all the other devotees followed them into the temple of Lord Jagannātha.

TEXT 210

দর্শন-লোভেতে করি' মর্যাদা লঙ্ঘন ।
ভোগ-মণ্ডপে যাঞা করে শ্রীমুখ দর্শন ॥ ২১০ ॥

darśana-lobhete kari' maryādā laṅghana
bhoga-maṇḍape yāñā kare śrī-mukha darśana

SYNONYMS

darśana-lobhete—being very anxious to see; *kari'*—doing; *maryādā laṅghana*—transgressions of regulative principles; *bhoga-maṇḍape*—in the room for offering food; *yāñā*—going; *kare*—do; *śrī-mukha darśana*—seeing the lotus face.

TRANSLATION

Out of great eagerness to see the Lord, they all neglected the regulative principles and, just to see the Lord's face, went to the place where the food was offered.

PURPORT

There are many regulative principles of Deity worship. For example, one is not allowed to enter the room where food is offered to Lord Jagannātha. However, in this case, being very anxious because of not having seen the Lord for fifteen days, all the people overruled the regulative principles and entered the room.

TEXT 211

তৃষার্ত প্রভুর নেত্র - ভ্রমর-যুগল ।
গাঢ় তৃষ্ণায় পিয়ে কৃষ্ণের বদন-কমল ॥ ২১১ ॥

tṛṣārta prabhura netra——bhramara-yugala
gāḍha tṛṣṇāya piye kṛṣṇera vadana-kamala

SYNONYMS

tṛṣā-ārta—thirsty; *prabhura*—of Lord Śrī Caitanya Mahāprabhu; *netra*—eyes; *bhramara-yugala*—like two bumblebees; *gāḍha*—deep; *tṛṣṇāya*—in thirst; *piye*—drinks; *kṛṣṇera*—of Lord Kṛṣṇa; *vadana-kamala*—the lotuslike face.

TRANSLATION

Śrī Caitanya Mahāprabhu was very thirsty to see the Lord, and His eyes became like two bumblebees drinking the honey from the lotuslike eyes of Lord Jagannātha, who is Kṛṣṇa Himself.

TEXT 212

প্রফুল্ল-কমল জিনি' নয়ন-যুগল ।
নীলমণি-দর্পণ-কান্তি গণ্ড ঝলমল ॥ ২১২ ॥

praphulla-kamala jini' nayana-yugala
nīlamaṇi-darpaṇa-kānti gaṇḍa jhalamala

SYNONYMS

praphulla-kamala—blossoming lotus flower; *jini'*—conquering; *nayana-yugala*—two eyes; *nīlamaṇi*—sapphire; *darpaṇa*—mirror; *kānti*—luster; *gaṇḍa*—neck; *jhalamala*—bright.

TRANSLATION

The eyes of Lord Jagannātha conquered the beauty of blossoming lotus flowers, and His neck was as lustrous as a mirror made of sapphires.

PURPORT

Lord Śrī Caitanya Mahāprabhu usually saw Lord Jagannātha from a distance, standing behind the column of Garuḍa. However, upon not seeing Lord Jagannātha for fifteen days, Caitanya Mahāprabhu felt great separation from Him. In great anxiety, Caitanya Mahāprabhu crossed the meeting hall and entered the room where food was offered, just to see the face of Lord Jagannātha. In verse 210, this action is called *maryādā-laṅghana,* a violation of the regulative principles. This indicates that one should not come very near a superior. The Deity of the Lord and the spiritual master should be seen from a distant place. This is called *maryādā*. Otherwise, as is said, familiarity breeds contempt. Sometimes coming too near the Deity or the spiritual master degrades the neophyte devotee. Personal servants of the Deity and the spiritual master should therefore always be very careful, for negligence may overcome them in their duty.

Lord Śrī Caitanya Mahāprabhu's eyes have been compared to thirsty bumblebees, and Śrī Jagannātha's eyes have been compared to blossoming lotus flowers. The author has made these comparisons in order to describe Lord Śrī Caitanya Mahāprabhu while the Lord was deeply absorbed in ecstatic love for Lord Jagannātha.

TEXT 213

বান্ধুলীর ফুল জিনি' অধর সুরঙ্গ ।
ঈষৎ হসিত কান্তি—অমৃত-তরঙ্গ ॥ ২১৩ ॥

bāndhulīra phula jini' adhara suraṅga
īṣat hasita kānti——amṛta-taraṅga

SYNONYMS

bāndhulīra phula—a kind of red flower named *bāndhulī; jini'*—conquering; *adhara*—chin; *su-raṅga*—buff color; *īṣat*—mild; *hasita*—smiling; *kānti*—luster; *amṛta*—nectar; *taraṅga*—waves.

TRANSLATION

The chin of the Lord, tinged with buff color, conquered the beauty of the bāndhulī flower. This increased the beauty of His mild smiling, which was like lustrous waves of nectar.

TEXT 214

শ্রীমুখ-সুন্দরকান্তি বাঢ়ে ক্ষণে ক্ষণে ।
কোটিভক্ত-নেত্র-ভৃঙ্গ করে মধুপানে ॥ ২১৪ ॥

śrī-mukha-sundara-kānti bāḍhe kṣaṇe kṣaṇe
koṭi-bhakta-netra-bhṛṅga kare madhu-pāne

SYNONYMS

śrī-mukha—of His beautiful face; *sundara-kānti*—attractive luster; *bāḍhe*—increases; *kṣaṇe kṣaṇe*—at every moment; *koṭi-bhakta*—of millions of devotees; *netra-bhṛṅga*—eyes like bumblebees; *kare*—engaged; *madhu-pāne*—in drinking the honey.

TRANSLATION

The luster of His beautiful face increased at every moment, and the eyes of hundreds and thousands of devotees drank its honey like bumblebees.

TEXT 215

যত পিয়ে তত তৃষ্ণা বাঢ়ে নিরন্তর ।
মুখাম্বুজ ছাড়ি' নেত্র না যায় অন্তর ॥ ২১৫ ॥

yata piye tata tṛṣṇā bāḍhe nirantara
mukhāmbuja chāḍi' netra nā yāya antara

SYNONYMS

yata—as much; *piye*—they drink; *tata*—so much; *tṛṣṇā*—thirst; *bāḍhe*—increases; *nirantara*—incessantly; *mukha-ambuja*—the lotuslike face; *chāḍi'*—giving up; *netra*—the eyes; *nā*—do not; *yāya*—go; *antara*—separate.

TRANSLATION

As their eyes began to drink the nectarean honey of His lotus face, their thirst increased. Thus their eyes did not leave Him.

PURPORT

In the *Laghu-bhāgavatāmṛta* (1.5.538), Śrīla Rūpa Gosvāmī has described the beauty of the Lord in this way:

asamānordhva-mādhurya-
taraṅgāmṛta-vāridhiḥ
jaṅgama-sthāvarollāsi-
rūpo gopendra-nandanaḥ

"The beauty of the son of Mahārāja Nanda is incomparable. Nothing is higher than His beauty, and nothing can equal it. His beauty is like waves in an ocean of nectar. This beauty is attractive both for moving and for nonmoving objects."

Similarly, in the *Tantra-śāstra,* there is another description of the Lord's beauty:

kandarpa-koṭy-arbuda-rūpa-śobha-
nīrājya-pādābja-nakhāṁ calasya
kutrāpy adṛṣṭa-śruta-ramya-kānter
dhyānaṁ paraṁ nanda-sutasya vakṣye

"I shall relate the supreme meditation upon Lord Śrī Kṛṣṇa, the son of Nanda Mahārāja. The tips of the toes of His lotus feet reflect the beauty of the bodies of unlimited millions of Cupids, and His bodily luster has never been seen or heard of anywhere."

One may also consult *Śrīmad-Bhāgavatam* (10.29.14) in this connection.

TEXT 216

এইমত মহাপ্রভু লঞা ভক্তগণ ।
মধ্যাহ্ন পর্যন্ত কৈল শ্রীমুখ দরশন ॥ ২১৬ ॥

ei-mata mahāprabhu lañā bhakta-gaṇa
madhyāhna paryanta kaila śrī-mukha daraśana

SYNONYMS

ei-mata—in this way; *mahāprabhu*—Śrī Caitanya Mahāprabhu; *lañā*—taking; *bhakta-gaṇa*—His associates; *madhyāhna paryanta*—up to midday; *kaila*—performs; *śrī-mukha daraśana*—seeing the face of Lord Jagannātha.

TRANSLATION

Thus Śrī Caitanya Mahāprabhu and His devotees enjoyed transcendental bliss upon seeing the face of Jagannātha. This continued to midday.

TEXT 217

স্বেদ, কম্প, অশ্রু-জল বহে সর্বক্ষণ ।
দর্শনের লোভে প্রভু করে সম্বরণ ॥ ২১৭ ॥

sveda, kampa, aśru-jala vahe sarva-kṣaṇa
darśanera lobhe prabhu kare saṁvaraṇa

SYNONYMS

sveda—perspiring; *kampa*—trembling; *aśru-jala*—tears from the eyes; *vahe*—flowed; *sarva-kṣaṇa*—always; *darśanera*—of seeing; *lobhe*—by greed; *prabhu*—Śrī Caitanya Mahāprabhu; *kare*—does; *saṁvaraṇa*—checking.

TRANSLATION

As usual, there were transcendental blissful symptoms in Caitanya Mahāprabhu's body. He perspired and trembled, and a constant flow of tears fell from His eyes. However, the Lord checked these tears so they would not disturb His seeing the face of the Lord.

TEXT 218

মধ্যে মধ্যে ভোগ লাগে, মধ্যে দরশন ।
ভোগের সময়ে প্রভু করেন কীর্তন ॥ ২১৮ ॥

madhye madhye bhoga lāge, madhye daraśana
bhogera samaye prabhu karena kīrtana

SYNONYMS

madhye madhye—at intervals; *bhoga lāge*—there were offerings of food; *madhye*—sometimes; *daraśana*—seeing; *bhogera samaye*—at the time of offering *prasāda; prabhu*—Śrī Caitanya Mahāprabhu; *karena kīrtana*—performed congregational chanting.

TRANSLATION

Their looking at the face of Lord Jagannātha was interrupted only when He was offered food. Afterwards they would again look upon His face. When the food was being offered to the Lord, Śrī Caitanya Mahāprabhu performed His kīrtana.

TEXT 219

দর্শন-আনন্দে প্রভু সব পাসরিলা ।
ভক্তগণ মধ্যাহ্ন করিতে প্রভুরে লঞা গেলা ॥ ২১৯ ॥

darśana-ānande prabhu saba pāsarilā
bhakta-gaṇa madhyāhna karite prabhure lañā gelā

SYNONYMS

darśana-ānande—because of pleasure due to seeing the face of the Lord; *prabhu*—Śrī Caitanya Mahāprabhu; *saba*—everything; *pāsarilā*—forgot; *bhakta-gaṇa*—the devotees; *madhyāhna*—noontime lunch; *karite*—to accept; *prabhure*—Śrī Caitanya Mahāprabhu; *lañā gelā*—took.

TRANSLATION

Feeling such great pleasure upon seeing the face of Lord Jagannātha, Śrī Caitanya Mahāprabhu forgot everything. The devotees, however, took Him to His lunch at noontime.

TEXT 220

প্রাতঃকালে রথযাত্রা হবেক জানিয়া ।
সেবক লাগায় ভোগ দ্বিগুণ করিয়া ॥ ২২০ ॥

prātaḥ-kāle ratha-yātrā habeka jāniyā
sevaka lāgāya bhoga dviguṇa kariyā

SYNONYMS

prātaḥ-kāle—in the morning; *ratha-yātrā*—the car festival; *habeka*—would take place; *jāniyā*—knowing; *sevaka*—the priestly servants of the Lord; *lāgāya*—offer; *bhoga*—food; *dvi-guṇa kariyā*—increasing to double.

TRANSLATION

Knowing that the car festival would take place in the morning, all the servants of Lord Jagannātha were doubling their offerings of food.

TEXT 221

গুণ্ডিচা-মার্জন-লীলা সংক্ষেপে কহিল ।
যাহা দেখি' শুনি' পাপীর কৃষ্ণভক্তি হৈল ॥ ২২১ ॥

guṇḍicā-mārjana-līlā saṅkṣepe kahila
yāhā dekhi' śuni' pāpīra kṛṣṇa-bhakti haila

SYNONYMS

guṇḍicā-mārjana-līlā—the pastimes of washing the Guṇḍicā temple; *saṅkṣepe kahila*—I have described in brief; *yāhā dekhi' śuni'*—by seeing and hearing which; *pāpīra*—of sinful men; *kṛṣṇa-bhakti haila*—there was awakening of Kṛṣṇa consciousness.

TRANSLATION

I have briefly described the pastimes of the Lord in washing and cleansing the Guṇḍicā temple. By seeing or hearing these pastimes, even sinful men can awaken their Kṛṣṇa consciousness.

TEXT 222

শ্রীরূপ-রঘুনাথ-পদে যার আশ ।
চৈতন্যচরিতামৃত কহে কৃষ্ণদাস ॥ ২২২ ॥

śrī-rūpa-raghunātha-pade yāra āśa
caitanya-caritāmṛta kahe kṛṣṇadāsa

SYNONYMS

śrī-rūpa—Śrīla Rūpa Gosvāmī; *raghunātha*—Śrīla Raghunātha dāsa Gosvāmī; *pade*—at the lotus feet; *yāra*—whose; *āśa*—expectation; *caitanya-caritāmṛta*—the book named *Caitanya-caritāmṛta; kahe*—describes; *kṛṣṇadāsa*—Śrīla Kṛṣṇadāsa Kavirāja Gosvāmī.

TRANSLATION

Praying at the lotus feet of Śrī Rūpa and Śrī Raghunātha, always desiring their mercy, I, Kṛṣṇadāsa, narrate Śrī Caitanya-caritāmṛta, following in their footsteps.

Thus end the Bhaktivedanta purports to the Śrī Caitanya-caritāmṛta, Madhya-līlā, *Chapter Twelve, describing the washing and cleansing of the Guṇḍicā temple.*

CHAPTER 13

The Ecstatic Dancing of the Lord at Ratha-yātrā

A summary of this chapter is given by Śrīla Bhaktivinoda Ṭhākura in his *Amṛta-pravāha-bhāṣya* as follows. After bathing early in the morning, Śrī Caitanya Mahāprabhu saw the Deities (Jagannātha, Baladeva and Subhadrā) get aboard Their three carts. This function is called Pāṇḍu-vijaya. At that time, King Pratāparudra took a broom with a golden handle and began to cleanse the road. Lord Jagannātha took permission from the goddess of fortune and then started in the car for the Guṇḍicā temple. The road to the temple led along a broad, sandy beach, and on both sides of the road were residential quarters, houses and gardens. Along that road the servants called *gauḍas* began to pull the cars. Śrī Caitanya Mahāprabhu divided His *saṅkīrtana* party into seven divisions. With two *mṛdaṅgas* in each division, there were altogether fourteen *mṛdaṅgas*. While performing *kīrtana,* Śrī Caitanya Mahāprabhu exhibited various symptoms of transcendental ecstasy, and Jagannātha and Śrī Caitanya Mahāprabhu exchanged Their feelings very blissfully. When the cars reached the place known as Balagaṇḍi, the devotees offered the Deities simple food. At this time, in a nearby garden, Śrī Caitanya Mahāprabhu and His devotees took a brief rest from the dancing.

TEXT 1

স জীয়াৎ কৃষ্ণচৈতন্যঃ শ্রীরথাগ্রে ননর্ত যঃ ।
যেনাসীজ্জগতাং চিত্রং জগন্নাথোঽপি বিস্মিতঃ ॥ ১ ॥

sa jīyāt kṛṣṇa-caitanyaḥ
śrī-rathāgre nanarta yaḥ
yenāsīj jagatāṁ citraṁ
jagannātho 'pi vismitaḥ

SYNONYMS

saḥ—He; *jīyāt*—may live long; *kṛṣṇa-caitanyaḥ*—Lord Śrī Caitanya Mahāprabhu; *śrī-ratha-agre*—in the front of the car; *nanarta*—danced; *yaḥ*—who; *yena*—by whom; *āsīt*—there was; *jagatām*—of the whole universe;

citram—wonder; *jagannāthaḥ*—Lord Jagannātha; *api*—also; *vismitaḥ*—was astonished.

TRANSLATION

May the Supreme Personality of Godhead, Śrī Kṛṣṇa Caitanya, who danced in front of the car of Śrī Jagannātha, be all glorified! By seeing His dancing, not only was the whole universe held in wonder, but Lord Jagannātha Himself became very much astonished.

TEXT 2

জয় জয় শ্রীকৃষ্ণচৈতন্য নিত্যানন্দ ।
জয়াদ্বৈতচন্দ্র জয় গৌরভক্তবৃন্দ ॥ ২ ॥

jaya jaya śrī-kṛṣṇa-caitanya nityānanda
jayādvaita-candra jaya gaura-bhakta-vṛnda

SYNONYMS

jaya jaya—all glories; *śrī-kṛṣṇa-caitanya*—to Lord Śrī Kṛṣṇa Caitanya Mahāprabhu; *nityānanda*—to Nityānanda Prabhu; *jaya*—all glories; *advaita-candra*—to Advaita Ācārya; *jaya*—all glories; *gaura-bhakta-vṛnda*—to the devotees of Lord Caitanya Mahāprabhu.

TRANSLATION

All glories to Śrī Kṛṣṇa Caitanya and Prabhu Nityānanda! All glories to Advaitacandra! And all glories to the devotees of Lord Śrī Caitanya Mahāprabhu!

TEXT 3

জয় শ্রোতাগণ, শুন, করি' এক মন ।
রথযাত্রায় নৃত্য প্রভুর পরম মোহন ॥ ৩ ॥

jaya śrotā-gaṇa, śuna, kari' eka mana
ratha-yātrāya nṛtya prabhura parama mohana

SYNONYMS

jaya—all glories; *śrotā-gaṇa*—to the listeners; *śuna*—please hear; *kari'*—keeping yourself; *eka mana*—in one attention; *ratha-yātrāya*—in the car festival; *nṛtya*—dancing; *prabhura*—of Śrī Caitanya Mahāprabhu; *parama*—extremely; *mohana*—enchanting.

TRANSLATION

All glories to the listeners of Caitanya-caritāmṛta. Please hear the description of the dancing of Lord Caitanya Mahāprabhu at the Ratha-yātrā festival. His dancing is very enchanting. Please hear of it with great attention.

TEXT 4

আর দিন মহাপ্রভু হঞা সাবধান।
রাত্রে উঠি' গণ-সঙ্গে কৈল প্রাতঃস্নান ॥ ৪ ॥

āra dina mahāprabhu hañā sāvadhāna
rātre uṭhi' gaṇa-saṅge kaila prātaḥ-snāna

SYNONYMS

āra dina—the next day; *mahāprabhu*—Śrī Caitanya Mahāprabhu; *hañā*—becoming; *sāvadhāna*—very careful; *rātre uṭhi'*—getting up at night; *gaṇa-saṅge*—with His personal devotees; *kaila*—took; *prātaḥ-snāna*—bathing early in the morning.

TRANSLATION

The next day, Śrī Caitanya Mahaprabhu and His personal associates got up in the dark and attentively took their early morning baths.

TEXT 5

পাণ্ডু বিজয় দেখিবারে করিল গমন।
জগন্নাথ যাত্রা কৈল ছাড়ি' সিংহাসন ॥ ৫ ॥

pāṇḍu-vijaya dekhibāre karila gamana
jagannātha yātrā kaila chāḍi' siṁhāsana

SYNONYMS

pāṇḍu-vijaya—the ceremony named Pāṇḍu-vijaya; *dekhibāre*—for seeing; *karila*—did; *gamana*—go; *jagannātha*—Lord Jagannātha; *yātrā*—departure; *kaila*—did; *chāḍi'*—leaving; *siṁhāsana*—the throne.

TRANSLATION

Śrī Caitanya Mahāprabhu and His personal associates then went to see the ceremony of Pāṇḍu-vijaya. During this ceremony, Lord Jagannātha leaves His throne and gets up onto the car.

TEXT 6

আপনি প্রতাপরুদ্র লঞা পাত্রগণ ।
মহাপ্রভুর গণে করায় বিজয়-দর্শন ॥ ৬ ॥

āpani pratāparudra lañā pātra-gaṇa
mahāprabhura gaṇe karāya vijaya-darśana

SYNONYMS

āpani—personally; *pratāparudra*—King Pratāparudra; *lañā*—taking with him; *pātra-gaṇa*—his associates; *mahāprabhura*—of Śrī Caitanya Mahāprabhu; *gaṇe*—associates; *karāya*—causes; *vijaya-darśana*—seeing the Pāṇḍu-vijaya ceremony.

TRANSLATION

King Pratāparudra in person, as well as his entourage, allowed the Pāṇḍu-vijaya ceremony to be seen by all the associates of Śrī Caitanya Mahāprabhu.

TEXT 7

অদ্বৈত, নিতাই আদি সঙ্গে ভক্তগণ ।
সুখে মহাপ্রভু দেখে ঈশ্বর-গমন ॥ ৭ ॥

advaita, nitāi ādi saṅge bhakta-gaṇa
sukhe mahāprabhu dekhe īśvara-gamana

SYNONYMS

advaita—Advaita Ācārya; *nitāi*—Lord Nityānanda Prabhu; *ādi*—headed by; *saṅge*—with; *bhakta-gaṇa*—devotees; *sukhe*—in great happiness; *mahāprabhu*—Śrī Caitanya Mahāprabhu; *dekhe*—sees; *īśvara-gamana*—how the Lord is starting.

TRANSLATION

Śrī Caitanya Mahāprabhu and His prominent devotees—Advaita Ācārya, Nityānanda Prabhu and others—were very happy to observe how Lord Jagannātha began the Ratha-yātrā.

TEXT 8

বলিষ্ঠ দয়িতা'গণ—যেন মত্ত হাতী ।
জগন্নাথ বিজয় করায় করি' হাতাহাতি ॥ ৮ ॥

baliṣṭha dayitā' gaṇa——yena matta hātī
jagannātha vijaya karāya kari' hātāhāti

SYNONYMS

baliṣṭha dayitā' gaṇa—very strong *dayitās,* or carriers of Jagannātha; *yena*—as if; *matta hātī*—drunken elephants; *jagannātha*—of Lord Jagannātha; *vijaya*—departure; *karāya*—cause; *kari'*—performing; *hātāhāti*—hand to hand.

TRANSLATION

The very strongly built dayitās [carriers of the Jagannātha Deity] were as powerful as drunken elephants. They manually carried Lord Jagannātha from the throne to the car.

PURPORT

The word *dayitā* refers to one who has received the mercy of the Lord. Lord Jagannātha has a number of stalwart servants known as *dayitās.* These servants do not come from very high-caste families (*brāhmaṇas, kṣatriyas* or *vaiśyas*), but because they are engaged in the service of the Lord, they have been elevated to a respected position. Thus they are known as *dayitās.* These servants of Lord Jagannātha take care of the Lord from the day of the Snāna-yātrā up to the time the Lord is carried from the throne to the Ratha car. In the *Kṣetra-māhātmya* these *dayitās* are said to come from the *śabaras,* a caste that keeps and sells pigs. However, among the *dayitās* there are also many who come from the *brāhmaṇa* caste. Those *dayitās* coming from the *brāhmaṇa* families are called *dayitā-patis,* or leaders of the *dayitās.* The *dayitā-patis* offer food such as sweetmeats to Lord Jagannātha during the *anavasara,* the resting period after Snāna-yātrā. They also make the early morning offering of sweetmeats daily. It is said that during the *anavasara* Lord Jagannātha suffers from fever and that the *dayitā-patis* offer Him an infusion of drugs represented by fruit juice. It is said that in the beginning Lord Jagannātha was worshiped by the *śabaras* and was known as the Deity Nīla Mādhava. Later, when the Deity was established in the temple, the Lord became known as Jagannātha. Because the Deities were taken from the *śabaras,* all the *śabara* devotees were elevated to the position of *dayitās.*

TEXT 9

কতক দয়িতা করে স্কন্ধ আলম্বন ।
কতক দয়িতা ধরে শ্রীপদ্ম-চরণ ॥ ৯ ॥

kataka dayitā kare skandha ālambana
kataka dayitā dhare śrī-padma-caraṇa

SYNONYMS

kataka dayitā—some of the *dayitās; kare*—do; *skandha*—of the shoulders; *ālambana*—capturing; *kataka*—some; *dayitā*—servants called *dayitās; dhare*—catch; *śrī-padma-caraṇa*—the lotus feet of the Lord.

TRANSLATION

While carrying the Deity of Lord Jagannātha, some of the dayitās took hold of the shoulders of the Lord, and some caught His lotus feet.

TEXT 10

কটিতটে বদ্ধ, দৃঢ় স্থূল পট্টডোরী ।
তুই দিকে দয়িতাগণ উঠায় তাহা ধরি' ॥ ১০ ॥

kaṭi-taṭe baddha, dṛḍha sthūla paṭṭa-ḍorī
dui dike dayitā-gaṇa uṭhāya tāhā dhari'

SYNONYMS

kaṭi-taṭe—on the waist; *baddha*—bound; *dṛḍha*—strong; *sthūla*—thick; *paṭṭa-ḍorī*—rope made of silk; *dui dike*—from two sides; *dayitā-gaṇa*—the *dayitās; uṭhāya*—raise; *tāhā*—that rope; *dhari'*—catching.

TRANSLATION

The Lord Jagannātha Deity was bound at the waist by a strong, thick rope made of silk. From two sides the dayitās caught hold of this rope and raised the Deity.

TEXT 11

উচ্চ দৃঢ় তুলী সব পাতি' স্থানে স্থানে ।
এক তুলী হৈতে ত্বরায় আর তুলীতে আনে ॥ ১১ ॥

ucca dṛḍha tulī saba pāti' sthāne sthāne
eka tulī haite tvarāya āra tulīte āne

SYNONYMS

ucca—puffed up; *dṛḍha*—strong; *tulī*—pads made of cotton; *saba*—all; *pāti'*—spreading; *sthāne sthāne*—from one place to another; *eka tulī*—one pad; *haite*—from; *tvarāya*—very soon; *āra*—next; *tulīte*—on the pad; *āne*—bring.

TRANSLATION

Strong, puffed-up cotton pads called tulīs were spread out from the throne to the car, and the heavy Deity of Lord Jagannātha was carried from one pillow-like pad to the next by the dayitās.

TEXT 12

প্রভু-পদাঘাতে তুলী হয় খণ্ড খণ্ড।
তুলা সব উড়ি' যায়, শব্দ হয় প্রচণ্ড ॥ ১২ ॥

prabhu-padāghāte tulī haya khaṇḍa khaṇḍa
tulā saba uḍi' yāya, śabda haya pracaṇḍa

SYNONYMS

prabhu-pada-āghāte—by the kicking of Lord Jagannātha; *tulī*—the pads; *haya*—become; *khaṇḍa khaṇḍa*—broken to pieces; *tulā*—cotton from inside; *saba*—all; *uḍi' yāya*—rises; *śabda*—sound; *haya*—there is; *pracaṇḍa*—very much.

TRANSLATION

While the dayitās carried the heavy Jagannātha Deity from one pad to the next, some of the pads broke, and the cotton contents floated into the air. When they broke, they made a heavy, cracking sound.

TEXT 13

বিশ্বম্ভর জগন্নাথে কে চালাইতে পারে ?
আপন ইচ্ছায় চলে করিতে বিহারে ॥ ১৩ ॥

viśvambhara jagannāthe ke cālāite pāre?
āpana icchāya cale karite vihāre

SYNONYMS

viśvambhara—the maintainer of the universe; *jagannāthe*—Lord Jagannātha; *ke*—who; *cālāite*—cause to be carried; *pāre*—can; *āpana*—personal; *icchāya*—by His will; *cale*—moves; *karite*—to act; *vihāre*—in pastimes.

TRANSLATION

Lord Jagannātha is the maintainer of the whole universe. Who can carry Him from one place to another? However, the Lord moves by His personal will just to perform His pastimes.

TEXT 14

মহাপ্রভু 'মণিমা' 'মণিমা' করে ধ্বনি ।
নানা-বাদ্য-কোলাহলে কিছুই না শুনি ॥ ১৪ ॥

mahāprabhu 'maṇimā' 'maṇimā' kare dhvani
nānā-vādya-kolāhale kichui nā śuni

SYNONYMS

mahāprabhu—Śrī Caitanya Mahāprabhu; *maṇimā*—Maṇimā; *maṇimā*—Maṇimā; *kare*—makes; *dhvani*—the sound; *nānā*—various; *vādya*—of musical instruments; *kolāhale*—by the tumultuous sound; *kichui*—anything; *nā*—not; *śuni*—can hear.

TRANSLATION

While the Lord was transported from the throne to the car, tumultuous sounds were made on various musical instruments. Śrī Caitanya Mahāprabhu was chanting "Maṇimā Maṇimā," but He could not be heard.

PURPORT

The word *maṇimā* is used to address a respectable person in Orissa. Lord Jagannātha was being respectfully addressed by Śrī Caitanya in this way.

TEXT 15

তবে প্রতাপরুদ্র করে আপনে সেবন ।
সুবর্ণ-মার্জনী লঞা করে পথ সম্মার্জন ॥ ১৫ ॥

tabe pratāparudra kare āpane sevana
suvarṇa-mārjanī lañā kare patha sammārjana

SYNONYMS

tabe—at this time; *pratāparudra*—King Pratāparudra; *kare*—does; *āpane*—personally; *sevana*—service; *suvarṇa*—golden; *mārjanī*—broom; *lañā*—taking; *kare*—does; *patha*—road; *sammārjana*—cleansing.

TRANSLATION

While the Lord was being carried from the throne to the car, King Pratāparudra personally engaged in the Lord's service by cleansing the road with a broom that had a golden handle.

TEXT 16

চন্দন-জলেতে করে পথ নিষেচনে ।
তুচ্ছ সেবা করে বসি' রাজ-সিংহাসনে ॥ ১৬ ॥

candana-jalete kare patha niṣecane
tuccha sevā kare vasi' rāja-siṁhāsane

SYNONYMS

candana-jalete—with sandalwood water; *kare*—does; *patha*—road; *niṣecane*—sprinkling; *tuccha*—insignificant, menial; *sevā*—service; *kare*—performs; *vasi'*—although in possession of; *rāja-siṁhāsane*—the royal throne.

TRANSLATION

The King sprinkled the road with sandalwood-scented water. Although he was the owner of the royal throne, he engaged in menial service for the sake of Lord Jagannātha.

TEXT 17

উত্তম হঞা রাজা করে তুচ্ছ সেবন ।
অতএব জগন্নাথের কৃপার ভাজন ॥ ১৭ ॥

uttama hañā rājā kare tuccha sevana
ataeva jagannāthera kṛpāra bhājana

SYNONYMS

uttama hañā—although very respectable; *rājā*—the King; *kare*—accepts; *tuccha*—menial; *sevana*—service; *ataeva*—therefore; *jagannāthera*—of Lord Jagannātha; *kṛpāra*—in the matter of mercy; *bhājana*—suitable candidate.

TRANSLATION

Although the King was the most exalted respectable person, still he accepted menial service for the Lord; he, therefore, became a suitable candidate for receiving the Lord's mercy.

TEXT 18

মহাপ্রভু সুখ পাইল সে-সেবা দেখিতে ।
মহাপ্রভুর কৃপা হৈল সে-সেবা হইতে ॥ ১৮ ॥

mahāprabhu sukha pāila se-sevā dekhite
mahāprabhura kṛpā haila se-sevā ha-ite

SYNONYMS

mahāprabhu—Śrī Caitanya Mahāprabhu; *sukha pāila*—felt very happy; *se-sevā*—that kind of service; *dekhite*—to see; *mahāprabhura*—of Śrī Caitanya Mahāprabhu; *kṛpā*—mercy; *haila*—there was; *se-sevā ha-ite*—because of that service.

TRANSLATION

Upon seeing the King engaged in such menial service, Caitanya Mahāprabhu became very happy. Simply by rendering this service, the King received the mercy of the Lord.

PURPORT

Unless one receives the mercy of the Lord, he cannot understand the Supreme Personality of Godhead or engage in His devotional service.

athāpi te deva padāmbuja-dvaya-
prasāda-leśānugṛhīta eva hi
jānāti tattvaṁ bhagavan-mahimno
na cānya eko 'pi ciraṁ vicinvan
(*Bhāg.* 10.14.29)

Only a devotee who has received a small fraction of the mercy of the Lord can understand Him. Others may engage in theoretical speculation to understand the Lord, but they can not know anything about Him. Although Mahārāja Pratāparudra was very eager to see Śrī Caitanya Mahāprabhu, the Lord refused to see him. However, when Śrī Caitanya Mahāprabhu saw the King engaged in menial service for Lord Jagannātha, He became very happy. Thus the King became eligible to receive Śrī Caitanya Mahāprabhu's mercy. If a devotee accepts Lord Śrī Caitanya Mahāprabhu as the universal *guru* and Lord Jagannātha as the Supreme Personality of Godhead Kṛṣṇa, he is benefited by the combined mercy of Kṛṣṇa and *guru*. That is stated by Śrī Caitanya Mahāprabhu in His instructions to Rūpa Gosvāmī. (Cc. *Madhya* 19.151)

brahmāṇḍa bhramite kona bhāgyavān jīva
guru-kṛṣṇa-prasāde pāya bhakti-latā-bīja

The seed of devotional service fructifies and becomes a transcendental creeper. Finally it reaches the lotus feet of the Lord in the spiritual sky. This seed is obtained by the mercy of the Lord and the *guru.* By the Lord's mercy one gets the association of a bona fide *guru,* and by the mercy of the *guru,* one gets a chance to render devotional service. Devotional service, the science of *bhakti-yoga,* carries one from this material world to the spiritual world.

TEXT 19

রথের সাজনি দেখি' লোকে চমৎকার ।
নব হেমময় রথ—সুমেরু-আকার ॥ ১৯ ॥

rathera sājani dekhi' loke camatkāra
nava hemamaya ratha——sumeru-ākāra

SYNONYMS

rathera—of the car; *sājani*—decoration; *dekhi'*—by seeing; *loke*—everyone; *camatkāra*—astonished; *nava*—new; *hema-maya*—golden; *ratha*—chariot car; *sumeru-ākāra*—as high as the mountain Sumeru.

TRANSLATION

Everyone was astonished to see the decorations on the Ratha car. The car appeared to be newly made of gold, and it was as high as Mount Sumeru.

PURPORT

In the year 1973 there was a gorgeous Ratha-yātrā festival in London, England, and the car was brought to Trafalgar Square. The London daily newspaper the *Guardian* published a front-page photo caption: "ISKCON Ratha-yātrā is rival to the Nelson Column in Trafalgar Square." The Nelson Column is a very impressive statue of Lord Nelson and can be seen from a good distance. Just as the residents of Purī compared the Ratha-yātrā car to Mount Sumeru, the residents of London considered the car rival to the Nelson Monument.

TEXT 20

শত শত সু-চামর-দর্পণে উজ্জ্বল ।
উপরে পতাকা শোভে চাঁদোয়া নির্মল ॥ ২০ ॥

śata śata su-cāmara-darpaṇe ujjvala
upare patākā śobhe cāṅdoyā nirmala

SYNONYMS

śata śata—hundreds upon hundreds; *su-cāmara*—beautiful white whisks; *darpaṇe*—with mirrors; *ujjvala*—very bright; *upare*—on the top; *patākā*—flag; *śobhe*—looks beautiful; *cāṅdoyā*—canopy; *nirmala*—thoroughly cleansed.

TRANSLATION

The decorations included bright mirrors and hundreds and hundreds of cāmaras [white whisks made of yak tails]. On top of the car were a neat and clean canopy and very beautiful flag.

TEXT 21

ঘাঘর, কিঙ্কিণী বাজে, ঘণ্টার ক্বণিত ।
নানা চিত্র-পট্টবস্ত্রে রথ বিভূষিত ॥ ২১ ॥

ghāghara, kiṅkiṇī bāje, ghaṇṭāra kvaṇita
nānā citra-paṭṭa-vastre ratha vibhūṣita

SYNONYMS

ghāghara—gongs; *kiṅkiṇī*—ankle bells; *bāje*—were sounding; *ghaṇṭāra*—of bells; *kvaṇita*—tinkling sound; *nānā*—various; *citra*—pictures; *paṭṭa-vastre*—with silken cloth; *ratha*—the car; *vibhūṣita*—decorated.

TRANSLATION

The car was also decorated with silken cloth and various pictures. Many brass bells, gongs and ankle bells rang.

TEXT 22

লীলায় চড়িল ঈশ্বর রথের উপর ।
আর দুই রথে চড়ে সুভদ্রা, হলধর ॥ ২২ ॥

līlāya caḍila īśvara rathera upara
āra dui rathe caḍe subhadrā, haladhara

SYNONYMS

līlāya—for the matter of pastimes; *caḍila*—got up; *īśvara*—the Supreme Personality of Godhead; *rathera*—a car; *upara*—aboard; *āra dui*—another two; *rathe*—in the cars; *caḍe*—got up; *subhadrā*—the sister of Lord Jagannātha; *haladhara*—Balarāma.

TRANSLATION

For the pastimes of the Ratha-yātrā ceremony, Lord Jagannātha got aboard one car, and His sister, Subhadrā, and elder brother, Balarāma, got aboard two other cars.

TEXT 23

পঞ্চদশ দিন ঈশ্বর মহালক্ষ্মী লঞা ।
তাঁর সঙ্গে ক্রীড়া কৈল নিভৃতে বসিয়া ॥ ২৩ ॥

pañca-daśa dina īśvara mahā-lakṣmī lañā
tāṅra saṅge krīḍā kaila nibhṛte vasiyā

SYNONYMS

pañca-daśa dina—fifteen days; *īśvara*—the Lord; *mahā-lakṣmī*—the supreme goddess of fortune; *lañā*—with; *tāṅra saṅge*—in her company; *krīḍā*—enjoyment; *kaila*—performed; *nibhṛte*—in a solitary place; *vasiyā*—sitting.

TRANSLATION

For fifteen days the Lord had remained in a secluded place with the supreme goddess of fortune and had performed His pastimes with her.

PURPORT

The fifteen-day period of *anavasara* is also called *nibhṛta,* in honor of the solitary place where the supreme goddess of fortune lives. After living there a fortnight, Lord Jagannātha took permission from the goddess of fortune to leave.

TEXT 24

তাঁহার সম্মতি লঞা ভক্তে সুখ দিতে ।
রথে চড়ি' বাহির হৈল বিহার করিতে ॥ ২৪ ॥

tāṅhāra sammati lañā bhakte sukha dite
rathe caḍi' bāhira haila vihāra karite

SYNONYMS

tāṅhāra sammati—her permission; *lañā*—taking; *bhakte*—the devotees; *sukha dite*—to please; *rathe caḍi'*—riding on the car; *bāhira haila*—came out; *vihāra karite*—to perform pastimes.

TRANSLATION

Having taken permission from the goddess of fortune, the Lord came out to ride on the Ratha car and perform His pastimes for the pleasure of the devotees.

PURPORT

In this connection, Śrīla Bhaktisiddhānta Sarasvatī Ṭhākura comments that as an ideal husband, Lord Jagannātha remained fifteen days in a secluded place with His wife, the supreme goddess of fortune. Nonetheless, the Lord wanted to come out of seclusion to give happiness to His devotees. The Lord enjoys Himself in two ways, known as *svakīya* and *parakīya.* The Lord's conjugal love in the *svakīya-rasa* relates to the regulative principles observed in Dvārakā. There the Lord has many married queens, but in Vṛndāvana the conjugal love of the Lord is not with His married wives but with His girl friends, the *gopīs.* Conjugal love with the *gopīs* is called *parakīya-rasa.* Lord Jagannātha leaves the secluded place where He enjoys the company of the supreme goddess of fortune in *svakīya-rasa,* and He goes to Vṛndāvana where He enjoys the *parakīya-rasa.* Bhaktisiddhānta Sarasvatī Ṭhākura therefore reminds us that the Lord's pleasure in *parakīya-rasa* is superior to His pleasure in *svakīya-rasa.*

In the material world, *parakīya-rasa,* or loving affairs with unmarried girl friends, is a most degraded relationship, but in the spiritual world this type of loving affair is considered the supreme enjoyment. In the material world everything is but a reflection of the spiritual world, and that reflection is perverted. We cannot understand the affairs of the spiritual world on the basis of our experience in the material world. The Lord's pastimes with the *gopīs* are therefore misunderstood by mundane scholars and word-wranglers. The *parakīya-rasa* of the spiritual world should not be discussed except by one who is very advanced in pure devotional service. The *parakīya-rasa* in the spiritual world and that in the material world are not comparable. The former is like gold, and the latter is like iron. Because the difference between the two is so great, they cannot actually be compared. However, one can easily distinguish the value of gold by seeing the value of iron. One who has the proper realization can easily distinguish the transcendental activities of the spiritual world from material activities.

TEXT 25

সূক্ষ্ম শ্বেতবালু পথে পুলিনের সম ।
দুই দিকে টোটা, সব—যেন বৃন্দাবন ॥ ২৫ ॥

sūkṣma śveta-bālu pathe pulinera sama
dui dike ṭoṭā, saba——yena vṛndāvana

SYNONYMS

sūkṣma—fine; *śveta-bālu*—white sand; *pathe*—on the path; *pulinera sama*—just like the bank of the Yamunā; *dui dike*—on two sides; *ṭoṭā*—gardens; *saba*—all; *yena*—like; *vṛndāvana*—the holy place Vṛndāvana.

TRANSLATION

The fine, white sand spread all over the path resembled the bank of the Yamunā, and the small gardens on both sides looked just like those in Vṛndāvana.

TEXT 26

রথে চড়ি' জগন্নাথ করিলা গমন ।
দুইপার্শ্বে দেখি' চলে আনন্দিত-মন ॥ ২৬ ॥

rathe caḍi' jagannātha karilā gamana
dui-pārśve dekhi' cale ānandita-mana

SYNONYMS

rathe caḍi'—riding on the car; *jagannātha*—Lord Jagannātha; *karilā gamana*—was passing; *dui-pārśve*—on both sides; *dekhi'*—seeing; *cale*—goes; *ānandita*—full of pleasure; *mana*—mind.

TRANSLATION

As Lord Jagannātha rode in His car and saw the beauty on both sides, His mind was filled with pleasure.

TEXT 27

'গৌড়' সব রথ টানে করিয়া আনন্দ ।
ক্ষণে শীঘ্র চলে রথ, ক্ষণে চলে মন্দ ॥ ২৭ ॥

'gauḍa' saba ratha ṭāne kariyā ānanda
kṣaṇe śīghra cale ratha, kṣaṇe cale manda

SYNONYMS

gauḍa—the pullers of the car; *saba*—all; *ratha*—the car; *ṭāne*—pull; *kariyā*—feeling; *ānanda*—happiness; *kṣaṇe*—sometimes; *śīghra cale*—goes very fast; *ratha*—the car; *kṣaṇe*—sometimes; *cale*—goes; *manda*—very slow.

TRANSLATION

The pullers of the car were known as gauḍas, and they pulled with great pleasure. However, the car sometimes went very fast and sometimes very slow.

TEXT 28

ক্ষণে স্থির হঞা রহে, টানিলেহ না চলে ।
ঈশ্বর-ইচ্ছায় চলে, না চলে কারো বলে ॥ ২৮ ॥

kṣaṇe sthira hañā rahe, ṭānileha nā cale
īśvara-icchāya cale, nā cale kāro bale

SYNONYMS

kṣaṇe—sometimes; *sthira*—still; *hañā*—becoming; *rahe*—stays; *ṭāṅileha*—in spite of being pulled; *nā cale*—does not go; *īśvara-icchāya*—by the will of the Lord; *cale*—goes; *nā cale*—does not go; *kāro*—of anyone; *bale*—by the strength.

TRANSLATION

Sometimes the car would stand still and not move, even though it was pulled very vigorously. The chariot therefore moved by the will of the Lord, not by the strength of any ordinary person.

TEXT 29

তবে মহাপ্রভু সব লঞা ভক্তগণ ।
স্বহস্তে পরাইল সবে মাল্য-চন্দন ॥ ২৯ ॥

tabe mahāprabhu saba lañā bhakta-gaṇa
svahaste parāila sabe mālya-candana

SYNONYMS

tabe—at that time; *mahāprabhu*—Śrī Caitanya Mahāprabhu; *saba*—all; *lañā*—taking; *bhakta-gaṇa*—devotees; *sva-haste*—by His own hand; *parāila*—decorated; *sabe*—everyone; *mālya-candana*—with flower garlands and pulp of sandalwood.

TRANSLATION

As the car stood still, Śrī Caitanya Mahāprabhu gathered all His devotees and, with His own hand, decorated them with flower garlands and sandalwood pulp.

TEXT 30

পরমানন্দ পুরী, আর ভারতী ব্রহ্মানন্দ ।
শ্রীহস্তে চন্দন পাঞা বাড়িল আনন্দ ॥ ৩০ ॥

paramānanda purī, āra bhāratī brahmānanda
śrī-haste candana pāñā bāḍila ānanda

SYNONYMS

paramānanda purī—Paramānanda Purī; *āra*—and; *bhāratī brahmānanda*—Brahmānanda Bhāratī; *śrī-haste*—by the hand of Lord Caitanya Mahāprabhu; *candana*—sandalwood pulp; *pāñā*—getting; *bāḍila*—increased; *ānanda*—transcendental bliss.

TRANSLATION

Paramānanda Purī and Brahmānanda Bhāratī were both personally given garlands and sandalwood pulp from the very hands of Śrī Caitanya Mahāprabhu. This increased their transcendental pleasure.

TEXT 31

অদ্বৈত-আচার্য, আর প্রভু-নিত্যানন্দ ।
শ্রীহস্ত-স্পর্শে দুঁহার হইল আনন্দ ॥ ৩১ ॥

advaita-ācārya, āra prabhu-nityānanda
śrī-hasta-sparśe duṅhāra ha-ila ānanda

SYNONYMS

advaita-ācārya—Advaita Ācārya; *āra*—and; *prabhu-nityānanda*—Lord Nityānanda Prabhu; *śrī-hasta-sparśe*—by the touch of the transcendental hand of Lord Caitanya; *duṅhāra*—of both of Them; *ha-ila*—there was; *ānanda*—transcendental bliss.

TRANSLATION

Similarly, when Advaita Ācārya and Nityānanda Prabhu felt the touch of the transcendental hand of Śrī Caitanya Mahāprabhu, They were both very pleased.

TEXT 32

কীর্তনীয়াগণে দিল মাল্য-চন্দন ।
স্বরূপ, শ্রীবাস,—যাহাঁ মুখ্য দুইজন ॥ ৩২ ॥

kīrtanīyā-gaṇe dila mālya-candana
svarūpa, śrīvāsa,——yāhāṅ mukhya dui-jana

SYNONYMS

kīrtanīyā-gaṇe—unto the performers of *saṅkīrtana; dila*—gave; *mālya-candana*—garlands and sandalwood pulp; *svarūpa*—Svarūpa; *śrīvāsa*—Śrīvāsa; *yāhāṅ*—where; *mukhya*—principal; *dui-jana*—two persons.

TRANSLATION

The Lord also gave garlands and sandalwood pulp to the performers of saṅkīrtana. The chief two performers were Svarūpa Dāmodara and Śrīvāsa Ṭhākura.

TEXT 33

চারি সম্প্রদায়ে হৈল চব্বিশ গায়ন ।
দুই দুই মার্দঙ্গিক হৈল অষ্ট জন ॥ ৩৩ ॥

cāri sampradāye haila cabbiśa gāyana
dui dui mārdaṅgika haila aṣṭa jana

SYNONYMS

cāri sampradāye—in the four parties; *hāila*—there were; *cabbiśa*—twenty-four; *gāyana*—performers of *kīrtana; dui dui*—two in each party; *mārdaṅgika*—players of *mṛdaṅga* drums; *haila*—there were; *aṣṭa jana*—eight persons.

TRANSLATION

There were altogether four parties of kīrtana performers, comprising twenty-four chanters. In each party there were also two mṛdaṅga players, making an additional eight persons.

TEXT 34

তবে মহাপ্রভু মনে বিচার করিয়া ।
চারি সম্প্রদায় দিল গায়ন বাঁটিয়া ॥ ৩৪ ॥

tabe mahāprabhu mane vicāra kariyā
cāri sampradāya dila gāyana bāṅṭiyā

SYNONYMS

tabe—after this; *mahāprabhu*—Śrī Caitanya Mahāprabhu; *mane*—in the mind; *vicāra kariyā*—considering; *cāri sampradāya*—four parties; *dila*—gave; *gāyana bāṅṭiyā*—dividing the singers.

TRANSLATION

When the four parties were formed, Śrī Caitanya Mahāprabhu, after some consideration, divided the chanters.

TEXT 35

নিত্যানন্দ, অদ্বৈত, হরিদাস, বক্রেশ্বরে ।
চারি জনে আজ্ঞা দিল নৃত্য করিবারে ॥ ৩৫ ॥

nityānanda, advaita, haridāsa, vakreśvare
cāri jane ājñā dila nṛtya karibāre

SYNONYMS

nityānanda—Lord Nityānanda; *advaita*—Advaita Ācārya; *haridāsa*—Haridāsa Ṭhākura; *vakreśvare*—Vakreśvara Paṇḍita; *cāri jane*—to these four persons; *ājñā dila*—the Lord gave an order; *nṛtya karibāre*—to dance.

TRANSLATION

Śrī Caitanya Mahāprabhu ordered Nityānanda Prabhu, Advaita Ācārya, Haridāsa Ṭhākura and Vakreśvara Paṇḍita to dance in each of the four respective parties.

TEXT 36

প্রথম সম্প্রদায়ে কৈল স্বরূপ—প্রধান ।
আর পঞ্চজন দিল তাঁর পালিগান ॥ ৩৬ ॥

prathama sampradāye kaila svarūpa——pradhāna
āra pañca-jana dila tāṅra pāligāna

SYNONYMS

prathama sampradāye—in the first party; *kaila*—fixed; *svarūpa*—Svarūpa Dāmodara; *pradhāna*—as the chief; *āra*—another; *pañca-jana*—five persons; *dila*—gave; *tāṅra*—his; *pāligāna*—responders.

TRANSLATION

Svarūpa Dāmodara was chosen as the leader of the first party and was given five assistants to respond to his chanting.

TEXT 37

দামোদর, নারায়ণ, দত্ত গোবিন্দ ।
রাঘব পণ্ডিত, আর শ্রীগোবিন্দানন্দ ॥ ৩৭ ॥

dāmodara, nārāyaṇa, datta govinda
rāghava paṇḍita, āra śrī-govindānanda

SYNONYMS

dāmodara—Dāmodara Paṇḍita; *nārāyaṇa*—Nārāyaṇa; *datta govinda*—Govinda Datta; *rāghava paṇḍita*—Rāghava Paṇḍita; *āra*—and; *śrī-govindānanda*—Śrī Govindānanda.

TRANSLATION

The five who responded to the singing of Svarūpa Dāmodara were Dāmodara Paṇḍita, Nārāyaṇa, Govinda Datta, Rāghava Paṇḍita and Śrī Govindānanda.

TEXT 38

অদ্বৈতেরে নৃত্য করিবারে আজ্ঞা দিল।
শ্রীবাস—প্রধান আর সম্প্রদায় কৈল ॥ ৩৮ ॥

advaitere nṛtya karibāre ājñā dila
śrīvāsa——pradhāna āra sampradāya kaila

SYNONYMS

advaitere—unto Advaita Ācārya; *nṛtya*—dancing; *karibāre*—for performing; *ājñā*—order; *dila*—gave; *śrīvāsa*—Śrīvāsa Ṭhākura; *pradhāna*—chief; *āra*—another; *sampradāya*—group; *kaila*—formed.

TRANSLATION

Advaita Ācārya Prabhu was ordered to dance in the first group. The Lord then formed another group with Śrīvāsa Ṭhākura as the chief man.

PURPORT

In the first group, Dāmodara Svarūpa was appointed chief singer, and the responding singers were Dāmodara Paṇḍita, Nārāyaṇa, Govinda Datta, Rāghava Paṇḍita and Govindānanda. Śrī Advaita Ācārya was appointed as a dancer. The next group was formed, and the chief singer was Śrīvāsa Ṭhākura.

TEXT 39

গঙ্গাদাস, হরিদাস, শ্রীমান্, শুভানন্দ।
শ্রীরাম পণ্ডিত, তাহাঁ নাচে নিত্যানন্দ ॥ ৩৯ ॥

gaṅgādāsa, haridāsa, śrīmān, śubhānanda
śrī-rāma paṇḍita, tāhāṅ nāce nityānanda

SYNONYMS

gaṅgādāsa—Gaṅgādāsa; *haridāsa*—Haridāsa; *śrīmān*—Śrīmān; *śubhānanda*—Śubhānanda; *śrī-rāma paṇḍita*—Śrī Rāma Paṇḍita; *tāhāṅ*—there; *nāce*—dances; *nityānanda*—Lord Nityānanda.

TRANSLATION

The five singers who responded to the singing of Śrīvāsa Ṭhākura were Gaṅgādāsa, Haridāsa, Śrīmān, Śubhānanda and Śrī Rāma Paṇḍita. Śrī Nityānanda Prabhu was appointed as a dancer.

TEXT 40

বাসুদেব, গোপীনাথ, মুরারি যাহাঁ গায় ।
মুকুন্দ—প্রধান কৈল আর সম্প্রদায় ॥ ৪০ ॥

vāsudeva, gopīnātha, murāri yāhāṅ gāya
mukunda——pradhāna kaila āra sampradāya

SYNONYMS

vāsudeva—Vāsudeva; *gopīnātha*—Gopīnātha; *murāri*—Murāri; *yāhāṅ*—where; *gāya*—sing; *mukunda*—Mukunda; *pradhāna*—chief; *kaila*—formed; *āra*—another; *sampradāya*—group.

TRANSLATION

Another group was formed consisting of Vāsudeva, Gopīnātha, and Murāri. All these were responsive singers, and Mukunda was the chief singer.

TEXT 41

শ্রীকান্ত, বল্লভসেন আর দুই জন ।
হরিদাস-ঠাকুর তাহাঁ করেন নর্তন ॥ ৪১ ॥

śrīkānta, vallabha-sena āra dui jana
haridāsa-ṭhākura tāhāṅ karena nartana

SYNONYMS

śrīkānta, vallabha-sena—Śrīkānta and Vallabha Sena; *āra*—another; *dui jana*—two persons; *haridāsa-ṭhākura*—Haridāsa Ṭhākura; *tāhāṅ*—there; *karena*—performs; *nartana*—dancing.

TRANSLATION

Another two persons, Śrīkānta and Vallabha Sena, joined as responsive singers. In this group, Haridāsa Ṭhākura [the senior] was the dancer.

PURPORT

In the third group, Mukunda was appointed the chief singer. This party was composed of Vāsudeva, Gopīnātha, Murāri, Śrīkānta and Vallabha Sena. The senior Haridāsa Ṭhākura was the dancer.

TEXT 42

গোবিন্দ-ঘোষ—প্রধান কৈল আর সম্প্রদায়।
হরিদাস, বিষ্ণুদাস, রাঘব, যাহাঁ গায় ॥ ৪২ ॥

govinda-ghoṣa——pradhāna kaila āra sampradāya
haridāsa, viṣṇudāsa, rāghava, yāhāṅ gāya

SYNONYMS

govinda-ghoṣa—Govinda Ghosh; *pradhāna*—the chief; *kaila*—formed; *āra*—another; *sampradāya*—group; *haridāsa*—the younger Haridāsa; *viṣṇudāsa*—Viṣṇudāsa; *rāghava*—Rāghava; *yāhāṅ*—where; *gāya*—sing.

TRANSLATION

The Lord formed another group, appointing Govinda Ghosh as leader. In this group the younger Haridāsa, Viṣṇudāsa and Rāghava were the responding singers.

TEXT 43

মাধব, বাসুদেব-ঘোষ,—দুই সহোদর।
নৃত্য করেন তাহাঁ পণ্ডিত-বক্রেশ্বর ॥ ৪৩ ॥

mādhava, vāsudeva-ghoṣa,——dui sahodara
nṛtya karena tāhāṅ paṇḍita-vakreśvara

SYNONYMS

mādhava—Mādhava; *vāsudeva-ghoṣa*—Vāsudeva Ghosh; *dui sahodara*—two brothers; *nṛtya karena*—dances; *tāhāṅ*—there; *paṇḍita-vakreśvara*—Vakreśvara Paṇḍita.

TRANSLATION

Two brothers named Mādhava Ghosh and Vāsudeva Ghosh also joined this group as responsive singers. Vakreśvara Paṇḍita was the dancer.

TEXT 44

কুলীন-গ্রামের এক কীর্তনীয়া-সমাজ ।
তাহাঁ নৃত্য করেন রামানন্দ, সত্যরাজ ॥ ৪৪ ॥

kulīna-grāmera eka kīrtanīyā-samāja
tāhāṅ nṛtya karena rāmānanda, satyarāja

SYNONYMS

kulīna-grāmera—of the village known as Kulīna-grāma; *eka*—one; *kīrtanīyā-samāja*—*saṅkīrtana* party; *tāhāṅ*—there; *nṛtya karena*—dances; *rāmānanda*—Rāmānanda; *satyarāja*—Satyarāja Khān.

TRANSLATION

There was a saṅkīrtana party from the village known as Kulīna-grāma, and Rāmānanda and Satyarāja were appointed the dancers in this group.

TEXT 45

শান্তিপুরের আচার্যের এক সম্প্রদায় ।
অচ্যুতানন্দ নাচে তথা, আর সব গায় ॥ ৪৫ ॥

śāntipurera ācāryera eka sampradāya
acyutānanda nāce tathā, āra saba gāya

SYNONYMS

śāntipurera—of Śāntipura; *ācāryera*—of Advaita Ācārya; *eka*—one; *sampradāya*—group; *acyutānanda*—the son of Advaita Ācārya; *nāce*—dances; *tathā*—there; *āra*—the rest; *saba*—all; *gāya*—were singing.

TRANSLATION

There was another party that came from Śāntipura and was formed by Advaita Ācārya. Acyutānanda was the dancer, and the rest of the men were singers.

TEXT 46

খণ্ডের সম্প্রদায় করে অন্যত্র কীর্তন ।
নরহরি নাচে তাহাঁ শ্রীরঘুনন্দন ॥ ৪৬ ॥

khaṇḍera sampradāya kare anyatra kīrtana
narahari nāce tāhāṅ śrī-raghunandana

SYNONYMS

khaṇḍera—of the place named Khaṇḍa; *sampradāya*—party; *kare*—performs; *anyatra*—in a different place; *kīrtana*—chanting; *narahari*—Narahari; *nāce*—dances; *tāhāṅ*—there; *śrī-raghunandana*—Raghunandana.

TRANSLATION

Another party was formed by the people of Khaṇḍa. These people were singing in a different place. In that group, Narahari Prabhu and Raghunandana were dancing.

TEXT 47

জগন্নাথের আগে চারি সম্প্রদায় গায় ।
দুই পাশে দুই, পাছে এক সম্প্রদায় ॥ ৪৭ ॥

jagannāthera āge cāri sampradāya gāya
dui pāśe dui, pāche eka sampradāya

SYNONYMS

jagannāthera āge—in front of the Deity Lord Jagannātha; *cāri sampradāya gāya*—four groups were chanting; *dui pāśe*—on two sides; *dui*—another two groups; *pāche*—at the rear; *eka sampradāya*—another group.

TRANSLATION

Four parties chanted and danced in front of Lord Jagannātha, and on both sides were two other parties. Another was at the rear.

TEXT 48

সাত সম্প্রদায়ে বাজে চৌদ্দ মাদল ।
যার ধ্বনি শুনি' বৈষ্ণব হৈল পাগল ॥ ৪৮ ॥

sāta sampradāye bāje caudda mādala
yāra dhvani śuni' vaiṣṇava haila pāgala

SYNONYMS

sāta sampradāye—in seven groups; *bāje*—were beating; *caudda*—fourteen; *mādala*—drums; *yāra*—of which; *dhvani*—the sound; *śuni'*—hearing; *vaiṣṇava*—all the devotees; *haila*—became; *pāgala*—mad.

TRANSLATION

There were altogether seven parties of saṅkīrtana, and in each party two men were beating drums. Thus fourteen drums were being played at once. The sound was tumultuous, and all the devotees bacame mad.

TEXT 49

বৈষ্ণবের মেঘ-ঘটায় হইল বাদল ।
কীর্তনানন্দে সব বর্ষে নেত্র-জল ॥ ৪৯ ॥

vaiṣṇavera megha-ghaṭāya ha-ila bādala
kīrtanānande saba varṣe netra-jala

SYNONYMS

vaiṣṇavera—of the devotees; *megha-ghaṭāya*—by the assembly of clouds; *ha-ila*—there was; *bādala*—rainfall; *kīrtana-ānande*—in the blissful situation of chanting; *saba*—all of them; *varṣe*—rain; *netra-jala*—tears from the eyes.

TRANSLATION

All the Vaiṣṇavas came together like an assembly of clouds. As the devotees chanted the holy names, tears fell in great ecstasy like rainfall from their eyes.

TEXT 50

ত্রিভুবন ভরি' উঠে কীর্তনের ধ্বনি ।
অন্য বাদ্যাদির ধ্বনি কিছুই না শুনি ॥ ৫০ ॥

SYNONYMS

tri-bhuvana bhari'—filling the three worlds; *uṭhe*—arose; *kīrtanera dhvani*—vibration of *saṅkīrtana; anya*—other; *vādya-ādira*—of musical instruments; *dhvani*—the sound; *kichui*—anything; *nā*—not; *śuni*—hears.

TRANSLATION

When the saṅkīrtana resounded, it filled the three worlds. Indeed, no one could hear mundane sounds or musical instruments other than the saṅkīrtana.

TEXT 51

সাত ঠাঞি বুলে প্রভু 'হরি' 'হরি' বলি'।
'জয় জগন্নাথ', বলেন হস্তযুগ তুলি' ॥ ৫১ ॥

sāta ṭhāñi bule prabhu 'hari' 'hari' bali'
'jaya jagannātha', balena hasta-yuga tuli'

SYNONYMS

sāta ṭhāñi—in the seven places; *bule*—wanders; *prabhu*—Śrī Caitanya Mahāprabhu; *hari hari bali'*—chanting the holy names Hari, Hari; *jaya jagannātha*—all glories to Lord Jagannātha; *balena*—says; *hasta-yuga*—His two arms; *tuli'*—raising.

TRANSLATION

Lord Caitanya Mahāprabhu wandered through all seven groups chanting the holy name, "Hari, Hari!" Raising His arms, He shouted, "All glories to Lord Jagannātha!"

TEXT 52

আর এক শক্তি প্রভু করিল প্রকাশ।
এককালে সাত ঠাঞি করিল বিলাস ॥ ৫২ ॥

āra eka śakti prabhu karila prakāśa
eka-kāle sāta ṭhāñi karila vilāsa

SYNONYMS

āra—another; *eka*—one; *śakti*—mystic power; *prabhu*—Lord Śrī Caitanya Mahāprabhu; *karila*—made; *prakāśa*—manifest; *eka-kāle*—simultaneously; *sāta ṭhāñi*—in seven places; *karila*—performed; *vilāsa*—pastimes.

TRANSLATION

Lord Caitanya Mahāprabhu then exhibited another mystic power by performing pastimes simultaneously in all seven groups.

TEXT 53

সবে কহে,—প্রভু আছেন মোর সম্প্রদায় ।
অন্য ঠাঞি নাহি যা'ন আমারে দয়ায় ॥ ৫৩ ॥

sabe kahe,——prabhu ācchena mora sampradāya
anya ṭhāñi nāhi yā'na āmāre dayāya

SYNONYMS

sabe kahe—everyone said; *prabhu*—Śrī Caitanya Mahāprabhu; *āchena*—is present; *mora sampradāya*—in my group; *anya ṭhāñi*—in other places; *nāhi*—does not; *yā'na*—go; *āmāre*—unto me; *dayāya*—bestows His mercy.

TRANSLATION

Everyone said, "Lord Caitanya Mahāprabhu is present in my group. Indeed, He does not go anywhere else. He is bestowing His mercy upon us."

TEXT 54

কেহ লখিতে নারে প্রভুর অচিন্ত্য-শক্তি ।
অন্তরঙ্গ-ভক্ত জানে, যাঁর শুদ্ধভক্তি ॥ ৫৪ ॥

keha lakhite nāre prabhura acintya-śakti
antaraṅga-bhakta jāne, yāṅra śuddha-bhakti

SYNONYMS

keha—anyone; *lakhite*—see; *nāre*—cannot; *prabhura*—of Śrī Caitanya Mahāprabhu; *acintya*—inconceivable; *śakti*—power; *antaraṅga*—intimate; *bhakta*—devotee; *jāne*—knows; *yāṅra*—whose; *śuddha-bhakti*—pure devotional service.

TRANSLATION

Actually, no one could see the inconceivable potency of the Lord. Only the most confidential devotees, those in pure, unalloyed devotional service, could understand.

TEXT 55

কীর্তন দেখিয়া জগন্নাথ হরষিত ।
সংকীর্তন দেখে রথ করিয়া স্থগিত ॥ ৫৫ ॥

kīrtana dekhiyā jagannātha haraṣita
saṅkīrtana dekhe ratha kariyā sthagita

SYNONYMS

kīrtana dekhiyā—by seeing the performance of *saṅkīrtana; jagannātha*—Lord Jagannātha; *haraṣita*—very pleased; *saṅkīrtana*—performance of *saṅkīrtana; dekhe*—sees; *ratha*—the car; *kariyā sthagita*—stopping.

TRANSLATION

Lord Jagannātha was very pleased by the saṅkīrtana, and He brought His car to a standstill just to see the performance.

TEXT 56

প্রতাপরুদ্রের হৈল পরম বিস্ময় ।
দেখিতে বিবশ রাজা হৈল প্রেমময় ॥ ৫৬ ॥

pratāparudrera haila parama vismaya
dekhite vivaśa rājā haila premamaya

SYNONYMS

pratāparudrera—of King Pratāparudra; *haila*—there was; *parama*—very much; *vismaya*—astonishment; *dekhite*—to see; *vivaśa*—inactive; *rājā*—the King; *haila*—became; *prema-maya*—in ecstatic love.

TRANSLATION

King Pratāparudra also was astonished to see the saṅkīrtana. He became inactive and was converted to ecstatic love of Kṛṣṇa.

TEXT 57

কাশীমিশ্রে কহে রাজা প্রভুর মহিমা ।
কাশীমিশ্র কহে,—তোমার ভাগ্যের নাহি সীমা ॥৫৭॥

kāśī-miśre kahe rājā prabhura mahimā
kāśī-miśra kahe,——tomāra bhāgyera nāhi sīmā

SYNONYMS

kāśī-miśre—unto Kāśī Miśra; *kahe*—said; *rājā*—the King; *prabhura mahimā*—the glories of Śrī Caitanya Mahāprabhu; *kāśī-miśra kahe*—Kāśī Miśra said; *tomāra*—your; *bhāgyera*—of fortune; *nāhi*—there is not; *sīmā*—a limit.

TRANSLATION

When the King informed Kāśī Miśra of the glories of the Lord, Kāśī Miśra replied, "O King, your fortune has no limit!"

TEXT 58

সার্বভৌম-সঙ্গে রাজা করে ঠারাঠারি।
আর কেহ নাহি জানে চৈতন্যের চুরি ॥ ৫৮ ॥

sārvabhauma-saṅge rājā kare ṭhārāṭhāri
āra keha nāhi jāne caitanyera curi

SYNONYMS

sārvabhauma-saṅge—with Sārvabhauma Bhaṭṭācārya; *rājā*—the King; *kare*—does; *ṭhārāṭhāri*—indication; *āra*—further; *keha*—anyone; *nāhi*—not; *jāne*—knows; *caitanyera*—of Lord Śrī Caitanya Mahāprabhu; *curi*—tricks.

TRANSLATION

The King and Sārvabhauma Bhaṭṭācārya were both aware of the Lord's activities, but no one else could see the tricks of Lord Caitanya Mahāprabhu.

TEXT 59

যারে তাঁর কৃপা, সেই জানিবারে পারে।
কৃপা বিনা ব্রহ্মাদিক জানিবারে নারে ॥ ৫৯ ॥

yāre tāṅra kṛpā, sei jānibāre pāre
kṛpā vinā brahmādika jānibāre nāre

SYNONYMS

yāre—upon whom; *tāṅra*—His; *kṛpā*—mercy; *sei*—that person; *jānibāre*—to know; *pāre*—is able; *kṛpā*—mercy; *vinā*—without; *brahma-ādika*—the demigods, headed by Lord Brahmā; *jānibāre*—to know; *nāre*—are not able.

TRANSLATION

Only a person who has received the mercy of the Lord can understand. Without the Lord's mercy, even the demigods, headed by Lord Brahmā, cannot understand.

TEXT 60

রাজার তুচ্ছ সেবা দেখি' প্রভুর তুষ্ট মন।
সেই ত' প্রসাদে পাইল 'রহস্য-দর্শন' ॥ ৬০ ॥

rājāra tuccha sevā dekhi' prabhura tuṣṭa mana
sei ta' prasāde pāila 'rahasya-darśana'

SYNONYMS

rājāra—of the King; *tuccha*—insignificant, menial; *sevā*—service; *dekhi'*—seeing; *prabhura*—of Śrī Caitanya Mahāprabhu; *tuṣṭa*—satisfied; *mana*—mind; *sei*—that; *ta'*—indeed; *prasāde*—by mercy; *pāila*—got; *rahasya-darśana*—seeing of the mystery of the activities.

TRANSLATION

Śrī Caitanya Mahāprabhu was very satisfied to see the King accept the menial task of sweeping the street, and for this humility, the King received the mercy of Śrī Caitanya Mahāprabhu. He could therefore observe the mystery of Śrī Caitanya Mahāprabhu's activities.

PURPORT

The mystery of the Lord's activities is described by Śrīla Bhaktisiddhānta Sarasvatī Ṭhākura. Lord Jagannātha was astonished to see the transcendental dancing and chanting of Śrī Caitanya Mahāprabhu, and He stopped His car just to see the dancing. Lord Caitanya Mahāprabhu then danced in such a mystical way that He pleased Lord Jagannātha. The seer and the dancer were one and the same Supreme Person, but the Lord, being one and many at the same time, was exhibiting the variegatedness of His pastimes. This is the meaning behind His mysterious exhibition. By the mercy of Śrī Caitanya Mahāprabhu, the King could understand how both of Them were enjoying each other's activities. Another mysterious exhibition was Śrī Caitanya Mahāprabhu's simultaneous presence in seven groups. By the mercy of Śrī Caitanya Mahāprabhu, the King could understand that also.

TEXT 61

সাক্ষাতে না দেয় দেখা, পরোক্ষে ত' দয়া।
কে বুঝিতে পারে চৈতন্যচন্দ্রের মায়া ॥ ৬১ ॥

sākṣāte nā deya dekhā, parokṣe ta' dayā
ke bujhite pāre caitanya-candrera māyā

SYNONYMS

sākṣāte—directly; *nā*—not; *deya*—gives; *dekhā*—interview; *parokṣe*—indirectly; *ta'*—indeed; *dayā*—there was mercy; *ke*—who; *bujhite*—to understand; *pāre*—is able; *caitanya-candrera*—of Lord Śrī Caitanya Mahāprabhu; *māyā*—internal potency.

TRANSLATION

Although the King was refused an interview, he was indirectly bestowed causeless mercy. Who can understand the internal potency of Śrī Caitanya Mahāprabhu?

PURPORT

As Śrī Caitanya Mahāprabhu was playing the part of a world teacher, He did not agree to see the King because a king is a mundane person interested in money and women. Indeed, the very name "king" suggests one who is always surrounded by money and women. As a *sannyāsī*, Śrī Caitanya Mahāprabhu was afraid of both money and women. The very word "king" is repugnant to one who is in the renounced order of life. Śrī Caitanya Mahāprabhu refused to see the King, but indirectly, by the Lord's causeless mercy, the King was able to understand the Lord's mysterious activities. Lord Caitanya Mahāprabhu's activities were exhibited sometimes to reveal Him as the Supreme Personality of Godhead and sometimes to show Him as a devotee. Both kinds of activity are mysterious and appreciated only by pure devotees.

TEXT 62

সার্বভৌম, কাশীমিশ্র,—দুই মহাশয় ।
রাজারে প্রসাদ দেখি' হইলা বিস্ময় ॥ ৬২ ॥

sārvabhauma, kāśī-miśra,——dui mahāśaya
rājāre prasāda dekhi' ha-ilā vismaya

SYNONYMS

sārvabhauma—Sārvabhauma Bhaṭṭācārya; *kāśī-miśra*—Kāśī Miśra; *dui mahāśaya*—two great personalities; *rājāre*—unto the King; *prasāda*—mercy; *dekhi'*—seeing; *ha-ilā*—became; *vismaya*—astonished.

TRANSLATION

When the two great personalities Sārvabhauma Bhaṭṭācārya and Kāśī Miśra saw Caitanya Mahāprabhu's causeless mercy upon the King, they were astonished.

TEXT 63

এইমত লীলা প্রভু কৈল কতক্ষণ ।
আপনে গায়েন, নাচা'ন নিজ-ভক্তগণ ॥ ৬৩ ॥

ei-mata līlā prabhu kaila kata-kṣaṇa
āpane gāyena, nācā'na nija-bhakta-gaṇa

SYNONYMS

ei-mata—in this way; *līlā*—pastimes; *prabhu*—Śrī Caitanya Mahāprabhu; *kaila*—performed; *kata-kṣaṇa*—for some time; *āpane gāyena*—personally sings; *nācā'na*—made to dance; *nija-bhakta-gaṇa*—His own personal devotees.

TRANSLATION

Lord Śrī Caitanya Mahāprabhu performed His pastimes for some time in this way. He personally sang and induced His personal associates to dance.

TEXT 64

কভু এক মূর্তি, কভু হন বহু-মূর্তি ।
কার্য-অনুরূপ প্রভু প্রকাশয়ে শক্তি ॥ ৬৪ ॥

kabhu eka mūrti, kabhu hana bahu-mūrti
kārya-anurūpa prabhu prakāśaye śakti

SYNONYMS

kabhu—sometimes; *eka mūrti*—one form; *kabhu*—sometimes; *hana*—becomes; *bahu-mūrti*—many forms; *kārya-anurūpa*—according to the program of activities; *prabhu*—Lord Śrī Caitanya Mahāprabhu; *prakāśaye*—exhibits; *śakti*—His internal potency.

TRANSLATION

According to His need, the Lord sometimes exhibited one form and sometimes many. This was being executed by His internal potency.

TEXT 65

লীলাবেশে প্রভুর নাহি নিজানুসন্ধান।
ইচ্ছা জানি 'লীলা শক্তি' করে সমাধান ॥ ৬৫ ॥

līlāveśe prabhura nāhi nijānusandhāna
icchā jāni 'līlā śakti' kare samādhāna

SYNONYMS

līlā-āveśe—in the ecstasy of transcendental pastimes; *prabhura*—of Śrī Caitanya Mahāprabhu; *nāhi*—there was not; *nija-anusandhāna*—understanding about His personal self; *icchā jāni*—knowing His desire; *līlā śakti*—the potency known as *līlā-śakti; kare*—does; *samādhāna*—all arrangements.

TRANSLATION

Indeed, the Personality of Godhead forgot Himself in the course of His transcendental pastimes, but His internal potency [līlā-śakti], knowing the intentions of the Lord, made all arrangements.

PURPORT

It is stated in the *Upaniṣads:*

parāsya śaktir vividhaiva śrūyate
svābhāvikī jñāna-bala-kriyā ca

"The Supreme Lord has multi-potencies which act so perfectly that all consciousness, strength and activity are being directed solely by His will." (*Śvetāśvatara Upaniṣad* 6.8)

Śrī Caitanya Mahāprabhu exhibited His mystic power in presenting Himself simultaneously in each and every *saṅkīrtana* group. Most people thought that He was one, but some saw that He was many. The internal devotees could understand that the Lord, although one, was exhibiting Himself as many in the different *saṅkīrtana* groups. When Śrī Caitanya Mahāprabhu danced, He forgot Himself and was simply absorbed in ecstatic bliss. However, His internal potency arranged everything perfectly. This is the difference between the internal and external potency. In the material world, the external potency (material energy) can act only after one endeavors at great length, but when the Supreme Lord desires, everything is performed automatically by the internal potency. By His will, things happen so nicely and perfectly that they appear to be carried out automatically. Sometimes the activities of the internal potency are exhibited in the material world. In fact, all the activities of material nature are actually performed by the inconceivable energies of the Lord, but so-called scientists and students of material nature are unable to understand ultimately how things are happening. They evasively conclude that everything is being done by nature, but they do not know that behind nature is the potent Supreme Personality of Godhead. This is explained in *Bhagavad-gītā:*

mayādhyakṣeṇa prakṛtiḥ
sūyate sa-carācaram
hetunānena kaunteya
jagad viparivartate

"This material nature is working under My direction, O son of Kuntī, and it is producing all moving and unmoving beings. By its rule this manifestation is created and annihilated again and again." (Bg. 9.10)

TEXT 66

পূর্বে যৈছে রাসাদি লীলা কৈল বৃন্দাবনে।
অলৌকিক লীলা গৌর কৈল ক্ষণে ক্ষণে ॥ ৬৬ ॥

pūrve yaiche rāsādi līlā kaila vṛndāvane
alaukika līlā gaura kaila kṣaṇe kṣaṇe

SYNONYMS

pūrve—formerly; *yaiche*—as; *rāsa-ādi līlā*—the *rāsa-līlā* and other pastimes; *kaila*—performed; *vṛndāvane*—at Vṛndāvana; *alaukika*—uncommon; *līlā*—pastimes; *gaura*—Lord Śrī Caitanya Mahāprabhu; *kaila*—performed; *kṣaṇe kṣaṇe*—moment after moment.

TRANSLATION

Just as Lord Śrī Kṛṣṇa formerly performed the rāsa-līlā dance and other pastimes at Vṛndāvana, Lord Śrī Caitanya Mahāprabhu performed uncommon pastimes moment after moment.

TEXT 67

ভক্তগণ অনুভবে, নাহি জানে আন।
শ্রীভাগবত-শাস্ত্র তাহাতে প্রমাণ ॥ ৬৭ ॥

bhakta-gaṇa anubhave, nāhi jāne āna
śrī-bhāgavata-śāstra tāhāte pramāṇa

SYNONYMS

bhakta-gaṇa—all devotees; *anubhave*—could perceive; *nāhi jāne*—do not know; *āna*—others; *śrī-bhāgavata-śāstra*—the revealed scripture *Śrīmad-Bhāgavatam; tāhāte*—in that connection; *pramāṇa*—evidence.

TRANSLATION

Śrī Caitanya Mahāprabhu's dancing before the Ratha-yātrā car could be perceived only by pure devotees. Others could not understand. Descriptions of Lord Kṛṣṇa's uncommon dancing can be found in the revealed scripture Śrīmad-Bhāgavatam.

PURPORT

Lord Śrī Kṛṣṇa expanded Himself into many forms while engaged in the *rāsa-līlā* dance, and He also expanded Himself when He married 16,000 wives in Dvārakā. The same process was adopted by Śrī Caitanya Mahāprabhu when He expanded Himself into seven forms to dance in each and every group of the *saṅkīrtana* party. These expansions were appreciated by pure devotees, including King Pratāparudra. Although for reasons of external formality Śrī Caitanya Mahāprabhu refused to see King Pratāparudra because he was a king, King Pratāparudra became one of the Lord's most confidential devotees by the Lord's special mercy upon Him. The King could see Śrī Caitanya Mahāprabhu simultaneously present in all seven groups. As confirmed in *Śrīmad-Bhāgavatam,* one cannot see the expansions of the transcendental forms of the Lord unless one is a pure devotee of the Lord.

TEXT 68

এইমত মহাপ্রভু করে নৃত্য-রঙ্গে ।
ভাসাইল সব লোক প্রেমের তরঙ্গে ॥ ৬৮ ॥

ei-mata mahāprabhu kare nṛtya-raṅge
bhāsāila saba loka premera taraṅge

SYNONYMS

ei-mata—in this way; *mahāprabhu*—Śrī Caitanya Mahāprabhu; *kare*—performs; *nṛtya-raṅge*—dancing in great pleasure; *bhāsāila*—inundated; *saba*—all; *loka*—people; *premera taraṅge*—in waves of ecstatic love.

TRANSLATION

In this way Śrī Caitanya Mahāprabhu danced in great jubilation and inundated all the people with waves of ecstatic love.

TEXT 69

এইমত হৈল কৃষ্ণের রথে আরোহণ ।
তার আগে প্রভু নাচাইল ভক্তগণ ॥ ৬৯ ॥

ei-mata haila kṛṣṇera rathe ārohaṇa
tāra āge prabhu nācāila bhakta-gaṇa

SYNONYMS

ei-mata—in this way; *haila*—there was; *kṛṣṇera*—of Lord Śrī Kṛṣṇa; *rathe*—on the car; *ārohaṇa*—getting up; *tāra āge*—before it; *prabhu*—Śrī Caitanya Mahāprabhu; *nācāila*—caused to dance; *bhakta-gaṇa*—all devotees.

TRANSLATION

Thus Lord Jagannātha mounted His car, and Lord Śrī Caitanya Mahāprabhu inspired all His devotees to dance in front of it.

TEXT 70

আগে শুন জগন্নাথের গুণ্ডিচা-গমন ।
তার আগে প্রভু যৈছে করিলা নর্তন ॥ ৭০ ॥

āge śuna jagannāthera guṇḍicā-gamana
tāra āge prabhu yaiche karilā nartana

SYNONYMS

āge—ahead; *śuna*—hear; *jagannāthera*—of Lord Jagannātha; *guṇḍicā-gamana*—going to the Guṇḍicā temple; *tāra āge*—before that; *prabhu*—Śrī Caitanya Mahāprabhu; *yaiche*—as; *karilā*—did; *nartana*—dancing.

TRANSLATION

Now please hear about Lord Jagannātha's going to the Guṇḍicā temple while Śrī Caitanya Mahāprabhu danced before the Ratha car.

TEXT 71

এইমত কীর্তন প্রভু করিল কতক্ষণ ।
আপন-উদ্যোগে নাচাইল ভক্তগণ ॥ ৭১ ॥

ei-mata kīrtana prabhu karila kata-kṣaṇa
āpana-udyoge nācāila bhakta-gaṇa

SYNONYMS

ei-mata—in this way; *kīrtana*—chanting; *prabhu*—Śrī Caitanya Mahāprabhu; *karila*—performed; *kata-kṣaṇa*—for some time; *āpana*—personal; *udyoge*—by endeavor; *nācāila*—caused to dance; *bhakta-gaṇa*—all the devotees.

TRANSLATION

The Lord performed kīrtana for some time and, through His own endeavor, inspired all the devotees to dance.

TEXT 72

আপনি নাচিতে যবে প্রভুর মন হৈল ।
সাত সম্প্রদায় তবে একত্র করিল ॥ ৭২ ॥

āpani nācite yabe prabhura mana haila
sāta sampradāya tabe ekatra karila

SYNONYMS

āpani—personally; *nācite*—to dance; *yabe*—when; *prabhura*—of Lord Śrī Caitanya Mahāprabhu; *mana*—mind; *haila*—became; *sāta sampradāya*—all the seven parties; *tabe*—at that time; *ekatra karila*—combined.

TRANSLATION

When the Lord Himself wanted to dance, all seven groups combined together.

TEXT 73

শ্রীবাস, রামাই, রঘু, গোবিন্দ, মুকুন্দ ।
হরিদাস, গোবিন্দানন্দ, মাধব, গোবিন্দ ॥ ৭৩ ॥

śrīvāsa, rāmāi, raghu, govinda, mukunda
haridāsa, govindānanda, mādhava, govinda

SYNONYMS

śrīvāsa—Śrīvāsa; *rāmāi*—Rāmāi; *raghu*—Raghu; *govinda*—Govinda; *mukunda*—Mukunda; *haridāsa*—Haridāsa; *govindānanda*—Govindānanda; *mādhava*—Mādhava; *govinda*—Govinda.

TRANSLATION

The Lord's devotees—including Śrīvāsa, Rāmāi, Raghu, Govinda, Mukunda, Haridāsa, Govindānanda, Mādhava and Govinda—all combined together.

TEXT 74

উদ্দণ্ড-নৃত্যে প্রভুর যবে হৈল মন।
স্বরূপের সঙ্গে দিল এই নব জন ॥ ৭৪ ॥

uddaṇḍa-nṛtye prabhura yabe haila mana
svarūpera saṅge dila ei nava jana

SYNONYMS

uddaṇḍa-nṛtye—in the dancing with high jumps; *prabhura*—of Śrī Caitanya Mahāprabhu; *yabe*—when; *haila mana*—it was the mind; *svarūpera*—Svarūpa Dāmodara; *saṅge*—with; *dila*—gave; *ei*—these; *nava jana*—nine persons.

TRANSLATION

When Śrī Caitanya Mahāprabhu desired to jump high while dancing, He placed these nine people in the charge of Svarūpa Dāmodara.

TEXT 75

এই দশ জন প্রভুর সঙ্গে গায়, ধায়।
আর সব সম্প্রদায় চারি দিকে গায় ॥ ৭৫ ॥

ei daśa jana prabhura saṅge gāya, dhāya
āra saba sampradāya cāri dike gāya

SYNONYMS

ei daśa jana—these ten persons; *prabhura*—Śrī Caitanya Mahāprabhu; *saṅge*—with; *gāya*—chant; *dhāya*—run; *āra*—others; *saba*—all; *sampradāya*—groups of men; *cāri dike*—all around; *gāya*—chant.

TRANSLATION

These devotees [Svarūpa Dāmodara and the devotees in his charge] sang along with the Lord, and they also ran beside Him. All the other groups of men also sang.

TEXT 76

দণ্ডবৎ করি, প্রভু যুড়ি' দুই হাত।
ঊর্ধ্বমুখে স্তুতি করে দেখি' জগন্নাথ ॥ ৭৬ ॥

daṇḍavat kari, prabhu yuḍi' dui hāta
ūrdhva-mukhe stuti kare dekhi' jagannātha

SYNONYMS

daṇḍavat kari—offering obeisances; *prabhu*—Śrī Caitanya Mahāprabhu; *yuḍi'*—folding; *dui hāta*—two hands; *ūrdhva-mukhe*—raising the face upward; *stuti kare*—offers prayer; *dekhi'*—seeing; *jagannātha*—the Deity of Lord Jagannātha.

TRANSLATION

Offering obeisances to the Lord with folded hands, Śrī Caitanya Mahāprabhu raised His face toward Jagannātha and prayed as follows.

TEXT 77

নমো ব্রহ্মণ্যদেবায় গোব্রাহ্মণহিতায় চ।
জগদ্ধিতায় কৃষ্ণায় গোবিন্দায় নমো নমঃ ॥ ৭৭ ॥

namo brahmaṇya-devāya
go-brāhmaṇa-hitāya ca
jagad-dhitāya kṛṣṇāya
govindāya namo namaḥ

SYNONYMS

namaḥ—all obeisances; *brahmaṇya-devāya*—to the Lord worshipable by persons in brahminical culture; *go-brāhmaṇa*—for cows and *brāhmaṇas; hitāya*—beneficial; *ca*—also; *jagat-hitāya*—to one who always is benefiting the whole world; *kṛṣṇāya*—unto Kṛṣṇa; *govindāya*—unto Govinda; *namaḥ namaḥ*—repeated obeisances.

TRANSLATION

" 'Let me offer my respectful obeisances unto Lord Kṛṣṇa, who is the worshipable Deity for all brahminical men, who is the well-wisher of cows and brāhmaṇas, and who is always benefiting the whole world. I offer my repeated obeisances to the Personality of Godhead, known as Kṛṣṇa and Govinda.'

PURPORT

This is a quotation from the *Viṣṇu Purāṇa* (1.19.65).

TEXT 78

জয়তি জয়তি দেবো দেবকীনন্দনোঽসৌ
জয়তি জয়তি কৃষ্ণো বৃষ্ণিবংশপ্রদীপঃ।

জয়তি জয়তি মেঘশ্যামলঃ কোমলাঙ্গো
জয়তি জয়তি পৃথ্বীভারনাশো মুকুন্দঃ ॥ ৭৮ ॥

jayati jayati devo devakī-nandano 'sau
jayati jayati kṛṣṇo vṛṣṇi-vaṁśa-pradīpaḥ
jayati jayati megha-śyāmalaḥ komalāṅgo
jayati jayati pṛthvī-bhāra-nāśo mukundaḥ

SYNONYMS

jayati—all glories; *jayati*—all glories; *devaḥ*—to the Supreme Personality of Godhead; *devakī-nandanaḥ*—the son of Devakī; *asau*—He; *jayati jayati*—all glories; *kṛṣṇaḥ*—to Lord Kṛṣṇa; *vṛṣṇi-vaṁśa-pradīpaḥ*—the light of the dynasty of Vṛṣṇi; *jayati jayati*—all glories; *megha-śyāmalaḥ*—to the Surpeme Personality of Godhead, who looks like a blackish cloud; *komala-aṅgaḥ*—with a body as soft as a lotus flower; *jayati jayati*—all glories; *pṛthvī-bhāra-nāśaḥ*—to the deliverer of the whole world from its burden; *mukundaḥ*—the deliverer of liberation to everyone.

TRANSLATION

" 'All glories unto the Supreme Personality of Godhead who is known as the son of Devakī. All glories to the Supreme Personality of Godhead who is known as the light of the dynasty of Vṛṣṇi. All glories to the Supreme Personality of Godhead whose bodily luster is like that of a new cloud and whose body is as soft as a lotus flower. All glories to the Supreme Personality of Godhead who appeared on this planet to deliver the world from the burden of demons and who can offer liberation to everyone.'

PURPORT

This is a verse from the *Mukunda-mālā* (3).

TEXT 79

জয়তি জননিবাসো দেবকীজন্মবাদো
যদুবরপরিষৎ স্বৈর্দোর্ভিরস্যন্নধর্ম্মম্ ।
স্থিরচরবৃজিনঘ্নঃ সুস্মিত-শ্রীমুখেন
ব্রজপুরবনিতানাং বর্ধয়ন্ কামদেবম্ ॥ ৭৯ ॥

jayati jana-nivāso devakī-janma-vādo
yadu-vara-pariṣat svair dorbhir asyann adharmam
sthira-cara-vṛjina-ghnaḥ susmita-śrī-mukhena
vraja-pura-vanitānāṁ vardhayan kāma-devam

SYNONYMS

jayati—eternally lives gloriously; *jana-nivāsaḥ*—He who lives among human beings like the members of the Yadu dynasty and is the ultimate reasort of all living entities; *devakī-janma-vādaḥ*—known as the son of Devakī (No one can actually become the father or mother of the Supreme Personality of Godhead. Therefore *devakī-janma-vāda* means that He is *known* as the son of Devakī. Similarly, He is also known as the son of mother Yaśodā, Vasudeva or Nanda Mahārāja.); *yadu-vara-pariṣat*—served by the members of the Yadu dynasty or the cowherd men of Vṛndāvana (all of whom are constant associates of the Supreme Lord and are the Lord's eternal servants); *svaiḥ dorbhiḥ*—by His own arms, or by His devotees like Arjuna who are just like His own arms; *asyan*—killing; *adharmam*—demons or the impious; *sthira-cara-vṛjina-ghnaḥ*—the destroyer of all the ill fortune of all living entities, moving and not moving; *su-smita*—always smiling; *śrī-mukhena*—by His beautiful face; *vraja-pura-vanitānām*—of the damsels of Vṛndāvana; *vardhayan*—increasing; *kāma-devam*—the lusty desires.

TRANSLATION

" 'Lord Śrī Kṛṣṇa is He who is known as jana-nivāsa, the ultimate resort of all living entities, and who is also known as Devakī-nandana or Yaśodā-nandana, the son of Devakī and Yaśodā. He is the guide of the Yadu dynasty, and with His mighty arms He kills everything inauspicious as well as every man who is impious. By His presence He destroys all things inauspicious for all living entities, moving and inert. His blissful smiling face always increases the lusty desires of the gopīs of Vṛndāvana. May He be all glorious and happy!'

PURPORT

This is a quotation from *Śrīmad-Bhāgavatam* (10.90.48).

TEXT 80

নাহং বিপ্রো ন চ নরপতির্নাপি বৈশ্যো ন শূদ্রো
নাহং বর্ণী ন চ গৃহপতির্নো বনস্থো যতির্বা ।
কিন্তু প্রোদ্যন্নিখিলপরমানন্দপূর্ণামৃতাব্ধে-
র্গোপীভর্তুঃ পদকমলয়োর্দাসদাসানুদাসঃ ॥ ৮০ ॥

nāhaṁ vipro na ca nara-patir nāpi vaiśyo na śūdro
nāhaṁ varṇī na ca gṛha-patir no vanastho yatir vā
kintu prodyan-nikhila-paramānanda-pūrṇāmṛtābdher
gopī-bhartuḥ pada-kamalayor dāsa-dāsānudāsaḥ

SYNONYMS

na—not; *aham*—I; *vipraḥ*—a *brāhmaṇa; na*—not; *ca*—also; *nara-patiḥ*—a king or *kṣatriya; na*—not; *api*—also; *vaiśyaḥ*—belonging to the mercantile class; *na*—not; *śūdraḥ*—belonging to the worker class; *na*—not; *aham*—I; *varṇī*—belonging to any caste, or *brahmacārī* (A *brahmacārī* may belong to any caste. Anyone can become a *brahmacārī* or lead a life of celibacy.); *na*—not; *ca*—also; *gṛha-patiḥ*—householder; *no*—not; *vana-sthaḥ*—*vānaprastha,* one who, after retirement from family life, goes to the forest to learn how to be detached from family life; *yatiḥ*—mendicant or renunciant; *vā*—either; *kintu*—but; *prodyan*—brilliant; *nikhila*—universal; *parama-ānanda*—with transcendental bliss; *pūrṇa*—complete; *amṛta-abdheḥ*—who is the ocean of nectar; *gopī-bhartuḥ*—of the Supreme Person, who is the maintainer of the *gopīs; pada-kamalayoḥ*—of the two lotus feet; *dāsa*—of the servant; *dāsa-anudāsaḥ*—the servant of the servant.

TRANSLATION

" 'I am not a brāhmaṇa, I am not a kṣatriya, I am not a vaiśya or a śūdra. Nor am I a brahmacārī, a householder, a vānaprastha or a sannyāsī. I identify Myself only as the servant of the servant of the servant of the lotus feet of Lord Śrī Kṛṣṇa, the maintainer of the gopīs. He is like an ocean of nectar, and He is the cause of universal transcendental bliss. He is always existing with brilliance.' "

PURPORT

This verse is found in the *Padyāvalī* (74).

TEXT 81

এত পড়ি' পুনরপি করিল প্রণাম ।
যোড়হাতে ভক্তগণ বন্দে ভগবান্ ॥ ৮১ ॥

eta paḍi' punarapi karila praṇāma
yoḍa-hāte bhakta-gaṇa vande bhagavān

SYNONYMS

eta paḍi'—reciting these; *punarapi*—again; *karila*—the Lord offered; *praṇāma*—obeisances; *yoḍa-hāte*—with folded hands; *bhakta-gaṇa*—all the devotees; *vande*—offer prayer; *bhagavān*—unto the Supreme Personality of Godhead.

TRANSLATION

Having recited all these verses from scripture, the Lord again offered His obeisances, and all the devotees, with folded hands, also offered prayers to the Supreme Personality of Godhead.

TEXT 82

উদ্দণ্ড নৃত্য প্রভু করিয়া হুঙ্কার ।
চক্র-ভ্রমি ভ্রমে যৈছে অলাত-আকার ॥ ৮২ ॥

uddaṇḍa nṛtya prabhu kariyā huṅkāra
cakra-bhrami bhrame yaiche alāta-ākāra

SYNONYMS

uddaṇḍa—jumping; *nṛtya*—dancing; *prabhu*—Śrī Caitanya Mahāprabhu; *kariyā*—making; *huṅkāra*—loud vibration; *cakra-bhrami*—making a circular movement like a wheel; *bhrame*—moves; *yaiche*—as if; *alāta-ākāra*—circle of fire.

TRANSLATION

When Śrī Caitanya Mahāprabhu danced and jumped high, roaring like thunder and moving in a circle like a wheel, He appeared like a circling firebrand.

PURPORT

If a burning cinder of a firebrand is whirled about very swiftly, it gives the appearance of a circle of fire. This is called *alāta-ākāra,* or a firebrand circle. This whole circle is not actually made of fire but is a single fire in motion. Similarly, Lord Śrī Caitanya Mahāprabhu is a single personality, but when He danced and jumped high in a circle, He appeared like the *alāta-cakra.*

TEXT 83

নৃত্যে প্রভুর যাহাঁ যাঁহা পড়ে পদতল ।
সসাগর-শৈল মহী করে টলমল ॥ ৮৩ ॥

nṛtye prabhura yāhāṅ yāṅhā paḍe pada-tala
sasāgara-śaila mahī kare ṭalamala

SYNONYMS

nṛtye—while dancing; *prabhura*—of Śrī Caitanya Mahāprabhu; *yāhāṅ yāṅhā*—wherever; *paḍe*—steps; *pada-tala*—His foot; *sa-sāgara*—with the oceans; *śaila*—hills and mountains; *mahī*—the earth; *kare*—does; *ṭalamala*—tilting.

TRANSLATION

Wherever Śrī Caitanya Mahāprabhu stepped while dancing, the whole earth, with its hills and seas, appeared to tilt.

TEXT 84

স্তম্ভ, স্বেদ, পুলক, অশ্রু, কম্প, বৈবর্ণ্য ।
নানা-ভাবে বিবশতা, গর্ব, হর্ষ, দৈন্য ॥ ৮৪ ॥

stambha, sveda, pulaka, aśru, kampa, vaivarṇya
nānā-bhāve vivaśatā, garva, harṣa, dainya

SYNONYMS

stambha—being stunned; *sveda*—perspiration; *pulaka*—jubilation; *aśru*—tears; *kampa*—trembling; *vaivarṇya*—change of color; *nānā-bhāve*—in various ways; *vivaśatā*—helplessness; *garva*—pride; *harṣa*—exuberation; *dainya*—humility.

TRANSLATION

When Caitanya Mahāprabhu danced, He displayed various blissful transcendental changes in His body. Sometimes He appeared as though stunned. Sometimes the hairs of His body stood on end. Sometimes He perspired, cried, trembled and changed color, and sometimes He exhibited symptoms of helplessness, pride, exuberance and humility.

TEXT 85

আছাড় খাঞা পড়ে ভূমে গড়ি' যায় ।
সুবর্ণ-পর্বত যৈছে ভূমেতে লোটায় ॥ ৮৫ ॥

āchāḍa khāñā paḍe bhūme gaḍi' yāya
suvarṇa-parvata yaiche bhūmete loṭāya

SYNONYMS

āchāḍa khāñā—crashing; *paḍe*—falls; *bhūme*—on the ground; *gaḍi'*—rolling; *yāya*—goes; *suvarṇa-parvata*—a golden mountain; *yaiche*—as if; *bhūmete*—on the ground; *loṭāya*—rolls.

TRANSLATION

When Śrī Caitanya Mahāprabhu fell down with a crash while dancing, He would roll on the ground. At such times it appeared that a golden mountain was rolling on the ground.

TEXT 86

নিত্যানন্দপ্রভু দুই হাত প্রসারিয়া।
প্রভুরে ধরিতে চাহে আশপাশ ধাঞা ॥ ৮৬ ॥

nityānanda-prabhu dui hāta prasāriyā
prabhure dharite cāhe āśa-pāśa dhāñā

SYNONYMS

nityānanda-prabhu—Lord Nityānanda Prabhu; *dui*—two; *hāta*—hands; *prasāriyā*—stretching; *prabhure*—Lord Śrī Caitanya Mahāprabhu; *dharite*—to catch; *cāhe*—wants; *āśa-pāśa*—here and there; *dhāñā*—running.

TRANSLATION

Nityānanda Prabhu would stretch out His two hands and try to catch the Lord when He was running here and there.

TEXT 87

প্রভু-পাছে বুলে আচার্য করিয়া হুঙ্কার।
'হরিবোল' 'হরিবোল' বলে বার বার ॥ ৮৭ ॥

prabhu-pāche bule ācārya kariyā huṅkāra
'hari-bola' 'hari-bola' bale bāra bāra

SYNONYMS

prabhu-pāche—behind the Lord; *bule*—was walking; *ācārya*—Advaita Ācārya; *kariyā*—making; *huṅkāra*—a loud vibration; *hari-bola hari-bola*—chant the holy name of Hari; *bale*—says; *bāra bāra*—again and again.

TRANSLATION

Advaita Ācārya would walk behind the Lord and loudly chant "Hari bol! Hari bol!" again and again.

TEXT 88

লোক নিবারিতে হৈল তিন মণ্ডল।
প্রথম-মণ্ডলে নিত্যানন্দ মহাবল ॥ ৮৮ ॥

loka nivārite haila tina maṇḍala
prathama-maṇḍale nityānanda mahā-bala

SYNONYMS

loka—the people; *nivārite*—to check; *haila*—there were; *tina*—three; *maṇḍala*—circles; *prathama-maṇḍale*—in the first circle; *nityānanda*—Lord Nityānanda; *mahā-bala*—of great strength.

TRANSLATION

Just to check the crowds from coming too near the Lord, they formed three circles. The first circle was guided by Nityānanda Prabhu, who is Balarāma Himself, the possessor of great strength.

TEXT 89

কাশীশ্বর গোবিন্দাদি যত ভক্তগণ ।
হাতাহাতি করি' হৈল দ্বিতীয় আবরণ ॥ ৮৯ ॥

kāśīśvara govindādi yata bhakta-gaṇa
hātāhāti kari' haila dvitīya āvaraṇa

SYNONYMS

kāśīśvara—Kāśīśvara; *govinda-ādi*—headed by Govinda; *yata*—all; *bhakta-gaṇa*—devotees; *hātāhāti*—linked hand to hand; *kari'*—doing; *haila*—became; *dvitīya*—a second; *āvaraṇa*—covering circle.

TRANSLATION

All the devotees headed by Kāśīśvara and Govinda linked hands and formed a second circle around the Lord.

TEXT 90

বাহিরে প্রতাপরুদ্র লঞা পাত্রগণ ।
মণ্ডল হঞা করে লোক নিবারণ ॥ ৯০ ॥

bāhire pratāparudra lañā pātra-gaṇa
maṇḍala hañā kare loka nivāraṇa

SYNONYMS

bāhire—outside; *pratāparudra*—King Pratāparudra; *lañā*—taking; *pātra-gaṇa*—his own associates; *maṇḍala*—circle; *hañā*—becoming; *kare*—does; *loka*—of the crowd; *nivāraṇa*—checking.

TRANSLATION

Mahārāja Pratāparudra and his personal assistants formed a third circle around the two inner circles just to check the crowd from coming too near.

TEXT 91

হরিচন্দনের স্কন্ধে হস্ত আলম্বিয়া ।
প্রভুর নৃত্য দেখে রাজা আবিষ্ট হঞা ॥ ৯১ ॥

haricandanera skandhe hasta ālambiyā
prabhura nṛtya dekhe rājā āviṣṭa hañā

SYNONYMS

haricandanera—of Haricandana; *skandhe*—on the shoulder; *hasta*—hand; *ālambiyā*—putting; *prabhura*—of Śrī Caitanya Mahāprabhu; *nṛtya dekhe*—sees the dancing; *rājā*—Mahārāja Pratāparudra; *āviṣṭa hañā*—in great ecstasy.

TRANSLATION

With his hands on the shoulders of Haricandana, King Pratāparudra could see Lord Caitanya Mahāprabhu dancing, and the King felt great ecstasy.

TEXT 92

হেনকালে শ্রীনিবাস প্রেমাবিষ্ট-মন ।
রাজার আগে রহি' দেখে প্রভুর নর্তন ॥ ৯২ ॥

hena-kāle śrīnivāsa premāviṣṭa-mana
rājāra āge rahi' dekhe prabhura nartana

SYNONYMS

hena-kāle—at this time; *śrīnivāsa*—Śrīvāsa Ṭhākura; *prema-āviṣṭa-mana*—with a greatly ecstatic mind; *rājāra āge*—in front of the King; *rahi'*—keeping himself; *dekhe*—sees; *prabhura*—of Śrī Caitanya Mahāprabhu; *nartana*—the dancing.

TRANSLATION

While the King beheld the dancing, Śrīvāsa Ṭhākura, standing in front of him, became ecstatic as he saw the dancing of Śrī Caitanya Mahāprabhu.

TEXT 93

রাজার আগে হরিচন্দন দেখে শ্রীনিবাস।
হস্তে তাঁরে স্পর্শি' কহে,—হও এক-পাশ ॥ ৯৩ ॥

rājāra āge haricandana dekhe śrīnivāsa
haste tāṅre sparśi' kahe,——hao eka-pāśa

SYNONYMS

rājāra āge—in front of the King; *haricandana*—Haricandana; *dekhe*—sees; *śrīnivāsa*—Śrīvāsa Ṭhākura; *haste*—with his hand; *tāṅre*—him; *sparśi'*—touching; *kahe*—says; *hao*—please come; *eka-pāśa*—to one side.

TRANSLATION

Seeing Śrīvāsa Ṭhākura standing before the King, Haricandana touched Śrīvāsa with his hand and requested him to step aside.

TEXT 94

নৃত্যাবেশে শ্রীনিবাস কিছুই না জানে।
বার বার ঠেলে, তেঁহো ক্রোধ হৈল মনে ॥ ৯৪ ॥

nṛtyāveśe śrīnivāsa kichui nā jāne
bāra bāra ṭhele, teṅho krodha haila mane

SYNONYMS

nṛtya-āveśe—fully absorbed in seeing the dancing of Śrī Caitanya Mahāprabhu; *śrīnivāsa*—Śrīvāsa Ṭhākura; *kichui*—anything; *nā*—does not; *jāne*—know; *bāra bāra*—again and again; *ṭhele*—when he pushes; *teṅho*—Śrīvāsa; *krodha*—angry; *haila*—became; *mane*—in the mind.

TRANSLATION

Absorbed in watching Śrī Caitanya Mahāprabhu dance, Śrīvāsa Ṭhākura could not understand why he was being touched and pushed. After he was pushed again and again, he became angry.

TEXT 95

চাপড় মারিয়া তারে কৈল নিবারণ।
চাপড় খাঞা ক্রুদ্ধ হৈলা হরিচন্দন ॥ ৯৫ ॥

cāpaḍa māriyā tāre kaila nivāraṇa
cāpaḍa khāñā kruddha hailā haricandana

SYNONYMS

cāpaḍa māriyā—slapping; *tāre*—him; *kaila nivāraṇa*—stopped; *cāpaḍa khāñā*—getting the slap; *kruddha*—angry; *hailā*—became; *haricandana*—Haricandana.

TRANSLATION

Śrīvāsa Ṭhākura slapped Haricandana to stop him from pushing him. In turn, this made Haricandana angry.

TEXT 96

ক্রুদ্ধ হঞা তাঁরে কিছু চাহে বলিবারে ।
আপনি প্রতাপরুদ্র নিবারিল তারে ॥ ৯৬ ॥

kruddha hañā tāṅre kichu cāhe balibāre
āpani pratāparudra nivārila tāre

SYNONYMS

kruddha hañā—becoming angry; *tāṅre*—unto Śrīvāsa Ṭhākura; *kichu*—something; *cāhe*—wants; *balibāre*—to speak; *āpani*—personally; *pratāparudra*—King Pratāparudra; *nivārila*—stopped; *tāre*—unto him.

TRANSLATION

As the angered Haricandana was about to speak to Śrīvāsa Ṭhākura, Pratāparudra Mahārāja personally stopped him.

TEXT 97

ভাগ্যবান্ তুমি – ইঁহার হস্ত-স্পর্শ পাইলা ।
আমার ভাগ্যে নাহি, তুমি কৃতার্থ হৈলা ॥ ৯৭ ॥

bhāgyavān tumi——iṅhāra hasta-sparśa pāilā
āmāra bhāgye nāhi, tumi kṛtārtha hailā

SYNONYMS

bhāgyavān tumi—you are very fortunate; *iṅhāra*—of Śrīvāsa Ṭhākura; *hasta*—of the hand; *sparśa*—touch; *pāilā*—have received; *āmāra bhāgye*—in my fortune; *nāhi*—there is no such thing; *tumi*—you; *kṛta-artha hailā*—have become graced.

TRANSLATION

King Pratāparudra said, "You are very fortunate, for you have been graced by the touch of Śrīvāsa Ṭhākura. I am not so fortunate. You should feel obliged to him."

TEXT 98

প্রভুর নৃত্য দেখি' লোকে হৈল চমৎকার ।
অন্য আছুক্, জগন্নাথের আনন্দ অপার ॥ ৯৮ ॥

prabhura nṛtya dekhi' loke haila camatkāra
anya āchuk, jagannāthera ānanda apāra

SYNONYMS

prabhura—of Śrī Caitanya Mahāprabhu; *nṛtya*—dancing; *dekhi'*—seeing; *loke*—everyone; *haila*—became; *camatkāra*—astonished; *anya āchuk*—let alone others; *jagannāthera*—of Lord Jagannātha; *ānanda apāra*—there was extreme happiness.

TRANSLATION

Everyone was astonished by the dancing of Caitanya Mahāprabhu, and even Lord Jagannātha became extremely happy to see Him.

TEXT 99

রথ স্থির কৈল, আগে না করে গমন ।
অনিমিষ-নেত্রে করে নৃত্য দরশন ॥ ৯৯ ॥

ratha sthira kaila, āge nā kare gamana
animiṣa-netre kare nṛtya daraśana

SYNONYMS

ratha—the car; *sthira kaila*—stopped; *āge*—forward; *nā*—not; *kare*—does; *gamana*—moving; *animiṣa*—unblinking; *netre*—with eyes; *kare*—does; *nṛtya*—of the dancing; *daraśana*—seeing.

TRANSLATION

The car came to a complete standstill and remained immobile while Lord Jagannātha, with unblinking eyes, watched the dancing of Śrī Caitanya Mahāprabhu.

TEXT 100

সুভদ্রা-বলরামের হৃদয়ে উল্লাস ।
নৃত্য দেখি' দুই জনার শ্রীমুখেতে হাস ॥ ১০০ ॥

subhadrā-balarāmera hṛdaye ullāsa
nṛtya dekhi' dui janāra śrī-mukhete hāsa

SYNONYMS

subhadrā—of the goddess Subhadrā; *balarāmera*—and of Balarāma; *hṛdaye*—in the hearts; *ullāsa*—ecstasy; *nṛtya*—dancing; *dekhi'*—seeing; *dui janāra*—of the two persons; *śrī-mukhete*—in the beautiful mouths; *hāsa*—smiling.

TRANSLATION

The goddess of fortune, Subhadrā, and Lord Balarāma both felt great happiness and ecstasy within Their hearts. Indeed, They were seen smiling at the dancing.

TEXT 101

উদ্দণ্ড নৃত্যে প্রভুর অদ্ভুত বিকার ।
অষ্ট সাত্ত্বিক ভাব উদয় হয় সমকাল ॥ ১০১ ॥

uddaṇḍa nṛtye prabhura adbhuta vikāra
aṣṭa sāttvika bhāva udaya haya sama-kāla

SYNONYMS

uddaṇḍa—jumping; *nṛtye*—by dancing; *prabhura*—of Śrī Caitanya Mahāprabhu; *adbhuta*—wonderful; *vikāra*—transformations; *aṣṭa sāttvika*—eight transcendental kinds; *bhāva*—ecstasy; *udaya haya*—awaken; *sama-kāla*—simultaneously.

TRANSLATION

When Caitanya Mahāprabhu danced and jumped high, eight wonderful transformations indicative of divine ecstasy were seen in His body. All these symptoms were visible simultaneously.

TEXT 102

মাংস-ব্রণ সম রোমবৃন্দ পুলকিত ।
শিমুলীর বৃক্ষ যেন কণ্টক-বেষ্টিত ॥ ১০২ ॥

māṁsa-vraṇa sama roma-vṛnda pulakita
śimulīra vṛkṣa yena kaṇṭaka-veṣṭita

SYNONYMS

māṁsa—skin; *vraṇa*—pimples; *sama*—like; *roma-vṛnda*—the hairs of the body; *pulakita*—erupted; *śimulīra vṛkṣa*—cotton tree; *yena*—as if; *kaṇṭaka*—by thorns; *veṣṭita*—surrounded.

TRANSLATION

His skin erupted with goose pimples, and the hairs of His body stood on end. His body resembled the śimulī [silk cotton tree], all covered with thorns.

TEXT 103

এক এক দন্তের কম্প দেখিতে লাগে ভয় ।
লোকে জানে, দন্ত সব খসিয়া পড়য় ॥ ১০৩ ॥

eka eka dantera kampa dekhite lāge bhaya
loke jāne, danta saba khasiyā paḍaya

SYNONYMS

eka eka—one after another; *dantera*—of teeth; *kampa*—movement; *dekhite*—to see; *lāge*—there is; *bhaya*—fear; *loke jāne*—the people understood; *danta*—the teeth; *saba*—all; *khasiyā*—being loosened; *paḍaya*—fall down.

TRANSLATION

Indeed, the people became afraid just to see His teeth chatter, and they even thought that His teeth would fall out.

TEXT 104

সর্বাঙ্গে প্রস্বেদ ছুটে তাতে রক্তোদ্গম ।
'জজ গগ' 'জজ গগ'—গদ্গদ-বচন ॥ ১০৪ ॥

sarvāṅge prasveda chuṭe tāte raktodgama
'jaja gaga' 'jaja gaga'——gadgada-vacana

SYNONYMS

sarvāṅge—all over the body; *prasveda*—perspiration; *chuṭe*—flows; *tāte*—along with it; *rakta-udgama*—oozing out of blood; *jaja gaga jaja gaga*—a sound indicating the name Jagannātha; *gadgada*—choked up due to ecstasy; *vacana*—words.

TRANSLATION

Śrī Caitanya Mahāprabhu's whole body flowed with perspiration and at the same time oozed blood. He made the sounds "jaja gaga, jaja gaga" in a voice choked with ecstasy.

TEXT 105

জলযন্ত্র-ধারা যৈছে বহে অশ্রুজল ।
আশ-পাশে লোক যত ভিজিল সকল ॥ ১০৫ ॥

jalayantra-dhārā yaiche vahe aśru-jala
āśa-pāśe loka yata bhijila sakala

SYNONYMS

jala-yantra—from a syringe; *dhārā*—pouring of water; *yaiche*—as if; *vahe*—are flowing; *aśru-jala*—tears from the eyes; *āśa-pāśe*—on all sides; *loka*—people; *yata*—as many as there were; *bhijila*—become wet; *sakala*—all.

TRANSLATION

Tears came forcefully from the eyes of the Lord, as if from a syringe, and all the people surrounding Him became wet.

TEXT 106

দেহ-কান্তি গৌরবর্ণ দেখিয়ে অরুণ ।
কভু কান্তি দেখি যেন মল্লিকা-পুষ্পসম ॥ ১০৬ ॥

deha-kānti gaura-varṇa dekhiye aruṇa
kabhu kānti dekhi yena mallikā-puṣpa-sama

SYNONYMS

deha-kānti—of the luster of the body; *gaura-varṇa*—white complexion; *dekhiye*—everyone saw; *aruṇa*—pink; *kabhu*—sometimes; *kānti*—the luster; *dekhi*—seeing; *yena*—as if; *mallikā-puṣpa-sama*—resembling the *mallikā* flower.

TRANSLATION

Everyone saw the complexion of His body change from white to pink, so that His luster resembled that of the mallikā flower.

TEXT 107

কভু স্তম্ভ, কভু প্রভু ভূমিতে লোটায়।
শুষ্ককাষ্ঠসম পদ-হস্ত না চলয় ॥ ১০৭ ॥

kabhu stambha, kabhu prabhu bhūmite loṭāya
śuṣka-kāṣṭha-sama pada-hasta nā calaya

SYNONYMS

kabhu—sometimes; *stambha*—stunned; *kabhu*—sometimes; *prabhu*—Lord Caitanya Mahāprabhu; *bhūmite*—on the ground; *loṭāya*—rolls; *śuṣka*—dry; *kāṣṭha*—wood; *sama*—like; *pada-hasta*—legs and hands; *nā*—do not; *calaya*—move.

TRANSLATION

Sometimes He appeared stunned, and sometimes He rolled on the ground. Indeed, sometimes His legs and hands became as hard as dry wood, and He did not move.

TEXT 108

কভু ভূমে পড়ে, কভু শ্বাস হয় হীন।
যাহা দেখি' ভক্তগণের প্রাণ হয় ক্ষীণ ॥ ১০৮ ॥

kabhu bhūme paḍe, kabhu śvāsa haya hīna
yāhā dekhi' bhakta-gaṇera prāṇa haya kṣīṇa

SYNONYMS

kabhu—sometimes; *bhūme*—on the ground; *paḍe*—falls down; *kabhu*—sometimes; *śvāsa*—breathing; *haya*—becomes; *hīna*—nil; *yāhā dekhi'*—seeing which; *bhakta-gaṇera*—of the devotees; *prāṇa*—life; *haya*—becomes; *kṣīṇa*—feeble.

TRANSLATION

When the Lord fell on the ground, sometimes His breathing almost stopped. When the devotees saw this, their lives also became very feeble.

TEXT 109

কভু নেত্রে নাসায় জল, মুখে পড়ে ফেন।
অমৃতের ধারা চন্দ্রবিম্বে বহে যেন ॥ ১০৯ ॥

kabhu netre nāsāya jala, mukhe paḍe phena
amṛtera dhārā candra-bimbe vahe yena

SYNONYMS

kabhu—sometimes; *netre*—from the eyes; *nāsāya*—from the nostrils; *jala*—water; *mukhe*—from the mouth; *paḍe*—fell; *phena*—foam; *amṛtera*—of nectar; *dhārā*—torrents; *candra-bimbe*—from the moon; *vahe*—flow; *yena*—as if.

TRANSLATION

Water flowed from His eyes and sometimes through His nostrils, and foam fell from His mouth. These flowings appeared to be torrents of nectar descending from the moon.

TEXT 110

সেই ফেন লঞা শুভানন্দ কৈল পান ।
কৃষ্ণপ্রেমরসিক তেঁহো মহাভাগ্যবান্ ॥ ১১০ ॥

sei phena lañā śubhānanda kaila pāna
kṛṣṇa-prema-rasika teṅho mahā-bhāgyavān

SYNONYMS

sei phena—that foam; *lañā*—taking; *śubhānanda*—a devotee named Śubhānanda; *kaila*—did; *pāna*—drinking; *kṛṣṇa-prema-rasika*—relisher of ecstatic love of Kṛṣṇa; *teṅho*—he; *mahā-bhāgyavān*—very fortunate.

TRANSLATION

The foam which fell from the mouth of Śrī Caitanya Mahāprabhu was taken and drunk by Śubhānanda because he was very fortunate and expert in relishing the mellow of ecstatic love of Kṛṣṇa.

TEXT 111

এইমত তাণ্ডব-নৃত্য কৈল কতক্ষণ ।
ভাব-বিশেষে প্রভুর প্রবেশিল মন ॥ ১১১ ॥

ei-mata tāṇḍava-nṛtya kaila kata-kṣaṇa
bhāva-viśeṣe prabhura praveśila mana

SYNONYMS

ei-mata—in this way; *tāṇḍava-nṛtya*—devastating dancing; *kaila*—performed; *kata-kṣaṇa*—for some time; *bhāva-viśeṣe*—in a particular ecstasy; *prabhura*—of Lord Caitanya Mahāprabhu; *praveśila mana*—the mind entered.

TRANSLATION

After performing His devastating dance for some time, Śrī Caitanya Mahāprabhu's mind entered into a mood of ecstatic love.

TEXT 112

তাণ্ডব-নৃত্য ছাড়ি' স্বরূপেরে আজ্ঞা দিল ।
হৃদয় জানিয়া স্বরূপ গাইতে লাগিল ॥ ১১২ ॥

tāṇḍava-nṛtya chāḍi' svarūpere ājñā dila
hṛdaya jāniyā svarūpa gāite lāgila

SYNONYMS

tāṇḍava-nṛtya chāḍi'—giving up such devastating dancing; *svarūpere*—unto Svarūpa Dāmodara; *ājñā dila*—gave an order; *hṛdaya*—mind; *jāniyā*—knowing; *svarūpa*—Svarūpa Dāmodara; *gāite lāgila*—began to sing.

TRANSLATION

After abandoning the dancing, the Lord ordered Svarūpa Dāmodara to sing. Understanding His mind, Svarūpa Dāmodara began to sing as follows.

TEXT 113

"সেই ত পরাণ-নাথ পাইনু ।
যাহা লাগি' মদন-দহনে ঝুরি' গেনু ॥" ১১৩ ॥ ধ্রু ॥

"sei ta parāṇa-nātha pāinu
yāhā lāgi' madana-dahane jhuri' genu"

SYNONYMS

sei ta—that indeed; *parāṇa-nātha*—the master of My life; *pāinu*—I have gotten; *yāhā lāgi'*—for whom; *madana-dahane*—being burned by Cupid; *jhuri' genu*—I became dried up.

TRANSLATION

"Now I have gained the Lord of My life, in the absence of whom I was being burned by Cupid and was withering away."

PURPORT

This song refers to Śrīmatī Rādhārāṇī's meeting with Kṛṣṇa at the holy place of Kurukṣetra, where Lord Śrī Kṛṣṇa and His brother and sister came to visit when there was a solar eclipse. It is a song of separation from Kṛṣṇa. When Rādhārāṇī met Kṛṣṇa at Kurukṣetra, She remembered His intimate association in Vṛndāvana, and She thought, "Now I have gained the Lord of my life. In His absence I was being burned by the arrow of Cupid, and thus I was withering away. Now I have My life again."

TEXT 114

এই ধুয়া উচ্চৈঃস্বরে গায় দামোদর ।
আনন্দে মধুর নৃত্য করেন ঈশ্বর ॥ ১১৪ ॥

ei dhuyā uccaiḥ-svare gāya dāmodara
ānande madhura nṛtya karena īśvara

SYNONYMS

ei dhuyā—this refrain; *uccaiḥ-svare*—loudly; *gāya*—sings; *dāmodara*—Svarūpa Dāmodara; *ānande*—in great ecstasy; *madhura*—rhythmic; *nṛtya*—dancing; *karena*—performs; *īśvara*—the Lord.

TRANSLATION

When this refrain was loudly sung by Svarūpa Dāmodara, Śrī Caitanya Mahāprabhu again began rhythmically dancing in transcendental bliss.

TEXT 115

ধীরে ধীরে জগন্নাথ করেন গমন ।
আগে নৃত্য করি' চলেন শচীর নন্দন ॥ ১১৫ ॥

dhīre dhīre jagannātha karena gamana
āge nṛtya kari' calena śacīra nandana

SYNONYMS

dhīre dhīre—slowly, slowly; *jagannātha*—Lord Jagannātha; *karena*—does; *gamana*—movement; *āge*—in front; *nṛtya*—dancing; *kari'*—performing; *calena*—goes forward; *śacīra nandana*—the son of mother Śacī.

TRANSLATION

The car of Lord Jagannātha began to move slowly while the son of mother Śacī went ahead and danced in front.

TEXT 116

জগন্নাথে নেত্র দিয়া সবে নাচে, গায় ।
কীর্তনীয়া সহ প্রভু পাছে পাছে যায় ॥ ১১৬ ॥

jagannāthe netra diyā sabe nāce, gāya
kīrtanīyā saha prabhu pāche pāche yāya

SYNONYMS

jagannāthe—on Lord Jagannātha; *netra*—the eyes; *diyā*—keeping; *sabe*—all the devotees; *nāce gāya*—dance and sing; *kīrtanīyā*—the performers of *saṅkīrtana; saha*—with; *prabhu*—Śrī Caitanya Mahāprabhu; *pāche pāche*—at the rear; *yāya*—goes forward.

TRANSLATION

While dancing and singing, all the devotees in front of Lord Jagannātha kept their eyes on Him. Caitanya Mahāprabhu then went to the end of the procession with the saṅkīrtana performers.

TEXT 117

জগন্নাথে মগ্ন প্রভুর নয়ন-হৃদয় ।
শ্রীহস্তযুগে করে গীতের অভিনয় ॥ ১১৭ ॥

jagannāthe magna prabhura nayana-hṛdaya
śrī-hasta-yuge kare gītera abhinaya

SYNONYMS

jagannāthe—into Lord Jagannātha; *magna*—absorbed; *prabhura*—of Lord Caitanya Mahāprabhu; *nayana-hṛdaya*—the eyes and mind; *śrī-hasta-yuge*—with His two arms; *kare*—performed; *gītera*—of the song; *abhinaya*—dramatic movement.

TRANSLATION

His eyes and mind fully absorbed in Lord Jagannātha, Caitanya Mahāprabhu began to play the drama of the song with His two arms.

TEXT 118

গৌর যদি পাছে চলে, শ্যাম হয় স্থিরে ।
গৌর আগে চলে, শ্যাম চলে ধীরে-ধীরে ॥ ১১৮ ॥

gaura yadi pāche cale, śyāma haya sthire
gaura āge cale, śyāma cale dhīre-dhīre

SYNONYMS

gaura—Śrī Caitanya Mahāprabhu; *yadi*—if; *pāche cale*—goes behind; *śyāma*—Jagannātha; *haya*—becomes; *sthire*—still; *gaura*—Śrī Caitanya Mahāprabhu; *āge cale*—goes forward; *śyāma*—Lord Jagannātha; *cale*—goes; *dhīre-dhīre*—slowly.

TRANSLATION

When Caitanya Mahāprabhu was dramatically enacting the song, He would sometimes fall behind in the procession. At such times, Lord Jagannātha would come to a standstill. When Caitanya Mahāprabhu again went forward, Lord Jagannātha's car would slowly start again.

TEXT 119

এইমত গৌর-শ্যামে, দোঁহে ঠেলাঠেলি ।
স্বরথে শ্যামেরে রাখে গৌর মহাবলী ॥ ১১৯ ॥

ei-mata gaura-śyāme, doṅhe ṭhelāṭheli
svarathe śyāmere rākhe gaura mahā-balī

SYNONYMS

ei-mata—in this way; *gaura-śyāme*—Lord Jagannātha and Lord Śrī Caitanya Mahāprabhu; *doṅhe*—between both of Them; *ṭhelāṭheli*—competition of pushing forward; *sva-rathe*—in His own car; *śyāmere*—Lord Jagannātha; *rākhe*—keeps; *gaura*—Lord Śrī Caitanya Mahāprabhu; *mahā-balī*—greatly powerful.

TRANSLATION

Thus there was a sort of competition between Caitanya Mahāprabhu and Lord Jagannātha in seeing who would lead, but Caitanya Mahāprabhu was so strong that He made Lord Jagannātha wait in His car.

PURPORT

After giving up the company of the *gopīs* in Vṛndāvana, Śrī Kṛṣṇa, the son of Mahārāja Nanda, engaged in His pastimes at Dvārakā. When Kṛṣṇa went to Kurukṣetra with His brother and sister and others from Dvārakā, He again met the inhabitants of Vṛndāvana. Śrī Caitanya Mahāprabhu is *rādhā-bhāva-dyuti-suvalita,* that is, Kṛṣṇa Himself assuming the part of Śrīmatī Rādhārāṇī in order to understand Kṛṣṇa. Lord Jagannātha-deva is Kṛṣṇa, and Śrī Kṛṣṇa Caitanya Mahāprabhu is Śrīmatī Rādhārāṇī. Caitanya Mahāprabhu's leading Lord Jagannātha toward Guṇḍicā temple corresponded to Śrīmatī Rādhārāṇī's leading Kṛṣṇa toward Vṛndāvana. Śrī Kṣetra, Jagannātha Purī, was taken as the kingdom of Dvārakā, the place where Kṛṣṇa enjoys supreme opulence. However, He was being led by Śrī Caitanya Mahāprabhu to Vṛndāvana, the simple village where all the inhabitants are filled with ecstatic love for Kṛṣṇa. Śrī Kṣetra is a place of *aiśvarya-līlā,* just as Vṛndāvana is the place of *mādhurya-līlā.* Śrī Caitanya Mahāprabhu's following at the rear of the *ratha* indicated that Lord Jagannātha, Kṛṣṇa, was forgetting the inhabitants of Vṛndāvana. Although Kṛṣṇa neglected the inhabitants of Vṛndāvana, He could not forget them. Thus in His opulent Ratha-yātrā, He was returning to Vṛndāvana. In the role of Śrīmatī Rādhārāṇī, Śrī Caitanya Mahāprabhu was examining whether the Lord still remembered the inhabitants of Vṛndāvana. When Caitanya Mahāprabhu fell behind the Ratha car, Jagannātha-deva, Kṛṣṇa Himself, understood the mind of Śrīmatī Rādhārāṇī. Therefore, Jagannātha sometimes fell behind the dancing Śrī Caitanya Mahāprabhu to indicate to Śrīmatī Rādhārāṇī that He had not forgotten. Thus Lord Jagannātha would wait on the *ratha* for their forward march. In this way Lord Jagannātha agreed that without the ecstasy of Śrīmatī Rādhārāṇī He could not feel satisfied. While Jagannātha was thus waiting, Gaurasundara, Caitanya Mahāprabhu, in His ecstasy of Śrīmatī Rādhārāṇī, immediately came forward to Kṛṣṇa. At such times, Lord Jagannātha would proceed ahead very slowly. These competitive exchanges were all part of the love affair between Kṛṣṇa and Śrīmatī Rādhārāṇī. In that competition between Lord Caitanya's ecstasy for Jagannātha and Jagannātha's ecstasy for Śrīmatī Rādhārāṇī, Caitanya Mahāprabhu emerged successful.

TEXT 120

নাচিতে নাচিতে প্রভুর হৈলা ভাবান্তর ।
হস্ত তুলি' শ্লোক পড়ে করি' উচ্চৈঃস্বর ॥ ১২০ ॥

nācite nācite prabhura hailā bhāvāntara
hasta tuli' śloka paḍe kari' uccaiḥ-svara

SYNONYMS

nācite nācite—while dancing; *prabhura*—of Śrī Caitanya Mahāprabhu; *hailā*—there was; *bhāva-antara*—a change of ecstasy; *hasta tuli'*—raising the arms; *śloka paḍe*—recites one verse; *kari'*—making; *uccaiḥ-svara*—loud voice.

TRANSLATION

While Śrī Caitanya Mahāprabhu was dancing, His ecstasy changed. Raising His two arms, He began to recite the following verse in a loud voice.

TEXT 121

যঃ কৌমারহরঃ স এব হি বরস্তা এব চৈত্রক্ষপা-
স্তে চোন্মীলিতমালতীসুরভয়ঃ প্রৌঢ়াঃ কদম্বানিলাঃ ।
সা চৈবাস্মি তথাপি তত্র সুরতব্যাপারলীলাবিধৌ
রেবা-রোধসি বেতসীতরুতলে চেতঃ সমুৎকণ্ঠতে ॥ ১২১ ॥

yaḥ kaumāra-haraḥ sa eva hi varas tā eva caitra-kṣapās
te conmīlita-mālatī-surabhayaḥ prauḍhāḥ kadambānilāḥ
sā caivāsmi tathāpi tatra surata-vyāpāra-līlā-vidhau
revā-rodhasi vetasī-taru-tale cetaḥ samutkaṇṭhate

SYNONYMS

yaḥ—that same person who; *kaumāra-haraḥ*—the thief of my heart during youth; *saḥ*—he; *eva hi*—certainly; *varaḥ*—lover; *tāḥ*—these; *eva*—certainly; *caitra-kṣapāḥ*—moonlit nights of the month of Caitra; *te*—those; *ca*—and; *unmīlita*—fructified; *mālatī*—of *mālatī* flowers; *surabhayaḥ*—fragrances; *prauḍhāḥ*—full; *kadamba*—with the fragrance of the *kadamba* flower; *anilāḥ*—the breezes; *sā*—that one; *ca*—also; *eva*—certainly; *asmi*—I am; *tathāpi*—still; *tatra*—there; *surata-vyāpāra*—in intimate transactions; *līlā*—of pastimes; *vidhau*—in the manner; *revā*—of the river named Revā; *rodhasi*—on the bank; *vetasi*—of the name Vetasī; *taru-tale*—underneath the tree; *cetaḥ*—my mind; *samutkaṇṭhate*—is very eager to go.

TRANSLATION

"That very personality who stole away my heart during my youth is now again my master. These are the same moonlit nights of the month of Caitra. The same fragrance of mālatī flowers is there, and the same sweet breezes are blowing from the kadamba forest. In our intimate relationship, I am also the same lover, yet still my mind is not happy here. I am eager to go back to that place on the bank of the Revā under the Vetasī tree. That is my desire."

PURPORT

This verse appears in the *Padyāvalī* (382), by Śrīla Rūpa Gosvāmī.

TEXT 122

এই শ্লোক মহাপ্রভু পড়ে বার বার ।
স্বরূপ বিনা অর্থ কেহ না জানে ইহার ॥ ১২২ ॥

ei śloka mahāprabhu paḍe bāra bāra
svarūpa vinā artha keha nā jāne ihāra

SYNONYMS

ei śloka—this verse; *mahāprabhu*—Śrī Caitanya Mahāprabhu; *paḍe*—recites; *bāra bāra*—again and again; *svarūpa vinā*—except for Svarūpa Dāmodara; *artha*—meaning; *keha*—anyone; *nā jāne*—does not know; *ihāra*—of this.

TRANSLATION

This verse was recited by Śrī Caitanya Mahāprabhu again and again. But for Svarūpa Dāmodara, no one could understand its meaning.

TEXT 123

এই শ্লোকার্থ পূর্বে করিয়াছি ব্যাখ্যান।
শ্লোকের ভাবার্থ করি সংক্ষেপে আখ্যান ॥ ১২৩ ॥

ei ślokārtha pūrve kariyāchi vyākhyāna
ślokera bhāvārtha kari saṅkṣepe ākhyāna

SYNONYMS

ei śloka-artha—the meaning of this verse; *pūrve*—previously; *kariyāchi*—I have done; *vyākhyāna*—explanation; *ślokera*—of the same verse; *bhāva-artha*—purport; *kari*—I do; *saṅkṣepe*—in brief; *ākhyāna*—description.

TRANSLATION

I have already explained this verse. Now I shall simply describe it in brief.

PURPORT

In this connection, see *Madhya-līlā,* Chapter One, verses 53, 77-80 and 82-84.

TEXT 124

পূর্বে যৈছে কুরুক্ষেত্রে সব গোপীগণ।
কৃষ্ণের দর্শন পাঞা আনন্দিত মন ॥ ১২৪ ॥

pūrve yaiche kurukṣetre saba gopī-gaṇa
kṛṣṇera darśana pāñā ānandita mana

SYNONYMS

pūrve yaiche—as previously; *kuru-kṣetre*—in the holy place known as Kurukṣetra; *saba gopī-gaṇa*—all the *gopīs* of Vṛndāvana; *kṛṣṇera*—of Lord Kṛṣṇa; *darśana*—interview; *pāñā*—getting; *ānandita mana*—very much pleased within the mind.

TRANSLATION

Formerly, all the gopīs of Vṛndāvana were very pleased when they met with Kṛṣṇa in the holy place Kurukṣetra.

TEXT 125

জগন্নাথ দেখি' প্রভুর সে ভাব উঠিল ।
সেই ভাবাবিষ্ট হঞা ধুয়া গাওয়াইল ॥ ১২৫ ॥

jagannātha dekhi' prabhura se bhāva uṭhila
sei bhāvāviṣṭa hañā dhuyā gāoyāila

SYNONYMS

jagannātha dekhi'—by seeing Lord Jagannātha; *prabhura*—of Śrī Caitanya Mahāprabhu; *se bhāva*—that ecstasy; *uṭhila*—awakened; *sei*—that; *bhāva-āviṣṭa*—absorbed in that ecstasy; *hañā*—becoming; *dhuyā*—refrain; *gāoyāila*—caused to sing.

TRANSLATION

Similarly, after seeing Lord Jagannātha, Śrī Caitanya Mahāprabhu awoke with the ecstasy of the gopīs. Being absorbed in this ecstasy, He asked Svarūpa Dāmodara to sing the refrain.

TEXT 126

অবশেষে রাধা কৃষ্ণে করে নিবেদন ।
সেই তুমি, সেই আমি, সেই নব সঙ্গম ॥ ১২৬ ॥

aveśeṣe rādhā kṛṣṇe kare nivedana
sei tumi, sei āmi, sei nava saṅgama

SYNONYMS

avaśeṣe—at last; *rādhā*—Śrīmatī Rādhārāṇī; *kṛṣṇe*—unto Lord Kṛṣṇa; *kare*—does; *nivedana*—submission; *sei tumi*—You are the same Kṛṣṇa; *sei āmi*—I am the same Rādhārāṇī; *sei nava saṅgama*—We are meeting in the same new spirit as in the beginning.

TRANSLATION

Śrī Caitanya Mahāprabhu spoke thus to Lord Jagannātha: "You are the same Kṛṣṇa, and I am the same Rādhārāṇī. We are meeting again in the same way that We met in the beginning of Our lives.

TEXT 127

তথাপি আমার মন হরে বৃন্দাবন ।
বৃন্দাবনে উদয় করাও আপন-চরণ ॥ ১২৭ ॥

tathāpi āmāra mana hare vṛndāvana
vṛndāvane udaya karāo āpana-caraṇa

SYNONYMS

tathāpi—yet; *āmāra*—my; *mana*—mind; *hare*—attracts; *vṛndāvana*—Śrī Vṛndāvana; *vṛndāvane*—at Vṛndāvana; *udaya karāo*—please cause to reappear; *āpana-caraṇa*—the brilliance of Your lotus feet.

TRANSLATION

"Although We are both the same, My mind is still attracted to Vṛndāvana-dhāma. I wish that You will please again appear with Your lotus feet in Vṛndāvana.

TEXT 128

ইহাঁ লোকারণ্য, হাতী, ঘোড়া, রথধ্বনি ।
তাহাঁ পুষ্পারণ্য, ভৃঙ্গ-পিক-নাদ শুনি ॥ ১২৮ ॥

ihāṅ lokāraṇya, hātī, ghoḍā, ratha-dhvani
tāhāṅ puṣpāraṇya, bhṛṅga-pika-nāda śuni

SYNONYMS

ihāṅ—at this place, Kurukṣetra; *loka-araṇya*—too great a crowd of people; *hātī*—elephants; *ghoḍā*—horses; *ratha-dhvani*—the rattling sound of chariots; *tāhāṅ*—there, in Vṛndāvana; *puṣpa-araṇya*—the garden of flowers; *bhṛṅga*—of bumblebees; *pika*—of the birds; *nāda*—sound; *śuni*—I hear.

TRANSLATION

"Kurukṣetra is crowded with people, their elephants and horses, and the rattling of chariots. In Vṛndāvana, however, there are flower gardens, and the humming of the bees and chirping of the birds can be heard.

TEXT 129

ইহাঁ রাজ-বেশ, সঙ্গে সব ক্ষত্রিয়গণ ।
তাহাঁ গোপবেশ, সঙ্গে মুরলী-বাদন ॥ ১২৯ ॥

ihāṅ rāja-veśa, saṅge saba kṣatriya-gaṇa
tāhāṅ gopa-veśa, saṅge muralī-vādana

SYNONYMS

ihāṅ—here, at Kurukṣetra; *rāja-veśa*—dressed like a royal prince; *saṅge*—with You; *saba*—all; *kṣatriya-gaṇa*—great warriors; *tāhāṅ*—there, in Vṛndāvana; *gopa-veśa*—dressed like a cowherd boy; *saṅge*—with You; *muralī-vādana*—the blowing of Your transcendental flute.

TRANSLATION

"Here at Kurukṣetra You are dressed like a royal prince, accompanied by great warriors, but in Vṛndāvana You appeared just like an ordinary cowherd boy, accompanied only by Your beautiful flute.

TEXT 130

ব্রজে তোমার সঙ্গে যেই সুখ-আস্বাদন ।
সেই সুখসমুদ্রের ইহাঁ নাহি এক কণ ॥ ১৩০ ॥

vraje tomāra saṅge yei sukha-āsvādana
sei sukha-samudrera ihāṅ nāhi eka kaṇa

SYNONYMS

vraje—at Vṛndāvana; *tomāra*—of You; *saṅge*—in the company; *yei*—what; *sukha-āsvādana*—taste of transcendental bliss; *sei*—that; *sukha-sumudrera*—of the ocean of transcendental bliss; *ihāṅ*—here, at Kurukṣetra; *nāhi*—there is not; *eka*—one; *kaṇa*—drop.

TRANSLATION

"Here there is not even a drop of the ocean of transcendental happiness that I enjoyed with You in Vṛndāvana.

TEXT 131

আমা লঞা পুনঃ লীলা করহ বৃন্দাবনে ।
তবে আমার মনোবাঞ্ছা হয় ত' পূরণে ॥ ১৩১ ॥

āmā lañā punaḥ līlā karaha vṛndāvane
tabe āmāra mano-vāñchā haya ta' pūraṇe

SYNONYMS

āmā lañā—taking Me; *punaḥ*—again; *līlā*—pastimes; *karaha*—perform; *vṛndāvane*—at Vṛndāvana; *tabe*—then; *āmāra manaḥ-vāñchā*—the desire of My mind; *haya*—becomes; *ta'*—indeed; *pūraṇe*—in fulfillment.

TRANSLATION

"I therefore request You to come to Vṛndāvana and enjoy pastimes with Me. If You do so, My ambition will be fulfilled."

TEXT 132

ভাগবতে আছে যৈছে রাধিকা-বচন ।
পূর্বে তাহা সূত্রমধ্যে করিয়াছি বর্ণন ॥ ১৩২ ॥

bhāgavate āche yaiche rādhikā-vacana
pūrve tāhā sūtra-madhye kariyāchi varṇana

SYNONYMS

bhāgavate—in *Śrīmad-Bhāgavatam; āche*—there is; *yaiche*—as; *rādhikā-vacana*—the statement of Śrīmatī Rādhikā; *pūrve*—previously; *tāhā*—that; *sūtra-madhye*—in the synopsis; *kariyāchi varṇana*—I have described.

TRANSLATION

I have already described in brief Śrīmatī Rādhārāṇī's statement from Śrīmad-Bhāgavatam.

TEXT 133

সেই ভাবাবেশে প্রভু পড়ে আর শ্লোক ।
সেই সব শ্লোকের অর্থ নাহি বুঝে লোক ॥ ১৩৩ ॥

sei bhāvāveśe prabhu paḍe āra śloka
sei saba ślokera artha nāhi bujhe loka

SYNONYMS

sei—that; *bhāva-āveśe*—in ecstasy; *prabhu*—Śrī Caitanya Mahāprabhu; *paḍe*—recites; *āra*—another; *śloka*—verse; *sei*—those; *saba ślokera*—of all verses; *artha*—meaning; *nāhi*—do not; *bujhe*—understand; *loka*—people in general.

TRANSLATION

In that ecstatic mood, Śrī Caitanya Mahāprabhu recited many other verses, but people in general cannot understand their meaning.

TEXT 134

স্বরূপ-গোসাঞি জানে, না কহে অর্থ তার।
শ্রীরূপ-গোসাঞি কৈল সে অর্থ প্রচার ॥ ১৩৪ ॥

svarūpa-gosāñi jāne, nā kahe artha tāra
śrī-rūpa-gosāñi kaila se artha pracāra

SYNONYMS

svarūpa-gosāñi—Svarūpa Dāmodara Gosvāmī; *jāne*—knows; *nā*—does not; *kahe*—say; *artha*—the meaning; *tāra*—of those verses; *śrī-rūpa-gosāñi*—Śrī Rūpa Gosvāmī; *kaila*—did; *se*—that; *artha*—of meaning; *pracāra*—broadcasting.

TRANSLATION

The meaning of those verses was known to Svarūpa Dāmodara Gosvāmī, but he did not reveal it. However, Śrī Rūpa Gosvāmī has broadcast the meaning.

TEXT 135

স্বরূপ সঙ্গে যার অর্থ করে আস্বাদন।
নৃত্যমধ্যে সেই শ্লোক করেন পঠন ॥ ১৩৫ ॥

svarūpa saṅge yāra artha kare āsvādana
nṛtya-madhye sei śloka karena paṭhana

SYNONYMS

svarūpa saṅge—in the association of Svarūpa Dāmodara Gosvāmī; *yāra*—of which; *artha*—meaning; *kare*—does; *āsvādana*—taste; *nṛtya-madhye*—in the midst of dancing; *sei śloka*—that verse; *karena paṭhana*—recites.

TRANSLATION

While dancing, Śrī Caitanya Mahāprabhu again began to recite that verse, which He tasted in the association of Svarūpa Dāmodara Gosvāmī.

TEXT 136

আহুশ্চ তে নলিন-নাভ পদারবিন্দং
যোগেশ্বরৈর্হৃদি বিচিন্ত্যমগাধবোধৈঃ ।
সংসারকূপপতিতোত্তরণাবলম্বং
গেহং জুষামপি মনস্যুদিয়াৎ সদা নঃ ॥ ১৩৬ ॥

āhuś ca te nalina-nābha padāravindaṁ
yogeśvarair hṛdi vicintyam agādha-bodhaiḥ
saṁsāra-kūpa-patitottaraṇāvalambaṁ
gehaṁ juṣām api manasy udiyāt sadā naḥ

SYNONYMS

āhuḥ—the *gopīs* said; *ca*—and; *te*—Your; *nalina-nābha*—O Lord, whose navel is just like a lotus flower; *pada-aravindam*—lotus feet; *yoga-īśvaraiḥ*—by great mystic *yogīs; hṛdi*—within the heart; *vicintyam*—to be meditated upon; *agādha-bodhaiḥ*—who are highly learned philosophers; *saṁsāra-kūpa*—in the dark well of material existence; *patita*—of those fallen; *uttaraṇa*—for deliverance; *avalambam*—the only shelter; *geham*—in family affairs; *juṣām*—of those engaged; *api*—although; *manasi*—in the minds; *udiyāt*—let be awakened; *sadā*—always; *naḥ*—our.

TRANSLATION

"The gopīs spoke thus: 'Dear Lord, whose navel is just like a lotus flower, Your lotus feet are the only shelter for those who have fallen into the deep well of material existence. Your feet are worshiped and meditated upon by great mystic yogīs and highly learned philosophers. We wish that these lotus feet may also be awakened within our hearts, although we are only ordinary persons engaged in household affairs.' "

PURPORT

This is a quotation from *Śrīmad-Bhāgavatam* (10.82.49). The *gopīs* were never interested in *karma-yoga, jñāna-yoga,* or *dhyāna-yoga.* They were simply interested in *bhakti-yoga.* Unless they were forced, they never liked to meditate on the lotus feet of the Lord. Rather, they preferred to take the lotus feet of the Lord and place them on their breasts. Sometimes they regretted that their breasts were so hard, fearing that Kṛṣṇa might not be very pleased to keep His soft lotus feet there. When those lotus feet were pricked by the grains of sand in the Vṛndāvana pasturing ground, the *gopīs* were pained and began to cry. The *gopīs* wanted to keep Kṛṣṇa at home always, and in this way their minds were absorbed in Kṛṣṇa consciousness. Such pure Kṛṣṇa consciousness can arise only in Vṛndāvana. Thus Śrī Caitanya Mahāprabhu began to explain His own mind, which was saturated in the ecstasy of the *gopīs*.

TEXT 137

অন্যের হৃদয়—মন, মোর মন—বৃন্দাবন,
'মনে' 'বনে' এক করি' জানি ।
তাহাঁ তোমার পদদ্বয়, করাহ যদি উদয়,
তবে তোমার পূর্ণ কৃপা মানি ॥ ১৩৭ ॥

anyera hṛdaya——mana, mora mana——vṛndāvana,
'mane' 'vane' eka kari' jāni
tāhāṅ tomāra pada-dvaya, karāha yadi udaya,
tabe tomāra pūrṇa kṛpā māni

SYNONYMS

anyera—of others; *hṛdaya*—consciousness; *mana*—mind; *mora mana*—My mind; *vṛndāvana*—Vṛndāvana consciousness; *mane*—with the mind; *vane*—with Vṛndāvana; *eka kari'*—as one and the same; *jāni*—I know; *tāhāṅ*—there, at Vṛndāvana; *tomāra*—Your; *pada-dvaya*—two lotus feet; *karāha*—You do; *yadi*—if; *udaya*—appearance; *tabe*—then; *tomāra*—Your; *pūrṇa*—complete; *kṛpā*—mercy; *māni*—I accept.

TRANSLATION

Speaking in the mood of Śrīmatī Rādhārāṇī, Caitanya Mahāprabhu said, " 'For most people, the mind and heart are one, but because My mind is never separated from Vṛndāvana, I consider My mind and Vṛndāvana to be one. My mind is already Vṛndāvana, and since You like Vṛndāvana, will You please place Your lotus feet there? I would deem that Your full mercy.

PURPORT

Only when the mind is free from designations can one desire the association of the Supreme Personality of Godhead. The mind must have some occupation. If a person is to be free of material things, his mind cannot be vacant; there must be subject matters for thinking, feeling and willing. Unless one's mind is filled with thoughts of Kṛṣṇa, feelings for Kṛṣṇa and a desire to serve Kṛṣṇa, the mind will be filled with material activities. Those who have given up all material activities and have ceased thinking of them should always retain the ambition to think of Kṛṣṇa. Without Kṛṣṇa, one cannot live, just as a person cannot live without some enjoyment for his mind.

TEXT 138

প্রাণনাথ, শুন মোর সত্য নিবেদন ।
ব্রজ—আমার সদন, তাহাঁ তোমার সঙ্গম,
না পাইলে না রহে জীবন ॥ ১৩৮ ॥ ধ্রু ॥

prāṇa-nātha, śuna mora satya nivedana
vraja——āmāra sadana, tāhāṅ tomāra saṅgama,
nā pāile nā rahe jīvana

SYNONYMS

prāṇa-nātha—O My Lord, master of My life; *śuna*—please hear; *mora*—My; *satya*—true; *nivedana*—submission; *vraja*—Vṛndāvana; *āmāra*—My; *sadana*—place; *tāhāṅ*—there; *tomāra*—Your; *saṅgama*—association; *nā pāile*—if I do not get; *nā*—not; *rahe*—does remain; *jīvana*—life.

TRANSLATION

" 'My dear Lord, kindly hear My true submission. My home is Vṛndāvana, and I wish Your association there. But if I do not get it, then it will be very difficult for Me to keep My life.

TEXT 139

পূর্বে উদ্ধব-দ্বারে, এবে সাক্ষাৎ আমারে,
যোগ-জ্ঞানে কহিলা উপায় ।
তুমি—বিদগ্ধ, কৃপাময়, জানহ আমার হৃদয়,
মোরে ঐছে কহিতে না যুয়ায় ॥ ১৩৯ ॥

pūrve uddhava-dvāre, ebe sākṣāt āmāre,
yoga-jñāne kahilā upāya

tumi——vidagdha, kṛpāmaya, jānaha āmāra hṛdaya,
more aiche kahite nā yuyāya

SYNONYMS

pūrve—previously; *uddhava-dvāre*—through Uddhava; *ebe*—now; *sākṣāt*—directly; *āmāre*—unto Me; *yoga*—mystic yogic meditation; *jñāne*—philosophical speculation; *kahilā*—You have said; *upāya*—the means; *tumi*—You; *vidagdha*—very humorous; *kṛpā-maya*—merciful; *jānaha*—You know; *āmāra*—My; *hṛdaya*—mind; *more*—unto Me; *aiche*—in that way; *kahite*—to speak; *nā yuyāya*—is not at all befitting.

TRANSLATION

" 'My dear Kṛṣṇa, formerly, when You were staying in Mathurā, You sent Uddhava to teach Me speculative knowledge and mystic yoga. Now You Yourself are speaking the same thing, but My mind doesn't accept it. There is no place in My mind for jñāna-yoga or dhyāna-yoga. Although You know Me very well, You are still instructing Me in jñāna-yoga and dhyāna-yoga. It is not right for You to do so.' "

PURPORT

The process of mystic *yoga,* the speculative method for searching out the Supreme Absolute Truth, does not appeal to one who is always absorbed in thoughts of Kṛṣṇa. A devotee is not at all interested in speculative activities. Instead of cultivating speculative knowledge or practicing mystic *yoga,* a devotee should worship the Deity in the temple and continuously engage in the Lord's service. Temple Deity worship is realized by the devotees to be the same as direct service to the Lord. The Deity is known as *arcā-vigraha* or *arcā-avatāra,* an incarnation of the Supreme Lord in the form of a material manifestation (brass, stone or wood). Ultimately there is no difference between Kṛṣṇa manifest in matter or Kṛṣṇa manifest in spirit because both are His energies. For Kṛṣṇa, there is no distinction between matter and spirit. His manifestation in material form, therefore, is as good as His original form, *sac-cid-ānanda-vigraha.* A devotee constantly engaged in Deity worship according to the rules and regulations laid down in the *śāstras* and given by the spiritual master realizes gradually that he is in direct contact with the Supreme Personality of Godhead. Thus he loses all interest in so-called meditation, *yoga* practice and mental speculation.

TEXT 140

চিত্ত কাঢ়ি' তোমা হৈতে, বিষয়ে চাহি লাগাইতে,
যত্ন করি, নারি কাঢ়িবারে।

তারে ধ্যান শিক্ষা করাহ, লোক হাসাঞা মার,
স্থানাস্থান না কর বিচারে ॥ ১৪০ ॥

citta kāḍhi' tomā haite, viṣaye cāhi lāgāite,
yatna kari, nāri kāḍhibāre
tāre dhyāna śikṣā karāha, loka hāsāñā māra,
sthānāsthāna nā kara vicāre

SYNONYMS

citta kāḍhi'—withdrawing the consciousness; *tomā haite*—from You; *viṣaye*—in mundane subject matters; *cāhi*—I want; *lāgāite*—to engage; *yatna kari*—I endeavor; *nāri kāḍhibāre*—I cannot withdraw; *tāre*—to such a servant; *dhyāna*—of meditation; *śikṣā*—instruction; *karāha*—You give; *loka*—people in general; *hāsāñā*—laugh; *māra*—You kill; *sthāna-asthāna*—proper or improper place; *nā kara*—You do not make; *vicāre*—consideration.

TRANSLATION

Caitanya Mahāprabhu continued: " 'I would like to withdraw My consciousness from You and engage it in material activities, but even though I try, I cannot do so. I am naturally inclined to You only. Your instructions for Me to meditate on You are therefore simply ludicrous. In this way, You are killing Me. It is not very good for You to think of Me as a candidate for Your instructions.

PURPORT

Śrīla Rūpa Gosvāmī says in *Bhakti-rasāmṛta-sindhu* (1.1.11):

anyābhilāṣitā-śūnyaṁ
jñāna-karmādy-anāvṛtam
ānakūlyena kṛṣṇānu-
śīlanaṁ bhaktir uttamā

For a pure devotee, there is no scope for indulgence in mystic *yoga* practice or the cultivation of speculative philosophy. It is indeed impossible for a pure devotee to engage his mind in such unwanted activities. Even if a pure devotee wanted to, his mind would not allow him to do so. That is a characteristic of a pure devotee—he is transcendental to all fruitive activity, speculative philosophy and mystic *yoga* meditation. The *gopīs* therefore expressed themselves as follows.

TEXT 141

নহে গোপী যোগেশ্বর, পদকমল তোমার,
ধ্যান করি' পাইবে সন্তোষ ।
তোমার বাক্য-পরিপাটী, তার মধ্যে কুটিনাটী,
শুনি' গোপীর আরো বাঢ়ে রোষ ॥ ১৪১ ॥

nahe gopī yogeśvara, pada-kamala tomāra,
dhyāna kari' pāibe santoṣa
tomāra vākya-paripāṭī, tāra madhye kuṭināṭī,
śuni' gopīra āro bāḍhe roṣa

SYNONYMS

nahe—not; *gopī*—*gopīs;* *yogeśvara*—masters of mystic *yoga* practice; *pada-kamala tomāra*—Your lotus feet; *dhyāna kari'*—by meditation; *pāibe santoṣa*—we get satisfaction; *tomāra*—Your; *vākya*—words; *paripāṭī*—very kindly composed; *tāra madhye*—within that; *kuṭināṭī*—duplicity; *śuni'*—hearing; *gopīra*—of the *gopīs;* *āro*—more and more; *bāḍhe*—increases; *roṣa*—anger.

TRANSLATION

" 'The gopīs are not like the mystic yogīs. They will never be satisfied simply by meditating on Your lotus feet and imitating the so-called yogīs. Teaching the gopīs about meditation is another kind of duplicity. When they are instructed to undergo mystic yoga practice, they are not at all satisfied. On the contrary, they become more angry with You.' "

PURPORT

Śrīla Prabodhānanda Sarasvatī has stated (*Caitanya-candrāmṛta* 5):

kaivalyaṁ narakāyate tridaśa-pūr ākāśa-puṣpāyate
durdāntendriya-kāla-sarpa-paṭalī protkhāta-daṁṣṭrāyate
viśvaṁ pūrṇa-sukhāyate vidhi-mahendrādiś ca kīṭāyate
yat kāruṇya-katākṣa-vaibhava-vatāṁ taṁ gauram eva stumaḥ

For a pure devotee who has realized Kṛṣṇa consciousness through Śrī Caitanya Mahāprabhu, the monistic philosophy by which one becomes one with the Supreme appears hellish. The mystic *yoga* practice by which the mind is controlled and the senses subjugated also appears ludicrous to a pure devotee. The devotee's mind and senses are already engaged in the transcendental service of the Lord. In this way the poisonous effects of sense activities are removed. If one's mind is always engaged in the service of the Lord, there is no possibility that one will think, feel or act materially. Similarly, the fruitive workers' attempt to attain heavenly planets is nothing more than phantasmagoria for the devotee. After all, the heavenly planets are material, and in due course of time they will all be dissolved. Devotees do not care for such temporary things. They engage in transcendental devotional activities because they desire elevation to the spiritual world, where they can live eternally and peacefully and with full knowledge of Kṛṣṇa. In Vṛndāvana, the *gopīs,* cowherd boys and even the calves, cows, trees and water are fully conscious of Kṛṣṇa. They are never satisfied with anything but Kṛṣṇa.

TEXT 142

দেহ-স্মৃতি নাহি যার, সংসারকূপ কাহাঁ তার,
তাহা হৈতে না চাহে উদ্ধার ।
বিরহ-সমুদ্র-জলে, কাম-তিমিঙ্গিলে গিলে,
গোপীগণে নেহ' তার পার ॥ ১৪২ ॥

deha-smṛti nāhi yāra, saṁsāra-kūpa kāhāṅ tāra,
tāhā haite nā cāhe uddhāra
viraha-samudra-jale, kāma-timiṅgile gile,
gopī-gaṇe neha' tāra pāra

SYNONYMS

deha-smṛti—bodily concept of life; *nāhi*—not; *yāra*—one whose; *saṁsāra-kūpa*—blind well of material life; *kāhāṅ*—where is; *tāra*—his; *tāhā haite*—from that; *nā*—does not; *cāhe*—want; *uddhāra*—liberation; *viraha-samudra-jale*—in the water of the ocean of separation; *kāma-timiṅgile*—the transcendental Cupid in the form of *timiṅgila* fish; *gile*—swallow; *gopī-gaṇe*—the *gopīs; neha'*—please take out; *tāra pāra*—beyond that.

TRANSLATION

Śrī Caitanya Mahāprabhu continued: " 'The gopīs are fallen in the great ocean of separation, and they are being devoured by the timiṅgila fish, which represent their ambition to serve You. The gopīs are to be delivered from the mouths of these timiṅgila fish, for they are pure devotees. Since they have no material conception of life, why should they aspire for liberation? The gopīs do not want that liberation desired by yogīs and jñānīs, for they are already liberated from the ocean of material existence.

PURPORT

The bodily conception is created by the desire for material enjoyment. This is called *vipada-smṛti,* which is the opposite of real life. The living entity is eternally the servant of Kṛṣṇa, but when he desires to enjoy the material world, he cannot progress in spiritual life. One can never be happy by advancing materially. This is also stated in *Śrīmad-Bhāgavatam* (7.5.30): *adānta-gobhir viśatāṁ tamisraṁ punaḥ punaś carvita-carvaṇānām.* Through the uncontrolled senses, one may advance one's hellish condition. He may continue to chew the chewed; that is, repeatedly accept birth and death. The conditioned souls use the duration of life between birth and death only to engage in the same hackneyed activities—eating, sleeping, mating and defending. In the lower animal species, we find the same activities. Since these activities are repeated, engaging in them is like chewing that which has already been chewed. If one can give up his ambition to engage in hackneyed material life and take to Kṛṣṇa consciousness instead, he will be liberated from the stringent laws of material nature. One does not need to make a separate attempt to become liberated. If one simply engages in the service of the Lord, he will be liberated automatically. As Śrīla Bilvamaṅgala Ṭhākura therefore says, *muktiḥ svayaṁ mukulitāñjali sevate 'smān:* "Liberation stands before me with folded hands, begging to serve me."

TEXT 143

বৃন্দাবন, গোবর্ধন, যমুনা-পুলিন, বন,
সেই কুঞ্জে রাসাদিক লীলা ।
সেই ব্রজের ব্রজজন, মাতা, পিতা, বন্ধুগণ,
বড় চিত্র, কেমনে পাসরিলা ॥ ১৪৩ ॥

vṛndāvana, govardhana, yamunā-pulina, vana,
sei kuñje rāsādika līlā
sei vrajera vraja-jana, mātā, pitā, bandhu-gaṇa,
baḍa citra, kemane pāsarilā

SYNONYMS

vṛndāvana—the transcendental land known as Vṛndāvana; *govardhana*—Govardhana Hill; *yamunā-pulina*—the bank of the Yamunā; *vana*—all the forests where the pastimes of the Lord took place; *sei kuñje*—in the bushes in that forest; *rāsa-ādika līlā*—the pastimes of the *rāsa* dance; *sei*—that; *vrajera*—of Vṛndāvana; *vraja-jana*—inhabitants; *mātā*—mother; *pitā*—father; *bandhu-gaṇa*—friends; *baḍa citra*—most wonderful; *kemane pāsarilā*—how have You forgotten.

TRANSLATION

" 'It is amazing that You have forgotten the land of Vṛndāvana. And how is it that You have forgotten Your father, mother and friends? How have You forgotten Govardhana Hill, the bank of the Yamunā, and the forest where You enjoyed the rāsa-līlā dance?

TEXT 144

বিদগ্ধ, মৃদু, সদ্‌গুণ, সুশীল, স্নিগ্ধ, করুণ,
তুমি, তোমার নাহি দোষাভাস।
তবে যে তোমার মন, নাহি স্মরে ব্রজজন,
সে—আমার দুর্দৈব-বিলাস॥ ১৪৪ ॥

vidagdha, mṛdu, sad-guṇa, suśīla, snigdha, karuṇa,
tumi, tomāra nāhi doṣābhāsa
tabe ye tomāra mana, nāhi smare vraja-jana,
se——āmāra durdaiva-vilāsa

SYNONYMS

vidagdha—most refined; *mṛdu*—gentle; *sat-guṇa*—endowed with all good qualities; *su-śīla*—well-behaved; *snigdha*—softhearted; *karuṇa*—merciful; *tumi*—You; *tomāra*—Your; *nāhi*—there is not; *doṣa-ābhāsa*—even a tinge of fault; *tabe*—still; *ye*—indeed; *tomāra*—Your; *mana*—mind; *nāhi*—does not; *smare*—remember; *vraja-jana*—the inhabitants of Vṛndāvana; *se*—that; *āmāra*—My; *durdaiva-vilāsa*—suffering of past misdeeds.

TRANSLATION

" 'Kṛṣṇa, You are certainly a refined gentleman with all good qualities. You are well-behaved, softhearted and merciful. I know that there is not even a tinge of fault to be found in You, yet Your mind does not even remember the inhabitants of Vṛndāvana. This is only My misfortune, and nothing else.

TEXT 145

না গণি আপন-দুঃখ, দেখি' ব্রজেশ্বরী-মুখ,
ব্রজজনের হৃদয় বিদরে।
কিবা মার' ব্রজবাসী, কিবা জীয়াও ব্রজে আসি',
কেন জীয়াও দুঃখ সহাইবারে? ১৪৫ ॥

nā gaṇi āpana-duḥkha, dekhi' vrajeśvarī-mukha,
vraja-janera hṛdaya vidare
kibā māra' vraja-vāsī, kibā jīyāo vraje āsi',
kena jīyāo duḥkha sahāibāre?

SYNONYMS

nā gaṇi—I do not care; *āpana-duḥkha*—My personal unhappiness; *dekhi'*—seeing; *vrajeśvarī-mukha*—the face of mother Yaśodā; *vraja-janera*—of all the inhabitants of Vṛndāvana; *hṛdaya vidare*—the hearts break; *kibā*—whether; *māra' vraja-vāsī*—You want to kill the inhabitants of Vṛndāvana; *kibā*—or; *jīyāo*—You want to keep their lives; *vraje āsi'*—coming in Vṛndāvana; *kena*—why; *jīyāo*—You let them live; *duḥkha sahāibāre*—just to cause to suffer unhappiness.

TRANSLATION

" 'I do not care for My personal unhappiness, but when I see the morose face of Your mother Yaśodā and the hearts of all the inhabitants of Vṛndāvana breaking because of You, I wonder whether You want to kill them all. Is it that You want to enliven them by coming there? Why is it You are simply keeping them alive in a state of suffering?

TEXT 146

তোমার যে অন্য বেশ, অন্য সঙ্গ, অন্য দেশ,
ব্রজজনে কভু নাহি ভায়।
ব্রজভূমি ছাড়িতে নারে, তোমা না দেখিলে মরে,
ব্রজজনের কি হবে উপায় ॥ ১৪৬ ॥

tomāra ye anya veśa, anya saṅga, anya deśa,
vraja-jane kabhu nāhi bhāya
vraja-bhūmi chāḍite nāre, tomā nā dekhile mare,
vraja-janera ki habe upāya

SYNONYMS

tomāra—Your; *ye*—that; *anya veśa*—different dress; *anya saṅga*—other associates; *anya deśa*—other countries; *vraja-jane*—to the inhabitants of Vṛndāvana; *kabhu*—at any time; *nāhi*—does not; *bhāya*—appeal; *vraja-bhūmi*—the land of Vṛndāvana; *chāḍite nāre*—they do not like to leave; *tomā*—You; *nā*—not; *dekhile*—seeing; *mare*—they die; *vraja-janera*—of the inhabitants of Vṛndāvana; *ki*—what; *habe*—will be; *upāya*—means.

TRANSLATION

" 'The inhabitants of Vṛndāvana do not want You dressed like a prince, nor do they want You to associate with great warriors in a different country. They cannot leave the land of Vṛndāvana, and without Your presence, they are all dying. What is their condition to be?

TEXT 147

তুমি—ব্রজের জীবন, ব্রজরাজের প্রাণধন,
তুমি ব্রজের সকল সম্পদ্ ।
কৃপার্দ্র তোমার মন, আসি' জীয়াও ব্রজজন,
ব্রজে উদয় করাও নিজ-পদ ॥ ১৪৭ ॥

tumi——vrajera jīvana, vraja-rājera prāṇa-dhana,
tumi vrajera sakala sampad
kṛpārdra tomāra mana, āsi' jīyāo vraja-jana,
vraje udaya karāo nija-pada

SYNONYMS

tumi—You; *vrajera jīvana*—the life and soul of Vṛndāvana; *vraja-rājera*—and of the King of Vraja, Nanda Mahārāja; *prāṇa-dhana*—the only life; *tumi*—You; *vrajera*—of Vṛndāvana; *sakala sampad*—all opulence; *kṛpā-ardra*—melting with kindness; *tomāra mana*—Your mind; *āsi'*—coming; *jīyāo*—give life; *vraja-jana*—to all the inhabitants of Vṛndāvana; *vraje*—in Vṛndāvana; *udaya karāo*—cause to appear; *nija-pada*—Your lotus feet.

TRANSLATION

" 'My dear Kṛṣṇa, You are the life and soul of Vṛndāvana-dhāma. You are especially the life of Nanda Mahārāja. You are the only opulence in the land of Vṛndāvana, and You are very merciful. Please come and let them all live. Kindly keep Your lotus feet again in Vṛndāvana.'

PURPORT

Śrīmatī Rādhārāṇī did not express Her personal unhappiness at being separated from Kṛṣṇa. She wanted to evoke Kṛṣṇa's feelings for the condition of all others in Vṛndāvana-dhāma—mother Yaśodā, Mahārāja Nanda, the cowherd boys, the *gopīs,* the birds and bees on the banks of the Yamunā, the water of the Yamunā, the trees, forests and all other paraphernalia associated with Kṛṣṇa before He left Vṛndāvana for Mathurā. These feelings of Śrīmatī Rādhārāṇī were manifested by Śrī Caitanya Mahāprabhu, and therefore He invited Lord Jagannātha, Kṛṣṇa, to return to Vṛndāvana. That is the purport of the Ratha-yātrā car's going from Jagannātha Purī to the Guṇḍicā temple.

TEXT 148

শুনিয়া রাধিকা-বাণী, ব্রজপ্রেম মনে আনি,
ভাবে ব্যাকুলিত দেহ-মন ।
ব্রজলোকের প্রেম শুনি', আপনাকে 'ঋণী' মানি',
করে কৃষ্ণ তাঁরে আশ্বাসন ॥ ১৪৮ ॥

śuniyā rādhikā-vāṇī, vraja-prema mane āni,
bhāve vyākulita deha-mana
vraja-lokera prema śuni', āpanāke 'ṛṇī' māni',
kare kṛṣṇa tāṅre āśvāsana

SYNONYMS

śuniyā—after hearing; *rādhikā-vāṇī*—the statement of Śrīmatī Rādhārāṇī; *vraja-prema*—the love of Vraja; *mane āni*—remembering; *bhāve*—in that ecstasy; *vyākulita*—very much perturbed; *deha-mana*—the body and mind; *vraja-lokera*—of the inhabitants of Vṛndāvana; *prema śuni'*—after hearing of the loving affairs; *āpanāke*—Himself; *ṛṇī māni'*—considering very indebted; *kare*—does; *kṛṣṇa*—Lord Kṛṣṇa; *tāṅre*—unto Her; *āśvāsana*—pacification.

TRANSLATION

"After hearing Śrīmatī Rādhārāṇī's statements, Lord Kṛṣṇa's love for the inhabitants of Vṛndāvana was evoked, and His body and mind became very perturbed. After hearing of their love for Him, He immediately thought Himself to be always indebted to the residents of Vṛndāvana. Then Kṛṣṇa began to pacify Śrīmatī Rādhārāṇī as follows.

TEXT 149

প্রাণপ্রিয়ে, শুন, মোর এ-সত্য-বচন ।
তোমা-সবার স্মরণে, ঝুরোঁ মুঞি রাত্রিদিনে,
মোর দুঃখ না জানে কোন জন ॥ ১৪৯ ॥ ধ্রু ॥

prāṇa-priye, śuna, mora e-satya-vacana
tomā-sabāra smaraṇe, jhuroṅ muñi rātri-dine,
mora duḥkha nā jāne kona jana

SYNONYMS

prāṇa-priye—O My dearmost; *śuna*—please hear; *mora*—of Me; *e-satya-vacana*—this true statement; *tomā-sabāra*—of all of you; *smaraṇe*—by remembrance; *jhuroṅ*—cry; *muñi*—I; *rātri-dine*—both day and night; *mora duḥkha*—My distress; *nā jāne*—does not know; *kona jana*—anyone.

TRANSLATION

" 'My dearest Śrīmatī Rādhārāṇī, please hear Me. I am speaking the truth. I cry day and night simply upon remembering all you inhabitants of Vṛndāvana. No one knows how unhappy this makes Me.'

PURPORT

It is said: *vṛndāvanaṁ parityajya padam ekaṁ na gacchati.* In one sense, Kṛṣṇa, the original Personality of Godhead (*īśvaraḥ paramaḥ kṛṣṇaḥ sac-cid-ānanda-vigrahaḥ*), does not even take one step away from Vṛndāvana. However, in order to take care of various duties, Kṛṣṇa had to leave Vṛndāvana. He had to go to Mathurā to kill Kaṁsa, and then He was taken by His father to Dvārakā, where He was busy with state affairs and disturbances created by demons. Kṛṣṇa was away from Vṛndāvana, and He was not at all happy, as He plainly disclosed to Śrīmatī Rādhārāṇī. She is the dearmost life and soul of Śrī Kṛṣṇa, and He expressed His mind to Her as follows.

TEXT 150

ব্রজবাসী যত জন, মাতা, পিতা, সখাগণ,
সবে হয় মোর প্রাণসম ।
তাঁর মধ্যে গোপীগণ, সাক্ষাৎ মোর জীবন,
তুমি মোর জীবনের জীবন ॥ ১৫০ ॥

vraja-vāsī yata jana, mātā, pitā, sakhā-gaṇa,
sabe haya mora prāṇa-sama
tāṅra madhye gopī-gaṇa, sākṣāt mora jīvana,
tumi mora jīvanera jīvana

SYNONYMS

vraja-vāsī yata jana—all the inhabitants of Vṛndāvana-dhāma; *mātā*—mother; *pitā*—father; *sakhā-gaṇa*—boy friends; *sabe*—all; *haya*—are; *mora prāṇa-sama*—as good as My life; *tāṅra madhye*—among them; *gopī-gaṇa*—the *gopīs; sākṣāt*—directly; *mora jīvana*—My life and soul; *tumi*—You; *mora jīvanera jīvana*—the life of My life.

TRANSLATION

"Śrī Kṛṣṇa continued: 'All the inhabitants of Vṛndāvana-dhāma—My mother, father, cowherd boy friends and everything else—are like My life and soul. And among all the inhabitants of Vṛndāvana, the gopīs are My very life and soul. Among the gopīs, You, Śrīmatī Rādhārāṇī, are the chief. Therefore You are the very life of My life.

PURPORT

Śrīmatī Rādhārāṇī is the center of all Vṛndāvana's activities. In Vṛndāvana, Kṛṣṇa is the instrument of Śrīmatī Rādhārāṇī; therefore all the inhabitants of Vṛndāvana still chant "Jaya Rādhe." From Kṛṣṇa's own statement given herein, it appears that Rādhārāṇī is the Queen of Vṛndāvana and that Kṛṣṇa is simply Her decoration. Kṛṣṇa is known as Madana-mohana, the enchanter of Cupid, but Śrīmatī Rādhārāṇī is the enchanter of Kṛṣṇa. Consequently Śrīmatī Rādhārāṇī is called Madana-mohana-mohinī, the enchanter of the enchanter of Cupid.

TEXT 151

তোমা-সবার প্রেমরসে, আমাকে করিল বশে,
আমি তোমার অধীন কেবল ।
তোমা-সবা ছাড়াঞা, আমা দূর-দেশে লঞা,
রাখিয়াছে দুর্দৈব প্রবল ॥ ১৫১ ॥

tomā-sabāra prema-rase, āmāke karila vaśe,
āmi tomāra adhīna kevala
tomā-sabā chāḍāñā, āmā dūra-deśe lañā,
rākhiyāche durdaiva prabala

SYNONYMS

tomā-sabāra—of all of you; *prema-rase*—by the ecstasy and mellows of loving affairs; *āmāke*—Me; *karila*—you have made; *vaśe*—subservient; *āmi*—I; *tomāra*—of you; *adhīna*—subservient; *kevala*—only; *tomā-sabā*—from all of you; *chāḍāñā*—separating; *āmā*—Me; *dūra-deśe*—to distant countries; *lañā*—taking; *rākhiyāche*—has kept; *durdaiva*—misfortune; *prabala*—very powerful.

TRANSLATION

" 'My dear Śrīmatī Rādhārāṇī, I am always subservient to the loving affairs of all of you. I am under your control only. My separation from you and residence in distant places have occurred due to My strong misfortune.

TEXT 152

প্রিয়া প্রিয়-সঙ্গহীনা, প্রিয় প্রিয়া-সঙ্গ বিনা,
নাহি জীয়ে,—এ সত্য প্রমাণ ।
মোর দশা শোনে যবে, তাঁর এই দশা হবে,
এই ভয়ে দুঁহে রাখে প্রাণ ॥ ১৫২ ॥

priyā priya-saṅga-hīnā, priya priyā-saṅga vinā,
nāhi jīye,——e satya pramāṇa
mora daśā śone yabe, tāṅra ei daśā habe,
ei bhaye duṅhe rākhe prāṇa

SYNONYMS

priyā—a woman beloved; *priya-saṅga-hīnā*—being separated from the man beloved; *priya*—the man beloved; *priyā-saṅga vinā*—being separated from the woman beloved; *nāhi jīye*—cannot live; *e satya pramāṇa*—this is factual evidence; *mora*—My; *daśā*—situation; *śone yabe*—when one hears; *tāṅra*—his; *ei*—this; *daśā*—situation; *habe*—there will be; *ei bhaye*—out of this fear; *duṅhe*—both; *rākhe prāṇa*—keep their life.

TRANSLATION

" 'When a woman is separated from the man she loves or a man is separated from his beloved woman, neither of them can live. It is a fact that they live only for one another, for if one dies and the other hears of it, he or she will die also.

TEXT 153

সেই সতী প্রেমবতী, প্রেমবান্ সেই পতি,
বিয়োগে যে বাঞ্ছে প্রিয়-হিতে ।
না গণে আপন-দুঃখ, বাঞ্ছে প্রিয়জন-সুখ,
সেই দুই মিলে অচিরাতে ॥ ১৫৩ ॥

sei satī premavatī, premavān sei pati,
viyoge ye vāñche priya-hite
nā gaṇe āpana-duḥkha, vāñche priyajana-sukha,
sei dui mile acirāte

SYNONYMS

sei satī—that chaste wife; *prema-vatī*—full of love; *prema-vān*—loving; *sei pati*—that husband; *viyoge*—in separation; *ye*—who; *vāñche*—desire; *priya-*

hite—for the welfare of the other; *nā gaṇe*—and do not care; *āpana-duḥkha*—for personal unhappiness; *vāñche*—desire; *priya-jana-sukha*—the happiness of the dearmost beloved; *sei*—those; *dui*—two; *mile*—meet; *acirāte*—without delay.

TRANSLATION

" 'A loving, chaste wife and a loving husband who desire all welfare for each other in separation and do not care for personal happiness, desire only one another's well-being. Such a pair certainly meet again without delay.

TEXT 154

রাখিতে তোমার জীবন, সেবি আমি নারায়ণ,
তাঁর শক্ত্যে আসি নিতি-নিতি।
তোমা-সনে ক্রীড়া করি', নিতি যাই যদুপুরী,
তাহা তুমি মানহ মোর স্ফূর্তি ॥ ১৫৪ ॥

rākhite tomāra jīvana, sevi āmi nārāyaṇa,
tāṅra śaktye āsi niti-niti
tomā-sane krīḍā kari', niti yāi yadu-purī,
tāhā tumi mānaha mora sphūrti

SYNONYMS

rākhite—just to keep; *tomāra jīvana*—Your life; *sevi āmi nārāyaṇa*—I always worship Lord Nārāyaṇa; *tāṅra śaktye*—by His potency; *āsi niti-niti*—I come to You daily; *tomā-sane*—with You; *krīḍā kari'*—enjoying pastimes; *niti*—daily; *yāi yadu-purī*—I return to Dvārakā-dhāma, known as Yadu-purī; *tāhā*—that; *tumi*—You; *mānaha*—experience; *mora*—My; *sphūrti*—manifestation.

TRANSLATION

" 'You are My most dear, and I know that in My absence You cannot live for a moment. Just to keep You living, I worship Lord Nārāyaṇa. By His merciful potency, I come to Vṛndāvana every day to enjoy pastimes with You. I then return to Dvārakā-dhāma. Thus You can always feel My presence here in Vṛndāvana.

TEXT 155

মোর ভাগ্য মো-বিষয়ে, তোমার যে প্রেম হয়ে,
সেই প্রেম—পরম প্রবল।
লুকাঞা আমা আনে, সঙ্গ করায় তোমা-সনে,
প্রকটেহ আনিবে সত্বর ॥ ১৫৫ ॥

mora bhāgya mo-viṣaye, tomāra ye prema haye,
sei prema——parama prabala
lukāñā āmā āne, saṅga karāya tomā-sane,
prakaṭeha ānibe satvara

SYNONYMS

mora bhāgya—My fortune; *mo-viṣaye*—in relation with Me; *tomāra*—Your; *ye*—whatever; *prema*—love; *haye*—there is; *sei prema*—that love; *parama prabala*—very powerful; *lukāñā*—secretly; *āmā āne*—brings Me; *saṅga karāya*—obliges Me to associate; *tomā-sane*—with You; *prakaṭeha*—directly manifested; *ānibe*—will bring; *satvara*—very soon.

TRANSLATION

" 'Our love affair is more powerful because of My good fortune in receiving Nārāyaṇa's grace. This allows Me to come here unseen by others. I hope that very soon I will be visible to everyone.

PURPORT

Kṛṣṇa has two kinds of presence—*prakaṭa* and *aprakaṭa,* manifest and unmanifest. Both are identical to the sincere devotee. Even if Kṛṣṇa is not physically present, the devotee's absorption in the affairs of Kṛṣṇa makes Him present. This is confirmed in *Brahma-saṁhitā* (5.38):

premāñjana-cchurita-bhakti-vilocanena
santaḥ sadaiva hṛdayeṣu vilokayanti
yaṁ śyāmasundaram acintya-guṇa-svarūpaṁ
govindam ādi-puruṣaṁ tam ahaṁ bhajāmi

Due to his intense love, the pure devotee always sees Lord Kṛṣṇa present within his heart. All glories to Govinda, the primeval Personality of Godhead! When Kṛṣṇa is not manifest before the inhabitants of Vṛndāvana, they are always absorbed in thoughts of Him. Therefore even though Kṛṣṇa was living at that time at Dvārakā, He was simultaneously present before all the inhabitants of Vṛndāvana. This was His *aprakaṭa* presence. Devotees who are always absorbed in thoughts of Kṛṣṇa will soon see Kṛṣṇa face to face without a doubt. Devotees who are always engaged in Kṛṣṇa consciousness and are fully absorbed in thoughts of Kṛṣṇa certainly return home, back to Godhead. They then see Kṛṣṇa directly, face to face, take *prasāda* with Him and enjoy His company. This is confirmed in *Bhagavad-gītā: tyaktvā dehaṁ punar janma naiti mām eti so 'rjuna* (Bg. 4.9).

During his lifetime, a pure devotee is always speaking of Kṛṣṇa and engaging in His service, and as soon as he gives up his body, he immediately returns to Goloka Vṛndāvana, where Kṛṣṇa is personally present. He then meets Kṛṣṇa directly. This is successful human life. This is the meaning of *prakaṭeha ānibe satvara*. The pure devotee will soon see the personal manifestation of Lord Śrī Kṛṣṇa.

TEXT 156

যাদবের বিপক্ষ, যত দুষ্ট কংসপক্ষ,
তাহা আমি কৈলুঁ সব ক্ষয়।
আছে দুই-চারি জন, তাহা মারি' বৃন্দাবন,
আইলাম আমি, জানিহ নিশ্চয় ॥ ১৫৬ ॥

yādavera vipakṣa, yata duṣṭa kaṁsa-pakṣa,
tāhā āmi kailuṅ saba kṣaya
āche dui-cāri jana, tāhā māri' vṛndāvana,
āilāma āmi, jāniha niścaya

SYNONYMS

yādavera vipakṣa—all the enemies of the Yadu dynasty; *yata*—all; *duṣṭa*—mischievous; *kaṁsa-pakṣa*—the party of Kaṁsa; *tāhā*—them; *āmi*—I; *kailuṅ saba kṣaya*—have annihilated all; *āche*—there are still; *dui-cāri jana*—two or four demons; *tāhā māri'*—after killing them; *vṛndāvana*—to Vṛndāvana; *āilāma āmi*—I am coming very soon; *jāniha niścaya*—please know it very well.

TRANSLATION

" 'I have already killed all the mischievous demons who are enemies of the Yadu dynasty, and I have also killed Kaṁsa and his allies. However, there are two or four demons still living. I want to kill them, and after doing so I shall very soon return to Vṛndāvana. Please know this for certain.

PURPORT

Just as Kṛṣṇa does not take a step away from Vṛndāvana, Kṛṣṇa's devotee also does not like to leave Vṛndāvana. However, when he has to tend to Kṛṣṇa's business, he leaves Vṛndāvana. After finishing his mission, a pure devotee returns home, back to Vṛndāvana, back to Godhead. Kṛṣṇa assured Rādhārāṇī that after killing the demons outside Vṛndāvana, He would return. "I am coming back very soon," He promised, "as soon as I have killed the few remaining demons."

TEXT 157

সেই শত্রুগণ হৈতে, ব্রজজন রাখিতে,
রহি রাজ্যে উদাসীন হঞা।

যেবা স্ত্রী-পুত্র-ধনে, করি রাজ্য আবরণে,
যদুগণের সন্তোষ লাগিয়া ॥ ১৫৭ ॥

sei śatru-gaṇa haite, vraja-jana rākhite,
rahi rājye udāsīna hañā
yebā strī-putra-dhane, kari rājya āvaraṇe,
yadu-gaṇera santoṣa lāgiyā

SYNONYMS

sei—those; *śatru-gaṇa haite*—from enemies; *vraja-jana*—to the inhabitants of Vṛndāvana; *rākhite*—to give protection; *rahi*—I remain; *rājye*—in My kingdom; *udāsīna*—indifferent; *hañā*—becoming; *yebā*—whatever; *strī-putra-dhane*—with wives, sons and wealth; *kari rājya āvaraṇe*—I decorate My kingdom; *yadu-gaṇera*—of the Yadu dynasty; *santoṣa*—satisfaction; *lāgiyā*—for the matter of.

TRANSLATION

" 'I wish to protect the inhabitants of Vṛndāvana from the attacks of My enemies. That is why I remain in My kingdom; otherwise I am indifferent to My royal position. Whatever wives, sons and wealth I maintain in the kingdom are only for the satisfaction of the Yadus.

TEXT 158

তোমার যে প্রেমগুণ, করে আমা আকর্ষণ,
আনিবে আমা দিন দশ বিশে।
পুনঃ আসি' বৃন্দাবনে, ব্রজবধূ তোমা-সনে,
বিলসিব রজনী-দিবসে ॥ ১৫৮ ॥

tomāra ye prema-guṇa, kare āmā ākarṣaṇa,
ānibe āmā dina daśa biśe
punaḥ āsi' vṛndāvane, vraja-vadhū tomā-sane,
vilasiba rajanī-divase

SYNONYMS

tomāra—Your; *ye*—whatever; *prema-guṇa*—qualities in ecstatic love; *kare*—do; *āmā*—Me; *ākarṣaṇa*—attracting; *ānibe*—will bring; *āmā*—Me; *dina daśa biśe*—within ten or twenty days; *punaḥ*—again; *āsi'*—coming; *vṛndāvane*—to Vṛndāvana; *vraja-vadhū*—all the damsels of Vṛndāvana; *tomā-sane*—with You; *vilasiba*—I shall enjoy; *rajanī-divase*—both day and night.

TRANSLATION

" 'Your loving qualities always attract Me to Vṛndāvana. Indeed, they will bring Me back within ten or twenty days, and when I return I shall enjoy both day and night with You and all the damsels of Vrajabhūmi.'

TEXT 159

এত তাঁরে কহি কৃষ্ণ, ব্রজে যাইতে সতৃষ্ণ,
এক শ্লোক পড়ি' শুনাইল।
সেই শ্লোক শুনি' রাধা, খণ্ডিল সকল বাধা,
কৃষ্ণপ্রাপ্ত্যে প্রতীতি হইল ॥ ১৫৯ ॥

eta tāṅre kahi kṛṣṇa, vraje yāite satṛṣṇa,
eka śloka paḍi' śunāila
sei śloka śuni' rādhā, khāṇḍila sakala bādhā,
kṛṣṇa-prāptye pratīti ha-ila

SYNONYMS

eta—so much; *tāṅre*—unto Rādhārāṇī; *kahi*—speaking; *kṛṣṇa*—Lord Kṛṣṇa; *vraje*—in Vṛndāvana; *yāite*—to go; *sa-tṛṣṇa*—very anxious; *eka śloka*—one verse; *paḍi'*—reciting; *śunāila*—making Her hear; *sei śloka*—that verse; *śuni'*—hearing; *rādhā*—Śrīmatī Rādhārāṇī; *khāṇḍila*—disappeared; *sakala*—all kinds of; *bādhā*—hindrances; *kṛṣṇa-prāptye*—in achieving Kṛṣṇa; *pratīti ha-ila*—there was assurance.

TRANSLATION

"While speaking to Śrīmatī Rādhārāṇī, Kṛṣṇa became very anxious to return to Vṛndāvana. He made Her listen to a verse which banished all Her difficulties and which assured Her that She would again attain Kṛṣṇa.

TEXT 160

ময়ি ভক্তির্হি ভূতানামমৃতত্বায় কল্পতে।
দিষ্ট্যা যদাসীন্মৎস্নেহো ভবতীনাং মদাপনঃ ॥ ১৬০ ॥

mayi bhaktir hi bhūtānām
amṛtatvāya kalpate
diṣṭyā yad āsīn mat-sneho
bhavatīnāṁ mad-āpanaḥ

SYNONYMS

mayi—unto Me; *bhaktiḥ*—the nine kinds of devotional service, such as *śravaṇa, kīrtana* and *smaraṇa; hi*—certainly; *bhūtānām*—of all living entities; *amṛtatvāya*—for becoming eternal associates of the Lord; *kalpate*—is quite befitting; *diṣṭyā*—by good fortune; *yat*—whatever; *āsīt*—there was; *mat-snehaḥ*—love and affection for Me; *bhavatīnām*—of all you *gopīs; mat-āpanaḥ*—the cause for getting Me back.

TRANSLATION

"Lord Śrī Kṛṣṇa said: 'Devotional service unto Me is the only way to attain Me. My dear gopīs, whatever love and affection you have attained for Me by good fortune is the only reason for My returning to you.' "

PURPORT

This is a verse from *Śrīmad-Bhāgavatam* (10.82.45).

TEXT 161

এই সব অর্থ প্রভু স্বরূপের সনে।
রাত্রি-দিনে ঘরে বসি' করে আস্বাদনে ॥ ১৬১ ॥

ei saba artha prabhu svarūpera sane
rātri-dine ghare vasi' kare āsvādane

SYNONYMS

ei saba—all these; *artha*—meanings; *prabhu*—Śrī Caitanya Mahāprabhu; *svarūpera sane*—with Svarūpa Dāmodara; *rātri-dine*—both day and night; *ghare vasi'*—sitting within His room; *kare*—does; *āsvādane*—taste.

TRANSLATION

Śrī Caitanya Mahāprabhu would sit in His room with Svarūpa Dāmodara and taste the topics of these verses day and night.

TEXT 162

নৃত্যকালে সেই ভাবে আবিষ্ট হঞা।
শ্লোক পড়ি' নাচে জগন্নাথ-মুখ চাঞা ॥ ১৬২ ॥

nṛtya-kāle sei bhāve āviṣṭa hañā
śloka paḍi' nāce jagannātha-mukha cāñā

SYNONYMS

nṛtya-kāle—while dancing; *sei bhāve*—in such ecstasy; *āviṣṭa*—absorbed; *hañā*—becoming; *śloka paḍi'*—reciting these verses; *nāce*—dances; *jagannātha-mukha*—the face of Jagannātha; *cāñā*—looking upon.

TRANSLATION

Śrī Caitanya Mahāprabhu danced completely absorbed in ecstatic emotion. While looking at the face of Lord Jagannātha, He danced and recited these verses.

TEXT 163

স্বরূপ-গোসাঞির ভাগ্য না যায় বর্ণন ।
প্রভুতে আবিষ্ট যাঁর কায়, বাক্য, মন ॥ ১৬৩ ॥

svarūpa-gosāñira bhāgya nā yāya varṇana
prabhute āviṣṭa yāṅra kāya, vākya, mana

SYNONYMS

svarūpa-gosāñira—of Svarūpa Dāmodara Gosvāmī; *bhāgya*—the fortune; *nā*—not; *yāya varṇana*—can be described; *prabhute*—in the service of the Lord; *āviṣṭa*—fully absorbed; *yāṅra*—of whom; *kāya*—body; *vākya*—words; *mana*—mind.

TRANSLATION

No one can describe the good fortune of Svarūpa Dāmodara Gosvāmī, for he is always absorbed in the service of the Lord with his body, mind and words.

TEXT 164

স্বরূপের ইন্দ্রিয়ে প্রভুর নিজেন্দ্রিয়গণ ।
আবিষ্ট হঞা করে গান-আস্বাদন ॥ ১৬৪ ॥

svarūpera indriye prabhura nijendriya-gaṇa
āviṣṭa hañā kare gāna-āsvādana

SYNONYMS

svarūpera—of Svarūpa Dāmodara; *indriye*—in the senses; *prabhura*—of Śrī Caitanya Mahāprabhu; *nija-indriya-gaṇa*—own senses; *āviṣṭa hañā*—being fully absorbed; *kare*—does; *gāna*—the singing; *āsvādana*—tasting.

TRANSLATION

The senses of Lord Śrī Caitanya Mahāprabhu were identical with the senses of Svarūpa. Therefore Caitanya Mahāprabhu used to become fully absorbed in tasting the singing of Svarūpa Dāmodara.

TEXT 165

ভাবের আবেশে কভু ভূমিতে বসিয়া ।
তর্জনীতে ভূমে লিখে অধোমুখ হঞা ॥ ১৬৫ ॥

bhāvera āveśe kabhu bhūmite vasiyā
tarjanīte bhūme likhe adhomukha hañā

SYNONYMS

bhāvera āveśe—because of ecstatic emotion; *kabhu*—sometimes; *bhūmite*—on the ground; *vasiyā*—sitting; *tarjanīte*—with the ring finger; *bhūme*—on the ground; *likhe*—writes; *adhomukha hañā*—looking down.

TRANSLATION

In emotional ecstasy, Caitanya Mahāprabhu would sometimes sit on the ground and, looking down, would write on the ground with His finger.

TEXT 166

অঙ্গুলিতে ক্ষত হবে জানি' দামোদর ।
ভয়ে নিজ-করে নিবারয়ে প্রভু-কর ॥ ১৬৬ ॥

aṅgulite kṣata habe jāni' dāmodara
bhaye nija-kare nivāraye prabhu-kara

SYNONYMS

aṅgulite—on the finger; *kṣata*—injury; *habe*—will take place; *jāni'*—knowing; *dāmodara*—Svarūpa Dāmodara; *bhaye*—out of fear; *nija-kare*—by his own hand; *nivāraye*—checks; *prabhu-kara*—the hand of the Lord.

TRANSLATION

Feeling that the Lord would injure His finger by writing in this way, Svarūpa Dāmodara checked Him with his own hand.

TEXT 167

প্রভুর ভাবানুরূপ স্বরূপের গান ।
যবে যেই রস তাহা করে মূর্তিমান্ ॥ ১৬৭ ॥

prabhura bhāvānurūpa svarūpera gāna
yabe yei rasa tāhā kare mūrtimān

SYNONYMS

prabhura—of Śrī Caitanya Mahāprabhu; *bhāva-anurūpa*—following the ecstatic emotions; *svarūpera*—of Svarūpa Dāmodara; *gāna*—the singing; *yabe*—when; *yei*—whatever; *rasa*—mellow; *tāhā*—that; *kare*—makes; *mūrtimān*—personified.

TRANSLATION

Svarūpa Dāmodara used to sing exactly according to the ecstatic emotion of the Lord. Whenever a particular mellow was being tasted by Śrī Caitanya Mahāprabhu, Svarūpa Dāmodara would personify it by singing.

TEXT 168

শ্রীজগন্নাথের দেখে শ্রীমুখ-কমল ।
তাহার উপর সুন্দর নয়নযুগল ॥ ১৬৮ ॥

śrī-jagannāthera dekhe śrī-mukha-kamala
tāhāra upara sundara nayana-yugala

SYNONYMS

śrī-jagannāthera—of Lord Jagannātha; *dekhe*—sees; *śrī-mukha-kamala*—the lotuslike face; *tāhāra upara*—upon this; *sundara*—beautiful; *nayana-yugala*—a pair of eyes.

TRANSLATION

Śrī Caitanya Mahāprabhu looked upon the beautiful lotuslike face and eyes of Lord Jagannātha.

TEXT 169

সূর্যের কিরণে মুখ করে ঝলমল ।
মাল্য, বস্ত্র, দিব্য অলঙ্কার, পরিমল ॥ ১৬৯ ॥

sūryera kiraṇe mukha kare jhalamala
mālya, vastra, divya alaṅkāra, parimala

SYNONYMS

sūryera—of the sun; *kiraṇe*—by the rays of sunshine; *mukha*—the face; *kare*—does; *jhalamala*—glittering; *mālya*—garland; *vastra*—garments; *divya alaṅkāra*—beautiful ornaments; *parimala*—surrounded by a fragrance.

TRANSLATION

Lord Jagannātha was garlanded, dressed with nice garments and adorned with beautiful ornaments. His face was glittering from the rays of sunshine, and the entire atmosphere was fragrant.

TEXT 170

প্রভুর হৃদয়ে আনন্দসিন্ধু উথলিল ।
উন্মাদ, ঝঞ্ঝা-বাত তৎক্ষণে উঠিল ॥ ১৭০ ॥

prabhura hṛdaye ānanda-sindhu uthalila
unmāda, jhañjhā-vāta tat-kṣaṇe uṭhila

SYNONYMS

prabhura hṛdaye—in the heart of Śrī Caitanya Mahāprabhu; *ānanda-sindhu*—the ocean of transcendental bliss; *uthalila*—arose; *unmāda*—madness; *jhañjhā-vāta*—hurricane; *tat-kṣaṇe*—immediately; *uṭhila*—intensified.

TRANSLATION

An ocean of transcendental bliss expanded in the heart of Lord Śrī Caitanya Mahāprabhu, and symptoms of madness immediately intensified like a hurricane.

TEXT 171

আনন্দোন্মাদে উঠায় ভাবের তরঙ্গ ।
নানা-ভাব-সৈন্যে উপজিল যুদ্ধ-রঙ্গ ॥ ১৭১ ॥

ānandonmāde uṭhāya bhāvera taraṅga
nānā-bhāva-sainye upajila yuddha-raṅga

SYNONYMS

ānanda-unmāde—the madness of transcendental bliss; *uṭhāya*—causes to arise; *bhāvera*—of emotion; *taraṅga*—waves; *nānā*—various; *bhāva*—emotions; *sainye*—among soldiers; *upajila*—there appeared; *yuddha-raṅga*—fighting.

TRANSLATION

The madness of transcendental bliss created waves of various emotions. The emotions appeared like opposing soldiers staging a fight.

TEXT 172

ভাবোদয়, ভাবশান্তি, সন্ধি, শাবল্য ।
সঞ্চারী, সাত্ত্বিক, স্থায়ী স্বভাব-প্রাবল্য ॥ ১৭২ ॥

bhāvodaya, bhāva-śānti, sandhi, śābalya
sañcārī, sāttvika, sthāyī svabhāva-prābalya

SYNONYMS

bhāva-udaya—awakening of emotion; *bhāva-śānti*—emotions of peace; *sandhi*—the junction of different emotions; *śābalya*—mixing of all emotions; *sañcārī*—impetuses for all kinds of emotion; *sāttvika*—transcendental; *sthāyī*—prevalent; *svabhāva*—natural emotion; *prābalya*—increase.

TRANSLATION

There was an increase in all the natural emotional symptoms. Thus there were awakening emotions, peacefulness, joined, mixed, transcendental and prevalent emotions, and impetuses for emotion.

TEXT 173

প্রভুর শরীর যেন শুদ্ধ-হেমাচল ।
ভাব-পুষ্পদ্রুম তাহে পুষ্পিত সকল ॥ ১৭৩ ॥

prabhura śarīra yena śuddha-hemācala
bhāva-puṣpa-druma tāhe puṣpita sakala

SYNONYMS

prabhura—of Śrī Caitanya Mahāprabhu; *śarīra*—body; *yena*—as if; *śuddha*—transcendental; *hemācala*—Himalayan mountain; *bhāva*—emotional; *puṣpa-druma*—flower trees; *tāhe*—in that situation; *puṣpita*—blooming with flowers; *sakala*—all.

TRANSLATION

Śrī Caitanya Mahāprabhu's body appeared like a transcendental Himalayan mountain bearing ecstatic emotional flower trees, all of them blooming.

TEXT 174

দেখিতে আকর্ষয়ে সবার চিত্ত-মন ।
প্রেমামৃতবৃষ্ট্যে প্রভু সিঞ্চে সবার মন ॥ ১৭৪ ॥

dekhite ākarṣaye sabāra citta-mana
premāmṛta-vṛṣṭye prabhu siñce sabāra mana

SYNONYMS

dekhite—by seeing; *ākarṣaye*—attracts; *sabāra*—of everyone; *citta-mana*—mind and consciousness; *prema-amṛta-vṛṣṭye*—by pouring of the nectar of transcendental love for God; *prabhu*—Śrī Caitanya Mahāprabhu; *siñce*—sprinkled; *sabāra*—everyone's; *mana*—mind.

TRANSLATION

Upon seeing all these symptoms, everyone's mind and consciousness were attracted. Indeed, the Lord sprinkled everyone's mind with the nectar of transcendental love of Godhead.

TEXT 175

জগন্নাথ-সেবক যত রাজপাত্রগণ ।
যাত্রিক লোক, নীলাচলবাসী যত জন ॥ ১৭৫ ॥

jagannātha-sevaka yata rāja-pātra-gaṇa
yātrika loka, nīlācala-vāsī yata jana

SYNONYMS

jagannātha-sevaka—the servants of Lord Jagannātha; *yata*—all; *rāja-pātra-gaṇa*—and the government officers; *yātrika*—pilgrim visitors; *loka*—people in general; *nīlācala-vāsī*—the residents of Jagannātha Purī; *yata jana*—as many people as there were.

TRANSLATION

He sprinkled the minds of the servants of Lord Jagannātha, the government officers, the pilgrim visitors, the general populace and all the residents of Jagannātha Purī.

TEXT 176

প্রভুর নৃত্য প্রেম দেখি' হয় চমৎকার ।
কৃষ্ণপ্রেম উছলিল হৃদয়ে সবার ॥ ১৭৬ ॥

prabhura nṛtya prema dekhi' haya camatkāra
kṛṣṇa-prema uchalila hṛdaye sabāra

SYNONYMS

prabhura—of Śrī Caitanya Mahāprabhu; *nṛtya*—dancing; *prema*—love; *dekhi'*—seeing; *haya*—become; *camatkāra*—astonished; *kṛṣṇa-prema*—love of Kṛṣṇa; *uchalila*—infatuated; *hṛdaye*—in the hearts; *sabāra*—of everyone.

TRANSLATION

After seeing the dancing and ecstatic love of Śrī Caitanya Mahāprabhu, everyone became astonished. In their hearts they became infatuated with love of Kṛṣṇa.

TEXT 177

প্রেমে নাচে, গায়, লোক, করে কোলাহল ।
প্রভুর নৃত্য দেখি' সবে আনন্দে বিহ্বল ॥ ১৭৭ ॥

preme nāce, gāya, loka, kare kolāhala
prabhura nṛtya dekhi' sabe ānande vihvala

SYNONYMS

preme—in ecstatic love; *nāce*—dance; *gāya*—chant; *loka*—people in general; *kare*—make; *kolāhala*—a great noise; *prabhura*—of Śrī Caitanya Mahāprabhu; *nṛtya*—dancing; *dekhi'*—seeing; *sabe*—everyone; *ānande*—in transcendental bliss; *vihvala*—overwhelmed.

TRANSLATION

Everyone danced and chanted in ecstatic love, and a great noise resounded. Everyone was overwhelmed with transcendental bliss just to see the dancing of Śrī Caitanya Mahāprabhu.

TEXT 178

অন্যের কি কায, জগন্নাথ-হলধর ।
প্রভুর নৃত্য দেখি' সুখে চলিলা মন্থর ॥ ১৭৮ ॥

anyera ki kāya, jagannātha-haladhara
prabhura nṛtya dekhi' sukhe calilā manthara

SYNONYMS

anyera ki kāya—apart from the actions of others; *jagannātha*—Lord Jagannātha; *haladhara*—Balarāma; *prabhura*—of Śrī Caitanya Mahāprabhu; *nṛtya*—the dancing; *dekhi'*—seeing; *sukhe*—in great happiness; *calilā*—moved; *manthara*—slowly.

TRANSLATION

Apart from the others, even Lord Jagannātha and Lord Balarāma, with great happiness, began to move very slowly upon seeing the dancing of Śrī Caitanya Mahāprabhu.

TEXT 179

কভু সুখে নৃত্যরঙ্গ দেখে রথ রাখি' ।
সে কৌতুক যে দেখিল, সেই তার সাক্ষী ॥ ১৭৯ ॥

kabhu sukhe nṛtya-raṅga dekhe ratha rākhi'
se kautuka ye dekhila, sei tāra sākṣī

SYNONYMS

kabhu—sometimes; *sukhe*—in great happiness; *nṛtya-raṅga*—amusement in dancing; *dekhe*—sees; *ratha*—the car; *rākhi'*—stopping; *se kautuka*—that amusement; *ye*—anyone who; *dekhila*—saw; *sei*—he; *tāra*—of that; *sākṣī*—witness.

TRANSLATION

Lord Jagannātha and Lord Balarāma sometimes stopped the car and happily observed Lord Caitanya's dancing. Anyone who was able to see Them stop and watch the dancing bore witness to Their pastimes.

TEXT 180

এইমত প্রভু নৃত্য করিতে ভ্রমিতে ।
প্রতাপরুদ্রের আগে লাগিলা পড়িতে ॥ ১৮০ ॥

ei-mata prabhu nṛtya karite bhramite
pratāparudrera āge lāgilā paḍite

SYNONYMS

ei-mata—in this way; *prabhu*—Lord Śrī Caitanya Mahāprabhu; *nṛtya karite*—dancing; *bhramite*—wandering; *pratāparudrera*—of King Pratāparudra; *āge*—in front; *lāgilā*—began; *paḍite*—to fall down.

TRANSLATION

When Lord Śrī Caitanya Mahāprabhu was dancing and wandering in this way, He fell down in front of Mahārāja Pratāparudra.

TEXT 181

সম্ভ্রমে প্রতাপরুদ্র প্রভুকে ধরিল ।
তাঁহাকে দেখিতে প্রভুর বাহ্যজ্ঞান হইল ॥ ১৮১ ॥

sambhrame pratāparudra prabhuke dharila
tāṅhāke dekhite prabhura bāhya-jñāna ha-ila

SYNONYMS

sambhrame—with great respect; *pratāparudra*—King Pratāparudra; *prabhuke*—Lord Śrī Caitanya Mahāprabhu; *dharila*—picked up; *tāṅhāke*—Him; *dekhite*—to see; *prabhura*—of Śrī Caitanya Mahāprabhu; *bāhya-jñāna*—external consciousness; *ha-ila*—there was.

TRANSLATION

Mahārāja Pratāparudra picked the Lord up with great respect, but upon seeing the King, Lord Caitanya Mahāprabhu came to His external senses.

TEXT 182

রাজা দেখি' মহাপ্রভু করেন ধিক্কার ।
ছি, ছি, বিষয়ীর স্পর্শ হইল আমার ॥ ১৮২ ॥

rājā dekhi' mahāprabhu karena dhikkāra
chi, chi, viṣayīra sparśa ha-ila āmāra

SYNONYMS

rājā dekhi'—by seeing the King; *mahāprabhu*—Śrī Caitanya Mahāprabhu; *karena*—does; *dhik-kāra*—condemnation; *chi chi*—how pitiable it is; *viṣayīra*—of a person interested in mundane affairs; *sparśa ha-ila*—there has been touching; *āmāra*—of Me.

TRANSLATION

After seeing the King, Śrī Caitanya Mahāprabhu condemned Himself, saying, "Oh, how pitiful it is that I have touched a person who is interested in mundane affairs."

TEXT 183

আবেশেতে নিত্যানন্দ না হৈলা সাবধানে ।
কাশীশ্বর-গোবিন্দ আছিলা অন্য-স্থানে ॥ ১৮৩ ॥

āveśete nityānanda nā hailā sāvadhāne
kāśīśvara-govinda āchilā anya-sthāne

SYNONYMS

āveśete—in great ecstasy; *nityānanda*—Nityānanda Prabhu; *nā*—not; *hailā*—became; *sāvadhāne*—careful; *kāśīśvara*—Kāśīśvara; *govinda*—Govinda; *āchilā*—were; *anya-sthāne*—in another place.

TRANSLATION

Not even Lord Nityānanda Prabhu, Kāśīśvara or Govinda took care of Lord Caitanya Mahāprabhu when He fell down. Nityānanda was in great ecstasy, and Kāśīśvara and Govinda were elsewhere.

TEXT 184

যদ্যপি রাজার দেখি' হাড়ির সেবন ।
প্রসন্ন হঞাছে তাঁরে মিলিবারে মন ॥ ১৮৪ ॥

yadyapi rājāra dekhi' hāḍira sevana
prasanna hañāche tāṅre milibāre mana

SYNONYMS

yadyapi—although; *rājāra*—of the King; *dekhi'*—seeing; *hāḍira sevana*—the service of a sweeper; *prasanna hañāche*—was satisfied; *tāṅre milibāre*—to see him; *mana*—His mind.

TRANSLATION

Śrī Caitanya Mahāprabhu had already been satisfied by the King's behavior, for the King had accepted the service of a sweeper for Lord Jagannātha. Therefore Lord Caitanya Mahāprabhu actually desired to see the King.

TEXT 185

তথাপি আপন-গণে করিতে সাবধান ।
বাহ্যে কিছু রোষাভাস কৈলা ভগবান্ ॥ ১৮৫ ॥

tathāpi āpana-gaṇe karite sāvadhāna
bāhye kichu roṣābhāsa kailā bhagavān

SYNONYMS

tathāpi—still; *āpana-gaṇe*—to personal associates; *karite*—to do; *sāvadhāna*—warning; *bāhye*—externally; *kichu*—some; *roṣa-ābhāsa*—apparent anger; *kailā*—showed; *bhagavān*—the Supreme Personality of Godhead.

TRANSLATION

However, just to warn His personal associates, the Supreme Personality of Godhead, Śrī Caitanya Mahāprabhu, externally expressed feelings of anger.

PURPORT

When Mahārāja Pratāparudra asked to see the Lord, Śrī Caitanya Mahāprabhu immediately refused, saying:

niṣkiñcanasya bhagavad-bhajanonmukhasya
pāraṁ paraṁ jigamiṣor bhava-sāgarasya
sandarśanaṁ viṣayiṇām atha yoṣitāṁ ca
hā hanta hanta viṣa-bhakṣaṇato 'py asādhu
(Cc. *Madhya* 11.8)

The word *niṣkiñcanasya* refers to a person who has finished his material activities. Such a person can begin to execute his activities in Kṛṣṇa consciousness to cross over the ocean of nescience. It is very dangerous for such a person to have intimate relationships with mundane people or to become intimately related with women. This formality is to be observed by anyone who is serious about going back home, back to Godhead. To teach His personal associates these principles, Śrī Caitanya Mahāprabhu expressed external anger when touched by the King. Since the Lord was very satisfied with the humble behavior of the King, He intentionally allowed the King to touch Him, but externally He expressed anger just to warn His personal associates.

TEXT 186

প্রভুর বচনে রাজার মনে হৈল ভয় ।
সার্বভৌম কহে,—তুমি না কয় সংশয় ॥ ১৮৬ ॥

prabhura vacane rājāra mane haila bhaya
sārvabhauma kahe,——tumi nā kaya saṁśaya

SYNONYMS

prabhura vacane—by the words of Śrī Caitanya Mahāprabhu; *rājāra*—of the King; *mane*—in the mind; *haila*—there was; *bhaya*—fear; *sārvabhauma kahe*—Sārvabhauma Bhaṭṭācārya said; *tumi*—you (the King); *nā kaya saṁśaya*—do not be worried.

TRANSLATION

King Pratāparudra became frightened when Lord Caitanya showed external anger, but Sārvabhauma Bhaṭṭācārya told the King, "Don't worry."

TEXT 187

তোমার উপরে প্রভুর সুপ্রসন্ন মন ।
তোমা লক্ষ্য করি' শিখায়েন নিজ গণ ॥ ১৮৭ ॥

tomāra upare prabhura suprasanna mana
tomā lakṣya kari' śikhāyena nija gaṇa

SYNONYMS

tomāra upare—upon you; *prabhura*—of Lord Śrī Caitanya Mahāprabhu; *suprasanna*—very satisfied; *mana*—the mind; *tomā*—you; *lakṣya kari'*—pointing out; *śikhāyena*—He teaches; *nija gaṇa*—His personal associates.

TRANSLATION

Sārvabhauma Bhaṭṭācārya informed the King, "The Lord is very satisfied with you. By pointing you out, He was teaching His personal associates how to behave with mundane people."

PURPORT

Although outwardly the King was a mundane man interested in money and women, internally he was purified by devotional activities. He showed this by engaging as a street sweeper to please Lord Jagannātha. A person may appear to be a pounds-and-shillings man interested in money and women, but if he is actually very meek and humble and surrendered to the Supreme Personality of Godhead, he is not mundane. Such a judgment can be made only by Śrī Caitanya Mahāprabhu and His very confidential devotees. As a general principle, however, no devotee should intimately mix with mundane people interested in money and women.

TEXT 188

অবসর জানি' আমি করিব নিবেদন ।
সেইকালে যাই' করিহ প্রভুর মিলন ॥ ১৮৮ ॥

avasara jāni' āmi kariba nivedana
sei-kāle yāi' kariha prabhura milana

SYNONYMS

avasara jāni'—understanding an opportune moment; *āmi*—I; *kariba*—shall do; *nivedana*—submission; *sei-kāle*—at that time; *yāi'*—coming; *kariha*—you do; *prabhura milana*—meeting with Lord Śrī Caitanya Mahāprabhu.

TRANSLATION

Sārvabhauma Bhaṭṭācārya continued, "I shall submit your petition when there is an opportune moment. It will then be easy for you to come and meet the Lord."

TEXT 189

তবে মহাপ্রভু রথ প্রদক্ষিণ করিয়া ।
রথ-পাছে যাই' ঠেলে রথে মাথা দিয়া ॥ ১৮৯ ॥

tabe mahāprabhu ratha pradakṣiṇa kariyā
ratha-pāche yāi' ṭhele rathe māthā diyā

SYNONYMS

tabe—at that time; *mahāprabhu*—Śrī Caitanya Mahāprabhu; *ratha*—the car; *pradakṣiṇa*—circumambulation; *kariyā*—doing; *ratha-pāche*—to the rear of the car; *yāi'*—going; *ṭhele*—pushes; *rathe*—on the car; *māthā diyā*—by placing the head.

TRANSLATION

After circumambulating Jagannātha, Śrī Caitanya Mahāprabhu went behind the car and began pushing it with His head.

TEXT 190

ঠেলিতেই চলিল রথ 'হড়' 'হড়' করি' ।
চতুর্দিকে লোক সব বলে 'হরি' 'হরি' ॥ ১৯০ ॥

ṭhelitei calila ratha 'haḍa' 'haḍa' kari'
catur-dike loka saba bale 'hari' 'hari'

SYNONYMS

ṭhelitei—as soon as He pushed; *calila*—departed; *ratha*—the car; *haḍa haḍa kari'*—making a rattling noise; *catuḥ-dike*—all around; *loka*—people in general; *saba*—all; *bale*—chant; *hari hari*—the holy name of the Lord, Hari Hari.

TRANSLATION

As soon as He pushed, the car immediately started to move, making a rattling noise. The people all around began to chant the holy name of the Lord, "Hari! Hari!"

TEXT 191

তবে প্রভু নিজ-ভক্তগণ লঞা সঙ্গে ।
বলদেব-সুভদ্রাগ্রে নৃত্য করে রঙ্গে ॥ ১৯১ ॥

tabe prabhu nija-bhakta-gaṇa lañā saṅge
baladeva-subhadrāgre nṛtya kare raṅge

SYNONYMS

tabe—at that time; *prabhu*—Śrī Caitanya Mahāprabhu; *nija*—personal; *bhakta-gaṇa*—devotees; *lañā*—taking; *saṅge*—with Him; *baladeva*—of Lord Balarāma; *subhadrā*—of the goddess of fortune Subhadrā; *agre*—in front; *nṛtya*—dancing; *kare*—performed; *raṅge*—in great amusement.

TRANSLATION

As the car began to move, Śrī Caitanya Mahāprabhu took His personal associates in front of the cars occupied by Lord Balarāma and Subhadrā, the goddess of fortune. Greatly inspired, He then began to dance in front of Them.

TEXT 192

তাহাঁ নৃত্য করি' জগন্নাথ আগে আইলা ।
জগন্নাথ দেখি' নৃত্য করিতে লাগিলা ॥ ১৯২ ॥

tāhāṅ nṛtya kari' jagannātha āge āilā
jagannātha dekhi' nṛtya karite lāgilā

SYNONYMS

tāhāṅ—there; *nṛtya kari'*—after performing the dance; *jagannātha*—of Lord Jagannātha; *āge*—in front; *āilā*—appeared; *jagannātha dekhi'*—seeing Lord Jagannātha; *nṛtya*—dancing; *karite*—to perform; *lāgilā*—began.

TRANSLATION

After finishing the dance before Lord Baladeva and Subhadrā, Śrī Caitanya Mahāprabhu came before Lord Jagannātha's car. Upon seeing Lord Jagannātha, He began to dance again.

TEXT 193

চলিয়া আইল রথ 'বলগণ্ডি'-স্থানে ।
জগন্নাথ রথ রাখি' দেখে ডাহিনে বামে ॥ ১৯৩ ॥

caliyā āila ratha 'balagaṇḍi'-sthāne
jagannātha ratha rākhi' dekhe ḍāhine vāme

SYNONYMS

caliyā—moving; *āila*—came; *ratha*—the car; *balagaṇḍi-sthāne*—at the place known as Balagaṇḍi; *jagannātha*—Lord Jagannātha; *ratha*—car; *rākhi'*—after stopping; *dekhe*—sees; *ḍāhine vāme*—left and right.

TRANSLATION

When they reached the place called Balagaṇḍi, Lord Jagannātha stopped His car and began to look left and right.

TEXT 194

বামে—'বিপ্রশাসন', নারিকেল-বন ।
ডাহিনে ত' পুষ্পোত্থান যেন বৃন্দাবন ॥ ১৯৪ ॥

vāme——'vipra-śāsana' nārikela-vana
ḍāhine ta' puṣpodyāna yena vṛndāvana

SYNONYMS

vāme—on the left; *vipra-śāsana*—the place known as *vipra-śāsana; nārikela-vana*—coconut grove; *ḍāhine*—on the right side; *ta'*—indeed; *puṣpa-udyāna*—flower gardens; *yena*—as if; *vṛndāvana*—Vṛndāvana.

TRANSLATION

On the left side, Lord Jagannātha saw the neighborhood of brāhmaṇas known as vipra-śāsana and the coconut tree grove. On the right side, He saw nice flower gardens resembling those in the holy place Vṛndāvana.

PURPORT

Vipra-śāsana is a name generally used in the Orissa province for the quarters where *brāhmaṇas* live.

TEXT 195

আগে নৃত্য করে গৌর লঞা ভক্তগণ ।
রথ রাখি' জগন্নাথ করেন দরশন ॥ ১৯৫ ॥

āge nṛtya kare gaura lañā bhakta-gaṇa
ratha rākhi' jagannātha karena daraśana

SYNONYMS

āge—in front; *nṛtya kare*—dances; *gaura*—Śrī Caitanya Mahāprabhu; *lañā*—accompanied by; *bhakta-gaṇa*—the devotees; *ratha rākhi'*—after stopping the car; *jagannātha*—Lord Jagannātha; *karena daraśana*—sees.

TRANSLATION

Śrī Caitanya Mahāprabhu and His devotees were dancing in front of the car, and, having stopped the car, Lord Jagannātha watched the dancing.

TEXT 196

সেই স্থলে ভোগ লাগে,—আছয়ে নিয়ম ।
কোটি ভোগ জগন্নাথ করে আস্বাদন ॥ ১৯৬ ॥

sei sthale bhoga lāge,——ācchaye niyama
koṭi bhoga jagannātha kare āsvādana

SYNONYMS

sei sthale—in that place; *bhoga lāge*—food is offered; *ācchaye niyama*—it is the custom; *koṭi bhoga*—millions of dishes; *jagannātha*—Lord Jagannātha; *kare*—does; *āsvādana*—tasting.

TRANSLATION

It was customary that food be offered to the Lord at vipra-śāsana. Indeed, innumerable dishes of food were offered, and Lord Jagannātha tasted each one of them.

TEXT 197

জগন্নাথের ছোট-বড় যত ভক্তগণ ।
নিজ নিজ উত্তম-ভোগ করে সমর্পণ ॥ ১৯৭ ॥

jagannāthera choṭa-baḍa yata bhakta-gaṇa
nija nija uttama-bhoga kare samarpaṇa

SYNONYMS

jagannāthera—of Lord Jagannātha; *choṭa*—neophyte; *baḍa*—advanced; *yata*—all; *bhakta-gaṇa*—devotees; *nija nija*—personally cooked; *uttama-bhoga*—first-class food; *kare*—do; *samarpaṇa*—offering.

TRANSLATION

All kinds of devotees of Lord Jagannātha—from neophytes to the most advanced—offered their best cooked food to the Lord.

TEXT 198

রাজা, রাজমহিষীবৃন্দ, পাত্র, মিত্রগণ।
নীলাচলবাসী যত ছোট-বড় জন॥ ১৯৮॥

rājā, rāja-mahiṣī-vṛnda, pātra, mitra-gaṇa
nīlācala-vāsī yata choṭa-baḍa jana

SYNONYMS

rājā—the King; *rāja-mahiṣī-vṛnda*—the queens of the King; *pātra*—ministers; *mitra-gaṇa*—friends; *nīlācala-vāsī*—all the residents of Jagannātha Purī; *yata*—as many; *choṭa-baḍa*—small and big; *jana*—persons.

TRANSLATION

This included the King, his queens, his ministers and friends and all other big and small residents of Jagannātha Purī.

TEXT 199

নানা-দেশের দেশী যত যাত্রিক জন।
নিজ-নিজ-ভোগ তাহাঁ করে সমর্পণ॥ ১৯৯॥

nānā-deśera deśī yata yātrika jana
nija-nija-bhoga tāhāṅ kare samarpaṇa

SYNONYMS

nānā-deśera—of various countries; *deśī*—local; *yata*—all kinds of; *yātrika*—visiting; *jana*—people; *nija-nija*—personally cooked; *bhoga*—food; *tāhāṅ*—there; *kare*—do; *samarpaṇa*—offering.

TRANSLATION

All the visitors who had come from different countries to Jagannātha Purī, as well as the local devotees, offered their personally cooked food to the Lord.

TEXT 200

আগে পাছে, দুই পার্শ্বে পুষ্পোদ্যান-বনে।
যেই যাহা পায়, লাগায়,—নাহিক নিয়মে ॥ ২০০ ॥

āge pāche, dui pārśve puṣpodyāna-vane
yei yāhā pāya, lāgāya,——nāhika niyame

SYNONYMS

āge pāche—in front or at the end; *dui pārśve*—on two sides; *puṣpa-udyāna-vane*—in the flower gardens; *yei*—one who; *yāhā pāya*—gets the opportunity; *lāgāya*—offers; *nāhika niyame*—there are no hard-and-fast rules.

TRANSLATION

The devotees offered their foods everywhere, in front and behind the car, on the two sides and within the flower garden. Wherever possible, they made their offering to the Lord, for there were no hard-and-fast rules.

TEXT 201

ভোগের সময় লোকের মহা ভিড় হৈল।
নৃত্য ছাড়ি' মহাপ্রভু উপবনে গেল ॥ ২০১ ॥

bhogera samaya lokera mahā bhiḍa haila
nṛtya chāḍi' mahāprabhu upavane gela

SYNONYMS

bhogera samaya—at the time the food was offered; *lokera*—of all the people; *mahā*—great; *bhiḍa*—crowd; *haila*—there was; *nṛtya chāḍi'*—giving up His dancing; *mahāprabhu*—Śrī Caitanya Mahāprabhu; *upavane gela*—went to a nearby garden.

TRANSLATION

While the food was being offered, a large crowd of people gathered. At that time Śrī Caitanya Mahāprabhu stopped His dancing and went to a nearby garden.

TEXT 202

প্রেমাবেশে মহাপ্রভু উপবন পাঞা ।
পুষ্পোদ্যানে গৃহপিণ্ডায় রহিলা পড়িয়া ॥ ২০২ ॥

premāveśe mahāprabhu upavana pāñā
puṣpodyāne gṛha-piṇḍāya rahilā paḍiyā

SYNONYMS

prema-āveśe—in ecstatic love; *mahāprabhu*—Śrī Caitanya Mahāprabhu; *upavana pāñā*—having come to a nice nearby garden; *puṣpa-udyāne*—in that flower garden; *gṛha-piṇḍāya*—on the raised platform; *rahilā*—remained; *paḍiyā*—falling flat.

TRANSLATION

Śrī Caitanya Mahāprabhu went to the garden. Immersed in a great ecstatic emotion, He fell flat on a raised platform there.

TEXT 203

নৃত্য-পরিশ্রমে প্রভুর দেহে ঘন ঘর্ম।
সুগন্ধি শীতল-বায়ু করেন সেবন ॥ ২০৩ ॥

nṛtya-pariśrame prabhura dehe ghana gharma
sugandhi śītala-vāyu karena sevana

SYNONYMS

nṛtya-pariśrame—by fatigue due to dancing; *prabhura*—of Śrī Caitanya Mahāprabhu; *dehe*—on the body; *ghana gharma*—much perspiration; *sugandhi*—fragrant; *śītala-vāyu*—cool breeze; *karena sevana*—enjoyed very much.

TRANSLATION

The Lord was very fatigued from the hard labor of dancing, and there was perspiration all over His body. He therefore enjoyed the fragrant, cool breeze of the garden.

TEXT 204

যত ভক্ত কীর্তনীয়া আসিয়া আরামে ।
প্রতিবৃক্ষতলে সবে করেন বিশ্রামে ॥ ২০৪ ॥

yata bhakta kīrtanīyā āsiyā ārāme
prati-vṛkṣa-tale sabe karena viśrāme

SYNONYMS

yata bhakta—all the devotees; *kīrtanīyā*—who were performing *saṅkīrtana;* *āsiyā*—coming; *ārāme*—in the resting place; *prati-vṛkṣa-tale*—under each and every tree; *sabe*—all of them; *karena*—take; *viśrāme*—rest.

TRANSLATION

All the devotees who were performing saṅkīrtana came there and took rest under each and every tree.

TEXT 205

এই ত' কহিল প্রভুর মহাসংকীর্তন ।
জগন্নাথের আগে যৈছে করিল নর্তন ॥ ২০৫ ॥

ei ta' kahila prabhura mahā-saṅkīrtana
jagannāthera āge yaiche karila nartana

SYNONYMS

ei ta'—in this way; *kahila*—I have described; *prabhura*—of Lord Śrī Caitanya Mahāprabhu; *mahā-saṅkīrtana*—the great congregational chanting; *jagannāthera āge*—in front of Lord Jagannātha; *yaiche*—as; *karila*—He did; *nartana*—dancing.

TRANSLATION

Thus I have described the great performance of congregational chanting by Lord Śrī Caitanya Mahāprabhu as He danced in front of Lord Jagannātha.

TEXT 206

রথাগ্রেতে প্রভু যৈছে করিলা নর্তন ।
চৈতন্যাষ্টকে রূপ-গোসাঞি কর্যাছে বর্ণন ॥ ২০৬ ॥

rathāgrete prabhu yaiche karilā nartana
caitanyāṣṭake rūpa-gosāñi karyāche varṇana

SYNONYMS

ratha-agrete—in front of the car; *prabhu*—Śrī Caitanya Mahāprabhu; *yaiche*—as; *karilā*—performed; *nartana*—dancing; *caitanya-aṣṭake*—in the prayer named

Caitanyāṣṭaka; rūpa-gosāñi—Rūpa Gosvāmī; *karyāche*—has done; *varṇana*—a vivid description.

TRANSLATION

In his prayer known as the Caitanyāṣṭaka, Śrīla Rūpa Gosvāmī has given a vivid description of the Lord's dancing before the car of Jagannātha.

PURPORT

Śrīla Rūpa Gosvāmī composed three prayers, each with the title *Caitanyāṣṭaka.* The verse next quoted is from the first of the *Caitanyāṣṭaka* prayers included in the book *Stava-mālā.*

TEXT 207

রথারূঢ়স্যারাদধিপদবি নীলাচলপতে-
রদভ্রপ্রেমোর্মিস্ফুরিতনটনোল্লাসবিবশঃ ।
সহর্ষং গায়দ্ভিঃ পরিবৃত-তনুর্বৈষ্ণবজনৈঃ
স চৈতন্যঃ কিং মে পুনরপি দৃশোর্যাস্যতি পদম্ ॥ ২০৭ ॥

rathārūḍhasyārād adhipadavi nīlācala-pater
adabhra-premormi-sphurita-naṭanollāsa-vivaśaḥ
saharṣaṁ gāyadbhiḥ parivṛta-tanur vaiṣṇava-janaiḥ
sa caitanyaḥ kiṁ me punar api dṛśor yāsyati padam

SYNONYMS

ratha-ārūḍhasya—of the Supreme Lord, who was placed aboard the car; *ārāt*—in front; *adhipadavi*—on the main road; *nīlācala-pateḥ*—of Lord Jagannātha, the Lord of Nīlācala; *adabhra*—great; *prema-urmi*—by waves of love of Godhead; *sphurita*—which was manifested; *naṭana-ullāsa-vivaśaḥ*—being overwhelmed by the transcendental bliss of dancing; *sa-harṣam*—with great pleasure; *gāyadbhiḥ*—who were singing; *parivṛta*—surrounded; *tanuḥ*—body; *vaiṣṇava-janaiḥ*—by the devotees; *saḥ caitanyaḥ*—that Lord Śrī Caitanya Mahāprabhu; *kim*—whether; *me*—my; *punaḥ api*—again; *dṛśoḥ*—of vision; *yāsyati*—will enter; *padam*—the path.

TRANSLATION

"Śrī Caitanya Mahāprabhu danced down the main road in great ecstasy before Lord Jagannātha, the master of Nīlācala, who was sitting on His car. Overwhelmed by the transcendental bliss of dancing and surrounded by Vaiṣṇavas who sang the holy names, He manifested waves of ecstatic love of Godhead. When will Śrī Caitanya Mahāprabhu again be visible to my vision?"

TEXT 208

ইহা যেই শুনে সেই শ্রীচৈতন্য পায় ।
সুদৃঢ় বিশ্বাস-সহ প্রেমভক্তি হয় ॥ ২০৮ ॥

ihā yei śune sei śrī-caitanya pāya
sudṛḍha viśvāsa-saha prema-bhakti haya

SYNONYMS

ihā—this; *yei*—anyone who; *śune*—hears; *sei*—that person; *śrī-caitanya pāya*—will achieve Śrī Caitanya Mahāprabhu; *su-dṛḍha*—firm; *viśvāsa*—conviction; *saha*—with; *prema-bhakti*—devotional service in great love; *haya*—there is.

TRANSLATION

Anyone who hears this description of the car festival will attain Śrī Caitanya Mahāprabhu. He will also attain the elevated state by which he will have firm conviction in devotional service and love of Godhead.

TEXT 209

শ্রীরূপ-রঘুনাথ-পদে যার আশ ।
চৈতন্যচরিতামৃত কহে কৃষ্ণদাস ॥ ২০৯ ॥

śrī-rūpa-raghunātha-pade yāra āśa
caitanya-caritāmṛta kahe kṛṣṇadāsa

SYNONYMS

śrī-rūpa—Śrīla Rūpa Gosvāmī; *raghunātha*—Śrīla Raghunātha dāsa Gosvāmī; *pade*—at the lotus feet; *yāra*—whose; *āśa*—expectation; *caitanya-caritāmṛta*—the book named *Caitanya-caritāmṛta; kahe*—describes; *kṛṣṇadāsa*—Śrīla Kṛṣṇadāsa Kavirāja Gosvāmī.

TRANSLATION

Praying at the lotus feet of Śrī Rūpa and Śrī Raghunātha, always desiring their mercy, I, Kṛṣṇadāsa, narrate Śrī Caitanya-caritāmṛta, following in their footsteps.

Thus end the Bhaktivedanta purports to the Śrī Caitanya-caritāmṛta, Madhya-līlā, *Thirteenth Chapter, describing Śrī Caitanya Mahāprabhu's ecstatic dancing at Lord Jagannātha's car festival.*

CHAPTER 14

Performance of the Vṛndāvana Pastimes

Dressing himself as a Vaiṣṇava, Mahārāja Pratāparudra entered a garden alone and began reciting verses from *Śrīmad-Bhāgavatam.* He then took the opportunity to massage the lotus feet of the Lord. The Lord, in His ecstatic love for Kṛṣṇa, immediately embraced the King and thus bestowed mercy upon him. When there was an offering of *prasāda* in the garden, Lord Caitanya also partook of it. After this, when Lord Jagannātha's Ratha car stopped moving, King Pratāparudra called for many elephants to pull it, but they were unsuccessful. Seeing this, Lord Caitanya began to push the car from behind with His head, and the chariot began moving. Then the devotees began pulling the chariot with ropes. Near the Guṇḍicā temple is a place known as Āiṭoṭā. This place was fixed up for Śrī Caitanya Mahāprabhu to rest in. When Lord Jagannātha was seated at Sundarācala, Śrī Caitanya Mahāprabhu saw it as Vṛndāvana. He performed sporting pastimes in the water of the lake known as Indradyumna. For nine continuous days during Ratha-yātrā, the Lord remained at Jagannātha Purī, and on the fifth day He and Svarūpa Dāmodara observed the pastimes of Lakṣmī, the goddess of fortune. During that time, there was much talk about the pastimes of the *gopīs.* When the *ratha* was again being drawn and the chanting resumed, Rāmānanda Vasu of Kulīna-grāma and Satyarāja Khān were requested to bring silk ropes every year for the Ratha-yātrā ceremony.

TEXT 1

গৌরঃ পশ্যন্নাত্মবৃন্দৈঃ শ্রীলক্ষ্মীবিজয়োৎসবম্ ।
শ্রুত্বা গোপীরসোল্লাসং হৃষ্টঃ প্রেম্ণা ননর্ত সঃ ॥ ১ ॥

gauraḥ paśyann ātma-vṛndaiḥ
śrī-lakṣmī-vijayotsavam
śrutvā gopī-rasollāsaṁ
hṛṣṭaḥ premṇā nanarta saḥ

SYNONYMS

gauraḥ—Lord Śrī Caitanya Mahāprabhu; *paśyan*—by seeing; *ātma-vṛndaiḥ*—with His personal associates; *śrī-lakṣmī*—of the goddess of fortune; *vijaya*--

utsavam—the grand festival; *śrutvā*—by hearing; *gopī*—of the *gopīs; rasa-ullāsam*—the superexcellence of the mellows; *hṛṣṭaḥ*—being very pleased; *prem-ṇā*—in great ecstatic love; *nanarta*—danced; *saḥ*—He, Śrī Caitanya Mahāprabhu.

TRANSLATION

Accompanied by His personal devotees, Śrī Caitanya Mahāprabhu went to the festival known as Lakṣmī-vijayotsava. There He discussed the superexcellent love of the gopīs. Just by hearing about them, He became very pleased and danced in great ecstatic love for the Lord.

TEXT 2

জয় জয় গৌরচন্দ্র শ্রীকৃষ্ণচৈতন্য ।
জয় জয় নিত্যানন্দ জয়াদ্বৈত ধন্য ॥ ২ ॥

jaya jaya gauracandra śrī-kṛṣṇa-caitanya
jaya jaya nityānanda jayādvaita dhanya

SYNONYMS

jaya jaya—all glories; *gauracandra*—to Gauracandra; *śrī-kṛṣṇa-caitanya*—Lord Śrī Caitanya Mahāprabhu; *jaya jaya*—all glories; *nityānanda*—to Nityānanda Prabhu; *jaya*—all glories; *advaita*—to Advaita Ācārya; *dhanya*—exalted.

TRANSLATION

All glories to Śrī Caitanya Mahāprabhu, known as Gauracandra! All glories to Lord Nityānanda Prabhu! All glories to Advaita Ācārya, who is so exalted!

TEXT 3

জয় জয় শ্রীবাসাদি গৌরভক্তগণ ।
জয় শ্রোতাগণ,—যাঁর গৌর প্রাণধন ॥ ৩ ॥

jaya jaya śrīvāsādi gaura-bhakta-gaṇa
jaya śrotā-gaṇa, ——yāṅra gaura prāṇa-dhana

SYNONYMS

jaya jaya—all glories; *śrīvāsa-ādi*—headed by Śrīvāsa; *gaura-bhakta-gaṇa*—to the devotees of Lord Caitanya; *jaya*—all glories; *śrotā-gaṇa*—to the hearers; *yāṅra*—of whom; *gaura*—Śrī Caitanya Mahāprabhu; *prāṇa-dhana*—the life and soul.

TRANSLATION

All glories to all the devotees, headed by Śrīvāsa Ṭhākura! All glories to the readers who have taken Śrī Caitanya Mahāprabhu as their life and soul.

TEXT 4

এইমত প্রভু আছেন প্রেমের আবেশে ।
হেনকালে প্রতাপরুদ্র করিল প্রবেশে ॥ ৪ ॥

ei-mata prabhu āchena premera āveśe
hena-kāle pratāparudra karila praveśe

SYNONYMS

ei-mata—in this way; *prabhu*—Lord Śrī Caitanya Mahāprabhu; *āchena*—was; *premera āveśe*—in the ecstatic emotion of love; *hena-kāle*—at this time; *pratāparudra*—King Pratāparudra; *karila praveśe*—entered.

TRANSLATION

While Śrī Caitanya Mahāprabhu was resting in ecstatic love, Mahārāja Pratāparudra entered the garden.

TEXT 5

সার্বভৌম-উপদেশে ছাড়ি' রাজবেশ ।
একলা বৈষ্ণব-বেশে করিল প্রবেশ ॥ ৫ ॥

sārvabhauma-upadeśe chāḍi' rāja-veśa
ekalā vaiṣṇava-veśe karila praveśa

SYNONYMS

sārvabhauma—of Sārvabhauma Bhaṭṭācārya; *upadeśe*—under instructions; *chāḍi'*—giving up; *rāja-veśa*—the royal dress; *ekalā*—alone; *vaiṣṇava-veśe*—in the dress of a Vaiṣṇava; *karila praveśa*—entered.

TRANSLATION

Following Sārvabhauma Bhaṭṭācārya's instructions, the King had given up his royal dress. He now entered the garden in the dress of a Vaiṣṇava.

PURPORT

Sometimes members of the International Society for Krishna Consciousness—especially in the Western countries—find it difficult to approach people to distribute books because people are unfamiliar with the traditional saffron robes of the devotees. The devotees have therefore inquired whether they can wear European and American dress before the general public. From the instructions given to King Pratāparudra by Sārvabhauma Bhaṭṭācārya, we can understand that we may change our dress in any way to facilitate our service. When our members change their dress to meet the public or to introduce our books, they are not breaking the devotional principles. The real principle is to spread this Kṛṣṇa consciousness movement, and if one has to change into regular Western dress for this purpose, there should be no objection.

TEXT 6

সব-ভক্তের আজ্ঞা নিল যোড়-হাত হঞা।
প্রভু-পদ ধরি' পড়ে সাহস করিয়া ॥ ৬ ॥

saba-bhaktera ājñā nila yoḍa-hāta hañā
prabhu-pada dhari' paḍe sāhasa kariyā

SYNONYMS

saba-bhaktera—of all the devotees; *ājñā nila*—took permission; *yoḍa-hāta hañā*—with folded hands; *prabhu-pada dhari'*—catching the feet of Śrī Caitanya Mahāprabhu; *paḍe*—falls; *sāhasa kariyā*—with great courage.

TRANSLATION

Mahārāja Pratāparudra was so humble that with folded hands he first took permission from all the devotees. Then, with great courage, he fell down and touched the lotus feet of the Lord.

TEXT 7

আঁখি মুদি' প্রভু প্রেমে ভূমিতে শয়ান।
নৃপতি নৈপুণ্যে করে পাদ-সম্বাহন ॥ ৭ ॥

āṅkhi mudi' prabhu preme bhūmite śayāna
nṛpati naipuṇye kare pāda-saṁvāhana

SYNONYMS

āṅkhi mudi'—with closed eyes; *prabhu*—Śrī Caitanya Mahāprabhu; *preme*—in ecstatic love; *bhūmite*—on the ground; *śayāna*—lying down; *nṛpati*—the King; *naipuṇye*—very expertly; *kare*—performs; *pāda-saṁvāhana*—massaging the legs.

TRANSLATION

Śrī Caitanya Mahāprabhu was lying on the ground with His eyes closed in ecstatic love and emotion, and the King very expertly began to massage His legs.

TEXT 8

রাসলীলার শ্লোক পড়ি' করেন স্তবন ।
"জয়তি তেঽধিকং" অধ্যায় করেন পঠন ॥ ৮ ॥

rāsa-līlāra śloka paḍi' karena stavana
"jayati te 'dhikaṁ" adhyāya karena paṭhana

SYNONYMS

rāsa-līlāra—of the *rāsa-līlā* dance; *śloka*—verses; *paḍi'*—reciting; *karena*—offers; *stavana*—prayers; *jayati te 'dhikam*—beginning with the words *jayati te 'dhikam; adhyāya*—chapter; *karena*—does; *paṭhana*—recitation.

TRANSLATION

The King began to recite verses about the rāsa-līlā from Śrīmad-Bhāgavatam. He recited the chapter beginning with the words "jayati te 'dhikam."

PURPORT

These verses from *Śrīmad-Bhāgavatam,* Canto Ten, Chapter Thirty-one, constitute what is known as the *Gopī-gītā.*

TEXT 9

শুনিতে শুনিতে প্রভুর সন্তোষ অপার ।
'বল, বল' বলি' প্রভু বলে বার বার ॥ ৯ ॥

śunite śunite prabhura santoṣa apāra
'bala, bala' bali' prabhu bale bāra bāra

SYNONYMS

śunite śunite—by hearing; *prabhura*—of Lord Śrī Caitanya Mahāprabhu; *santoṣa apāra*—great satisfaction; *bala bala*—go on reciting; *bali'*—saying; *prabhu*—Lord Śrī Caitanya Mahāprabhu; *bale*—says; *bāra bāra*—again and again.

TRANSLATION

When Śrī Caitanya Mahāprabhu heard these verses, He was pleased beyond limits, and He said again and again, "Go on reciting, go on reciting."

TEXT 10

"তব কথামৃতং" শ্লোক রাজা যে পড়িল ।
উঠি' প্রেমাবেশে প্রভু আলিঙ্গন কৈল ॥ ১০ ॥

"tava kathāmṛtaṁ" śloka rājā ye paḍila
uṭhi' premāveśe prabhu āliṅgana kaila

SYNONYMS

tava kathāmṛtam—beginning with the words *tava kathāmṛtam; śloka*—the verse; *rājā*—the King; *ye paḍila*—as he recited; *uṭhi'*—getting up; *prema-āveśe*—in ecstatic love; *prabhu*—Śrī Caitanya Mahāprabhu; *āliṅgana kaila*—embraced.

TRANSLATION

As soon as the King recited the verse beginning with the words "tava kathāmṛtam," the Lord immediately arose in ecstatic love and embraced him.

TEXT 11

তুমি মোরে দিলে বহু অমূল্য রতন ।
মোর কিছু দিতে নাহি, দিলুঁ আলিঙ্গন ॥ ১১ ॥

tumi more dile bahu amūlya ratana
mora kichu dite nāhi, diluṅ āliṅgana

SYNONYMS

tumi—you; *more*—unto Me; *dile*—delivered; *bahu*—various; *amūlya*—incalculable; *ratana*—gems; *mora*—of Me; *kichu*—anything; *dite*—to give; *nāhi*—there is not; *diluṅ*—I give; *āliṅgana*—embracing.

TRANSLATION

Upon hearing the verses recited by the King, Śrī Caitanya Mahāprabhu said, "You have given Me invaluable gems, but I have nothing to give you in return. Therefore I am simply embracing you."

TEXT 12

এত বলি' সেই শ্লোক পড়ে বার বার।
দুইজনার অঙ্গে কম্প, নেত্রে জলধার ॥ ১২ ॥

eta bali' sei śloka paḍe bāra bāra
dui-janāra aṅge kampa, netre jala-dhāra

SYNONYMS

eta bali'—saying this; *sei śloka*—that verse; *paḍe*—recites; *bāra bāra*—again and again; *dui-janāra*—of both of them (Śrī Caitanya Mahāprabhu and the King Pratāparudra); *aṅge*—in the bodies; *kampa*—trembling; *netre*—in the eyes; *jala-dhāra*—flow of water.

TRANSLATION

After saying this, Śrī Caitanya Mahāprabhu began to recite the same verse again and again. Both the King and Śrī Caitanya Mahāprabhu were trembling, and tears were flowing from their eyes.

TEXT 13

তব কথামৃতং তপ্তজীবনং, কবিভিরীড়িতং কল্মষাপহম্।
শ্রবণমঙ্গলং শ্রীমদাততং, ভুবি গৃণন্তি যে ভূরিদা জনাঃ ॥১৩

tava kathāmṛtaṁ tapta-jīvanaṁ
kavibhir īḍitaṁ kalmaṣāpaham
śravaṇa-maṅgalaṁ śrīmad-ātataṁ
bhuvi gṛṇanti ye bhūridā janāḥ

SYNONYMS

tava—Your; *kathā-amṛtam*—the nectar of words; *tapta-jīvanam*—life for persons very much aggrieved in the material world; *kavibhiḥ*—by greatly exalted persons; *īḍitam*—described; *kalmaṣa-apaham*—that which drives away all kinds of sinful reaction; *śravaṇa-maṅgalam*—giving all spiritual benefit to anyone who hears; *śrī-mat*—filled with all spiritual power; *ātatam*—broadcast all over the world; *bhuvi*—in the material world; *gṛṇanti*—chant and spread; *ye*—those who; *bhūri-dāḥ*—most beneficent; *janāḥ*—persons.

TRANSLATION

"My Lord, the nectar of Your words and the descriptions of Your activities are the life and soul of those who are always aggrieved in this material world.

These narrations are transmitted by exalted personalities, and they eradicate all sinful reactions. Whoever hears these narrations attains all good fortune. These narrations are broadcast all over the world and are filled with spiritual power. Those who spread the message of Godhead are certainly the most munificent welfare workers."

PURPORT

This verse is from *Śrīmad-Bhāgavatam* (10.31.9).

TEXT 14

'ভূরিদা' 'ভূরিদা' বলি' করে আলিঙ্গন।
ইঁহো নাহি জানে, ইহোঁ হয় কোন্ জন ॥ ১৪ ॥

'bhūridā' 'bhūridā' bali' kare āliṅgana
iṅho nāhi jāne, —ihoṅ haya kon jana

SYNONYMS

bhūri-dā—the most munificent; *bhūri-dā*—the most munificent; *bali'*—crying; *kare*—does; *āliṅgana*—embracing; *iṅho*—Śrī Caitanya Mahāprabhu; *nāhi jāne*—does not know; *ihoṅ*—Pratāparudra Mahārāja; *haya*—is; *kon jana*—who.

TRANSLATION

After hearing the recitation of this verse, Śrī Caitanya Mahāprabhu immediately embraced the reciter, King Pratāparudra, and cried, "You are the most munificent! You are the most munificent!" At this point Śrī Caitanya Mahāprabhu did not even know who the King was.

TEXT 15

পূর্ব-সেবা দেখি' তাঁরে কৃপা উপজিল।
অনুসন্ধান বিনা কৃপা-প্রসাদ করিল ॥ ১৫ ॥

pūrva-sevā dekhi' tāṅre kṛpā upajila
anusandhāna vinā kṛpā-prasāda karila

SYNONYMS

pūrva-sevā—previous service; *dekhi'*—seeing; *tāṅre*—unto him; *kṛpā*—mercy; *upajila*—awakened; *anusandhāna*—inquiry; *vinā*—without; *kṛpā*—of mercy; *prasāda*—grace; *karila*—bestowed.

TRANSLATION

Śrī Caitanya Mahāprabhu's mercy was aroused because of the King's previous service. Therefore without even asking who he was, the Lord immediately bestowed His mercy upon him.

TEXT 16

এই দেখ,—চৈতন্যের কৃপা-মহাবল।
তার অনুসন্ধান বিনা করায় সফল ॥ ১৬ ॥

ei dekha, —caitanyera kṛpā-mahābala
tāra anusandhāna vinā karāya saphala

SYNONYMS

ei—this; *dekha*—just see; *caitanyera*—of Śrī Caitanya Mahāprabhu; *kṛpā-mahā-bala*—how greatly powerful is the mercy; *tāra anusandhāna*—inquiring about him; *vinā*—without; *karāya*—He makes; *sa-phala*—successful.

TRANSLATION

How powerful is the mercy of Śrī Caitanya Mahāprabhu! Without even inquiring about the King, the Lord made everything successful.

PURPORT

Śrī Caitanya Mahāprabhu's mercy is so powerful that it acts automatically. If a person renders loving service to Kṛṣṇa, it never goes in vain. It is recorded in a spiritual account, and in due time it will fructify. This is confirmed by *Bhagavad-gītā* (2.40). *Svalpam apy asya dharmasya trāyate mahato bhayāt:* "In this endeavor there is no loss or diminution, and a little advancement on this path can protect one from the most dangerous type of fear."

Śrī Caitanya Mahāprabhu has particularly bestowed upon all fallen souls in this age the most potent method of devotional service, and whoever takes to it through the mercy of Śrī Caitanya Mahāprabhu is immediately elevated to the transcendental position. *Śrīmad-Bhāgavatam* recommends: *yajñaiḥ saṅkīrtana-prāyair yajanti hi su-medhasaḥ* (*Bhāg.* 11.5.32).

A student of Kṛṣṇa consciousness must receive Śrī Caitanya Mahāprabhu's mercy; then his devotional service will quickly succeed. This was the case with King Pratāparudra. One has to be noticed by Śrī Caitanya Mahāprabhu, and a little service with sincere efforts will convince the Lord that one is a proper candidate for returning home, back to Godhead. Mahārāja Pratāparudra did not have a chance to meet Śrī Caitanya Mahāprabhu, but when the Lord saw that the King was serving Lord Jagannātha as a menial sweeper, the Lord's mercy upon the King became a solid fact. When Mahārāja Pratāparudra, in the dress of a Vaiṣṇava, was serving the Lord, the Lord did not even inquire who he was. Rather, He had compassion upon him and began to embrace him.

Kṛṣṇadāsa Kavirāja Gosvāmī wants to point out that nothing could compare to the Lord's mercy toward Mahārāja Pratāparudra; therefore he uses the word *dekha* ("just see") and *caitanyera kṛpā-mahābala* ("how powerful is the mercy of Śrī Caitanya Mahāprabhu"). This is also confirmed by Prabodhānanda Sarasvatī: *yat-kāruṇya-kaṭākṣa-vaibhava-vatām* (*Caitanya-candrāmṛta,* 5). Even a little of Śrī Caitanya Mahāprabhu's mercy serves as a great asset for spiritual advancement. Therefore the Kṛṣṇa consciousness movement must be spread through the mercy of Śrī Caitanya Mahāprabhu. When Rūpa Gosvāmī experienced the mercy and magnanimity of Śrī Caitanya Mahāprabhu, he said:

namo mahā-vadānyāya
kṛṣṇa-prema-pradāya te
kṛṣṇāya kṛṣṇa-caitanya-
nāmne gaura-tviṣe namaḥ

"I offer my respectful obeisances unto the Supreme Lord Śrī Kṛṣṇa Caitanya who is more magnanimous than any other *avatāra,* even Kṛṣṇa Himself, because He is bestowing freely what no one else has ever given—pure love of Kṛṣṇa." Śrīla Locana dāsa Ṭhākura has also sung, *parama karuṇa, pahuṅ dui jana, nitāi-gaura-candra:* "The two brothers Nitāi and Gaura are so kind that no one can compare to them." Similarly, Śrīla Narottama dāsa Ṭhākura has sung:

vrajendra-nandana yei, śacī-suta haila sei,
balarāma ha-ila nitāi,
dīna-hīna yata chila, hari-nāme uddhārila,
tā'ra sākṣī jagāi-mādhāi

Śrī Caitanya Mahāprabhu's special mission is the deliverance of all fallen souls in Kali-yuga. Devotees of Kṛṣṇa must persistently seek the favor and mercy of Śrī Caitanya Mahāprabhu to become fit to return home, back to Godhead.

TEXT 17

প্রভু বলে,—কে তুমি, করিলা মোর হিত ?
আচম্বিতে আসি' পিয়াও কৃষ্ণলীলামৃত ? ১৭ ॥

prabhu bale, ——ke tumi, karilā mora hita?
ācambite āsi' piyāo kṛṣṇa-līlāmṛta?

SYNONYMS

prabhu bale—the Lord said; *ke tumi*—who are you; *karilā*—you have done; *mora*—My; *hita*—welfare; *ācambite*—all of a sudden; *āsi'*—coming; *piyāo*—you make Me drink; *kṛṣṇa-līlā-amṛta*—the nectar of the pastimes of Lord Kṛṣṇa.

TRANSLATION

Finally Śrī Caitanya Mahāprabhu said, "Who are you? You have done so much for Me. All of a sudden you have come here and made me drink the nectar of the pastimes of Lord Kṛṣṇa."

TEXT 18

রাজা কহে,—আমি তোমার দাসের অনুদাস।
ভৃত্যের ভৃত্য কর,—এই মোর আশ ॥ ১৮ ॥

rājā kahe, ——āmi tomāra dāsera anudāsa
bhṛtyera bhṛtya kara, ——ei mora āśa

SYNONYMS

rājā kahe—the King said; *āmi*—I; *tomāra*—Your; *dāsera anudāsa*—most obedient servant of Your servant; *bhṛtyera bhṛtya*—servant of the servant; *kara*—make (me); *ei*—this; *mora āśa*—my desire.

TRANSLATION

The King replied, "My Lord, I am the most obedient servant of Your servants. It is my ambition that You will accept me as the servant of Your servants."

PURPORT

The greatest achievement for a devotee is to become a servant of the servants. Actually no one should desire to become the direct servant of the Lord. That is not a very good idea. When Prahlāda Mahārāja was offered a benediction by Nṛsiṁhadeva, Prahlāda rejected all kinds of material benediction, but he prayed to become the servant of the servant of the Lord. When Dhruva Mahārāja was offered a benediction by Kuvera, the treasurer of the demigods, Dhruva could have asked for unlimited material opulence, but he simply asked for the benediction of becoming the servant of the servants of the Lord. Kholāvecā Śrīdhara was a very poor man, but when Śrī Caitanya Mahāprabhu wanted to give him a benediction, he also prayed to the Lord to be allowed to remain a servant of the servants of the Lord. The conclusion is that being the servant of the servants of the Supreme Personality of Godhead is the highest benediction one can desire.

TEXT 19

তবে মহাপ্রভু তাঁরে ঐশ্বর্য দেখাইল ।
'কারেহ না কহিবে' এই নিষেধ করিল ॥ ১৯ ॥

tabe mahāprabhu tāṅre aiśvarya dekhāila
'kāreha nā kahibe' ei niṣedha karila

SYNONYMS

tabe—at that time; *mahāprabhu*—Śrī Caitanya Mahāprabhu; *tāṅre*—to the King; *aiśvarya*—divine power; *dekhāila*—showed; *kāreha nā kahibe*—do not speak to anyone; *ei*—this; *niṣedha karila*—forbade.

TRANSLATION

At that time, Śrī Caitanya Mahāprabhu displayed some of His divine opulences to the King, and He forbade him to disclose this to anyone.

TEXT 20

'রাজা'—হেন জ্ঞান কভু না কৈল প্রকাশ ।
অন্তরে সকল জানেন, বাহিরে উদাস ॥ ২০ ॥

'rājā'——hena jñāna kabhu nā kaila prakāśa
antare sakala jānena, bāhire udāsa

SYNONYMS

rājā—the King; *hena jñāna*—such knowledge; *kabhu*—at any time; *nā*—not; *kaila prakāśa*—manifested; *antare*—within the heart; *sakala*—everything; *jānena*—knows; *bāhire*—externally; *udāsa*—indifferent.

TRANSLATION

Although within His heart Caitanya Mahāprabhu knew everything that was happening, externally He did not disclose it. Nor did He disclose that he knew He was talking with King Pratāparudra.

TEXT 21

প্রতাপরুদ্রের ভাগ্য দেখি' ভক্তগণে ।
রাজারে প্রশংসে সবে আনন্দিত-মনে ॥ ২১ ॥

pratāparudrera bhāgya dekhi' bhakta-gaṇe
rājāre praśaṁse sabe ānandita-mane

SYNONYMS

pratāparudrera—of King Pratāparudra; *bhāgya*—the fortune; *dekhi'*—seeing; *bhakta-gaṇe*—all the devotees; *rājāre*—the King; *praśaṁse*—praised; *sabe*—all; *ānandita-mane*—with blissful minds.

TRANSLATION

Seeing the Lord's special mercy upon King Pratāparudra, the devotees praised the King's fortune, and their minds became open and blissful.

PURPORT

This is a characteristic of a Vaiṣṇava. He is never envious if one receives the mercy and strength of Śrī Caitanya Mahāprabhu. A pure Vaiṣṇava is very happy to see a person elevated in devotional service. Unfortunately, there are many so-called Vaiṣṇavas who become envious to see someone actually recognized by Śrī Caitanya Mahāprabhu. It is a fact that no one can preach Caitanya Mahāprabhu's message without receiving the special mercy of the Lord. This is known to every Vaiṣṇava, yet there are some envious people who cannot tolerate the expansion of this Kṛṣṇa consciousness movement all over the world. They find fault with a pure devotee preacher and do not praise him for the excellent service he renders in fulfilling Śrī Caitanya Mahāprabhu's mission.

TEXT 22

দণ্ডবৎ করি' রাজা বাহিরে চলিলা ।
যোড় হস্ত করি' সব ভক্তেরে বন্দিলা ॥ ২২ ॥

daṇḍavat kari' rājā bāhire calilā
yoḍa hasta kari' saba bhaktere vandilā

SYNONYMS

daṇḍavat kari'—offering obeisances; *rājā*—the King; *bāhire*—outside; *calilā*—departed; *yoḍa*—folded; *hasta*—hands; *kari'*—making; *saba*—all; *bhaktere*—unto the devotees; *vandilā*—offered prayers.

TRANSLATION

Submissively offering prayers to the devotees with folded hands and offering obeisances to Śrī Caitanya Mahāprabhu, the King went outside.

TEXT 23

মধ্যাহ্ন করিলা প্রভু লঞা ভক্তগণ ।
বাণীনাথ প্রসাদ লঞা কৈল আগমন ॥ ২৩ ॥

madhyāhna karilā prabhu lañā bhakta-gaṇa
vāṇīnātha prasāda lañā kaila āgamana

SYNONYMS

madhyāhna karilā—accepted lunch; *prabhu*—Śrī Caitanya Mahāprabhu; *lañā*—accompanied by; *bhakta-gaṇa*—all the devotees; *vāṇīnātha*—Vāṇīnātha; *prasāda lañā*—taking all kinds of remnants of Jagannātha's food; *kaila*—did; *āgamana*—arrival.

TRANSLATION

After this, Vāṇīnātha Rāya brought all kinds of prasāda, and Śrī Caitanya Mahāprabhu accepted lunch with the devotees.

TEXT 24

সার্বভৌম-রামানন্দ-বাণীনাথে দিয়া ।
প্রসাদ পাঠা'ল রাজা বহুত করিয়া ॥ ২৪ ॥

sārvabhauma-rāmānanda-vāṇīnāthe diyā
prasāda pāṭhā'la rājā bahuta kariyā

SYNONYMS

sārvabhauma—Sārvabhauma Bhaṭṭācārya; *rāmānanda*—Rāmānanda Rāya; *vāṇīnāthe diyā*—through Vāṇīnātha Rāya; *prasāda*—*prasāda; pāṭhā'la*—had sent; *rājā*—the King; *bahuta kariyā*—in a large quantity.

TRANSLATION

The King also sent a large quantity of prasāda through Sārvabhauma Bhaṭṭācārya, Rāmānanda Rāya and Vāṇīnātha Rāya.

TEXT 25

'বলগণ্ডি ভোগে'র প্রসাদ—উত্তম, অনন্ত ।
'নি-সকড়ি' প্রসাদ আইল, যার নাহি অন্ত ॥ ২৫ ॥

'balagaṇḍi bhoge'ra prasāda——uttama, ananta
'ni-sakaḍi' prasāda āila, yāra nāhi anta

SYNONYMS

balagaṇḍi bhogera—of food offered at Balagaṇḍi; *prasāda*—remnants; *uttama*—all of the foremost quality; *ananta*—of all varieties; *ni-sakaḍi*—uncooked food like milk products and fruits; *prasāda*—remnants of food; *āila*—arrived; *yāra*—of which; *nāhi*—there is not; *anta*—end.

TRANSLATION

The prasāda sent by the King had been offered at the Balagaṇḍi festival and included uncooked milk products and fruits. It was all of the finest quality, and there was no end to the variety.

TEXT 26

ছানা, পানা, পৈড়, আম্র, নারিকেল, কাঁঠাল ।
নানাবিধ কদলক, আর বীজ-তাল ॥ ২৬ ॥

chānā, pānā, paiḍa, āmra, nārikela, kāṅṭhāla
nānā-vidha kadalaka, āra bīja-tāla

SYNONYMS

chānā—curd; *pānā*—fruit juice; *paiḍa*—coconut; *āmra*—mango; *nārikela*—dried coconut; *kāṅṭhāla*—jackfruit; *nānā-vidha*—various kinds of; *kadalaka*—bananas; *āra*—and; *bīja-tāla*—palm fruit seeds.

TRANSLATION

There was curd, fruit juice, coconut, mango, dried coconut, jackfruit, various kinds of bananas and palm fruit seeds.

PURPORT

This is the first list of *prasāda* offered to Lord Jagannātha.

TEXT 27

নারঙ্গ, ছোলঙ্গ, টাবা, কমলা, বীজপূর ।
বাদাম, ছোহারা, দ্রাক্ষা, পিণ্ডখর্জুর ॥ ২৭ ॥

nāraṅga, cholaṅga, ṭābā, kamalā, bīja-pūra
bādāma, chohārā, drākṣā, piṇḍa-kharjura

SYNONYMS

nāraṅga—oranges; *cholaṅga*—grapefruits; *ṭābā*—another type of orange; *kamalā*—tangerines; *bīja-pūra*—another type of tangerine; *bādāma*—almonds; *chohārā*—dried fruit; *drākṣā*—raisins; *piṇḍa-kharjura*—dates.

TRANSLATION

There were also oranges, grapefruit, tangerines, almonds, dried fruit, raisins and dates.

TEXT 28

মনোহরা-লাড়ু আদি শতেক প্রকার ।
অমৃতগুটিকা-আদি, ক্ষীরসা অপার ॥ ২৮ ॥

manoharā-lāḍu ādi śateka prakāra
amṛta-guṭikā-ādi, kṣīrasā apāra

SYNONYMS

manoharā-lāḍu—a kind of *sandeśa; ādi*—and others; *śateka prakāra*—hundreds of varieties; *amṛta-guṭikā*—round sweetmeats; *ādi*—and others; *kṣīrasā*—condensed milk; *apāra*—of various qualities.

TRANSLATION

There were hundreds of different types of sweetmeats like manoharā-lāḍu, sweets like amṛta-guṭikā and various types of condensed milk.

TEXT 29

অমৃতমণ্ডা, সরবতী, আর কুম্ড়া-কুরী ।
সরামৃত, সরভাজা, আর সরপুরী ॥ ২৯ ॥

amṛta-maṇḍā, saravatī, āra kumḍā-kurī
sarāmṛta, sarabhājā, āra sarapurī

SYNONYMS

amṛta-maṇḍā—a variety of papaya; *saravatī*—a kind of orange; *āra*—and; *kumḍā-kurī*—crushed squash; *sarāmṛta*—cream; *sara-bhājā*—fried cream; *āra*—and; *sara-purī*—a kind of *purī* made with cream.

TRANSLATION

There were also papayas and saravatī, a type of orange, and also crushed squash. There was also regular cream, fried cream and a type of purī made with cream.

TEXT 30

হরিবল্লভ, সেঁওতি, কর্পূর, মালতী।
ডালিমা মরিচ-লাড়ু, নবাত, অমৃতি ॥ ৩০ ॥

hari-vallabha, seṅoti, karpūra, mālatī
ḍālimā marica-lāḍu, navāta, amṛti

SYNONYMS

hari-vallabha—a sweetmeat like bread fried in ghee (like a doughnut); *seṅoti*—a sweetmeat made of a kind of fragrant flower; *karpūra*—a flower; *mālatī*—another flower; *ḍālimā*—pomegranate; *marica-lāḍu*—a sweetmeat made with black pepper; *navāta*—another kind of sweetmeat, made with fused sugar; *amṛti*—a preparation generally called *amṛti-jilipi,* made with rice powder and chick-pea flour, mixed with yogurt, fried in ghee and immersed in sugar water.

TRANSLATION

There were also sweets like hari-vallabha and sweets made of seṅoti flowers, karpūra flowers and mālatī flowers. There were pomegranates, sweets made with black pepper, sweets made with fused sugar, and amṛti-jilipi.

TEXT 31

পদ্মচিনি, চন্দ্রকান্তি, খাজা, খণ্ডসার।
বিয়রি, কদ্‌মা, তিলাখাজার প্রকার ॥ ৩১ ॥

padmacini, candrakānti, khājā, khaṇḍasāra
viyari, kadmā, tilākhājāra prakāra

SYNONYMS

padma-cini—sugar obtained from lotus flowers; *candra-kānti*—a kind of bread made from urad dahl; *khājā*—a crispy sweetmeat; *khaṇḍa-sāra*—sugar candy; *viyari*—a sweetmeat made from fried rice; *kadmā*—a sweetmeat made from sesame seeds; *tilākhājāra*—cookies made from sesame seeds; *prakāra*—all varieties.

TRANSLATION

There was lotus flower sugar, a kind of bread made from urad dahl, crispy sweetmeats, sugar candy, fried rice sweets, sesame seed sweets and cookies made from sesame seeds.

TEXT 32

নারঙ্গ-ছোলঙ্গ-আম্র-বৃক্ষের আকার ।
ফুল-ফল-পত্রযুক্ত খণ্ডের বিকার ॥ ৩২ ॥

nāraṅga-cholaṅga-āmra-vṛkṣera ākāra
phula-phala-patra-yukta khaṇḍera vikāra

SYNONYMS

nāraṅga-cholaṅga-āmra-vṛkṣera ākāra—sweetmeats in the shape of varieties of oranges, lemons and mangoes; *phula-phala-patra-yukta*—dressed with fruits, flowers and leaves; *khaṇḍera vikāra*—made from sugar candy.

TRANSLATION

There were sweetmeats made from sugarcane candy in the form of oranges, lemons and mangoes along with fruits, flowers and leaves.

TEXT 33

দধি, দুগ্ধ, ননী, তক্র, রসালা, শিখরিণী ।
স-লবণ মুদ্গাঙ্কুর, আদা খানি খানি ॥ ৩৩ ॥

dadhi, dugdha, nanī, takra, rasālā, śikhariṇī
sa-lavaṇa mudgāṅkura, ādā khāni khāni

SYNONYMS

dadhi—yogurt; *dugdha*—milk; *nanī*—butter; *takra*—buttermilk; *rasālā*—fruit juice; *śikhariṇī*—a preparation made of fried yogurt and sugar candy; *sa-lavaṇa*—salty; *mudga-aṅkura*—mung dahl sprouts; *ādā*—ginger; *khāni khāni*—cut into pieces.

TRANSLATION

There was yogurt, milk, butter, buttermilk, fruit juice, a preparation made of fried yogurt and sugar candy, and salty mung dahl sprouts with shredded ginger.

TEXT 34

লেম্বু-কুল-আদি নানা-প্রকার আচার ।
লিখিতে না পারি প্রসাদ কতেক প্রকার ॥ ৩৪ ॥

lembu-kula-ādi nānā-prakāra ācāra
likhite nā pāri prasāda kateka prakāra

SYNONYMS

lembu—lemon; *kula*—berries; *ādi*—and so on; *nānā-prakāra*—varieties of; *ācāra*—pickles; *likhite*—to write; *nā*—not; *pāri*—I am able; *prasāda*—food offered to Jagannātha; *kateka prakāra*—how many varieties.

TRANSLATION

There were also various types of pickles—lemon pickle, berry pickle and so on. Indeed, I am not able to describe the variety of food offered to Lord Jagannātha.

PURPORT

In verses 26-34, the author describes the various foods offered to Lord Jagannātha. He has described them as far as possible, but he finally admits his inability to describe them completely.

TEXT 35

প্রসাদে পুরিত হইল অর্ধ উপবন ।
দেখিয়া সন্তোষ হৈল মহাপ্রভুর মন ॥ ৩৫ ॥

prasāde pūrita ha-ila ardha upavana
dekhiyā santoṣa haila mahāprabhura mana

SYNONYMS

prasāde—with all the *prasāda; pūrita ha-ila*—became filled; *ardha upavana*—half of the garden; *dekhiyā*—seeing; *santoṣa*—satisfaction; *haila*—there was; *mahāprabhura mana*—in the mind of Śrī Caitanya Mahāprabhu.

TRANSLATION

When Śrī Caitanya Mahāprabhu saw half the garden filled with a variety of prasāda, He was very satisfied.

TEXT 36

এইমত জগন্নাথ করেন ভোজন ।
এই সুখে মহাপ্রভুর জুড়ায় নয়ন ॥ ৩৬ ॥

ei-mata jagannātha karena bhojana
ei sukhe mahāprabhura juḍāya nayana

SYNONYMS

ei-mata—in this way; *jagannātha*—Lord Jagannātha; *karena bhojana*—accepts His food; *ei sukhe*—in this happiness; *mahāprabhura*—of Lord Śrī Caitanya Mahāprabhu; *juḍāya*—become fully satisfied; *nayana*—the eyes.

TRANSLATION

Indeed, Śrī Caitanya Mahāprabhu was fully satisfied just to see how Lord Jagannātha accepted all the food.

PURPORT

Following in the footsteps of Śrī Caitanya Mahāprabhu, a Vaiṣṇava should be fully satisfied simply to see a variety of food offered to the Deity of Jagannātha or Rādhā-Kṛṣṇa. A Vaiṣṇava should not hunger for a variety of food for his own sake; rather, his satisfaction is in seeing various foods being offered to the Deity. In his *Gurv-aṣṭaka,* Śrīla Viśvanātha Cakravartī Ṭhākura writes:

catur-vidha-śrī-bhagavat-prasāda-
svādv-anna-tṛptān hari-bhakta-saṅghān
kṛtvaiva tṛptiṁ bhajataḥ sadaiva
vande guroḥ śrī-caraṇāravindam

"The spiritual master is always offering Kṛṣṇa four kinds of delicious food [analyzed as that which is licked, chewed, drunk and sucked]. When the spiritual master sees that the devotees are satisfied by eating *bhagavat-prasāda,* he is satisfied. I offer my respectful obeisances unto the lotus feet of such a spiritual master."

The spiritual master's duty is to engage his disciples in preparing varieties of nice food to offer the Deity. After being offered, this food is distributed as *prasāda* to the devotees. These activities satisfy the spiritual master, although he himself does not eat or require such a variety of *prasāda.* By seeing to the offering and distribution of *prasāda,* he himself is encouraged in devotional service.

TEXT 37

কেয়াপত্র-দ্রোণী আইল বোঝা পাঁচ-সাত।
এক এক জনে দশ দোনা দিল,—এত পাত ॥ ৩৭ ॥

keyā-patra-droṇī āila bojhā pāṅca-sāta
eka eka jane daśa donā dila,——eta pāta

SYNONYMS

keyā-patra-droṇī—plates made of leaves of the *ketakī* tree; *āila*—arrived; *bojhā*—in loads; *pāṅca-sāta*—five or seven; *eka eka jane*—to each and every man; *daśa donā dila*—ten such plates were given; *eta pāta*—so many dishes.

TRANSLATION

There then arrived five or seven loads of plates made of the leaves of the ketakī tree. Each man was supplied ten of these plates, and in this way the dishes were served.

TEXT 38

কীর্তনীয়ার পরিশ্রম জানি' গৌররায়।
তাঁ-সবারে খাওয়াইতে প্রভুর মন ধায়॥ ৩৮॥

kīrtanīyāra pariśrama jāni' gaurarāya
tāṅ-sabāre khāoyāite prabhura mana dhāya

SYNONYMS

kīrtanīyāra—of all the singers; *pariśrama*—labor; *jāni'*—knowing; *gaurarāya*—Śrī Caitanya Mahāprabhu; *tāṅ-sabāre*—all of them; *khāoyāite*—to fill; *prabhura*—of Śrī Caitanya Mahāprabhu; *mana dhāya*—the mind was very eager.

TRANSLATION

Śrī Caitanya Mahāprabhu understood the labor of all the kīrtana chanters; therefore He was very eager to feed them sumptuously.

TEXT 39

পাঁতি পাঁতি করি' ভক্তগণে বসাইলা।
পরিবেশন করিবারে আপনে লাগিলা॥ ৩৯॥

pāṅti pāṅti kari' bhakta-gaṇe vasāilā
pariveśana karibāre āpane lāgilā

SYNONYMS

pāṅti pāṅti kari'—in different lines; *bhakta-gaṇe*—all the devotees; *vasāilā*—made seated; *pariveśana*—distribution; *karibāre*—to do; *āpane*—personally; *lāgilā*—began.

TRANSLATION

All the devotees sat down in lines, and Śrī Caitanya Mahāprabhu personally began to distribute the prasāda.

TEXT 40

প্রভু না খাইলে, কেহ না করে ভোজন।
স্বরূপ-গোসাঞি তবে কৈল নিবেদন॥ ৪০॥

prabhu nā khāile, keha nā kare bhojana
svarupa-gosāñi tabe kaila nivedana

SYNONYMS

prabhu—Śrī Caitanya Mahāprabhu; *nā khāile*—without eating; *keha*—anyone; *nā*—not; *kare bhojana*—accepts the *prasāda; svarūpa-gosāñi*—Svarūpa Dāmodara Gosvāmī; *tabe*—at that time; *kaila nivedana*—submitted.

TRANSLATION

However, the devotees could not accept the prasāda until Caitanya Mahāprabhu took it. It was Svarūpa Gosvāmī who informed the Lord of this.

TEXT 41

আপনে বৈস, প্রভু, ভোজন করিতে।
তুমি না খাইলে, কেহ না পারে খাইতে॥ ৪১॥

āpane vaisa, prabhu, bhojana karite
tumi nā khāile, keha nā pāre khāite

SYNONYMS

āpane vaisa—You personally sit down; *prabhu*—my Lord; *bhojana karite*—to eat; *tumi nā khāile*—without Your eating; *keha*—anyone; *nā pāre*—is not able; *khāite*—to eat.

TRANSLATION

Svarūpa Dāmodara said, "My Lord, would You please sit down. No one will eat until You do."

TEXT 42

তবে মহাপ্রভু বৈসে নিজগণ লঞা।
ভোজন করাইল সবাকে আকণ্ঠ পূরিয়া॥ ৪২॥

tabe mahāprabhu vaise nija-gaṇa lañā
bhojana karāila sabāke ākaṇṭha pūriyā

SYNONYMS

tabe—at that time; *mahāprabhu*—Śrī Caitanya Mahāprabhu; *vaise*—sits; *nija-gaṇa lañā*—with His personal associates; *bhojana karāila*—fed; *sabāke*—all of them; *ākaṇṭha pūriyā*—filling to the neck.

TRANSLATION

At that time, Śrī Caitanya Mahāprabhu sat down with His personal associates and fed everyone of them very sumptuously until they were filled to the necks.

TEXT 43

ভোজন করি' বসিলা প্রভু করি' আচমন।
প্রসাদ উবরিল, খায় সহস্রেক জন ॥ ৪৩ ॥

bhojana kari' vasilā prabhu kari' ācamana
prasāda ubarila, khāya sahasreka jana

SYNONYMS

bhojana kari'—after eating; *vasilā prabhu*—the Lord sat down; *kari'*—finishing; *ācamana*—washing the mouth; *prasāda*—remnants of food; *ubarila*—there was so much excess; *khāya*—ate; *sahasreka jana*—thousands of men.

TRANSLATION

After finishing, the Lord washed His mouth and sat down. There was so much extra prasāda that it was distributed to thousands.

TEXT 44

প্রভুর আজ্ঞায় গোবিন্দ দীন-হীন জনে।
দুঃখী কাঙ্গাল আনি' করায় ভোজনে ॥ ৪৪ ॥

prabhura ājñāya govinda dīna-hīna jane
duḥkhī kāṅgāla āni' karāya bhojane

SYNONYMS

prabhura ājñāya—on the order of Śrī Caitanya Mahāprabhu; *govinda*—His personal servant; *dīna-hīna jane*—unto all poor men; *duḥkhī*—unhappy; *kāṅgāla*—beggars; *āni'*—inviting; *karāya bhojane*—fed sumptuously.

TRANSLATION

Following the orders of Śrī Caitanya Mahāprabhu, Govinda, His personal servant, called for all the poor beggars, who were unhappy due to their poverty, and fed them sumptuously.

TEXT 45

কাঙ্গালের ভোজন-রঙ্গ দেখে গৌরহরি ।
'হরিবোল' বলি' তারে উপদেশ করি ॥ ৪৫ ॥

kāṅgālera bhojana-raṅga dekhe gaurahari
'hari-bola' bali' tāre upadeśa kari

SYNONYMS

kāṅgālera—of the beggars; *bhojana-raṅga*—process of eating; *dekhe*—sees; *gaurahari*—Śrī Caitanya Mahāprabhu; *hari-bola bali'*—chanting "Hari bol"; *tāre*—them; *upadeśa kari*—instructs.

TRANSLATION

Observing the beggars eating prasāda, Śrī Caitanya Mahāprabhu chanted, "Hari bol!" and instructed them to chant the holy name.

PURPORT

In a song, Śrīla Bhaktivinoda Ṭhākura chants:

miche māyāra vaśe, yāccha bhese',
khāccha hābuḍubu, bhāi
jīva kṛṣṇa-dāsa, e viśvāsa,
ka'rle ta' āra duḥkha nāi

"Everyone is captivated by the waves of the ocean of nescience, but if everyone would immediately accept Lord Śrī Kṛṣṇa as their eternal master, there would be no chance of being carried away by the waves of illusion. Then all sufferings would stop." Kṛṣṇa conducts the material world under the three modes of material nature, and consequently there are three platforms of life—higher, middle and lower. On whatever platform one may be situated, one is tossed by the waves of material nature. Someone may be rich, someone may be middle class, and someone may be a poor beggar—it doesn't matter. As long as one is under the spell of the three modes of material nature, he must continue to experience these divisions.

Śrī Caitanya Mahāprabhu therefore advised the beggars to chant "Hari bol!" while taking *prasāda*. Chanting means accepting one's self as the eternal servant of Kṛṣṇa. This is the only solution, regardless of social position. Everyone is suffering under the spell of *māyā;* therefore the best course is to learn how to get out of the clutches of *māyā.* That is the verdict of *Bhagavad-gītā* (14.26):

māṁ ca yo 'vyabhicāreṇa
bhakti-yogena sevate
sa guṇān samatītyaitān
brahma-bhūyāya kalpate

"One who engages in full devotional service, who does not fall down in any circumstance, at once transcends the modes of material nature and thus comes to the level of Brahman."

One can overcome the spell of *māyā* and attain the transcendental platform by agreeing to engage in the devotional service of the Lord. Devotional service begins with *śravaṇaṁ kīrtanam;* therefore Śrī Caitanya Mahāprabhu advised the beggars to chant the Hare Kṛṣṇa *mahā-mantra* for elevation to the transcendental position. On the transcendental platform, there is no distinction between the rich, the middle class and the poor.

TEXT 46

'হরিবোল' বলি' কাঙ্গাল প্রেমে ভাসি' যায় ।
ঐছন অদ্ভুত লীলা করে গৌররায় ॥ ৪৬ ॥

'hari-bola' bali' kāṅgāla preme bhāsi' yāya
aichana adbhuta līlā kare gaurarāya

SYNONYMS

hari-bola bali'—by chanting "Hari bol"; *kāṅgāla*—the poor section of people; *preme*—in ecstatic love; *bhāsi' yāya*—began to float; *aichana*—such; *adbhuta*—wonderful; *līlā*—pastimes; *kare*—performs; *gaurarāya*—Śrī Caitanya Mahāprabhu.

TRANSLATION

As soon as the beggars chanted the holy name, "Hari bol," they were immediately absorbed in ecstatic love of Godhead. In this way Śrī Caitanya Mahāprabhu performed wonderful pastimes.

PURPORT

To feel the emotion of ecstatic love of God is to be on the transcendental platform. If one can keep himself in that transcendental position, he will surely return home, back to Godhead. In the spiritual world there are no higher, middle or lower classes. This is confirmed by *Īśopaniṣad, Mantra* Seven:

yasmin sarvāṇi bhūtāny
ātmaivābhūd vijānataḥ
tatra ko mohaḥ kaḥ śoka
ekatvam anupaśyataḥ

"One who always sees all living entities as spiritual sparks, in quality one with the Lord, becomes a true knower of things. What, then, can be illusion or anxiety for him?"

TEXT 47

ইহাঁ জগন্নাথের রথ-চলন-সময়।
গৌড় সব রথ টানে, আগে নাহি যায়॥ ৪৭॥

ihāṅ jagannāthera ratha-calana-samaya
gauḍa saba ratha ṭāne, āge nāhi yāya

SYNONYMS

ihāṅ—outside the garden; *jagannāthera*—of Lord Jagannātha; *ratha-calana-samaya*—at the time of drawing the car; *gauḍa*—the workers named *gauḍas* who draw the car; *saba*—all; *ratha ṭāne*—pull the car; *āge*—forward; *nāhi yāya*—it does not go.

TRANSLATION

Outside the garden, when it was time to pull Jagannātha's car, all the workers called gauḍas tried to pull it, but it would not move forward.

TEXT 48

টানিতে না পারে গৌড়, রথ ছাড়ি' দিল।
পাত্র-মিত্র লঞা রাজা ব্যগ্র হঞা আইল॥ ৪৮॥

ṭānite nā pāre gauḍa, ratha chāḍi' dila
pātra-mitra lañā rājā vyagra hañā āila

SYNONYMS

ṭānite nā pāre—they could not pull; *gauḍa*—the *gauḍas; ratha chāḍi' dila*—gave up the attempt; *pātra-mitra*—all the officers and friends; *lañā*—taking with him; *rājā*—the King; *vyagra*—in great anxiety; *hañā*—being; *āila*—arrived.

TRANSLATION

When the gauḍas saw that they could not budge the car, they abandoned the attempt. Then the King arrived in great anxiety, and he was accompanied by his officers and friends.

TEXT 49

মহামল্লগণে দিল রথ চালাইতে।
আপনে লাগিলা রথ, না পারে টানিতে ॥ ৪৯ ॥

mahā-malla-gaṇe dila ratha cālāite
āpane lāgilā ratha, nā pāre ṭānite

SYNONYMS

mahā-malla-gaṇe—unto the big wrestlers; *dila*—gave; *ratha*—the car; *cālāite*—to pull out; *āpane*—personally; *lāgilā*—engaged; *ratha*—the car; *nā pāre ṭānite*—could not move.

TRANSLATION

The King then arranged for big wrestlers to try to pull the car, and even the King himself joined in, but the car could not be moved.

TEXT 50

ব্যগ্র হঞা আনে রাজা মত্ত-হাতীগণ।
রথ চালাইতে রথে করিল যোজন ॥ ৫০ ॥

vyagra hañā āne rājā matta-hātī-gaṇa
ratha cālāite rathe karila yojana

SYNONYMS

vyagra hañā—with eagerness; *āne*—brings; *rājā*—the King; *matta-hātī-gaṇa*—very strong elephants; *ratha cālāite*—to make the car move; *rathe*—to the car; *karila yojana*—harnessed.

TRANSLATION

Becoming even more eager to move the car, the King had very strong elephants brought forth and harnessed to it.

TEXT 51

মত্ত-হস্তিগণ টানে যার যত বল।
এক পদ না চলে রথ, হইল অচল ॥ ৫১ ॥

matta-hasti-gaṇa ṭāne yāra yata bala
eka pada nā cale ratha, ha-ila acala

SYNONYMS

matta-hasti-gaṇa—the strong elephants; *ṭāne*—started pulling; *yāra yata bala*—with whatever strength they had; *eka pada*—a single step; *nā cale*—does not move; *ratha*—the car; *ha-ila*—was; *acala*—still.

TRANSLATION

The strong elephants pulled with all their strength, but still the car remained at a standstill, not budging an inch.

TEXT 52

শুনি' মহাপ্রভু আইলা নিজগণ লঞা ।
মত্তহস্তী রথ টানে,—দেখে দাণ্ডাঞা ॥ ৫২ ॥

śuni' mahāprabhu āilā nija-gaṇa lañā
matta-hastī ratha ṭāne,——dekhe dāṇḍāñā

SYNONYMS

śuni'—after hearing; *mahāprabhu*—Śrī Caitanya Mahāprabhu; *āilā*—came; *nija-gaṇa lañā*—with His personal devotees; *matta-hastī*—strong elephants; *ratha ṭāne*—trying to pull the car; *dekhe*—He saw; *dāṇḍāñā*—standing there.

TRANSLATION

As soon as Śrī Caitanya Mahāprabhu heard this news, He went there with all His personal associates. They then stood there and watched the elephants try to pull the car.

TEXT 53

অঙ্কুশের ঘায় হস্তী করয়ে চিৎকার ।
রথ নাহি চলে, লোকে করে হাহাকার ॥ ৫৩ ॥

aṅkuśera ghāya hastī karaye citkāra
ratha nāhi cale, loke kare hāhākāra

SYNONYMS

aṅkuśera—of the elephant-goad; *ghāya*—by striking; *hastī*—the elephants; *karaye*—made; *citkāra*—crying; *ratha*—the car; *nāhi cale*—does not move; *loke*—all the people; *kare*—exclaim; *hāhā-kāra*—alas.

TRANSLATION

The elephants, being beaten by the elephant-goad, were crying, but still the car would not move. The assembled people cried out, "Alas!"

TEXT 54

তবে মহাপ্রভু সব হস্তী ঘুচাইল ।
নিজগণে রথ-কাছি টানিবারে দিল ॥ ৫৪ ॥

tabe mahāprabhu saba hastī ghucāila
nija-gaṇe ratha-kāchi ṭānibāre dila

SYNONYMS

tabe—at that time; *mahāprabhu*—Śrī Caitanya Mahāprabhu; *saba*—all; *hastī*—the elephants; *ghucāila*—let free; *nija-gaṇe*—to His own men; *ratha-kāchi*—the rope of the car; *ṭānibāre dila*—gave to pull.

TRANSLATION

At that time, Śrī Caitanya Mahāprabhu let all the elephants go free and placed the car's ropes in the hands of His own men.

TEXT 55

আপনে রথের পাছে ঠেলে মাথা দিয়া ।
হড়্ হড়্ করি, রথ চলিল ধাইয়া ॥ ৫৫ ॥

āpane rathera pāche ṭhele māthā diyā
haḍ haḍ kari, ratha calila dhāiyā

SYNONYMS

āpane—personally; *rathera pāche*—at the back of the car; *ṭhele*—pushes; *māthā diyā*—with His head; *haḍ haḍ kari*—making a rattling sound; *ratha*—the car; *calila*—began to move; *dhāiyā*—running.

TRANSLATION

Śrī Caitanya Mahāprabhu then went to the back of the car and began to push with His head. It was then that the car began to move and ramble along, making a rattling sound.

TEXT 56

ভক্তগণ কাছি হাতে করি' মাত্র ধায়।
আপনে চলিল রথ, টানিতে না পায় ॥ ৫৬ ॥

bhakta-gaṇa kāchi hāte kari' mātra dhāya
āpane calila ratha, ṭānite nā pāya

SYNONYMS

bhakta-gaṇa—all the devotees; *kāchi*—the rope; *hāte*—in the hand; *kari'*—taking; *mātra*—only; *dhāya*—run; *āpane*—automatically; *calila*—moved; *ratha*—the car; *ṭānite*—to pull; *nā pāya*—they had no chance.

TRANSLATION

Indeed, the car began to move automatically, and the devotees simply carried the rope in their hands. Since it was moving effortlessly, they did not need to pull it.

TEXT 57

আনন্দে করয়ে লোক 'জয়' 'জয়'-ধ্বনি।
'জয় জগন্নাথ' বই আর নাহি শুনি ॥ ৫৭ ॥

ānande karaye loka 'jaya' 'jaya'-dhvani
'jaya jagannātha' ba-i āra nāhi śuni

SYNONYMS

ānande—in great pleasure; *karaye*—do; *loka*—all the people; *jaya jaya-dhvani*—the sound of "all glories, all glories"; *jaya jagannātha*—all glories to Lord Jagannātha; *ba-i*—except for this; *āra nāhi śuni*—no one could hear anything else.

TRANSLATION

When the car moved forward, everyone began to chant with great pleasure, "All glories! All glories!" and "All glories to Lord Jagannātha!" No one could hear anything else.

TEXT 58

নিমেষে ত' গেল রথ গুণ্ডিচার দ্বার।
চৈতন্য-প্রতাপ দেখি' লোকে চমৎকার ॥ ৫৮ ॥

nimeṣe ta' gela ratha guṇḍicāra dvāra
caitanya-pratāpa dekhi' loke camatkāra

SYNONYMS

nimeṣe—in a moment; *ta'*—indeed; *gela*—arrived; *ratha*—the car; *guṇḍicāra dvāra*—at the door of the Guṇḍicā temple; *caitanya-pratāpa*—the strength of Śrī Caitanya Mahāprabhu; *dekhi'*—seeing; *loke*—all the people; *camatkāra*—astonished.

TRANSLATION

In a moment the car reached the door of the Guṇḍicā temple. Upon seeing the uncommon strength of Śrī Caitanya Mahāprabhu, all the people were struck with wonder.

TEXT 59

'জয় গৌরচন্দ্র', 'জয় শ্রীকৃষ্ণচৈতন্য' ।
এইমত কোলাহল লোকে ধন্য ধন্য ॥ ৫৯ ॥

'jaya gauracandra', 'jaya śrī-kṛṣṇa-caitanya'
ei-mata kolāhala loke dhanya dhanya

SYNONYMS

jaya gauracandra—all glories to Gaurahari; *jaya śrī-kṛṣṇa-caitanya*—all glories to Lord Śrī Kṛṣṇa Caitanya Mahāprabhu; *ei-mata*—in this way; *kolāhala*—a tumultuous sound; *loke*—people in general; *dhanya dhanya*—began to chant, "Wonderful, wonderful!"

TRANSLATION

The crowd made a tumultuous vibration, chanting, "Jaya Gauracandra! Jaya Śrī Kṛṣṇa Caitanya!" Then the people began to chant, "Wonderful! Wonderful!"

TEXT 60

দেখিয়া প্রতাপরুদ্র পাত্র-মিত্র-সঙ্গে ।
প্রভুর মহিমা দেখি' প্রেমে ফুলে অঙ্গে ॥ ৬০ ॥

dekhiyā pratāparudra pātra-mitra-saṅge
prabhura mahimā dekhi' preme phule aṅge

SYNONYMS

dekhiyā—seeing; *pratāparudra*—King Pratāparudra; *pātra-mitra-saṅge*—with his ministers and friends; *prabhura*—of Śrī Caitanya Mahāprabhu; *mahimā*—the greatness; *dekhi'*—by seeing; *preme*—in love; *phule*—eruptions; *aṅge*—on the body.

TRANSLATION

Seeing the greatness of Śrī Caitanya Mahāprabhu, Pratāparudra Mahārāja and his ministers and friends were so moved by ecstatic love that their hair stood on end.

TEXT 61

পাণ্ডুবিজয় তবে করে সেবকগণে ।
জগন্নাথ বসিলা গিয়া নিজ-সিংহাসনে ॥ ৬১ ॥

pāṇḍu-vijaya tabe kare sevaka-gaṇe
jagannātha vasilā giyā nija-siṁhāsane

SYNONYMS

pāṇḍu-vijaya—the getting down from the car; *tabe*—at that time; *kare*—do; *sevaka-gaṇe*—all the servants; *jagannātha*—Lord Jagannātha; *vasilā*—sat; *giyā*—going; *nija-siṁhāsane*—on His own throne.

TRANSLATION

All the servants of Lord Jagannātha then took Him down from the car, and the Lord went to sit on His throne.

TEXT 62

সুভদ্রা-বলরাম নিজ-সিংহাসনে আইলা ।
জগন্নাথের স্নানভোগ হইতে লাগিলা ॥ ৬২ ॥

subhadrā-balarāma nija-siṁhāsane āilā
jagannāthera snāna-bhoga ha-ite lāgilā

SYNONYMS

subhadrā-balarāma—Subhadrā and Balarāma; *nija*—own; *siṁhāsane*—on thrones; *āilā*—arrived; *jagannāthera*—of Lord Jagannātha; *snāna-bhoga*—bathing and offering food; *ha-ite lāgilā*—began to take place.

TRANSLATION

Subhadrā and Balarāma also sat on their respective thrones. There followed the bathing of Lord Jagannātha and finally the offering of food.

TEXT 63

আঙ্গিনাতে মহাপ্রভু লঞা ভক্তগণ ।
আনন্দে আরম্ভ কৈল নর্তন-কীর্তন ॥ ৬৩ ॥

āṅgināte mahāprabhu lañā bhakta-gaṇa
ānande ārambha kaila nartana-kīrtana

SYNONYMS

āṅgināte—in the yard of the temple; *mahāprabhu*—Śrī Caitanya Mahāprabhu; *lañā bhakta-gaṇa*—with His devotees; *ānande*—in great pleasure; *ārambha kaila*—began; *nartana-kīrtana*—chanting and dancing.

TRANSLATION

While Lord Jagannātha, Lord Balarāma and Subhadrā sat on their respective thrones, Śrī Caitanya Mahāprabhu and His devotees began to perform saṅkīrtana with great pleasure, chanting and dancing in the yard of the temple.

TEXT 64

আনন্দে মহাপ্রভুর প্রেম উথলিল ।
দেখি' সব লোক প্রেম-সাগরে ভাসিল ॥ ৬৪ ॥

ānande mahāprabhura prema uthalila
dekhi' saba loka prema-sāgare bhāsila

SYNONYMS

ānande—in great ecstasy; *mahāprabhura*—of Śrī Caitanya Mahāprabhu; *prema*—love; *uthalila*—flooded; *dekhi'*—seeing; *saba loka*—all people; *prema-sāgare*—in the ocean of love of Godhead; *bhāsila*—were flooded.

TRANSLATION

While Śrī Caitanya Mahāprabhu was chanting and dancing, He was overwhelmed with ecstatic love, and all the people who saw Him were also flooded in the ocean of love of Godhead.

TEXT 65

নৃত্য করি' সন্ধ্যাকালে আরতি দেখিল ।
আইটোটা আসি' প্রভু বিশ্রাম করিল ॥ ৬৫ ॥

nṛtya kari' sandhyā-kāle ārati dekhila
āiṭoṭā āsi' prabhu viśrāma karila

SYNONYMS

nṛtya kari'—after dancing; *sandhyā-kāle*—in the evening; *ārati dekhila*—observed the *ārati* ceremony; *āiṭoṭā āsi'*—coming to the place known as Āiṭoṭā; *prabhu*—Śrī Caitanya Mahāprabhu; *viśrāma karila*—took rest for the night.

TRANSLATION

In the evening, after finishing His dancing in the yard of the Guṇḍicā temple, the Lord observed the ārati ceremony. Thereafter He went to a place called Āiṭoṭā and took rest for the night.

TEXT 66

অদ্বৈতাদি ভক্তগণ নিমন্ত্রণ কৈল ।
মুখ্য মুখ্য নব জন নব দিন পাইল ॥ ৬৬ ॥

advaitādi bhakta-gaṇa nimantraṇa kaila
mukhya mukhya nava jana nava dina pāila

SYNONYMS

advaita-ādi—headed by Advaita Ācārya; *bhakta-gaṇa*—the devotees; *nimantraṇa kaila*—invited Lord Caitanya Mahāprabhu; *mukhya mukhya*—chief and important; *nava jana*—nine persons; *nava dina*—nine days; *pāila*—got.

TRANSLATION

For nine days, nine chief devotees, headed by Advaita Ācārya, got an opportunity to invite the Lord to their homes.

TEXT 67

আর ভক্তগণ চাতুর্মাস্যে যত দিন ।
এক এক দিন করি' করিল বণ্টন ॥ ৬৭ ॥

āra bhakta-gaṇa cāturmāsye yata dina
eka eka dina kari' karila baṇṭana

SYNONYMS

āra bhakta-gaṇa—the remaining devotees; *cāturmāsye*—in the four months of the rainy season; *yata dina*—all the days; *eka eka dina kari'*—one day each; *karila banṭana*—shared.

TRANSLATION

During the four months of the rainy season, the remaining devotees extended invitations to the Lord for one day each. In this way they shared invitations.

TEXT 68

চারি মাসের দিন মুখ্যভক্ত বাঁটি' নিল ।
আর ভক্তগণ অবসর না পাইল ॥ ৬৮ ॥

cāri māsera dina mukhya-bhakta bāṅṭi' nila
āra bhakta-gaṇa avasara nā pāila

SYNONYMS

cāri māsera dina—the days of four months; *mukhya-bhakta*—the chief devotees; *bāṅṭi' nila*—shared among themselves; *āra bhakta-gaṇa*—other devotees; *avasara*—opportunity; *nā pāila*—did not get.

TRANSLATION

For the four-month period, all the daily invitations were shared among the important devotees. The rest of the devotees did not get an opportunity to extend an invitation to the Lord.

TEXT 69

এক দিন নিমন্ত্রণ করে দুই-তিনে মিলি' ।
এইমত মহাপ্রভুর নিমন্ত্রণ-কেলি ॥ ৬৯ ॥

eka dina nimantraṇa kare dui-tine mili'
ei-mata mahāprabhura nimantraṇa-keli

SYNONYMS

eka dina—one day; *nimantraṇa*—invitation; *kare*—make; *dui-tine*—two or three persons; *mili'*—combining; *ei-mata*—in this way; *mahāprabhura*—of Śrī Caitanya Mahāprabhu; *nimantraṇa*—invitation; *keli*—pastimes.

TRANSLATION

Since they could not get one day each, two or three devotees combined to extend an invitation. These are the pastimes of Lord Śrī Caitanya Mahāprabhu's acceptance of invitations.

TEXT 70

প্রাতঃকালে স্নান করি' দেখি' জগন্নাথ ।
সংকীর্তনে নৃত্য করে ভক্তগণ সাথ ॥ ৭০ ॥

prātaḥ-kāle snāna kari' dekhi' jagannātha
saṅkīrtane nṛtya kare bhakta-gaṇa sātha

SYNONYMS

prātaḥ-kāle—in the morning; *snāna kari'*—taking a bath; *dekhi'*—after seeing; *jagannātha*—Lord Jagannātha; *saṅkīrtane*—in the performance of *saṅkīrtana; nṛtya kare*—dances; *bhakta-gaṇa sātha*—with the devotees.

TRANSLATION

After taking His bath early in the morning, Śrī Caitanya Mahāprabhu would go see Lord Jagannātha in the temple. Then He would perform saṅkīrtana with His devotees.

TEXT 71

কভু অদ্বৈতে নাচায়, কভু নিত্যানন্দে ।
কভু হরিদাসে নাচায়, কভু অচ্যুতানন্দে ॥ ৭১ ॥

kabhu advaite nācāya, kabhu nityānande
kabhu haridāse nācāya, kabhu acyutānande

SYNONYMS

kabhu—sometimes; *advaite*—Advaita Ācārya; *nācāya*—made dance; *kabhu nityānande*—sometimes Nityānanda Prabhu; *kabhu haridāse nācāya*—sometimes made Haridāsa Ṭhākura dance; *kabhu*—sometimes; *acyutānande*—Acyutānanda.

TRANSLATION

By chanting and dancing, Śrī Caitanya Mahāprabhu induced Advaita Ācārya to dance. Sometimes He induced Nityānanda, Haridāsa Ṭhākura and Acyutānanda to dance.

TEXT 72

**কভু বক্রেশ্বরে, কভু আর ভক্তগণে ।
ত্রিসন্ধ্যা কীর্তন করে গুণ্ডিচা-প্রাঙ্গণে ॥ ৭২ ॥**

kabhu vakreśvare, kabhu āra bhakta-gaṇe
trisandhyā kīrtana kare guṇḍicā-prāṅgaṇe

SYNONYMS

kabhu vakreśvare—sometimes Vakreśvara Paṇḍita; *kabhu*—sometimes; *āra bhakta-gaṇe*—other devotees; *tri-sandhyā*—three times (morning, evening and noon); *kīrtana kare*—performs *kīrtana; guṇḍicā-prāṅgaṇe*—in the yard of the Guṇḍicā temple.

TRANSLATION

Sometimes Śrī Caitanya Mahāprabhu engaged Vakreśvara and other devotees in chanting and dancing. Three times daily—morning, noon and evening—He would perform saṅkīrtana in the yard of the Guṇḍicā temple.

TEXT 73

**বৃন্দাবনে আইলা কৃষ্ণ—এই প্রভুর জ্ঞান ।
কৃষ্ণের বিরহ-স্ফূর্তি হৈল অবসান ॥ ৭৩ ॥**

vṛndāvane āilā kṛṣṇa——ei prabhura jñāna
kṛṣṇera viraha-sphūrti haila avasāna

SYNONYMS

vṛndāvane—at Vṛndāvana; *āilā kṛṣṇa*—Kṛṣṇa arrived; *ei prabhura jñāna*—this is consciousness of Lord Śrī Caitanya Mahāprabhu; *kṛṣṇera*—from Lord Kṛṣṇa; *viraha-sphūrti*—feelings of separation; *haila avasāna*—ended.

TRANSLATION

At this time Śrī Caitanya Mahāprabhu felt that Lord Kṛṣṇa had returned to Vṛndāvana. Thinking this, His feelings of separation from Kṛṣṇa subsided.

TEXT 74

**রাধা-সঙ্গে কৃষ্ণ-লীলা- এই হৈল জ্ঞানে ।
এই রসে মগ্ন প্রভু হইলা আপনে ॥ ৭৪ ॥**

rādhā-saṅge kṛṣṇa-līlā——ei haila jñāne
ei rase magna prabhu ha-ilā āpane

SYNONYMS

rādhā-saṅge—with Rādhārāṇī; *kṛṣṇa-līlā*—pastimes of Lord Kṛṣṇa; *ei haila jñāne*—this was His consciousness; *ei rase magna*—merged in this mellow; *prabhu*—Lord Caitanya Mahāprabhu; *ha-ilā āpane*—remained personally.

TRANSLATION

Śrī Caitanya Mahāprabhu was always thinking of the pastimes of Rādhā and Kṛṣṇa, and He remained personally merged in this consciousness.

TEXT 75

নানোদ্যানে ভক্তসঙ্গে বৃন্দাবন-লীলা ।
'ইন্দ্রদ্যুম্ন'-সরোবরে করে জলখেলা ॥ ৭৫ ॥

nānodyāne bhakta-saṅge vṛndāvana-līlā
'indradyumna'-sarovare kare jala-khelā

SYNONYMS

nānā-udyāne—in various gardens; *bhakta-saṅge*—with the devotees; *vṛndāvana-līlā*—pastimes of Vṛndāvana; *indradyumna*—Indradyumna; *sarovare*—in the lake; *kare jala-khelā*—performed sports in the water.

TRANSLATION

There were many gardens near the Guṇḍicā temple, and Śrī Caitanya Mahāprabhu and His devotees used to perform the pastimes of Vṛndāvana in each of them. In the lake named Indradyumna, He sported in the water.

TEXT 76

আপনে সকল ভক্তে সিঞ্চে জল দিয়া ।
সব ভক্তগণ সিঞ্চে চৌদিকে বেড়িয়া ॥ ৭৬ ॥

āpane sakala bhakte siñce jala diyā
saba bhakta-gaṇa siñce caudike beḍiyā

SYNONYMS

āpane—personally; *sakala bhakte*—all the devotees; *siñce*—sprinkles; *jala diyā*—with water; *saba bhakta-gaṇa*—all the devotees; *siñce*—sprinkle; *cau-dike beḍiyā*—surrounding the Lord on all sides.

TRANSLATION

The Lord personally splashed all the devotees with water, and the devotees, surrounding Him on all sides, also splashed the Lord.

TEXT 77

কভু এক মণ্ডল, কভু অনেক মণ্ডল ।
জলমণ্ডূক-বাদ্যে সবে বাজায় করতাল ॥ ৭৭ ॥

kabhu eka maṇḍala, kabhu aneka maṇḍala
jala-maṇḍūka-vādye sabe bājāya karatāla

SYNONYMS

kabhu eka maṇḍala—sometimes one circle; *kabhu*—sometimes; *aneka maṇḍala*—various circles; *jala-maṇḍūka-vādye*—like the croaking sound of frogs in the water; *sabe*—all of them; *bājāya*—play; *karatāla*—cymbals.

TRANSLATION

While in the water they sometimes formed a circle and sometimes many circles, and while in the water they used to play cymbals and imitate the croaking of frogs.

TEXT 78

দুই-দুই জনে মেলি' করে জল-রণ ।
কেহ হারে, কেহ জিনে—প্রভু করে দরশন ॥ ৭৮ ॥

dui-dui jane meli' kare jala-raṇa
keha hāre, keha jine——prabhu kare daraśana

SYNONYMS

dui-dui jane—forming a party of two men; *meli'*—joining; *kare*—do; *jala-raṇa*—fighting in the water; *keha hāre*—someone is defeated; *keha jine*—someone is victorious; *prabhu*—Śrī Caitanya Mahāprabhu; *kare daraśana*—sees.

TRANSLATION

Sometimes two would pair off to fight in the water. One would emerge victorious and the other defeated, and the Lord would watch all this fun.

TEXT 79

অদ্বৈত-নিত্যানন্দে জল-ফেলাফেলি ।
আচার্য হারিয়া পাছে করে গালাগালি ॥ ৭৯ ॥

advaita-nityānande jala-phelāpheli
ācārya hāriyā pāche kare gālāgāli

SYNONYMS

advaita-nityānande—both Advaita Ācārya and Nityānanda Prabhu; *jala-phelāpheli*—throwing water on each other; *ācārya hāriyā*—Advaita Ācārya, after being defeated; *pāche*—at the end; *kare*—does; *gālāgāli*—accusing.

TRANSLATION

The first sporting took place between Advaita Ācārya and Nityānanda Prabhu, who threw water upon one another. Advaita Ācārya was defeated, and He later began to rebuke Nityānanda Prabhu, calling Him bad names.

TEXT 80

বিদ্যানিধির জলকেলি স্বরূপের সনে ।
গুপ্ত-দত্তে জলকেলি করে দুই জনে ॥ ৮০ ॥

vidyānidhira jala-keli svarūpera sane
gupta-datte jala-keli kare dui jane

SYNONYMS

vidyānidhira—of Vidyānidhi; *jala-keli*—water sports; *svarūpera sane*—with Svarūpa Dāmodara; *gupta-datte*—both Murāri Gupta and Vāsudeva Datta; *jala-keli*—water sports; *kare*—do; *dui jane*—two persons.

TRANSLATION

Svarūpa Dāmodara and Vidyānidhi also threw water upon one another, and Murāri Gupta and Vāsudeva Datta also sported in that way.

TEXT 81

শ্রীবাস-সহিত জল খেলে গদাধর ।
রাঘব-পণ্ডিত সনে খেলে বক্রেশ্বর ॥ ৮১ ॥

śrīvāsa-sahita jala khele gadādhara
rāghava-paṇḍita sane khele vakreśvara

SYNONYMS

śrīvāsa-sahita—with Śrīvāsa Ṭhākura; *jala khele*—performs this water sport; *gadādhara*—Gadādhara Paṇḍita; *rāghava-paṇḍita sane*—with Rāghava Paṇḍita; *khele*—sports; *vakreśvara*—Vakreśvara Paṇḍita.

TRANSLATION

Another duel took place between Śrīvāsa Ṭhākura and Gadādhara Paṇḍita, and yet another between Rāghava Paṇḍita and Vakreśvara Paṇḍita. Thus they all engaged in throwing water.

TEXT 82

সার্বভৌম-সঙ্গে খেলে রামানন্দ-রায় ।
গাম্ভীর্য গেল দোঁহার, হৈল শিশুপ্রায় ॥ ৮২ ॥

sārvabhauma-saṅge khele rāmānanda-rāya
gāmbhīrya gela doṅhāra, haila śiśu-prāya

SYNONYMS

sārvabhauma-saṅge—with Sārvabhauma Bhaṭṭācārya; *khele*—sports; *rāmānanda-rāya*—Śrī Rāmānanda Rāya; *gāmbhīrya*—gravity; *gela*—disappeared; *doṅhāra*—of both of them; *haila*—became; *śiśu-prāya*—like children.

TRANSLATION

Indeed, Sārvabhauma Bhaṭṭācārya engaged in water sports with Śrī Rāmānanda Rāya, and they both lost their gravity and became like children.

TEXT 83

মহাপ্রভু তাঁ দোঁহার চাঞ্চল্য দেখিয়া ।
গোপীনাথাচার্যে কিছু কহেন হাসিয়া ॥ ৮৩ ॥

mahāprabhu tāṅ doṅhāra cāñcalya dekhiyā
gopīnāthācārye kichu kahena hāsiyā

SYNONYMS

mahāprabhu—Śrī Caitanya Mahāprabhu; *tāṅ doṅhāra*—of these two persons; *cāñcalya*—restlessness; *dekhiyā*—seeing; *gopīnātha-ācārye*—unto Gopīnātha Ācārya; *kichu*—something; *kahena*—says; *hāsiyā*—smiling.

TRANSLATION

When Śrī Caitanya Mahāprabhu saw the exuberance of Sārvabhauma Bhaṭṭācārya and Rāmānanda Rāya, He smiled and spoke to Gopīnātha Ācārya.

TEXT 84

পণ্ডিত, গম্ভীর, দুঁহে—প্রামাণিক জন।
বাল-চাঞ্চল্য করে, করাহ বর্জন ॥ ৮৪ ॥

paṇḍita, gambhīra, duṅhe——prāmāṇika jana
bāla-cāñcalya kare, karāha varjana

SYNONYMS

paṇḍita—learned scholars; *gambhīra*—very grave; *duṅhe*—both of them; *prāmāṇika jana*—authoritative persons; *bāla-cāñcalya kare*—sport like children; *karāha varjana*—ask them to stop.

TRANSLATION

"Tell Bhaṭṭācārya and Rāmānanda Rāya to stop their childish play because they are both learned scholars and very grave and great personalities."

TEXT 85

গোপীনাথ কহে,—তোমার কৃপা-মহাসিন্ধু।
উছলিত করে যবে তার এক বিন্দু ॥ ৮৫ ॥

gopīnātha kahe,——tomāra kṛpā-mahāsindhu
uchalita kare yabe tāra eka bindu

SYNONYMS

gopīnātha kahe—Gopīnātha Ācārya replied; *tomāra kṛpā*—of Your mercy; *mahā-sindhu*—the great ocean; *uchalita kare*—rises; *yabe*—when; *tāra*—of that; *eka bindu*—a drop.

TRANSLATION

Gopīnātha Ācārya replied, "I believe that one drop of the ocean of Your great mercy has swelled up upon them.

TEXT 86

মেরু-মন্দর-পর্বত ডুবায় যথা তথা।
এই দুই—গণ্ড-শৈল, ইহার কা কথা ॥ ৮৬ ॥

meru-mandara-parvata ḍubāya yathā tathā
ei dui——gaṇḍa-śaila, ihāra kā kathā

SYNONYMS

meru-mandara—Sumeru and Mandara; *parvata*—big mountains; *ḍubāya*—drowns; *yathā tathā*—anywhere; *ei dui*—these two; *gaṇḍa-śaila*—very small hills; *ihāra kā kathā*—what to speak of these.

TRANSLATION

"A drop from the ocean of Your mercy can drown great mountains like Sumeru and Mandara. Since these two gentlemen are little hills by comparison, there is no wonder that they are being drowned in the ocean of Your mercy.

TEXT 87

শুষ্কতর্ক-খলি খাইতে জন্ম গেল যাঁর ।
তাঁরে লীলামৃত পিয়াও,—এ কৃপা তোমার ॥ ৮৭ ॥

śuṣka-tarka-khali khāite janma gela yāṅra
tāṅre līlāmṛta piyāo,——e kṛpā tomāra

SYNONYMS

śuṣka-tarka—of dry logic; *khali*—oil cakes; *khāite*—eating; *janma*—the whole life; *gela*—passed; *yāṅra*—of whom; *tāṅre*—him; *līlā-amṛta*—the nectar of Your pastimes; *piyāo*—You caused to drink; *e*—this; *kṛpā*—mercy; *tomāra*—Your.

TRANSLATION

"Logic is like a dry oil cake from which all the oil has been extracted. Bhaṭṭācārya passed his life in eating such dry cakes, but now You have made him drink the nectar of transcendental pastimes. It is certainly Your great mercy upon him."

TEXT 88

হাসি' মহাপ্রভু তবে অদ্বৈতে আনিল ।
জলের উপরে তাঁরে শেষ-শয্যা কৈল ॥ ৮৮ ॥

hāsi' mahāprabhu tabe advaite ānila
jalera upare tāṅre śeṣa-śayyā kaila

SYNONYMS

hāsi'—smiling; *mahāprabhu*—Śrī Caitanya Mahāprabhu; *tabe*—at that time; *advaite ānila*—called for Advaita Ācārya; *jalera upare*—on the surface of the water; *tāṅre*—Him; *śeṣa-śayyā*—the Śeṣa Nāga bed; *kaila*—made.

TRANSLATION

After Gopīnātha Ācārya finished talking, Śrī Caitanya Mahāprabhu smiled and, calling for Advaita Ācārya, made Him act like the Śeṣa Nāga bed.

TEXT 89

আপনে তাঁহার উপর করিল শয়ন ।
'শেষশায়ী-লীলা' প্রভু কৈল প্রকটন ॥ ৮৯ ॥

āpane tāṅhāra upara karila śayana
'śeṣa-śāyī-līlā' prabhu kaila prakaṭana

SYNONYMS

āpane—personally; *tāṅhāra upara*—upon Advaita Ācārya; *karila śayana*—lay down; *śeṣa-śāyī-līlā*—the pastimes of Śeṣaśāyī Viṣṇu; *prabhu*—Śrī Caitanya Mahāprabhu; *kaila prakaṭana*—demonstrated.

TRANSLATION

Lying down on Advaita Prabhu, who was floating on the water, Śrī Caitanya Mahāprabhu demonstrated the pastime of Śeṣaśāyī Viṣṇu.

TEXT 90

অদ্বৈত নিজ-শক্তি প্রকট করিয়া ।
মহাপ্রভু লঞা বুলে জলেতে ভাসিয়া ॥ ৯০ ॥

advaita nija-śakti prakaṭa kariyā
mahāprabhu lañā bule jalete bhāsiyā

SYNONYMS

advaita—Advaita Ācārya; *nija-śakti*—His personal potency; *prakaṭa kariyā*—after manifesting; *mahāprabhu lañā*—carrying Śrī Caitanya Mahāprabhu; *bule*—moves; *jalete*—on the water; *bhāsiyā*—floating.

TRANSLATION

Manifesting His personal potency, Advaita Ācārya floated about on the water, carrying Śrī Caitanya Mahāprabhu.

TEXT 91

এইমত জলক্রীড়া করি' কতক্ষণ ।
আইটোটা আইলা প্রভু লঞা ভক্তগণ ॥ ৯১ ॥

ei-mata jala-krīḍā kari' kata-kṣaṇa
āiṭoṭā āilā prabhu lañā bhakta-gaṇa

SYNONYMS

ei-mata—in this way; *jala-krīḍā*—sporting in the water; *kari'*—after performing; *kata-kṣaṇa*—for some time; *āiṭoṭā*—to the place named Āiṭoṭā; *āilā*—came back; *prabhu*—Śrī Caitanya Mahāprabhu; *lañā bhakta-gaṇa*—accompanied by the devotees.

TRANSLATION

After sporting in the water for some time, Śrī Caitanya Mahāprabhu returned to His place at Āiṭoṭā, accompanied by His devotees.

TEXT 92

পুরী, ভারতী আদি যত মুখ্য ভক্তগণ ।
আচার্যের নিমন্ত্রণে করিলা ভোজন ॥ ৯২ ॥

purī, bhāratī ādi yata mukhya bhakta-gaṇa
ācāryera nimantraṇe karilā bhojana

SYNONYMS

purī—Paramānanda Purī; *bhāratī*—Brahmānanda Bhāratī; *ādi*—beginning with; *yata*—all; *mukhya*—chief; *bhakta-gaṇa*—devotees; *ācāryera*—of Advaita Ācārya; *nimantraṇe*—by the invitation; *karilā bhojana*—accepted their lunch.

TRANSLATION

Paramānanda Purī, Brahmānanda Bhāratī and all the other chief devotees of Śrī Caitanya Mahāprabhu took lunch at the invitation of Advaita Ācārya.

TEXT 93

বাণীনাথ আর যত প্রসাদ আনিল ।
মহাপ্রভুর গণে সেই প্রসাদ খাইল ॥ ৯৩ ॥

vāṇīnātha āra yata prasāda ānila
mahāprabhura gaṇe sei prasāda khāila

SYNONYMS

vāṇīnātha—Vāṇīnātha Rāya; *āra*—extra; *yata*—whatever; *prasāda*—remnants of food; *ānila*—brought; *mahāprabhura gaṇe*—the personal associates of Śrī Caitanya Mahāprabhu; *sei*—those; *prasāda*—remnants of food; *khāila*—ate.

TRANSLATION

Whatever extra prasāda was brought by Vāṇīnātha Rāya was taken by the other associates of Śrī Caitanya Mahāprabhu.

TEXT 94

অপরাহ্নে আসি' কৈল দর্শন, নর্তন ।
নিশাতে উদ্যানে আসি' করিলা শয়ন ॥ ৯৪ ॥

aparāhne āsi' kaila darśana, nartana
niśāte udyāne āsi' karilā śayana

SYNONYMS

aparāhne—in the afternoon; *āsi'*—coming; *kaila*—performed; *darśana nartana*—visiting the Lord and dancing; *niśāte*—at night; *udyāne*—in the garden; *āsi'*—coming; *karilā śayana*—took rest.

TRANSLATION

In the afternoon, the Lord went to the Guṇḍicā temple to visit the Lord and dance. At night He went to the garden to take rest.

TEXT 95

আর দিন আসি' কৈল ঈশ্বর দরশন ।
প্রাঙ্গণে নৃত্য-গীত কৈল কতক্ষণ ॥ ৯৫ ॥

āra dina āsi' kaila īśvara daraśana
prāṅgaṇe nṛtya-gīta kaila kata-kṣaṇa

SYNONYMS

āra dina—the next day; *āsi'*—coming; *kaila*—performed; *īśvara daraśana*—seeing the Lord; *prāṅgaṇe*—in the yard; *nṛtya-gīta*—chanting and dancing; *kaila*—performed; *kata-kṣaṇa*—for some time.

TRANSLATION

The next day, Śrī Caitanya Mahāprabhu also went to the temple of Guṇḍicā and saw the Lord. He then chanted and danced in the yard for some time.

TEXT 96

ভক্তগণ-সঙ্গে প্রভু উদ্যানে আসিয়া ।
বৃন্দাবন-বিহার করে ভক্তগণ লঞা ॥ ৯৬ ॥

bhakta-gaṇa-saṅge prabhu udyāne āsiyā
vṛndāvana-vihāra kare bhakta-gaṇa lañā

SYNONYMS

bhakta-gaṇa-saṅge—with the devotees; *prabhu*—Lord Śrī Caitanya Mahāprabhu; *udyāne*—in the garden; *āsiyā*—coming; *vṛndāvana-vihāra*—the pastimes of Vṛndāvana; *kare*—performs; *bhakta-gaṇa lañā*—with all the devotees.

TRANSLATION

Accompanied by His devotees, Śrī Caitanya Mahāprabhu then went into the garden and enjoyed the pastimes of Vṛndāvana.

PURPORT

Śrīla Bhaktisiddhānta Sarasvatī Ṭhākura has pointed out that this *vṛndāvana-vihāra*—the pastimes of Vṛndāvana—does not refer to Kṛṣṇa's mixing with the *gopīs* or the transcendental mellow of *parakīya-rasa.* Śrī Caitanya Mahāprabhu's *vṛndāvana-līlā* in the garden of Jagannātha Purī did not involve association with women or with other people's wives in the fashion transcendentally demonstrated by Śrī Kṛṣṇa. In His *vṛndāvana-līlā,* Śrī Caitanya Mahāprabhu conceived of Himself as the assistant of Śrīmatī Rādhārāṇī. When Śrīmatī Rādhārāṇī enjoyed the company of Kṛṣṇa, Her maidservants were very pleased. One should not compare Śrī Caitanya Mahāprabhu's *vṛndāvana-vihāra* in the garden of Jagannātha with the activities of the *gaurāṅga-nāgarīs.*

TEXT 97

বৃক্ষবল্লী প্রফুল্লিত প্রভুর দরশনে ।
ভৃঙ্গ-পিক গায়, বহে শীতল পবনে ॥ ৯৭ ॥

vṛkṣa-vallī praphullita prabhura daraśane
bhṛṅga-pika gāya, vahe śītala pavane

SYNONYMS

vṛkṣa-vallī—trees and creepers; *praphullita*—joyful; *prabhura*—of Śrī Caitanya Mahāprabhu; *daraśane*—by the sight; *bhṛṅga*—bumblebees; *pika*—birds; *gāya*—chant; *vahe*—were blowing; *śītala*—cool; *pavane*—breezes.

TRANSLATION

There were multifarious trees and creepers in the garden, and they were all jubilant to see Śrī Caitanya Mahāprabhu. Indeed, the birds were chirping, the bees were buzzing, and a cool breeze was blowing.

TEXT 98

প্রতি-বৃক্ষতলে প্রভু করেন নর্তন ।
বাসুদেব-দত্ত মাত্র করেন গায়ন ॥ ৯৮ ॥

prati-vṛkṣa-tale prabhu karena nartana
vāsudeva-datta mātra karena gāyana

SYNONYMS

prati-vṛkṣa-tale—underneath each tree; *prabhu*—Śrī Caitanya Mahāprabhu; *karena nartana*—dances; *vāsudeva-datta*—Vāsudeva Datta; *mātra*—only; *karena*—performs; *gāyana*—chanting.

TRANSLATION

As Śrī Caitanya Mahāprabhu danced beneath each and every tree, Vāsudeva Datta sang alone.

TEXT 99

এক এক বৃক্ষতলে এক এক গান গায় ।
পরম-আবেশে একা নাচে গৌররায় ॥ ৯৯ ॥

eka eka vṛkṣa-tale eka eka gāna gāya
parama-āveśe ekā nāce gaurarāya

SYNONYMS

eka eka vṛkṣa-tale—under each and every tree; *eka eka*—a different; *gāna*—song; *gāya*—sings; *parama-āveśe*—in great ecstasy; *ekā*—alone; *nāce*—dances; *gaurarāya*—Śrī Caitanya Mahāprabhu.

TRANSLATION

As Vāsudeva Datta sang a different song beneath each and every tree, Śrī Caitanya Mahāprabhu danced there alone in great ecstasy.

TEXT 100

তবে বক্রেশ্বরে প্রভু কহিলা নাচিতে ।
বক্রেশ্বর নাচে, প্রভু লাগিলা গাইতে ॥ ১০০ ॥

tabe vakreśvare prabhu kahilā nācite
vakreśvara nāce, prabhu lāgilā gāite

SYNONYMS

tabe—thereafter; *vakreśvare*—unto Vakreśvara Paṇḍita; *prabhu*—Lord Śrī Caitanya Mahāprabhu; *kahilā*—ordered; *nācite*—to dance; *vakreśvara nāce*—Vakreśvara Paṇḍita began to dance; *prabhu*—Śrī Caitanya Mahāprabhu; *lāgilā*—began; *gāite*—to sing.

TRANSLATION

Śrī Caitanya Mahāprabhu then ordered Vakreśvara Paṇḍita to dance, and as he began to dance, the Lord began to sing.

TEXT 101

প্রভু-সঙ্গে স্বরূপাদি কীর্তনীয়া গায় ।
দিক্‌বিদিক্ নাহি জ্ঞান প্রেমের বন্যায় ॥ ১০১ ॥

prabhu-saṅge svarūpādi kīrtanīyā gāya
dik-vidik nāhi jñāna premera vanyāya

SYNONYMS

prabhu-saṅge—with Śrī Caitanya Mahāprabhu; *svarūpa-ādi*—headed by Svarūpa Dāmodara; *kīrtanīyā*—chanters; *gāya*—sing; *dik-vidik*—of time and circumstances; *nāhi*—not; *jñāna*—knowledge; *premera*—of ecstatic love; *vanyāya*—by inundation.

TRANSLATION

Then devotees like Svarūpa Dāmodara and other kīrtana performers began to sing along with Śrī Caitanya Mahāprabhu. Being inundated with ecstatic love, they lost all consideration of time and circumstance.

TEXT 102

এই মত কতক্ষণ করি' বন-লীলা ।
নরেন্দ্র-সরোবরে গেলা করিতে জলখেলা ॥ ১০২ ॥

ei mata kata-kṣaṇa kari' vana-līlā
narendra-sarovare gelā karite jala-khelā

SYNONYMS

ei mata—in this way; *kata-kṣaṇa*—for some time; *kari'*—performing; *vana-līlā*—pastimes in the garden; *narendra-sarovare*—in the lake known as Narendra-sarovara; *gelā*—they went; *karite*—to do; *jala-khelā*—sporting in the water.

TRANSLATION

After thus performing pastimes in the garden for some time, they all went to a lake called Narendra-sarovara and there enjoyed sporting in the water.

TEXT 103

জলক্রীড়া করি' পুনঃ আইলা উদ্যানে ।
ভোজনলীলা কৈলা প্রভু লঞা ভক্তগণে ॥ ১০৩ ॥

jala-krīḍā kari' punaḥ āilā udyāne
bhojana-līlā kailā prabhu lañā bhakta-gaṇe

SYNONYMS

jala-krīḍā—sporting in the water; *kari'*—performing; *punaḥ*—again; *āilā*—came; *udyāne*—in the garden; *bhojana-līlā*—pastimes of accepting *prasāda;* *kailā*—performed; *prabhu*—Śrī Caitanya Mahāprabhu; *lañā bhakta-gaṇe*—with all the devotees.

TRANSLATION

After sporting in the water, Śrī Caitanya Mahāprabhu returned to the garden and accepted prasāda with the devotees.

TEXT 104

নব দিন গুণ্ডিচাতে রহে জগন্নাথ ।
মহাপ্রভু ঐছে লীলা করে ভক্ত-সাথ ॥ ১০৪ ॥

nava dina guṇḍicāte rahe jagannātha
mahāprabhu aiche līlā kare bhakta-sātha

SYNONYMS

nava dina—nine days; *guṇḍicāte*—in the temple of Guṇḍicā; *rahe*—stays; *jagannātha*—Lord Jagannātha; *mahāprabhu*—Śrī Caitanya Mahāprabhu; *aiche*—in the above-mentioned way; *līlā*—pastimes; *kare*—performs; *bhakta-sātha*—with His devotees.

TRANSLATION

For nine continuous days His Lordship Śrī Jagannātha-deva stayed at the Guṇḍicā temple. During this time Śrī Caitanya Mahāprabhu also stayed there and performed the pastimes with His devotees that have already been described.

TEXT 105

'জগন্নাথ-বল্লভ' নাম বড় পুষ্পারাম ।
নব দিন করেন প্রভু তথাই বিশ্রাম ॥ ১০৫ ॥

'jagannātha-vallabha' nāma baḍa puṣpārāma
nava dina karena prabhu tathāi viśrāma

SYNONYMS

jagannātha-vallabha—Jagannātha-vallabha; *nāma*—named; *baḍa*—very big; *puṣpa-ārāma*—garden; *nava dina*—nine days; *karena*—does; *prabhu*—Śrī Caitanya Mahāprabhu; *tathāi*—there; *viśrāma*—resting.

TRANSLATION

The garden of His pastimes was very large and was named Jagannātha-vallabha. Śrī Caitanya Mahāprabhu took his rest there for nine days.

TEXT 106

'হেরা-পঞ্চমী'র দিন আইল জানিয়া ।
কাশীমিশ্রে কহে রাজা সযত্ন করিয়া ॥ ১০৬ ॥

'herā-pañcamī'ra dina āila jāniyā
kāśī-miśre kahe rājā sayatna kariyā

SYNONYMS

herā-pañcamīra dina—the day of Herā-pañcamī; *āila*—was nearing; *jāniyā*—knowing; *kāśī-miśre*—unto Kāśī Miśra; *kahe*—says; *rājā*—the King; *sa-yatna kariyā*—with great attention.

TRANSLATION

Knowing that the Herā-pañcamī festival was drawing near, King Pratāparudra attentively talked with Kāśī Miśra.

TEXT 107

কল্য 'হেরা-পঞ্চমী' হবে লক্ষ্মীর বিজয় ।
ঐছে উৎসব কর যেন কভু নাহি হয় ॥ ১০৭ ॥

kalya 'herā-pañcamī' habe lakṣmīra vijaya
aiche utsava kara yena kabhu nāhi haya

SYNONYMS

kalya—tomorrow; *herā-pañcamī*—the function of Herā-pañcamī; *habe*—will be; *lakṣmīra*—of the goddess of fortune; *vijaya*—welcome; *aiche*—such; *utsava*—festival; *kara*—perform; *yena*—as; *kabhu*—at any time; *nāhi haya*—did not take place.

TRANSLATION

"Tomorrow will be the function of Herā-pañcamī or Lakṣmī-vijaya. Hold this festival in a way that it has never been held before."

PURPORT

This Herā-pañcamī festival takes place five days after the Ratha-yātrā festival. Lord Jagannātha has left His wife, the goddess of fortune, and gone to Vṛndāvana, which is the Guṇḍicā temple. Due to separation from the Lord, the goddess of fortune decides to come to see the Lord at Guṇḍicā. The coming of the goddess of fortune to Guṇḍicā is celebrated by Herā-pañcamī. Sometimes this is misspelled as Harā-pañcamī in the section known as *ativāḍī*. The word *herā* means "to see" and refers to the goddess of fortune going to see Lord Jagannātha. The word *pañcamī* means "the fifth day" and is used because this takes place on the fifth day of the moon.

TEXT 108

মহোৎসব কর তৈছে বিশেষ সম্ভার ।
দেখি' মহাপ্রভুর যৈছে হয় চমৎকার ॥ ১০৮ ॥

mahotsava kara taiche viśeṣa sambhāra
dekhi' mahāprabhura yaiche haya camatkāra

SYNONYMS

mahotsava—the festival; *kara*—perform; *taiche*—in such a way; *viśeṣa sambhāra*—with great gorgeousness; *dekhi'*—after seeing; *mahāprabhura*—of Lord Śrī Caitanya Mahāprabhu; *yaiche*—so that; *haya*—there is; *camatkāra*—astonishment.

TRANSLATION

King Pratāparudra said, "Hold this festival in such a gorgeous way that upon seeing it, Caitanya Mahāprabhu will be completely pleased and astonished.

TEXT 109

ঠাকুরের ভাণ্ডারে আর আমার ভাণ্ডারে ।
চিত্রবস্ত্র-কিঙ্কিণী, আর ছত্র-চামরে ॥ ১০৯ ॥

ṭhākurera bhāṇḍāre āra āmāra bhāṇḍāre
citra-vastra-kiṅkiṇī, āra chatra-cāmare

SYNONYMS

ṭhākurera—of the Deity; *bhāṇḍāre*—in the storehouse; *āra*—and; *āmāra*—my; *bhāṇḍāre*—in the storehouse; *citra-vastra*—printed cloth; *kiṅkiṇī*—small bells; *āra*—and; *chatra*—umbrellas; *cāmare*—yak-tail whisks.

TRANSLATION

"Take as many printed cloths, small bells, umbrellas and cāmaras as there are in my storehouse and in the Deity's storehouse.

TEXT 110

ধ্বজাবৃন্দ-পতাকা-ঘণ্টায় করহ মণ্ডন ।
নানাবাদ্য-নৃত্য-দোলায় করহ সাজন ॥ ১১০ ॥

dhvajāvṛnda-patākā-ghaṇṭāya karaha maṇḍana
nānā-vādya-nṛtya-dolāya karaha sājana

SYNONYMS

dhvajā-vṛnda—all kinds of flags; *patākā*—big flags; *ghaṇṭāya*—with ringing bells; *karaha*—make; *maṇḍana*—decoration; *nānā-vādya*—all kinds of musical parties; *nṛtya*—dancing; *dolāya*—on the carrier; *karaha sājana*—decorate attractively.

TRANSLATION

"Collect all kinds of small and large flags and ringing bells. Then decorate the carrier and have various musical and dancing parties accompany it. In this way decorate the carrier attractively.

TEXT 111

দ্বিগুণ করিয়া কর সব উপহার ।
রথযাত্রা হৈতে যৈছে হয় চমৎকার ॥ ১১১ ॥

dviguṇa kariyā kara saba upahāra
ratha-yātrā haite yaiche haya camatkāra

SYNONYMS

dvi-guṇa kariyā—making a double portion; *kara*—make; *saba*—all kinds of; *upahāra*—presentations; *ratha-yātrā haite*—than the car festival; *yaiche*—so that; *haya*—it becomes; *camatkāra*—more wonderful.

TRANSLATION

"You should also double the quantity of prasāda. Make so much that it will even surpass the Ratha-yātrā festival.

TEXT 112

সেইত' করিহ,- প্রভু লঞা ভক্তগণ ।
স্বচ্ছন্দে আসিয়া যৈছে করেন দরশন ॥ ১১২ ॥

seita' kariha,——prabhu lañā bhakta-gaṇa
svacchande āsiyā yaiche karena daraśana

SYNONYMS

seita' kariha—do that; *prabhu*—Śrī Caitanya Mahāprabhu; *lañā bhakta-gaṇa*—taking with Him all the devotees; *svacchande*—freely; *āsiyā*—coming; *yaiche*—as; *karena daraśana*—pays a visit to the temple.

TRANSLATION

"Arrange the festival in such a way that Śrī Caitanya Mahāprabhu may freely go with His devotees to visit the Deity without difficulty."

TEXT 113

প্রাতঃকালে মহাপ্রভু নিজগণ লঞা ।
জগন্নাথ দর্শন কৈল সুন্দরাচলে যাঞা ॥ ১১৩ ॥

prātaḥ-kāle mahāprabhu nija-gaṇa lañā
jagannātha darśana kaila sundarācale yāñā

SYNONYMS

prātaḥ-kāle—in the morning; *mahāprabhu*—Śrī Caitanya Mahāprabhu; *nija-gaṇa lañā*—taking His associates; *jagannātha darśana*—visiting Lord Jagannātha; *kaila*—performed; *sundarācale*—to the Guṇḍicā temple; *yāñā*—going.

TRANSLATION

In the morning, Śrī Caitanya Mahāprabhu took His personal associates with Him to see Lord Jagannātha at Sundarācala.

PURPORT

Sundarācala is the Guṇḍicā temple. The temple of Jagannātha at Jagannātha Purī is called Nīlācala, and the temple at Guṇḍicā is called Sundarācala.

TEXT 114

নীলাচলে আইলা পুনঃ ভক্তগণ-সঙ্গে ।
দেখিতে উৎকণ্ঠা হেরা-পঞ্চমীর রঙ্গে ॥ ১১৪ ॥

nīlācale āilā punaḥ bhakta-gaṇa-saṅge
dekhite utkaṇṭhā herā-pañcamīra raṅge

SYNONYMS

nīlācale—to Jagannātha Purī; *āilā*—returned; *punaḥ*—again; *bhakta-gaṇa-saṅge*—with His devotees; *dekhite*—to see; *utkaṇṭhā*—very eager; *herā-pañcamīra raṅge*—performance of the festival known as Herā-pañcamī.

TRANSLATION

Śrī Caitanya Mahāprabhu and His personal devotees returned to Nīlācala with great eagerness to see the Herā-pañcamī festival.

TEXT 115

কাশীমিশ্র প্রভুরে বহু আদর করিয়া ।
স্বগণ-সহ ভাল-স্থানে বসাইল লঞা ॥ ১১৫ ॥

kāśī-miśra prabhure bahu ādara kariyā
svagaṇa-saha bhāla-sthāne vasāila lañā

SYNONYMS

kāśī-miśra—Kāśī Miśra; *prabhure*—unto Śrī Caitanya Mahāprabhu; *bahu*—very much; *ādara kariyā*—offering respect; *sva-gaṇa-saha*—with His associates; *bhāla-sthāne*—in a nice place; *vasāila*—made seated; *lañā*—taking.

TRANSLATION

Kāśī Miśra received Caitanya Mahāprabhu with great respect, and taking the Lord and His associates to a very nice place, he had them seated.

TEXT 116

রসবিশেষ প্রভুর শুনিতে মন হৈল ।
ঈষৎ হাসিয়া প্রভু স্বরূপে পুছিল ॥ ১১৬ ॥

rasa-viśeṣa prabhura śunite mana haila
īṣat hāsiyā prabhu svarūpe puchila

SYNONYMS

rasa-viśeṣa—a particular mellow; *prabhura*—of Śrī Caitanya Mahāprabhu; *śunite*—to hear; *mana haila*—there was a desire; *īṣat hāsiyā*—smiling mildly; *prabhu*—Śrī Caitanya Mahāprabhu; *svarūpe puchila*—inquired from Svarūpa Dāmodara.

TRANSLATION

After taking His seat, Śrī Caitanya Mahāprabhu wanted to hear about a particular mellow of devotional service; therefore, mildly smiling, He began to question Svarūpa Dāmodara.

TEXTS 117-118

যদ্যপি জগন্নাথ করেন দ্বারকায় বিহার ।
সহজ প্রকট করে পরম উদার ॥ ১১৭ ॥
তথাপি বৎসর-মধ্যে হয় একবার ।
বৃন্দাবন দেখিতে তাঁর উৎকণ্ঠা অপার ॥ ১১৮ ॥

yadyapi jagannātha karena dvārakāya vihāra
sahaja prakaṭa kare parama udāra

tathāpi vatsara-madhye haya eka-bāra
vṛndāvana dekhite tāṅra utkaṇṭhā apāra

SYNONYMS

yadyapi—although; *jagannātha*—Lord Jagannātha; *karena*—does; *dvārakāya*—in Dvārakā-dhāma; *vihāra*—enjoyment; *sahaja*—natural; *prakaṭa*—manifestation; *kare*—does; *parama*—sublime; *udāra*—liberal; *tathāpi*—still; *vatsara-madhye*—within a year; *haya*—becomes; *eka-bāra*—once; *vṛndāvana dekhite*—to visit Vṛndāvana; *tāṅra*—His; *utkaṇṭhā*—eagerness; *apāra*—unlimited.

TRANSLATION

"Although Lord Jagannātha enjoys His pastimes at Dvārakā-dhāma and naturally manifests sublime liberality there, still, once a year, He becomes unlimitedly eager to see Vṛndāvana."

TEXT 119

বৃন্দাবন-সম এই উপবন-গণ ।
তাহা দেখিবারে উৎকণ্ঠিত হয় মন ॥ ১১৯ ॥

vṛndāvana-sama ei upavana-gaṇa
tāhā dekhibāre utkaṇṭhita haya mana

SYNONYMS

vṛndāvana-sama—exactly resembling Vṛndāvana; *ei*—all these; *upavana-gaṇa*—neighboring gardens; *tāhā*—those gardens; *dekhibāre*—for seeing; *utkaṇṭhita*—very eager; *haya mana*—His mind becomes.

TRANSLATION

Pointing out the neighboring gardens, Śrī Caitanya Mahāprabhu said, "All these gardens exactly resemble Vṛndāvana; therefore Lord Jagannātha is very eager to see them again.

TEXT 120

বাহির হইতে করে রথযাত্রা-ছল ।
সুন্দরাচলে যায় প্রভু ছাড়ি' নীলাচল ॥ ১২০ ॥

bāhira ha-ite kare ratha-yātrā-chala
sundarācale yāya prabhu chāḍi' nīlācala

SYNONYMS

bāhira ha-ite—externally; *kare*—makes; *ratha-yātrā-chala*—an excuse to enjoy the car festival; *sundarācale*—to Sundarācala, the Guṇḍicā temple; *yāya*—goes; *prabhu*—Lord Jagannātha; *chāḍi'*—leaving; *nīlācala*—Jagannātha Purī.

TRANSLATION

"Externally He gives the excuse that He wants to participate in the Ratha-yātrā festival, but actually He wants to leave Jagannātha Purī to go to Sundarācala, Guṇḍicā temple, the replica of Vṛndāvana.

TEXT 121

নানা-পুষ্পোদ্যানে তথা খেলে রাত্রি-দিনে।
লক্ষ্মীদেবীরে সঙ্গে নাহি লয় কি কারণে? ১২১ ॥

nānā-puṣpodyāne tathā khele rātri-dine
lakṣmīdevīre saṅge nāhi laya ki kāraṇe?

SYNONYMS

nānā-puṣpa-udyāne—in the various flower gardens; *tathā*—there; *khele*—He plays; *rātri-dine*—both day and night; *lakṣmī-devīre*—Lakṣmīdevī, the goddess of fortune; *saṅge*—with Him; *nāhi*—does not; *laya*—take; *ki kāraṇe*—what is the reason.

TRANSLATION

"The Lord enjoys His pastimes day and night in various flower gardens there. But why did He not take Lakṣmīdevī, the goddess of fortune, with Him?"

TEXT 122

স্বরূপ কহে,—শুন, প্রভু, কারণ ইহার।
বৃন্দাবন-ক্রীড়াতে লক্ষ্মীর নাহি অধিকার ॥ ১২২ ॥

svarūpa kahe,——śuna, prabhu, kāraṇa ihāra
vṛndāvana-krīḍāte lakṣmīra nāhi adhikāra

SYNONYMS

svarūpa kahe—Svarūpa replied; *śuna*—please hear; *prabhu*—O my Lord; *kāraṇa ihāra*—the reason for this; *vṛndāvana-krīḍāte*—in the pastimes of Vṛndāvana; *lakṣmīra*—of the goddess of fortune; *nāhi*—there is not; *adhikāra*—admission.

TRANSLATION

Svarūpa Dāmodara replied, "My dear Lord, please hear the reason for this. Lakṣmīdevī, the goddess of fortune, cannot be admitted to the pastimes of Vṛndāvana.

TEXT 123

বৃন্দাবন-লীলায় কৃষ্ণের সহায় গোপীগণ।
গোপীগণ বিনা কৃষ্ণের হরিতে নারে মন ॥ ১২৩ ॥

vṛndāvana-līlāya kṛṣṇera sahāya gopī-gaṇa
gopī-gaṇa vinā kṛṣṇera harite nāre mana

SYNONYMS

vṛndāvana-līlāya—in the pastimes of Vṛndāvana; *kṛṣṇera*—of Lord Kṛṣṇa; *sahāya*—assistants; *gopī-gaṇa*—all the *gopīs; gopī-gaṇa vinā*—except for the *gopīs; kṛṣṇera*—of Lord Kṛṣṇa; *harite*—to attract; *nāre*—no one is able; *mana*—the mind.

TRANSLATION

"In the pastimes of Vṛndāvana, the only assistants are the gopīs. But for the gopīs, no one can attract the mind of Kṛṣṇa."

TEXT 124

প্রভু কহে,—যাত্রা-ছলে কৃষ্ণের গমন ।
সুভদ্রা আর বলদেব, সঙ্গে দুই জন ॥ ১২৪ ॥

prabhu kahe,——yātrā-chale kṛṣṇera gamana
subhadrā āra baladeva, saṅge dui jana

SYNONYMS

prabhu kahe—Śrī Caitanya Mahāprabhu said; *yātrā-chale*—on the plea of the car festival; *kṛṣṇera*—of Lord Kṛṣṇa; *gamana*—departure; *subhadrā*—His sister; *āra*—and; *baladeva*—His brother; *saṅge*—with Him; *dui jana*—two persons.

TRANSLATION

The Lord said, "Using the car festival as an excuse, Kṛṣṇa goes there with Subhadrā and Baladeva.

TEXT 125

গোপী-সঙ্গে যত লীলা হয় উপবনে ।
নিগূঢ় কৃষ্ণের ভাব কেহ নাহি জানে ॥ ১২৫ ॥

gopī-saṅge yata līlā haya upavane
nigūḍha kṛṣṇera bhāva keha nāhi jāne

SYNONYMS

gopī-saṅge—with the *gopīs; yata līlā*—all pastimes; *haya upavane*—that are in those gardens; *nigūḍha*—very confidential; *kṛṣṇera*—of Lord Kṛṣṇa; *bhāva*—ecstasies; *keha*—anyone; *nāhi*—does not; *jāne*—know.

TRANSLATION

"All the pastimes with the gopīs that take place in those gardens are very confidential ecstasies of Lord Kṛṣṇa. No one knows them.

TEXT 126

অতএব কৃষ্ণের প্রাকট্যে নাহি কিছু দোষ।
তবে কেনে লক্ষ্মীদেবী করে এত রোষ? ১২৬॥

ataeva kṛṣṇera prākaṭye nāhi kichu doṣa
tabe kene lakṣmīdevī kare eta roṣa?

SYNONYMS

ataeva—since; *kṛṣṇera*—of Lord Kṛṣṇa; *prākaṭye*—by such a manifestation; *nāhi*—there is not; *kichu*—any; *doṣa*—fault; *tabe*—therefore; *kene*—why; *lakṣmī-devī*—the goddess of fortune; *kare*—does; *eta*—so much; *roṣa*—anger.

TRANSLATION

"Since there is no fault at all in Kṛṣṇa's pastimes, why does the goddess of fortune become angry?"

TEXT 127

স্বরূপ কহে,—প্রেমবতীর এই ত' স্বভাব।
কান্তের ঔদাস্য-লেশে হয় ক্রোধভাব॥ ১২৭॥

svarūpa kahe,——premavatīra ei ta' svabhāva
kāntera audāsya-leśe haya krodha-bhāva

SYNONYMS

svarūpa kahe—Svarūpa Dāmodara Gosvāmī replied; *prema-vatīra*—of the girl who is too afflicted by love; *ei*—this; *ta'*—indeed; *sva-bhāva*—the nature; *kāntera*—of the beloved; *audāsya*—of negligence; *leśe*—even by a fractional part; *haya*—there is; *krodha-bhāva*—anger.

TRANSLATION

Svarūpa Dāmodara replied, "It is the nature of a girl afflicted by love to become immediately angry upon finding neglect on the part of her lover."

TEXT 128

হেনকালে, খচিত যাহে বিবিধ রতন।
সুবর্ণের চৌদোলা করি' আরোহণ ॥ ১২৮ ॥

hena-kāle, khacita yāhe vividha ratana
suvarṇera caudolā kari' ārohaṇa

SYNONYMS

hena-kāle—while Svarūpa Dāmodara and Lord Caitanya Mahāprabhu were talking; *khacita*—were bedecked; *yāhe*—on which; *vividha*—varieties; *ratana*—gems; *suvarṇera*—made of gold; *caudolā*—a palanquin carried by four men; *kari' ārohaṇa*—riding upon.

TRANSLATION

While Svarūpa Dāmodara and Śrī Caitanya Mahāprabhu were talking, the procession of the goddess of fortune came by. She was riding upon a golden palanquin carried by four men and bedecked with a variety of jewels.

TEXT 129

ছত্র-চামর-ধ্বজা পতাকার গণ।
নানাবাদ্য-আগে নাচে দেবদাসীগণ ॥ ১২৯ ॥

chatra-cāmara-dhvajā patākāra gaṇa
nānā-vādya-āge nāce deva-dāsī-gaṇa

SYNONYMS

chatra—of umbrellas; *cāmara*—and whisks; *dhvajā*—and flags; *patākāra*—and big flags; *gaṇa*—congregation; *nānā-vādya*—varieties of musical parties; *āge*—in front; *nāce*—dance; *deva-dāsī-gaṇa*—dancing girls.

TRANSLATION

The palanquin was also surrounded by people carrying umbrellas, cāmara whisks and flags, and it was preceded by musicians and dancing girls.

TEXT 130

তাম্বূল-সম্পুট, ঝারি, ব্যজন, চামর।
সাথে দাসী শত, হার দিব্য ভূষাম্বর ॥ ১৩০ ॥

tāmbūla-sampuṭa, jhāri, vyajana, cāmara
sāthe dāsī śata, hāra divya bhūṣāmbara

SYNONYMS

tāmbūla-sampuṭa—boxes containing the ingredients for betel nut preparation; *jhāri*—water pitchers; *vyajana*—fans; *cāmara*—whisks; *sāthe*—along with; *dāsī*—maidservants; *śata*—hundreds; *hāra*—necklaces; *divya*—valuable; *bhūṣāmbara*—dresses.

TRANSLATION

The maidservants were carrying water pitchers, cāmara whisks and boxes for betel nuts. There were hundreds of maidservants, all attractively dressed with valuable necklaces.

TEXT 131

অলৌকিক ঐশ্বর্য সঙ্গে বহু-পরিবার ।
ক্রুদ্ধ হঞা লক্ষ্মীদেবী আইলা সিংহদ্বার ॥ ১৩১ ॥

alaukika aiśvarya saṅge bahu-parivāra
kruddha hañā lakṣmīdevī āilā siṁha-dvāra

SYNONYMS

alaukika—uncommon; *aiśvarya*—opulence; *saṅge*—accompanied by; *bahu-parivāra*—many members of the family; *kruddha hañā*—being angry; *lakṣmī-devī*—the goddess of fortune; *āilā*—arrived; *siṁha-dvāra*—at the main gate of the temple.

TRANSLATION

In an angry mood, the goddess of fortune arrived at the main gate of the temple accompanied by many members of her family, all of whom exhibited uncommon opulence.

TEXT 132

জগন্নাথের মুখ্য মুখ্য যত ভৃত্যগণে ।
লক্ষ্মীদেবীর দাসীগণ করেন বন্ধনে ॥ ১৩২ ॥

jagannāthera mukhya mukhya yata bhṛtya-gaṇe
lakṣmīdevīra dāsī-gaṇa karena bandhane

SYNONYMS

jagannāthera—of Lord Jagannātha; *mukhya mukhya*—the principal; *yata*—all; *bhṛtya-gaṇe*—servants; *lakṣmī-devīra*—of the goddess of fortune; *dāsī-gaṇa*—maidservants; *karena bandhane*—arrested.

TRANSLATION

When the procession arrived, the maidservants of the goddess of fortune began to arrest all the principal servants of Lord Jagannātha.

TEXT 133

বান্ধিয়া আনিয়া পাড়ে লক্ষ্মীর চরণে ।
চোরে যেন দণ্ড করি' লয় নানা-ধনে ॥ ১৩৩ ॥

bāndhiyā āniyā pāḍe lakṣmīra caraṇe
core yena daṇḍa kari' laya nānā-dhane

SYNONYMS

bāndhiyā—after binding; *āniyā*—bringing; *pāḍe*—make them fall down; *lakṣmīra caraṇe*—at the lotus feet of the goddess of fortune; *core*—a thief; *yena*—as if; *daṇḍa kari'*—after punishing; *laya*—take away; *nānā-dhane*—all kinds of riches.

TRANSLATION

The maidservants bound the servants of Jagannātha, handcuffed them, and made them fall down at the lotus feet of the goddess of fortune. Indeed, they were arrested just like thieves who have all their riches taken away.

PURPORT

When Lord Jagannātha starts His car festival, He gives assurance to the goddess of fortune that He will return the next day. When He does not return, the goddess of fortune, after waiting two or three days, begins to feel that her husband has neglected her. She naturally becomes quite angry. Gorgeously decorating herself and her associates, she comes out of the temple and stands before the main gate. All the principal servants of Lord Jagannātha are then arrested by her maidservants, brought before her and forced to fall down at her lotus feet.

TEXT 134

অচেতনবৎ তারে করেন তাড়নে ।
নানামত গালি দেন ভণ্ড-বচনে ॥ ১৩৪ ॥

acetanavat tāre karena tāḍane
nānā-mata gāli dena bhaṇḍa-vacane

SYNONYMS

acetana-vat—almost unconscious; *tāre*—unto the servants; *karena*—does; *tāḍane*—chastisement; *nānā-mata*—various kinds of; *gāli*—amusement; *dena*—speaks; *bhaṇḍa-vacane*—various loose language.

TRANSLATION

When the servants fall down before the lotus feet of the goddess of fortune, they almost fall unconscious. They are chastised and made the butt of jokes and loose language.

TEXT 135

লক্ষ্মী-সঙ্গে দাসীগণের প্রাগল্ভ্য দেখিয়া ।
হাসে মহাপ্রভুর গণ মুখে হস্ত দিয়া ॥ ১৩৫ ॥

lakṣmī-saṅge dāsī-gaṇera prāgalbhya dekhiyā
hāse mahāprabhura gaṇa mukhe hasta diyā

SYNONYMS

lakṣmī-saṅge—in the company of the goddess of fortune; *dāsī-gaṇera*—of the maidservants; *prāgalbhya*—impudence; *dekhiyā*—after seeing; *hāse*—smile; *mahāprabhura*—of Śrī Caitanya Mahāprabhu; *gaṇa*—the companions; *mukhe*—on their faces; *hasta*—hands; *diyā*—covering.

TRANSLATION

When Śrī Caitanya Mahāprabhu's associates saw such impudence exhibited by the maidservants of the goddess of fortune, they covered their faces with their hands and began to smile.

TEXT 136

দামোদর কহে,—ঐছে মানের প্রকার ।
ত্রিজগতে কাহাঁ নাহি দেখি শুনি আর ॥ ১৩৬ ॥

dāmodara kahe,—aiche mānera prakāra
trijagate kāhāṅ nāhi dekhi śuni āra

SYNONYMS

dāmodara kahe—Svarūpa Dāmodara Gosvāmī said; *aiche*—such; *mānera*—of egoistic pride; *prakāra*—kind; *tri-jagate*—within the three worlds; *kāhāṅ*—anywhere; *nāhi*—not; *dekhi*—I see; *śuni*—I hear; *āra*—other.

TRANSLATION

Svarūpa Dāmodara said, "There is no egoistic pride like this within the three worlds. At least I have neither seen nor heard of it.

TEXT 137

মানিনী নিরুৎসাহে ছাড়ে বিভূষণ ।
ভূমে বসি' নখে লেখে, মলিন-বদন ॥ ১৩৭ ॥

mānini nirutsāhe chāḍe vibhūṣaṇa
bhūme vasi' nakhe lekhe, malina-vadana

SYNONYMS

mānini—proud, egoistic woman; *nirutsāhe*—because of disappointment; *chāḍe*—gives up; *vibhūṣaṇa*—all kinds of ornaments; *bhūme vasi'*—sitting on the floor; *nakhe*—with the nails; *lekhe*—marks lines; *malina-vadana*—with a morose face.

TRANSLATION

"When a woman is neglected and disappointed, out of egoistic pride she gives up her ornaments and morosely sits down on the floor, marking lines on it with her nails.

TEXT 138

পূর্বে সত্যভামার শুনি এবম্বিধ মান ।
ব্রজে গোপীগণের মান—রসের নিধান ॥ ১৩৮ ॥

pūrve satyabhāmāra śuni evaṁ-vidha māna
vraje gopī-gaṇera māna——rasera nidhāna

SYNONYMS

pūrve—previously; *satyabhāmāra*—of Queen Satyabhāmā; *śuni*—I hear; *evaṁ-vidha māna*—this kind of egoistic pride; *vraje*—in Vṛndāvana; *gopī-gaṇera*—of the *gopīs;* *māna*—pride; *rasera nidhāna*—the reservoir of all humorous mellows.

TRANSLATION

"I have heard of this kind of pride in Satyabhāmā, Kṛṣṇa's proudest Queen, and I have also heard of it in the gopīs of Vṛndāvana, who are the reservoirs of all transcendental mellows.

TEXT 139

ইঁহো নিজ-সম্পত্তি সব প্রকট করিয়া ।
প্রিয়ের উপর যায় সৈন্য সাজাঞা ॥ ১৩৯ ॥

iṅho nija-sampatti saba prakaṭa kariyā
priyera upara yāya sainya sājāñā

SYNONYMS

iṅho—this; *nija-sampatti*—her opulence; *saba*—all; *prakaṭa kariyā*—manifesting; *priyera upara*—against her beloved husband; *yāya*—goes; *sainya sājāñā*—accompanied by soldiers.

TRANSLATION

"But in the case of the goddess of fortune, I see a different kind of pride. She manifests her own opulences and even goes with her soldiers to attack her husband."

PURPORT

After seeing the impudence of the goddess of fortune, Svarūpa Dāmodara Gosvāmī wanted to inform Śrī Caitanya Mahāprabhu about the superexcellence of the *gopīs'* loving affairs. He therefore said, "My Lord, I never experienced anything like the behavior of the goddess of fortune. We sometimes see a beloved wife becoming proud of her position and then frustrated due to some neglect. She then gives up caring for her appearance, accepts dirty clothes and morosely sits on the floor and draws lines with her nails. We have heard of such egoistic pride in Satyabhāmā and the *gopīs* of Vṛndāvana, but what we see in the goddess of fortune here at Jagannātha Purī is completely different. She becomes very angry with her husband, and attacks Him with her great opulence."

TEXT 140

প্রভু কহে,—কহ ব্রজের মানের প্রকার ।
স্বরূপ কহে,—গোপীমান-নদী শতধার ॥ ১৪০ ॥

prabhu kahe,——kaha vrajera mānera prakāra
svarūpa kahe,——gopī-māna-nadī śata-dhāra

SYNONYMS

prabhu kahe—the Lord said; *kaha*—please tell; *vrajera*—of Vṛndāvana; *mānera*—of the egoistic pride; *prakāra*—the varieties; *svarūpa kahe*—Svarūpa Dāmodara replied; *gopī-māna*—the pride of the *gopīs; nadī*—like a river; *śata-dhāra*—with hundreds of branches.

TRANSLATION

Śrī Caitanya Mahāprabhu said, "Please tell me of the varieties of egoistic pride manifest in Vṛndāvana." Svarūpa Dāmodara replied, "The pride of the gopīs is like a river flowing with hundreds of tributaries.

TEXT 141

নায়িকার স্বভাব, প্রেমবৃত্তে বহু ভেদ ।
সেই ভেদে নানা-প্রকার মানের উদ্ভেদ ॥ ১৪১ ॥

nāyikāra svabhāva, prema-vṛtte bahu bheda
sei bhede nānā-prakāra mānera udbheda

SYNONYMS

nāyikāra—of the heroine; *sva-bhāva*—nature; *prema-vṛtte*—in the matter of loving affairs; *bahu*—many; *bheda*—varieties; *sei*—that; *bhede*—in each variety; *nānā-prakāra*—various types; *mānera*—of the jealous anger of a woman; *udbheda*—subdivisions.

TRANSLATION

"The characteristics and modes of love are different in different women. Their jealous anger also takes on different varieties and qualities.

TEXT 142

সম্যক্ গোপিকার মান না যায় কথন ।
এক-দুই-ভেদে করি দিগ্-দরশন ॥ ১৪২ ॥

samyak gopikāra māna nā yāya kathana
eka-dui-bhede kari dig-daraśana

SYNONYMS

samyak—fully; *gopikāra*—of the *gopīs; māna*—jealous anger; *nā*—not; *yāya*—is possible; *kathana*—to speak; *eka-dui*—one, two; *bhede*—in different types; *kari*—I make; *dik-daraśana*—indication.

TRANSLATION

"It is not possible to give a complete statement about the different types of jealous anger manifest by the gopīs, but a few principles may serve as an indication.

TEXT 143

মানে কেহ হয় 'ধীরা', কেহ ত' 'অধীরা'।
এই তিন-ভেদে, কেহ হয় 'ধীরাধীরা' ॥ ১৪৩ ॥

māne keha haya 'dhīrā,' keha ta' 'adhīrā'
ei tina-bhede, keha haya 'dhīrādhīrā'

SYNONYMS

māne—on the platform of jealous anger; *keha*—some women; *haya dhīrā*—are very sober; *keha ta'*—and some of them; *adhīrā*—very restless; *ei tina-bhede*—and there is a third division; *keha haya*—some are; *dhīrā-adhīrā*—a mixture of sober and restless.

TRANSLATION

"There are three types of women experiencing jealous anger: sober women, restless women and women both restless and sober.

TEXT 144

'ধীরা' কান্তে দূরে দেখি' করে প্রত্যুত্থান।
নিকটে আসিলে, করে আসন প্রদান ॥ ১৪৪ ॥

'dhīrā' kānte dūre dekhi' kare pratyutthāna
nikaṭe āsile, kare āsana pradāna

SYNONYMS

dhīrā—the sober; *kānte*—the hero; *dūre*—from a distance; *dekhi'*—after seeing; *kare pratyutthāna*—stands up; *nikaṭe āsile*—when the hero comes nearby; *kare*—does; *āsana*—of a seat; *pradāna*—offering.

TRANSLATION

"When a sober heroine sees her hero approaching from a distance, she immediately stands up to recieve him. When he comes near, she immediately offers him a place to sit.

TEXT 145

হৃদয়ে কোপ, মুখে কহে মধুর বচন।
প্রিয় আলিঙ্গিতে, তারে করে আলিঙ্গন ॥ ১৪৫ ॥

hṛdaye kopa, mukhe kahe madhura vacana
priya āliṅgite, tāre kare āliṅgana

SYNONYMS

hṛdaye—within the heart; *kopa*—anger; *mukhe*—in the mouth; *kahe*—speaks; *madhura*—sweet; *vacana*—words; *priya*—lover; *āliṅgite*—when embracing; *tāre*—him; *kare āliṅgana*—embraces.

TRANSLATION

"The sober heroine conceals her anger within her heart and externally speaks sweet words. When her lover embraces her, she also returns his embrace.

TEXT 146

সরল ব্যবহার, করে মানের পোষণ।
কিম্বা সোল্লুণ্ঠ-বাক্যে করে প্রিয়-নিরসন ॥ ১৪৬ ॥

sarala vyavahāra, kare mānera poṣaṇa
kimvā solluṇṭha-vākye kare priya-nirasana

SYNONYMS

sarala vyavahāra—plain dealings; *kare*—does; *mānera*—of jealous anger; *poṣaṇa*—maintenance; *kimvā*—or; *solluṇṭha*—smiling a little; *vākye*—by words; *kare*—does; *priya*—of the lover; *nirasana*—refutation.

TRANSLATION

"The sober heroine is very simple in her behavior. She keeps her jealous anger within her heart, but with mild words and smiles she refutes the advances of her lover.

TEXT 147

'অধীরা' নিষ্ঠুর-বাক্যে করয়ে ভর্ৎসন।
কর্ণোৎপলে তাড়ে, করে মালায় বন্ধন ॥ ১৪৭ ॥

'adhīrā' niṣṭhura-vākye karaye bhartsana
karṇotpale tāḍe, kare mālāya bandhana

SYNONYMS

adhīrā—the restless heroine; *niṣṭhura-vākye*—by cruel words; *karaye*—does; *bhartsana*—chastisement; *karṇa-utpale tāḍe*—pulls the ear; *kare*—does; *mālāya*—with a garland; *bandhana*—binding.

TRANSLATION

"The restless heroine, however, sometimes chastises her lover with cruel words, sometimes pulls his ear and sometimes binds him with a flower garland.

TEXT 148

'ধীরাধীরা' বক্র-বাক্যে করে উপহাস ।
কভু স্তুতি, কভু নিন্দা, কভু বা উদাস ॥ ১৪৮ ॥

'dhīrādhīrā' vakra-vākye kare upahāsa
kabhu stuti, kabhu nindā, kabhu vā udāsa

SYNONYMS

dhīrā-adhīrā—the heroine who is a combination of sobriety and restlessness; *vakra-vākye kare upahāsa*—jokes with equivocal words; *kabhu stuti*—sometimes praise; *kabhu nindā*—sometimes blasphemy; *kabhu vā udāsa*—sometimes indifference.

TRANSLATION

"The heroine who is a combination of sobriety and restlessness always jokes with equivocal words. She sometimes praises her lover, sometimes blasphemes him and sometimes remains indifferent.

TEXT 149

'মুগ্ধা', 'মধ্যা', 'প্রগল্‌ভা',—তিন নায়িকার ভেদ ।
'মুগ্ধা' নাহি জানে মানের বৈদগ্ধ্য-বিভেদ ॥ ১৪৯ ॥

'mugdhā', 'madhyā', 'pragalbhā',—tina nāyikāra bheda
'mugdhā' nāhi jāne mānera vaidagdhya-vibheda

SYNONYMS

mugdhā—captivated; *madhyā*—intermediate; *pragalbhā*—impudent; *tina*—three; *nāyikāra*—of heroines; *bheda*—divisions; *mugdhā*—the captivated; *nāhi jāne*—does not know; *mānera*—of jealous anger; *vaidagdhya-vibheda*—the intricacies of cunning behavior.

TRANSLATION

"Heroines may also be classified as captivated, intermediate and impudent. The captivated heroine does not know very much about the cunning intricacies of jealous anger.

TEXT 150

মুখ আচ্ছাদিয়া করে কেবল রোদন ।
কান্তের প্রিয়বাক্য শুনি' হয় পরসন্ন ॥ ১৫০ ॥

mukha ācchādiyā kare kevala rodana
kāntera priya-vākya śuni' haya parasanna

SYNONYMS

mukha ācchādiyā—covering the face; *kare*—performs; *kevala*—only; *rodana*—crying; *kāntera*—of the lover; *priya-vākya*—sweet words; *śuni'*—hearing; *haya*—becomes; *parasanna*—satisfied.

TRANSLATION

"The captivated heroine simply covers her face and goes on crying. When she hears sweet words from her lover, she is very satisfied.

TEXT 151

'মধ্যা' 'প্রগল্‌ভা' ধরে ধীরাদি-বিভেদ ।
তার মধ্যে সবার স্বভাবে তিন ভেদ ॥ ১৫১ ॥

'madhyā' 'pragalbhā' dhare dhīrādi-vibheda
tāra madhye sabāra svabhāve tina bheda

SYNONYMS

madhyā—the intermediate; *pragalbhā*—the impudent; *dhare*—contain; *dhīrā-ādi-vibheda*—the three divisions of *dhīrā, adhīrā* and *dhīrādhīrā; tāra madhye*—among them; *sabāra*—of all of them; *sva-bhāve*—in nature; *tina bheda*—three divisions.

TRANSLATION

"Both the intermediate and impudent heroines can be classified as sober, restless and both sober and restless. All their characteristics can be further classified in three divisions.

TEXT 152

কেহ 'প্রখরা', কেহ 'মৃদু', কেহ হয় 'সমা'।
স্ব-স্বভাবে কৃষ্ণের বাড়ায় প্রেম-সীমা ॥ ১৫২ ॥

keha 'prakharā', keha 'mṛdu', keha haya 'samā'
sva-svabhāve kṛṣṇera bāḍāya prema-sīmā

SYNONYMS

keha—some; *prakharā*—very talkative; *keha*—some; *mṛdu*—very mild; *keha haya*—some of them are; *samā*—equipoised; *sva-svabhāve*—by their own characteristics; *kṛṣṇera*—of Lord Kṛṣṇa; *bāḍāya*—increases; *prema-sīmā*—limit of loving ecstasy.

TRANSLATION

"Some of them are very talkative, some are mild, and some are equipoised. Each heroine, according to her own character, increases Śrī Kṛṣṇa's loving ecstasy.

TEXT 153

প্রাখর্য, মার্দব, সাম্য স্বভাব নির্দোষ।
সেই সেই স্বভাবে কৃষ্ণে করায় সন্তোষ ॥ ১৫৩ ॥

prākharya, mārdava, sāmya svabhāva nirdoṣa
sei sei svabhāve kṛṣṇe karāya santoṣa

SYNONYMS

prākharya—talkativeness; *mārdava*—mildness; *sāmya*—being equipoised; *sva-bhāva*—nature; *nirdoṣa*—faultless; *sei sei sva-bhāve*—in those transcendental qualities; *kṛṣṇe*—Lord Kṛṣṇa; *karāya*—they make; *santoṣa*—happy.

TRANSLATION

"Although some of the gopīs are talkative, some mild and some equipoised, all of them are transcendental and faultless. They please Kṛṣṇa by their unique characteristics."

TEXT 154

একথা শুনিয়া প্রভুর আনন্দ অপার।
'কহ, কহ, দামোদর',—বলে বার বার ॥ ১৫৪ ॥

e-kathā śuniyā prabhura ānanda apāra
'kaha, kaha, dāmodara',——bale bāra bāra

SYNONYMS

e-kathā śuniyā—hearing this description; *prabhura*—of Śrī Caitanya Mahāprabhu; *ānanda apāra*—unlimited happiness; *kaha kaha*—please go on speaking; *dāmodara*—My dear Dāmodara; *bale bāra bāra*—He said again and again.

TRANSLATION

Śrī Caitanya Mahāprabhu felt unlimited happiness upon hearing these descriptions, and He again and again requested Svarūpa Dāmodara to continue speaking.

TEXT 155

দামোদর কহে,—কৃষ্ণ রসিকশেখর ।
রস-আস্বাদক, রসময়-কলেবর ॥ ১৫৫ ॥

dāmodara kahe,——kṛṣṇa rasika-śekhara
rasa-āsvādaka, rasamaya-kalevara

SYNONYMS

dāmodara kahe—Dāmodara said; *kṛṣṇa*—Lord Kṛṣṇa; *rasika-śekhara*—the master of transcendental mellows; *rasa-āsvādaka*—the taster of transcendental mellows; *rasa-maya-kalevara*—whose body is made of all transcendental bliss.

TRANSLATION

Dāmodara Gosvāmī said, "Kṛṣṇa is the master of all transcendental mellows. He is the taster of transcendental mellows, and His body is composed of transcendental bliss.

TEXT 156

প্রেমময়-বপু কৃষ্ণ ভক্ত-প্রেমাধীন ।
শুদ্ধপ্রেমে, রসগুণে, গোপিকা—প্রবীণ ॥ ১৫৬ ॥

premamaya-vapu kṛṣṇa bhakta-premādhīna
śuddha-preme, rasa-guṇe, gopikā——pravīṇa

SYNONYMS

prema-maya-vapu—body of love and ecstasy; *kṛṣṇa*—Lord Kṛṣṇa; *bhakta-prema-adhīna*—always subordinate to the loving feelings of His devotees; *śuddha-preme*—in pure uncontaminated love; *rasa-guṇe*—and in the qualities of transcendental mellows; *gopikā*—the *gopīs; pravīṇa*—very experienced.

TRANSLATION

"Kṛṣṇa is full of ecstatic love and always subordinate to the love of his devotees. The gopīs are very experienced in pure love and in the dealings of transcendental mellows.

TEXT 157

গোপিকার প্রেমে নাহি রসাভাস-দোষ ।
অতএব কৃষ্ণের করে পরম সন্তোষ ॥ ১৫৭ ॥

gopikāra preme nāhi rasābhāsa-doṣa
ataeva kṛṣṇera kare parama santoṣa

SYNONYMS

gopikāra—of the *gopīs; preme*—in the loving affairs; *nāhi*—there is not; *rasa-ābhāsa*—of an adulterated taste of mellow; *doṣa*—fault; *ataeva*—therefore; *kṛṣṇera*--of Lord Kṛṣṇa; *kare*—they do; *parama santoṣa*—highest satisfaction.

TRANSLATION

"There is no flaw or adulteration in the love of the gopīs; therefore they give Kṛṣṇa the highest pleasure.

PURPORT

Rasābhāsa occurs when one's relationship with Kṛṣṇa is adulterated. There are different types of *rasābhāsa*—first-, second- and third-class. The word *rasa* means "mellow," and *ābhāsa* means "a shadow." If one tastes one kind of mellow and something extra is imposed, that is *uparasa*. If something is derived from the original mellow, it is called *anurasa*. If something is appreciated that is far removed from the original mellow, it is called *aparasa*. *Uparasa, anurasa* and *aparasa* are, respectively, first-, second- and third-class *rasābhāsas*. As stated in *Bhakti-rasāmṛta-sindhu* (4.9):

pūrvam evānuśiṣṭena vikalā rasa-lakṣaṇā
rasā eva rasābhāsā rasa-jñair anukīrtitāḥ
syus tridhoparasāś cānurasāś cāparasāś ca te
uttamā madhyamāḥ proktāḥ kaniṣṭhāś cety amī kramāt

TEXT 158

এবং শশঙ্কাংশুবিরাজিতা নিশাঃ
স সত্যকামোঽনুরতাবলাগণঃ ।
সিষেব আত্মন্যবরুদ্ধ-সৌরতঃ
সর্বাঃ শরৎকাব্যকথারসাশ্রয়াঃ ॥ ১৫৮ ॥

evaṁ śaśaṅkāṁśu-virājitā niśāḥ
sa satya-kāmo 'nuratābalā-gaṇaḥ
siṣeva ātmany avaruddha-sauratah
sarvāḥ śarat-kāvya-kathā-rasāśrayāḥ

SYNONYMS

evam—thus; *śaśaṅka-aṁśu*—with rays of moonshine; *virājitāḥ*—beautifully existing; *niśāḥ*—nights; *saḥ*—He; *satya-kāmaḥ*—the Absolute Truth; *anurata*—to whom are attracted; *abalā-gaṇaḥ*—women; *siṣeva*—performed; *ātmani*—in His own self; *avaruddha-sauratah*—His transcendental erotic love was checked; *sarvāḥ*—all; *śarat*—in autumn; *kāvya*—poetic; *kathā*—words; *rasa-āśrayāḥ*—full of all transcendental mellows.

TRANSLATION

" 'Lord Śrī Kṛṣṇa, who is the Absolute Truth, enjoyed His rāsa dance every night during the autumn season. He performed this dance in the moonlight and with full transcendental mellows. He used poetic words and surrounded Himself with women who were very much attracted to Him.'

PURPORT

This verse is a quotation from *Śrīmad-Bhāgavatam* (10.33.26). The *gopīs* are all transcendental spirit souls. One should never think that the *gopīs* and Kṛṣṇa have material bodies. Vṛndāvana-dhāma is also a spiritual abode, and there the days and nights, the trees, flowers, water and everything else are spiritual. There is not even a trace of material contamination. Kṛṣṇa, who is the Supreme Brahman and Supersoul, is not at all interested in anything material. His activities with the *gopīs* are all spiritual and take place within the spiritual world. They have nothing to do with the material world. Lord Kṛṣṇa's lusty desires and all His dealings with the *gopīs* are on the spiritual platform. One has to be transcendentally realized before even considering relishing the pastimes of Kṛṣṇa with the *gopīs*. One who is on the mundane platform must first purify himself by following the regulative principles. Only then can he try to understand Kṛṣṇa and the *gopīs*. Śrī Caitanya Mahāprabhu and Svarūpa Dāmodara Gosvāmī are here talking about the relationship between Kṛṣṇa and the *gopīs:* therefore the subject matter is neither mundane nor erotic. Being a *sannyāsī*, Śrī Caitanya Mahāprabhu was very strict in His dealings with women. Unless the *gopīs* were on the spiritual platform, Śrī Caitanya Mahāprabhu would have never even mentioned them to Svarūpa Dāmodara Gosvāmī. Therefore these descriptions do not at all pertain to material activity.

TEXT 159

'বামা' এক গোপীগণ, 'দক্ষিণা' এক গণ ।
নানা-ভাবে করায় কৃষ্ণে রস আস্বাদন ॥ ১৫৯ ॥

'vāmā' eka gopī-gaṇa, 'dakṣiṇā' eka gaṇa
nānā-bhāve karāya kṛṣṇe rasa āsvādana

SYNONYMS

vāmā—left wing; *eka*—one; *gopī-gaṇa*—party of *gopīs; dakṣiṇā*—right wing; *eka*—another; *gaṇa*—party of *gopīs; nānā-bhāve*—in varieties of ecstatic love; *karāya*—cause to do; *kṛṣṇe*—unto Kṛṣṇa; *rasa āsvādana*—tasting of transcendental mellows.

TRANSLATION

"The gopīs can be divided into a left wing and a right wing. Both wings induce Kṛṣṇa to taste transcendental mellows by various manifestations of ecstatic love.

TEXT 160

গোপীগণ-মধ্যে শ্রেষ্ঠা রাধা-ঠাকুরাণী ।
নির্মল-উজ্জ্বল-রস-প্রেম-রত্নখনি ॥ ১৬০ ॥

gopī-gaṇa-madhye śreṣṭhā rādhā-ṭhākurāṇī
nirmala-ujjvala-rasa-prema-ratna-khani

SYNONYMS

gopī-gaṇa-madhye—of all the *gopīs; śreṣṭhā*—the chief; *rādhā-ṭhākurāṇī*—Śrīmatī Rādhārāṇī; *nirmala*—purified; *ujjvala*—brilliant; *rasa*—in mellows; *prema*—of ecstatic love; *ratna-khani*—the jewel mine.

TRANSLATION

"Of all the gopīs, Śrīmatī Rādhārāṇī is the chief. She is a jewel mine of ecstatic love and the source of all purified transcendental conjugal mellows.

TEXT 161

বয়সে 'মধ্যমা' তেঁহো স্বভাবেতে 'সমা' ।
গাঢ় প্রেমভাবে তেঁহো নিরন্তর 'বামা' ॥ ১৬১ ॥

vayase 'madhyamā' teṅho svabhāvete 'samā'
gāḍha prema-bhāve teṅho nirantara 'vāmā'

SYNONYMS

vayase madhyamā—grown up; *teṅho*—Śrīmatī Rādhārāṇī; *sva-bhāvete*—in character; *samā*—equipoised; *gāḍha*—deep; *prema-bhāve*—in ecstatic love; *teṅho*—She; *nirantara*—constantly; *vāmā*—of the group of the left-wing *gopīs.*

TRANSLATION

"Rādhārāṇī is grown up, and Her character is equipoised. She is always deeply absorbed in ecstatic love and always feeling in the mood of a left-wing gopī.

PURPORT

The left wing and right wing of the *gopīs* has been explained by Rūpa Gosvāmī in *Ujjvala-nīlamaṇi.* The left wing is described in this way:

mana-grahe sadodyuktā
tac-chaithilye ca kopanā
abhedyā nāyake prāyaḥ
krūrā vāmeti kīrtyate

"A *gopī* who is always eager to be jealously angered, who is very enthusiastic for that position, who immediately becomes angry when defeated, who is never under the control of a hero and who always opposes Him is called *vāmā,* or a left-wing *gopī.*"

Śrīla Rūpa Gosvāmī describes the right-wing *gopīs* in this way:

asahyā māna-nirbandhe
nāyake yukta-vādinī
sāmabhis tena bhedyā ca
dakṣiṇā parikīrtitā

"A *gopī* who cannot tolerate womanly anger, who speaks suitable words to the hero and who is satisfied by His sweet words is called a *dakṣiṇā,* or a right-wing *gopī.*"

TEXT 162

বাম্য-স্বভাবে মান উঠে নিরন্তর ।
তার মধ্যে উঠে কৃষ্ণের আনন্দ-সাগর ॥ ১৬২ ॥

vāmya-svabhāve māna uṭhe nirantara
tāra madhye uṭhe kṛṣṇera ānanda-sāgara

SYNONYMS

vāmya-svabhāve—because of left-wing character; *māna*—womanly anger; *uṭhe*—awakens; *nirantara*—always; *tāra madhye*—in that dealing; *uṭhe*—is awakening; *kṛṣṇera*—of Lord Kṛṣṇa; *ānanda-sāgara*—an ocean of transcendental bliss.

TRANSLATION

"Because She is a left-wing gopī, Her womanly anger is always awakening, but Kṛṣṇa derives transcendental bliss from Her activities.

TEXT 163

অহেরিব গতিঃ প্রেম্ণঃ স্বভাবকুটিলা ভবেৎ ।
অতো হেতোরহেতোশ্চ যূনোর্মান উদঞ্চতি ॥ ১৬৩ ॥

aher iva gatiḥ premṇaḥ
svabhāva-kuṭilā bhavet
ato hetor ahetoś ca
yūnor māna udañcati

SYNONYMS

aheḥ—of the snake; *iva*—like; *gatiḥ*—the movement; *premṇaḥ*—of the loving affairs; *sva-bhāva*—by nature; *kuṭilā*—crooked; *bhavet*—is; *ataḥ*—therefore; *hetoḥ*—from some cause; *ahetoḥ*—from the absence of a cause; *ca*—and; *yūnoḥ*—of the young couple; *mānaḥ*—anger; *udañcati*—appears.

TRANSLATION

" 'The progress of loving affairs between young couples is by nature crooked, like the movement of a snake. Because of this, two types of anger arise between young couples—anger with a cause and anger without a cause.' "

PURPORT

This is a quotation from Śrīla Rūpa Gosvāmī's *Ujjvala-nīlamaṇi* (*Śṛṅgāra-bheda-prakaraṇa,* 102).

TEXT 164

এত শুনি' বাড়ে প্রভুর আনন্দ-সাগর ।
'কহ, কহ' কহে প্রভু, বলে দামোদর ॥ ১৬৪ ॥

eta śuni' bāḍe prabhura ānanda-sāgara
'kaha, kaha' kahe prabhu, bale dāmodara

SYNONYMS

eta śuni'—hearing this; *bāḍe*—increased; *prabhura*—of Śrī Caitanya Mahāprabhu; *ānanda-sāgara*—the ocean of transcendental bliss; *kaha kaha*—go on speaking; *kahe prabhu*—Śrī Caitanya Mahāprabhu continued to request; *bale dāmodara*—Dāmodara Gosvāmī continued to reply.

TRANSLATION

When Śrī Caitanya Mahāprabhu heard these talks, His ocean of transcendental bliss increased. He therefore told Svarūpa Dāmodara, "Go on speaking, go on speaking." And thus Svarūpa Dāmodara continued.

TEXT 165

'অধিরূঢ় মহাভাব'—রাধিকার প্রেম ।
বিশুদ্ধ, নির্মল, যৈছে দশবাণ হেম ॥ ১৬৫ ॥

'adhirūḍha mahābhāva'——rādhikāra prema
viśuddha, nirmala, yaiche daśa-vāṇa hema

SYNONYMS

adhirūḍha mahā-bhāva—highly elevated ecstatic love; *rādhikāra prema*—the loving affairs of Śrīmatī Rādhārāṇī; *viśuddha*—completely uncontaminated; *nirmala*—purified; *yaiche*—as if; *daśa-vāṇa*—ten times purified; *hema*—gold.

TRANSLATION

"Śrīmatī Rādhārāṇī's love is a highly advanced ecstasy. All Her dealings are completely pure and devoid of material tinge. Indeed, Her dealings are ten times purer than gold.

TEXT 166

কৃষ্ণের দর্শন যদি পায় আচম্বিতে।
নানা-ভাব-বিভূষণে হয় বিভূষিতে ॥ ১৬৬ ॥

kṛṣṇera darśana yadi pāya ācambite
nānā-bhāva-vibhūṣaṇe haya vibhūṣite

SYNONYMS

kṛṣṇera—of Lord Kṛṣṇa; *darśana*—interview; *yadi*—if; *pāya*—gets; *ācambite*—all of a sudden; *nānā*—various; *bhāva*—ecstatic; *vibhūṣaṇe*—with ornaments; *haya*—is; *vibhūṣite*—decorated.

TRANSLATION

"As soon as Rādhārāṇī gets a chance to see Kṛṣṇa, Her body is suddenly decorated with various ecstatic ornaments.

TEXT 167

অষ্ট 'সাত্ত্বিক', হর্ষাদি 'ব্যভিচারী' যাঁর।
'সহজ প্রেম', বিংশতি 'ভাব'-অলঙ্কার ॥ ১৬৭ ॥

aṣṭa 'sāttvika', harṣādi 'vyabhicārī' yāṅra
'sahaja prema', viṁśati 'bhāva'-alaṅkāra

SYNONYMS

aṣṭa—eight; *sāttvika*—transcendental symptoms; *harṣa-ādi*—like jubilation; *vyabhicārī*—distinctive features; *yāṅra*—of whose; *sahaja prema*—natural love; *viṁśati*—twenty; *bhāva*—of ecstasy; *alaṅkāra*—ornaments.

TRANSLATION

"The transcendental ornaments of Śrīmatī Rādhārāṇī's body include the eight sāttvikas, or transcendental symptoms, the thirty-three vyabhicārī-bhāvas, beginning with harṣa, or jubilation in natural love, and the twenty bhāvas, or ecstatic emotional ornaments.

PURPORT

The thirty-three *vyabhicārī-bhāvas,* bodily symptoms manifest in ecstatic love, are as follows: (1) *nirveda,* indifference; (2) *viṣāda,* moroseness; (3) *dainya,* meekness; (4) *glāni,* a feeling that one is in a faulty position; (5) *śrama,* fatigue; (6)

mada, madness; (7) *garva,* pride; (8) *śaṅkā,* doubt; (9) *trāsa,* shock; (10) *āvega,* intense emotion; (11) *unmāda,* craziness; (12) *apasmāra,* forgetfulness; (13) *vyādhi,* disease; (14) *moha,* bewilderment; (15) *mṛti,* death; (16) *ālasya,* laziness; (17) *jāḍya,* invalidity; (18) *vrīḍā,* shame; (19) *avahitthā,* concealment; (20) *smṛti,* remembrance; (21) *vitarka,* argument; (22) *cintā,* contemplation; (23) *mati,* attention; (24) *dhṛti,* forbearance; (25) *harṣa,* jubilation; (26) *autsukya,* eagerness; (27) *augrya,* violence; (28) *amarṣa,* anger; (29) *asūyā,* jealousy; (30) *cāpalya,* impudence; (31) *nidrā,* sleep; (32) *supti,* deep sleep and (33) *prabodha,* awakening.

TEXT 168

'কিলকিঞ্চিত', 'কুট্টমিত', 'বিলাস', 'ললিত'।
'বিব্বোক','মোট্টায়িত', আর 'মৌগ্ধ্য', 'চকিত'॥১৬৮॥

'kila-kiñcita', 'kuṭṭamita', 'vilāsa', 'lalita'
'vivvoka', 'moṭṭāyita', āra 'maugdhya', 'cakita'

SYNONYMS

kila-kiñcita—a particular type of ornament at the time of seeing Kṛṣṇa; *kuṭṭamita*—the symptom explained in verse 197; *vilāsa*—the symptom explained in verse 187; *lalita*—the symptom explained in verse 192; *vivvoka*—neglecting the presentation given by the hero; *moṭṭāyita*—awakening of lusty desires by the remembrance and words of the hero; *āra*—and; *maugdhya*—assuming the position of not knowing things although everything is known; *cakita*—a position in which the heroine appears very afraid although she is not at all afraid.

TRANSLATION

"Some of the symptoms critically explained in the following verses are kila-kiñcita, kuṭṭamita, vilāsa, lalita, vivvoka, moṭṭāyita, maugdhya and cakita.

TEXT 169

এত ভাবভূষায় ভূষিত শ্রীরাধার অঙ্গ।
দেখিতে উথলে কৃষ্ণসুখাব্ধি-তরঙ্গ ॥ ১৬৯ ॥

eta bhāva-bhūṣāya bhūṣita śrī-rādhāra aṅga
dekhite uthale kṛṣṇa-sukhābdhi-taraṅga

SYNONYMS

eta—so many; *bhāva-bhūṣāya*—with the ornaments of ecstasy; *bhūṣita*—decorated; *śrī-rādhāra*—of Śrīmatī Rādhārāṇī; *aṅga*—the body; *dekhite*—to see;

uthale—awakens; *kṛṣṇa-sukha-abdhi*—of the ocean of Kṛṣṇa's happiness; *taraṅga*—waves.

TRANSLATION

"When Śrīmatī Rādhārāṇī's body manifests the ornaments of many ecstatic symptoms, the ocean of Kṛṣṇa's happiness immediately displays transcendental waves.

TEXT 170

কিলকিঞ্চিতাদি-ভাবের শুন বিবরণ ।
যে ভাব-ভূষায় রাধা হরে কৃষ্ণ-মন ॥ ১৭০ ॥

kila-kiñcitādi-bhāvera śuna vivaraṇa
ye bhāva-bhūṣāya rādhā hare kṛṣṇa-mana

SYNONYMS

kila-kiñcita-ādi—beginning with the ecstasy named *kila-kiñcita; bhāvera*—of ecstasies; *śuna*—hear; *vivaraṇa*—the description; *ye bhāva-bhūṣāya*—with these ecstatic ornaments; *rādhā*—Śrīmatī Rādhārāṇī; *hare*—enchants; *kṛṣṇa-mana*—the mind of Kṛṣṇa.

TRANSLATION

"Now hear a description of different ecstasies, beginning with kila-kiñcita. With these ecstatic ornaments, Śrīmatī Rādhārāṇī enchants the mind of Kṛṣṇa.

TEXT 171

রাধা দেখি' কৃষ্ণ যদি ছুঁইতে করে মন ।
দানঘাটি-পথে যবে বর্জেন গমন ॥ ১৭১ ॥

rādhā dekhi' kṛṣṇa yadi chuṅite kare mana
dāna-ghāṭi-pathe yabe varjena gamana

SYNONYMS

rādhā—Śrīmatī Rādhārāṇī; *dekhi'*—after seeing; *kṛṣṇa*—Lord Kṛṣṇa; *yadi*—if; *chuṅite*—to touch; *kare mana*—desires; *dāna-ghāṭi-pathe*—on the way leading toward the spot from where one crosses the river to the other side; *yabe*—when; *varjena*—prohibits; *gamana*—going.

TRANSLATION

"When Śrī Kṛṣṇa sees Śrīmatī Rādhārāṇī and wants to touch Her body, He prohibits Her from going to the spot where one can cross the River Yamunā.

TEXT 172

যবে আসি' মানা করে পুষ্প উঠাইতে।
সখী-আগে চাহে যদি গায়ে হাত দিতে ॥ ১৭২ ॥

yabe āsi' mānā kare puṣpa uṭhāite
sakhī-āge cāhe yadi gāye hāta dite

SYNONYMS

yabe—when; *āsi'*—coming nearby; *mānā kare*—prohibits; *puṣpa uṭhāite*—to pick up flowers; *sakhī-āge*—in front of the friends of Śrīmatī Rādhārāṇī; *cāhe*—wants; *yadi*—if; *gāye*—in the body; *hāta dite*—touch with the hand.

TRANSLATION

"Approaching Her, Kṛṣṇa prohibits Śrīmatī Rādhārāṇī from picking flowers. He may also touch Her in front of Her friends.

TEXT 173

এইসব স্থানে 'কিলকিঞ্চিত' উদ্গম।
প্রথমে 'হর্ষ' সঞ্চারী—মূল কারণ ॥ ১৭৩ ॥

ei-saba sthāne 'kila-kiñcita' udgama
prathame 'harṣa' sañcārī——mūla kāraṇa

SYNONYMS

ei-saba sthāne—in such places; *kila-kiñcita*—of the symptom of the ecstasy known as *kila-kiñcita; udgama*—awakening; *prathame*—in the beginning; *harṣa*—jubilation; *sañcārī*—ecstatic emotion; *mūla kāraṇa*—the root cause.

TRANSLATION

"At such times, the ecstatic symptoms of kila-kiñcita are awakened. First there is jubilation in ecstatic love, which is the root cause of these symptoms.

PURPORT

Whenever Śrīmatī Rādhārāṇī leaves Her house, She is always well-dressed and attractive. It is Her womanly nature to attract Śrī Kṛṣṇa's attention, and upon seeing Her so attractively dressed, Śrī Kṛṣṇa desires to touch Her body. The Lord then finds some fault in Her and prohibits Her from going to a river crossing and stops Her from picking flowers. Such are the pastimes between Śrīmatī Rādhārāṇī and Śrī Kṛṣṇa. Being a cowherd girl, Śrīmatī Rādhārāṇī regularly carries a container of milk and often goes to sell it on the other side of the Yamunā. To cross the river, She has to pay the boatman, and the spot where the boatman collects his fares is called the *dāna-ghāṭi*. Lord Śrī Kṛṣṇa stops Her from going, telling Her, "First You have to pay the fee; then You will be allowed to go." This pastime is called *dāna-keli-līlā*. Similarly, if Śrīmatī Rādhārāṇī wants to pick a flower, Śrī Kṛṣṇa claims to be the garden's proprietor and prohibits Her. This pastime is called *kila-kiñcita*. Rādhārāṇī's shyness arises due to Śrī Kṛṣṇa's prohibitions, and ecstatic loving bodily symptoms called *kila-kiñcita-bhāva* are manifest at this time. These ecstatic symptoms are explained in the following verse, which is from Śrīla Rūpa Gosvāmī's *Ujjvala-nīlamaṇi* (*Anubhāva-prakaraṇa,* 44).

TEXT 174

গর্বাভিলাষরুদিতস্মিতাসূয়াভয়ক্রুধাম্ ।
সঙ্করীকরণং হর্ষাদুচ্যতে কিলকিঞ্চিতম্ ॥ ১৭৪ ॥

garvābhilāṣa-rudita-
smitāsūyā-bhaya-krudhām
saṅkarī-karaṇaṁ harṣād
ucyate kila-kiñcitam

SYNONYMS

garva—pride; *abhilāṣa*—ambition; *rudita*—crying; *smita*—smiling; *asūyā*—envying; *bhaya*—fearing; *krudhām*—anger; *saṅkarī-karaṇam*—the act of shrinking away; *harṣāt*—because of jubilation; *ucyate*—is called; *kila-kiñcitam*—ecstatic symptoms known as *kila-kiñcita*.

TRANSLATION

" 'Pride, ambition, weeping, smiling, envy, fear and anger are the seven ecstatic loving symptoms manifest by a jubilant shrinking away, and these symptoms are called kila-kiñcita-bhāva.'

TEXT 175

আর সাত ভাব আসি' সহজে মিলয় ।
অষ্টভাব-সম্মিলনে 'মহাভাব' হয় ॥ ১৭৫ ॥

āra sāta bhāva āsi' sahaje milaya
aṣṭa-bhāva-sammilane 'mahābhāva' haya

SYNONYMS

āra—other; *sāta*—seven; *bhāva*—ecstatic symptoms; *āsi'*—coming together; *sahaje*—naturally; *milaya*—become mixed; *aṣṭa-bhāva*—of eight kinds of ecstatic emotional symptoms; *sammilane*—by the combining; *mahā-bhāva haya*—there is *mahābhāva.*

TRANSLATION

"There are seven other transcendental ecstatic symptoms, and when they combine on the platform of jubilation, the combination is called mahābhāva.

TEXT 176

গর্ব, অভিলাষ, ভয়, শুষ্করুদিত ।
ক্রোধ, অসূয়া হয়, আর মন্দস্মিত ॥ ১৭৬ ॥

garva, abhilāṣa, bhaya, śuṣka-rudita
krodha, asūyā haya, āra manda-smita

SYNONYMS

garva—pride; *abhilāṣa*—ambition; *bhaya*—fear; *śuṣka-rudita*—dry, artificial crying; *krodha*—anger; *asūyā*—envy; *haya*—there is; *āra*—also; *manda-smita*—mild smiling.

TRANSLATION

"The seven combined ingredients of mahābhāva are pride, ambition, fear, dry artificial crying, anger, envy and mild smiling.

TEXT 177

নানা-স্বাদু অষ্টভাব একত্র মিলন ।
যাহার আস্বাদে তৃপ্ত হয় কৃষ্ণ-মন ॥ ১৭৭ ॥

nānā-svādu aṣṭa-bhāva ekatra milana
yāhāra āsvāde tṛpta haya kṛṣṇa-mana

SYNONYMS

nānā—various; *svādu*—tasteful; *aṣṭa-bhāva*—eight kinds of ecstatic symptoms; *ekatra*—at one place; *milana*—meeting; *yāhāra*—of which; *āsvāde*—by the tasting; *tṛpta*—satisfied; *haya*—is; *kṛṣṇa-mana*—the mind of Kṛṣṇa.

TRANSLATION

"There are eight symptoms of ecstatic love on the platform of transcendental jubilation, and when they are combined and tasted by Kṛṣṇa, the Lord's mind is completely satisfied.

TEXT 178

দধি, খণ্ড, ঘৃত, মধু, মরীচ, কর্পূর।
এলাচি-মিলনে যৈছে রসালা মধুর ॥ ১৭৮ ॥

dadhi, khaṇḍa, ghṛta, madhu, marīca, karpūra
elāci-milane yaiche rasālā madhura

SYNONYMS

dadhi—yogurt; *khaṇḍa*—candy; *ghṛta*—ghee; *madhu*—honey; *marīca*—black pepper; *karpūra*—camphor; *elāci*—cardamom; *milane*—by combining together; *yaiche*—as; *rasālā*—very tasteful; *madhura*—and sweet.

TRANSLATION

"Indeed, they are compared to a combination of yogurt, candy, ghee, honey, black pepper, camphor and cardamom, which, when mixed together, are very tasty and sweet.

TEXT 179

এই ভাব-যুক্ত দেখি' রাধাস্য-নয়ন।
সঙ্গম হইতে সুখ পায় কোটি-গুণ ॥ ১৭৯ ॥

ei bhāva-yukta dekhi' rādhāsya-nayana
saṅgama ha-ite sukha pāya koṭi-guṇa

SYNONYMS

ei bhāva—with these ecstatic symptoms; *yukta*—combined together; *dekhi'*—seeing; *rādhā-asya-nayana*—the face and eyes of Śrīmatī Rādhārāṇī; *saṅgama ha-ite*—than direct embracing; *sukha pāya*—enjoys happiness; *koṭi-guṇa*—millions of times more.

TRANSLATION

"Lord Śrī Kṛṣṇa is thousands upon thousands of times more satisfied when He sees Śrīmatī Rādhārāṇī's face light up from this combination of ecstatic love than He is by direct union with Her.

PURPORT

This is further explained in the following verse from the *Ujjvala-nīlamaṇi* (*Anubhāva-prakaraṇa,* 46) of Śrīla Rūpa Gosvāmī.

TEXT 180

অন্তঃস্মেরতয়োজ্জ্বলা জলকণব্যাকীর্ণপক্ষ্মাঙ্কুরা
কিঞ্চিৎপাটলিতাঞ্চলা রসিকতোৎসিক্তা পুরঃ কুঞ্চতী।
রুদ্ধায়াঃ পথি মাধবেন মধুরব্যাভুগ্নতোরোত্তরা
রাধায়াঃ কিলকিঞ্চিতস্তবকিনী দৃষ্টিঃ শ্রিয়ং বঃ ক্রিয়াৎ॥১৮০॥

antaḥ smeratayojjvalā jala-kaṇa-vyākīrṇa-pakṣmāṅkurā
kiñcit pāṭalitāñcalā rasikatotsiktā puraḥ kuñcatī
ruddhāyāḥ pathi mādhavena madhura-vyābhugna-torottarā
rādhāyāḥ kila-kiñcita-stavakinī dṛṣṭiḥ śriyaṁ vaḥ kriyāt

SYNONYMS

antaḥ—internally or not manifested; *smeratayā ujjvala*—brightened by mild smiling; *jala-kaṇa*—with drops of water; *vyākīrṇa*—scattered; *pakṣma-aṅkurā*—from the eyelashes; *kiñcit*—very little; *pāṭalita-añcalā*—a tinge of redness, mixed with whiteness, on the borders of the eyes; *rasikata-utsiktā*—being merged in the cunning behavior of the Lord; *puraḥ*—in the front; *kuñcatī*—shrinks; *ruddhāyāḥ*—having been blocked; *pathi*—on the way; *mādhavena*—by Kṛṣṇa; *madhura*—sweet; *vyābhugna*—curved; *torā-uttarā*—the eyes; *rādhāyāḥ*—of Śrīmatī Rādhārāṇī; *kila-kiñcita*—the ecstatic symptom named *kila-kiñcita; stavakinī*—like a bouquet of flowers; *dṛṣṭiḥ*—glance; *śriyam*—good fortune; *vaḥ*—of all of you; *kriyāt*—may perform.

TRANSLATION

" 'May the sight of Śrīmatī Rādhārāṇī's kila-kiñcita ecstasy, which is like a bouquet, bring good fortune to all. When Śrī Kṛṣṇa blocked Rādhārāṇī's way to the dāna-ghāṭi, there was laughter within Her heart. Her eyes grew bright, and fresh tears flowed from Her eyes, reddening them. Due to Her sweet relationship with Kṛṣṇa, Her eyes were enthusiastic, and when Her crying subsided, She appeared even more beautiful.'

TEXT 181

বাষ্পব্যাকুলিতারুণাঞ্চলচলন্নেত্রং রসোল্লাসিতং
হেলোল্লাসচলাধরং কুটিলিতভ্রূযুগ্মমুদ্যৎস্মিতম্।

রাধায়াঃ কিলকিঞ্চিতাঞ্চিতমসৌ বীক্ষ্যাননং সঙ্গমা-
দানন্দং তমবাপ কোটিগুণিতং যোঽভূন্ন গীর্গোচরঃ ॥১৮১॥

bāṣpa-vyākulitāruṇāñcala-calan-netraṁ rasollāsitaṁ
helollāsa-calādharaṁ kuṭilita-bhrū-yugmam udyat-smitam
rādhāyāḥ kila-kiñcitāñcitam asau vīkṣyānanaṁ saṅgamād
ānandaṁ tam avāpa koṭi-guṇitaṁ yo 'bhūn na gīr-gocaraḥ

SYNONYMS

bāṣpa—by tears; *vyākulita*—agitated; *aruṇa-añcala*—with a reddish tinge; *calan*—moving; *netram*—eyes; *rasa-ullāsitam*—because of being agitated by transcendental mellows; *hela-ullāsa*—because of neglectful jubilation; *cala-adharam*—moving lips; *kuṭilita*—curved; *bhrū-yugmam*—two eyebrows; *udyat*—awakening; *smitam*—smiling; *rādhāyāḥ*—of Śrīmatī Rādhārāṇī; *kila-kiñcita*—with the ecstatic symptom named *kila-kiñcita; añcitam*—expression; *asau*—He (Kṛṣṇa); *vīkṣya*—after glancing over; *ānanam*—the face; *saṅgamāt*—even than embracing; *ānandam*—happiness; *tam*—that; *avāpa*—got; *koṭi-guṇitam*—millions upon millions times more; *yaḥ*—which; *abhūt*—became; *na*—not; *gīḥ-gocaraḥ*—the subject of being described.

TRANSLATION

" 'Agitated by tears, Śrīmatī Rādhārāṇī's eyes were tinged with red, just like the eastern horizon at sunrise. Her lips began to move with jubilation and lusty desire. Her eyebrows curved, and Her lotuslike face smiled mildly. Seeing Rādhārāṇī's face exhibit such emotion, Lord Śrī Kṛṣṇa felt a million times happier than when He embraced Her. Indeed, Lord Śrī Kṛṣṇa's happiness is not at all mundane.' "

PURPORT

This is a quotation from *Govinda-līlāmṛta* (9.18).

TEXT 182

এত শুনি' প্রভু হৈলা আনন্দিত মন।
সুখাবিষ্ট হঞা স্বরূপে কৈলা আলিঙ্গন ॥ ১৮২ ॥

eta śuni' prabhu hailā ānandita mana
sukhāviṣṭa hañā svarūpe kailā āliṅgana

SYNONYMS

eta śuni'—hearing this; *prabhu*—Śrī Caitanya Mahāprabhu; *hailā*—became; *ānandita mana*—very happy in His mind; *sukha-āviṣṭa hañā*—being absorbed in happiness; *svarūpe*—unto Svarūpa Dāmodara Gosvāmī; *kailā*—did; *āliṅgana*—embracing.

TRANSLATION

Upon hearing this, Śrī Caitanya Mahāprabhu became very happy, and, being absorbed in this happiness, He embraced Svarūpa Dāmodara Gosvāmī.

TEXT 183

'বিলাসাদি'-ভাব-ভূষার কহ ত' লক্ষণ ।
যেই ভাবে রাধা হরে গোবিন্দের মন ? ১৮৩ ॥

'vilāsādi'-bhāva-bhūṣāra kaha ta' lakṣaṇa
yei bhāve rādhā hare govindera mana?

SYNONYMS

vilāsa-ādi—beginning with transcendental enjoyment; *bhāva*—of ecstasy; *bhūṣāra*—of the ornaments; *kaha*—please speak; *ta'*—indeed; *lakṣaṇa*—the symptoms; *yei bhāve*—by which symptoms; *rādhā*—Śrīmatī Rādhārāṇī; *hare*—enchants; *govindera mana*—the mind of Śrī Govinda.

TRANSLATION

Śrī Caitanya Mahāprabhu then asked Svarūpa Dāmodara, "Please speak of the ecstatic ornaments decorating the body of Śrīmatī Rādhārāṇī, by which She enchants the mind of Śrī Govinda."

TEXT 184

তবে ত' স্বরূপ-গোসাঞি কহিতে লাগিলা ।
শুনি' প্রভুর ভক্তগণ মহাসুখ পাইলা ॥ ১৮৪ ॥

tabe ta' svarūpa-gosāñi kahite lāgilā
śuni' prabhura bhakta-gaṇa mahā-sukha pāilā

SYNONYMS

tabe—at that time; *ta'*—indeed; *svarūpa-gosāñi*—Svarūpa Dāmodara; *kahite lāgilā*—began to speak; *śuni'*—hearing; *prabhura*—of Śrī Caitanya Mahāprabhu; *bhakta-gaṇa*—all the devotees; *mahā-sukha pāilā*—achieved great happiness.

TRANSLATION

Being thus requested, Svarūpa Dāmodara began to speak. All the devotees of Śrī Caitanya Mahāprabhu were very happy to hear him.

TEXT 185

রাধা বসি' আছে, কিবা বৃন্দাবনে যায় ।
তাহাঁ যদি আচম্বিতে কৃষ্ণ-দরশন পায় ॥ ১৮৫ ॥

rādhā vasi' āche, kibā vṛndāvane yāya
tāhāṅ yadi ācambite kṛṣṇa-daraśana pāya

SYNONYMS

rādhā vasi' āche—Śrīmatī Rādhārāṇī is sitting; *kibā*—or; *vṛndāvane yāya*—is going to Vṛndāvana; *tāhāṅ*—there; *yadi*—if; *ācambite*—all of a sudden; *kṛṣṇa-daraśana pāya*—gets the opportunity to see Kṛṣṇa.

TRANSLATION

"Sometimes when Śrīmatī Rādhārāṇī is sitting or when She is going to Vṛndāvana, She sometimes sees Kṛṣṇa.

TEXT 186

দেখিতে নানা-ভাব হয় বিলক্ষণ ।
সে বৈলক্ষণ্যের নাম 'বিলাস'-ভূষণ ॥ ১৮৬ ॥

dekhite nānā-bhāva haya vilakṣaṇa
se vailakṣaṇyera nāma 'vilāsa'-bhūṣaṇa

SYNONYMS

dekhite—while seeing; *nānā-bhāva*—of various ecstasies; *haya*—there are; *vilakṣaṇa*—symptoms; *se*—those; *vailakṣaṇyera*—of different symptoms; *nāma*—the name; *vilāsa*—*vilāsa; bhūṣaṇa*—ornaments.

TRANSLATION

"The symptoms of various ecstasies that become manifest at that time are called vilāsa.

PURPORT

This is described in the following verse, taken from the *Ujjvala-nīlamaṇi* (*Anubhāva-prakaraṇa*, 31).

TEXT 187

গতিস্থানাসনাদীনাং মুখনেত্রাদিকর্মণাম্ ।
তাৎকালিকন্তু বৈশিষ্ট্যং বিলাসঃ প্রিয়সঙ্গজম্ ॥ ১৮৭ ॥

gati-sthānāsanādīnāṁ
mukha-netrādi-karmaṇām
tātkālikaṁ tu vaiśiṣṭyaṁ
vilāsaḥ priya-saṅgajam

SYNONYMS

gati—moving; *sthāna*—standing; *āsana-ādīnām*—and of sitting and so on; *mukha*—of the face; *netra*—of the eyes; *ādi*—and so on; *karmaṇām*—of the activities; *tāt-kālikam*—relating to that time; *tu*—then; *vaiśiṣṭyam*—various symptoms; *vilāsaḥ*—of the name *vilāsa; priya-saṅga-jam*—produced from meeting her beloved.

TRANSLATION

" 'The various symptoms manifested in a woman's face, eyes, and the other parts of her body and the way she moves, stands or sits when she meets her beloved are called vilāsa.' "

TEXT 188

লজ্জা, হর্ষ, অভিলাষ, সম্ভ্রম, বাম্য, ভয় ।
এত ভাব মিলি' রাধায় চঞ্চল করয় ॥ ১৮৮ ॥

lajjā, harṣa, abhilāṣa, sambhrama, vāmya, bhaya
eta bhāva mili' rādhāya cañcala karaya

SYNONYMS

lajjā—timidity; *harṣa*—jubilation; *abhilāṣa*—ambition; *sambhrama*—respect; *vāmya*—characteristics of the left-wing *gopīs; bhaya*—fear; *eta*—these; *bhāva*—ecstatic symptoms; *mili'*—coming together; *rādhāya*—Śrīmatī Rādhārāṇī; *cañcala karaya*—agitate.

TRANSLATION

Svarūpa Dāmodara said, "Timidity, jubilation, ambition, respect, fear and the characteristics of the left-wing gopīs were all ecstatic symptoms combined to agitate Śrīmatī Rādhārāṇī.

PURPORT

This is explained in the following verse found in the *Govinda-līlāmṛta* (9.11).

TEXT 189

পুরঃ কৃষ্ণালোকাৎ স্থগিতকুটিলাস্যা গতিরভূৎ
তিরশ্চীনং কৃষ্ণাম্বরদরবৃতং শ্রীমুখমপি ।

চলত্তারং স্ফারং নয়নযুগমাভুগ্নমিতি সা
বিলাসাখ্য-স্বালঙ্করণবলিতাসীৎ প্রিয়মুদে ॥ ১৮৯ ॥

puraḥ kṛṣṇālokāt sthagita-kuṭilāsyā gatir abhūt
tiraścīnaṁ kṛṣṇāmbara-dara-vṛtaṁ śrī-mukham api
calat-tāraṁ sphāraṁ nayana-yugam ābhugnam iti sā
vilāsākhya-svālaṅkaraṇa-valitāsīt priya-mude

SYNONYMS

puraḥ—in front of Her; *kṛṣṇa-ālokāt*—by seeing Lord Kṛṣṇa; *sthagita-kuṭilā*—stopped and assumed an attitude of crookedness; *asyāḥ*—of Śrīmatī Rādhārāṇī; *gatiḥ*—the progress; *abhūt*—became; *tiraścīnam*—being crooked; *kṛṣṇa-ambara*—by a blue cloth; *dara-vṛtam*—covered; *śrī-mukham api*—Her face also; *calat-tāram*—like moving stars; *sphāram*—wide; *nayana-yugam*—the pair of eyes; *ābhugnam*—very curved; *iti*—thus; *sā*—She (Rādhārāṇī); *vilāsa-ākhya*—named *vilāsa; sva-alaṅkaraṇa*—by personal ornaments; *valita*—decorated; *āsīt*—was; *priya-mude*—just to increase the pleasure of Śrī Kṛṣṇa.

TRANSLATION

" 'When Śrīmatī Rādhārāṇī saw Lord Kṛṣṇa just before Her, Her progress stopped, and She assumed an attitude of opposition. Although Her face was slightly covered by a blue garment, Her two starry eyes were agitated, being wide and curved. Thus She was decorated with the ornaments of vilāsa, and Her beauty increased to give pleasure to Śrī Kṛṣṇa, the Supreme Personality of Godhead.'

TEXT 190

কৃষ্ণ-আগে রাধা যদি রহে দাণ্ডাঞা ।
তিন-অঙ্গ-ভঙ্গে রহে ভ্রূ নাচাঞা ॥ ১৯০ ॥

kṛṣṇa-āge rādhā yadi rahe dāṇḍāñā
tina-aṅga-bhaṅge rahe bhrū nācāñā

SYNONYMS

kṛṣṇa-āge—in front of Kṛṣṇa; *rādhā*—Śrīmatī Rādhārāṇī; *yadi*—if; *rahe*—remains; *dāṇḍāñā*—standing; *tina-aṅga-bhaṅge*—with three bends in the body; *rahe*—remains; *bhrū*—eyebrows; *nācāñā*—dancing.

TRANSLATION

"When Śrīmatī Rādhārāṇī stands before Kṛṣṇa, She stands bent in three places—Her neck, waist and legs—and Her eyebrows dance.

TEXT 191

মুখে-নেত্রে হয় নানা-ভাবের উদ্গার ।
এই কান্তা-ভাবের নাম 'ললিত'-অলঙ্কার ॥১৯১ ॥

mukhe-netre haya nānā-bhāvera udgāra
ei kāntā-bhāvera nāma 'lalita'-alaṅkāra

SYNONYMS

mukhe—on the mouth; *netre*—on the eyes; *haya*—there are; *nānā-bhāvera*—of various ecstasies; *udgāra*—the awakening; *ei*—this; *kāntā-bhāvera*—of the condition of the female; *nāma*—the name; *lalita*—of *lalita; alaṅkāra*—the ornament.

TRANSLATION

"When there is an awakening of various ecstatic features on Śrīmatī Rādhārāṇī's face and in Her eyes, the lalita ornaments are manifest.

TEXT 192

বিন্যাস-ভঙ্গিরঙ্গানাং ভ্রূবিলাস-মনোহরা ।
সুকুমারা ভবেদ্যত্র ললিতং তদুদাহৃতম্ ॥ ১৯২ ॥

vinyāsa-bhaṅgir aṅgānāṁ
bhrū-vilāsa-manoharā
sukumārā bhaved yatra
lalitaṁ tad udāhṛtam

SYNONYMS

vinyāsa—in arrangement; *bhaṅgiḥ*—curvature; *aṅgānām*—of bodily limbs; *bhrū-vilāsa*—due to the pastimes of the eyebrows; *manoharā*—very beautiful; *su-kumārā*—delicate; *bhavet*—may be; *yatra*—where; *lalitam*—*lalita; tat*—that; *udāhṛtam*—called.

TRANSLATION

" 'When the bodily features are delicate and expertly curved, and when the eyebrows are very beautifully agitated, the ornament of charm, called lalita-alaṅkāra, is manifest.'

PURPORT

This verse is from *Ujjvala-nīlamaṇi* (*Anubhāva-prakaraṇa*, 56).

TEXT 193

ললিত-ভূষিত রাধা দেখে যদি কৃষ্ণ ।
দুঁহে দুঁহা মিলিবারে হয়েন সতৃষ্ণ ॥ ১৯৩ ॥

lalita-bhūṣita rādhā dekhe yadi kṛṣṇa
duṅhe duṅhā milibāre hayena satṛṣṇa

SYNONYMS

lalita-bhūṣita—decorated with *lalita-alaṅkāra; rādhā*—Śrīmatī Rādhārāṇī; *dekhe*—sees; *yadi*—if; *kṛṣṇa*—Lord Kṛṣṇa; *duṅhe*—both of Them; *duṅhā*—the two of Them; *milibāre*—to meet; *hayena*—become; *sa-tṛṣṇa*—very anxious.

TRANSLATION

"When Lord Śrī Kṛṣṇa happens to see Śrīmatī Rādhārāṇī decorated with these lalita ornaments, They both anxiously want to meet one another.

TEXT 194

হ্রিয়া তির্যগ্-গ্রীবা-চরণ-কটি-ভঙ্গী-সুমধুরা
চলচ্চিল্লী-বল্লী-দলিত-রতিনাথোর্জিত-ধনুঃ ।
প্রিয়-প্রেমোল্লাসোল্লসিত-ললিতালালিত-তনুঃ
প্রিয়প্রীত্যৈ সাসীদুদিতললিতালঙ্কৃতিযুতা ॥ ১৯৪ ॥

hriyā tiryag-grīvā-caraṇa-kaṭi-bhaṅgī-sumadhurā
calac-cillī-vallī-dalita-ratināthorjita-dhanuḥ
priya-premollāsollasita-lalitālālita-tanuḥ
priya-prītyai sāsīd udita-lalitālaṅkṛti-yutā

SYNONYMS

hriyā—by Her attitude of shyness; *tiryak*—going crosswise; *grīvā*—of the neck; *caraṇa*—of the knees; *kaṭi*—of the waist; *bhaṅgī*—by the curve; *su-madhurā*—very sweet; *calat-cillī*—of moving eyebrows; *vallī*—by the creepers; *dalita*—conquered; *rati-nātha*—of Cupid; *ūrjita*—powerful; *dhanuḥ*—by which the bow; *priya-prema-ullāsa*—because of the loving attitude of the beloved; *ullasita*—being inspired; *lalita*—by the mood known as *lalita; ālālita-tanuḥ*—whose body is covered; *priya-prītyai*—for the sake of pleasing the beloved; *sā*—Śrīmatī Rādhārāṇī; *āsīt*—was; *udita*—awakened; *lalita-alaṅkṛti–yutā*—possessing the *lalita-alaṅkāra.*

TRANSLATION

" 'When Śrīmatī Rādhārāṇī was decorated with the ornament of lalita-alaṅkāra, just to increase Śrī Kṛṣṇa's love, an attractive curve was manifest by Her neck, knees and waist. This was brought about by Her timidity and apparent desire to avoid Kṛṣṇa. The flickering movements of Her eyebrows could conquer the powerful bow of Cupid. To increase the joy of Her beloved's love, Her body was decorated with the ornaments of lalita-alaṅkāra.'

PURPORT

This verse is quoted from *Govinda-līlāmṛta* (9.14).

TEXT 195

লোভে আসি' কৃষ্ণ করে কঞ্চুকাকর্ষণ ।
অন্তরে উল্লাস, রাধা করে নিবারণ ॥ ১৯৫ ॥

lobhe āsi' kṛṣṇa kare kañcukākarṣaṇa
antare ullāsa, rādhā kare nivāraṇa

SYNONYMS

lobhe—in greed; *āsi'*—coming; *kṛṣṇa*—Lord Kṛṣṇa; *kare*—does; *kañcuka-ākarṣaṇa*—snatching the border of Her sari; *antare*—within; *ullāsa*—very much pleased; *rādhā*—Śrīmatī Rādhārāṇī; *kare*—does; *nivāraṇa*—stopping.

TRANSLATION

"When Kṛṣṇa comes forward and greedily snatches at the border of Rādhārāṇī's sari, She is actually very pleased within, but overtly She tries to stop Him.

TEXT 196

বাহিরে বামতা-ক্রোধ, ভিতরে সুখ মনে ।
'কুট্টমিত'-নাম এই ভাব-বিভূষণে ॥ ১৯৬ ॥

bāhire vāmatā-krodha, bhitare sukha mane
'kuṭṭamita'-nāma ei bhāva-vibhūṣaṇe

SYNONYMS

bāhire—externally; *vāmatā*—opposition; *krodha*—anger; *bhitare*—within; *sukha*—happiness; *mane*—in the mind; *kuṭṭamita*—*kuṭṭamita; nāma*—named; *ei*—this; *bhāva-vibhūṣaṇe*—ornament of an ecstatic attitude.

TRANSLATION

"This ecstatic dress of Śrīmatī Rādhārāṇī's is called kuṭṭamita. When it is manifest, She externally tries to avoid Kṛṣṇa, and She apparently becomes angry, although She is very happy within.

TEXT 197

স্তনাধরাদিগ্রহণে হৃৎপ্রীতাবপি সম্ভ্রমাৎ।
বহিঃক্রোধো ব্যথিতবৎ প্রোক্তং কুট্টমিতং বুধৈঃ ॥ ১৯৭ ॥

stanādharādi-grahaṇe
hṛt-prītāv api sambhramāt
bahiḥ krodho vyathitavat
proktaṁ kuṭṭamitaṁ budhaiḥ

SYNONYMS

stana—breasts; *adhara*—lips; *ādi*—and so on; *grahaṇe*—when capturing; *hṛt-prītau*—satisfaction of the heart; *api*—even though; *sambhramāt*—because of respectfulness; *bahiḥ*—externally; *krodhaḥ*—anger; *vyathita*—aggrieved; *vat*—as if; *proktam*—called; *kuṭṭamitam*—the technical term *kuṭṭamita; budhaiḥ*—by learned scholars.

TRANSLATION

" 'When the border of Her sari and the cloth veiling Her face are caught, She externally appears offended and angry, but within Her heart She is very happy. Learned scholars call this attitude kuṭṭamita.'

PURPORT

This is a quotation from *Ujjvala-nīlamaṇi* (*Anubhāva-prakaraṇa,* 49).

TEXT 198

কৃষ্ণ-বাঞ্ছা পূর্ণ হয়, করে পাণি-রোধ।
অন্তরে আনন্দ রাধা, বাহিরে বাম্য-ক্রোধ ॥ ১৯৮ ॥

kṛṣṇa-vāñchā pūrṇa haya, kare pāṇi-rodha
antare ānanda rādhā, bāhire vāmya-krodha

SYNONYMS

kṛṣṇa-vāñchā—the desire of Lord Kṛṣṇa; *pūrṇa*—fulfilled; *haya*—let it be; *kare*—does; *pāṇi-rodha*—checking with Her hand; *antare*—within the heart;

ānanda—transcendental bliss; *rādhā*—Śrīmatī Rādhārāṇī; *bāhire*—externally; *vāmya*—opposition; *krodha*—and anger.

TRANSLATION

"Although Śrīmatī Rādhārāṇī was checking Her sari with Her hand, internally She was thinking, 'Let Kṛṣṇa satisfy His desires.' In this way She was very pleased within, although She externally displayed opposition and anger.

TEXT 199

ব্যথা পাঞা' করে যেন শুষ্ক রোদন ।
ঈষৎ হাসিয়া কৃষ্ণে করেন ভর্ৎসন ॥ ১৯৯ ॥

vyathā pāñā' kare yena śuṣka rodana
īṣat hāsiyā kṛṣṇe karena bhartsana

SYNONYMS

vyathā pāñā'—being offended; *kare*—does; *yena*—as if; *śuṣka*—dry; *rodana*—crying; *īṣat*—mildly; *hāsiyā*—smiling; *kṛṣṇe*—unto Kṛṣṇa; *karena*—does; *bhartsana*—admonition.

TRANSLATION

"Śrīmatī Rādhārāṇī externally displays a kind of dry crying, as if She is offended. Then She mildly smiles and admonishes Lord Kṛṣṇa.

TEXT 200

পাণিরোধমবিরোধিতবাঞ্ছং ভর্ৎসনাশ্চ মধুরস্মিতগর্ভাঃ ।
মাধবস্য কুরুতে করভোরুর্হারি শুষ্করুদিতঞ্চ মুখেঽপি ॥ ২০০ ॥

pāṇi-rodham avirodhita-vāñchaṁ
bhartsanāś ca madhura-smita-garbhāḥ
mādhavasya kurute karabhorur
hāri śuṣka-ruditaṁ ca mukhe 'pi

SYNONYMS

pāṇi—the hand; *rodham*—obstructing; *avirodhita*—unobstructed; *vāñcham*—the desire of Kṛṣṇa; *bhartsanāḥ*—admonitions; *ca*—and; *madhura*—sweet; *smita-garbhāḥ*—containing a gentle smiling attitude; *mādhavasya*—of Śrī Kṛṣṇa; *kurute*—does; *karabha-ūruḥ*—whose thigh is like the trunk of a baby elephant; *hāri*—charming; *śuṣka-ruditam*—dry crying; *ca*—and; *mukhe*—on the face; *api*—also.

TRANSLATION

" 'Actually She has no desire to stop Kṛṣṇa's endeavor to touch Her body with His hands, yet Śrīmatī Rādhārāṇī, whose thighs are like the trunk of a baby elephant, protests His advances and, sweetly smiling, admonishes Him. At such times She cries without tears on Her charming face.'

TEXT 201

এইমত আর সব ভাব-বিভূষণ ।
যাহাতে ভূষিত রাধা হরে কৃষ্ণ মন ॥ ২০১ ॥

ei-mata āra saba bhāva-vibhūṣaṇa
yāhāte bhūṣita rādhā hare kṛṣṇa mana

SYNONYMS

ei-mata—in this way; *āra*—also; *saba*—all; *bhāva-vibhūṣaṇa*—ecstatic ornaments; *yāhāte*—by which; *bhūṣita*—being decorated; *rādhā*—Śrīmatī Rādhārāṇī; *hare*—attracts; *kṛṣṇa mana*—the mind of Kṛṣṇa.

TRANSLATION

"In this way, Śrīmatī Rādhārāṇī is ornamented and decorated with various ecstatic symptoms, which attract the mind of Śrī Kṛṣṇa.

TEXT 202

অনন্ত কৃষ্ণের লীলা না যায় বর্ণন ।
আপনে বর্ণেন যদি 'সহস্রবদন' ॥ ২০২ ॥

ananta kṛṣṇera līlā nā yāya varṇana
āpane varṇena yadi 'sahasra-vadana'

SYNONYMS

ananta—unlimited; *kṛṣṇera*—of Lord Kṛṣṇa; *līlā*—pastimes; *nā*—not; *yāya*—is possible; *varṇana*—description; *āpane*—personally; *varṇena*—describes; *yadi*—if; *sahasra-vadana*—the thousand-mouthed Śeṣa.

TRANSLATION

"It is not at all possible to describe the unlimited pastimes of Śrī Kṛṣṇa, even though He Himself describes them in His incarnation of Sahasra-vadana, the thousand-mouthed Śeṣa Nāga."

TEXT 203

শ্রীবাস হাসিয়া কহে,—শুন, দামোদর।
আমার লক্ষ্মীর দেখ সম্পত্তি বিস্তর ॥ ২০৩ ॥

śrīvāsa hāsiyā kahe,——śuna, dāmodara
āmāra lakṣmīra dekha sampatti vistara

SYNONYMS

śrīvāsa—Śrīvāsa Ṭhākura; *hāsiyā*—smiling; *kahe*—says; *śuna*—please hear; *dāmodara*—O Dāmodara Gosvāmī; *āmāra lakṣmīra*—of my goddess of fortune; *dekha*—just see; *sampatti vistara*—the great opulence.

TRANSLATION

This time, Śrīvāsa Ṭhākura smiled and told Dāmodara Paṇḍita, "My dear sir, please hear! Just see how opulent my goddess of fortune is!

TEXT 204

বৃন্দাবনের সম্পদ্ দেখ,—পুষ্প-কিসলয়।
গিরিধাতু-শিখিপিচ্ছ-গুঞ্জাফল-ময় ॥ ২০৪ ॥

vṛndāvanera sampad dekha,——puṣpa-kisalaya
giridhātu-śikhipiccha-guñjāphala-maya

SYNONYMS

vṛndāvanera—of Vṛndāvana; *sampad*—the opulence; *dekha*—see; *puṣpa-kisalaya*—a few flowers and twigs; *giri-dhātu*—some minerals from the hills; *śikhi-piccha*—some peacock feathers; *guñjā-phala-maya*—some *guñjā-phala.*

TRANSLATION

"As far as Vṛndāvana's opulence is concerned, it consists of a few flowers and twigs, some minerals from the hills, a few peacock feathers and the plant known as guñjā.

TEXT 205

বৃন্দাবন দেখিবারে গেলা জগন্নাথ।
শুনি' লক্ষ্মী-দেবীর মনে হৈল আসোয়াথ ॥ ২০৫ ॥

vṛndāvana dekhibāre gelā jagannātha
śuni' lakṣmī-devīra mane haila āsoyātha

SYNONYMS

vṛndāvana—Vṛndāvana-dhāma; *dekhibāre*—to see; *gelā*—went; *jagannātha*—Lord Jagannātha; *śuni'*—hearing; *lakṣmī-devīra*—of the goddess of fortune; *mane*—in the mind; *haila*—there was; *āsoyātha*—envy.

TRANSLATION

"When Jagannātha decided to see Vṛndāvana, He went there, and upon hearing this, the goddess of fortune experienced restlessness and jealousy.

TEXT 206

এত সম্পত্তি ছাড়ি' কেনে গেলা বৃন্দাবন ।
তাঁরে হাস্য করিতে লক্ষ্মী করিলা সাজন ॥ ২০৬ ॥

eta sampatti chāḍi' kene gelā vṛndāvana
tāṅre hāsya karite lakṣmī karilā sājana

SYNONYMS

eta sampatti—so much opulence; *chāḍi'*—giving up; *kene*—why; *gelā*—He went; *vṛndāvana*—to Vṛndāvana; *tāṅre hāsya karite*—to make Him a laughingstock; *lakṣmī*—the goddess of fortune; *karilā*—made; *sājana*—so much decoration.

TRANSLATION

"She wondered, 'Why did Lord Jagannātha give up so much opulence and go to Vṛndāvana?' To make Him a laughingstock, the goddess of fortune made arrangements for much decoration.

TEXT 207

"তোমার ঠাকুর, দেখ এত সম্পত্তি ছাড়ি' ।
পত্র-ফল-ফুল-লোভে গেলা পুষ্পবাড়ী ॥ ২০৭ ॥

"tomāra ṭhākura, dekha eta sampatti chāḍi'
patra-phala-phula-lobhe gelā puṣpa-bāḍī

SYNONYMS

tomāra ṭhākura—your Lord; *dekha*—just see; *eta sampatti chāḍi'*—giving so much opulence; *patra-phala-phula*—leaves, fruits and flowers; *lobhe*—for the sake of; *gelā*—went; *puṣpa-bāḍī*—to the flower garden of Guṇḍicā.

TRANSLATION

"Then the maidservants of the goddess of fortune said to the servants of Lord Jagannātha, 'Why did your Lord Jagannātha abandon the great opulence of the goddess of fortune and, for the sake of a few leaves, fruits and flowers, go see the flower garden of Śrīmatī Rādhārāṇī?

TEXT 208

এই কর্ম করে কাহাঁ বিদগ্ধ-শিরোমণি ?
লক্ষ্মীর অগ্রেতে নিজ প্রভুরে দেহ' আনি' ॥"২০৮ ॥

ei karma kare kāhāṅ vidagdha-śiromaṇi?
lakṣmīra agrete nija prabhure deha' āni' "

SYNONYMS

ei—this; *karma*—work; *kare*—does; *kāhāṅ*—where; *vidagdha-śiromaṇi*—the chief of all experts; *lakṣmīra*—of the goddess of fortune; *agrete*—in front; *nija*—your own; *prabhure*—master; *deha'*—present; *āni'*—bringing.

TRANSLATION

" 'Your master is so expert at everything, but why does He do such things? Please bring your master before the goddess of fortune.'

TEXT 209

এত বলি' মহালক্ষ্মীর সব দাসীগণে ।
কটি-বস্ত্রে বান্ধি' আনে প্রভুর নিজগণে ॥ ২০৯ ॥

eta bali' mahā-lakṣmīra saba dāsī-gaṇe
kaṭi-vastre bāndhi' āne prabhura nija-gaṇe

SYNONYMS

eta bali'—saying this; *mahā-lakṣmīra*—of the goddess of fortune; *saba*—all; *dāsī-gaṇe*—maidservants; *kaṭi-vastre*—by their waist clothes; *bāndhi'*—binding; *āne*—bring; *prabhura*—of Jagannātha; *nija-gaṇe*—personal servants.

TRANSLATION

"In this way all the maidservants of the goddess of fortune arrested the servants of Jagannātha, bound them around the waist and brought them before the goddess of fortune.

TEXT 210

লক্ষ্মীর চরণে আনি' করায় প্রণতি ।
ধন-দণ্ড লয়, আর করায় মিনতি ॥ ২১০ ॥

lakṣmīra caraṇe āni' karāya praṇati
dhana-daṇḍa laya, āra karāya minati

SYNONYMS

lakṣmīra caraṇe—at the lotus feet of the goddess of fortune; *āni'*—bringing; *karāya praṇati*—made to bow down; *dhana-daṇḍa laya*—take a fine; *āra*—also; *karāya*—make them perform; *minati*—submission.

TRANSLATION

"When all the maidservants brought Lord Jagannātha's servants before the lotus feet of the goddess of fortune, the Lord's servants were fined and forced to submit.

TEXT 211

রথের উপরে করে দণ্ডের তাড়ন ।
চোর-প্রায় করে জগন্নাথের সেবকগণ ॥ ২১১ ॥

rathera upare kare daṇḍera tāḍana
cora-prāya kare jagannāthera sevaka-gaṇa

SYNONYMS

rathera upare—on the car; *kare*—do; *daṇḍera tāḍana*—chastisement by sticks; *cora-prāya*—almost like thieves; *kare*—they treated; *jagannāthera*—of Lord Jagannātha; *sevaka-gaṇa*—the personal servants.

TRANSLATION

"All the maidservants began to beat the Ratha car with sticks, and they treated the servants of Lord Jagannātha almost like thieves.

TEXT 212

সব ভৃত্যগণ কহে,—যোড় করি' হাত।
কালি আনি দিব তোমার আগে জগন্নাথ' ॥ ২১২ ॥

saba bhṛtya-gaṇa kahe,——yoḍa kari' hāta
'kāli āni diba tomāra āge jagannātha'

SYNONYMS

saba bhṛtya-gaṇa kahe—all the servants said; *yoḍa kari' hāta*—folding the hands; *kāli*—tomorrow; *āni*—bringing; *diba*—we shall give; *tomāra*—of you; *āge*—in front; *jagannātha*—Lord Jagannātha.

TRANSLATION

"Finally all of Lord Jagannātha's servants submitted to the goddess of fortune with folded hands, assuring her that they would bring Lord Jagannātha before her the very next day.

TEXT 213

তবে শান্ত হঞা লক্ষ্মী যায় নিজ ঘর।
আমার লক্ষ্মীর সম্পদ্—বাক্য-অগোচর ॥ ২১৩ ॥

tabe śānta hañā lakṣmī yāya nija ghara
āmāra lakṣmīra sampad——vākya-agocara

SYNONYMS

tabe—then; *śānta hañā*—being pacified; *lakṣmī*—the goddess of fortune; *yāya*—goes back; *nija ghara*—to her own apartment; *āmāra*—my; *lakṣmīra*—of the goddess of fortune; *sampad*—the opulence; *vākya-agocara*—beyond description.

TRANSLATION

"Being thus pacified, the goddess of fortune returned to her apartment. Just see! My goddess of fortune is opulent beyond all description."

TEXT 214

দুগ্ধ আউটি' দধি মথে তোমার গোপীগণে।
আমার ঠাকুরাণী বৈসে রত্নসিংহাসনে ॥ ২১৪ ॥

dugdha āuṭi' dadhi mathe tomāra gopī-gaṇe
āmāra ṭhākurāṇī vaise ratna-siṁhāsane

SYNONYMS

dugdha āuṭi'—boiling milk; *dadhi*—into yogurt; *mathe*—churn; *tomāra*—your; *gopī-gaṇe*—*gopīs;* *āmāra*—my; *ṭhākurāṇī*—mistress; *vaise*—sits down; *ratna-siṁhāsane*—on a throne of gems.

TRANSLATION

Śrīvāsa Ṭhākura continued to address Svarūpa Dāmodara: "Your gopīs are engaged in boiling milk and churning it to turn it into yogurt, but my mistress, the goddess of fortune, sits on a throne made of jewels and gems."

TEXT 215

নারদ-প্রকৃতি শ্রীবাস করে পরিহাস ।
শুনি' হাসে মহাপ্রভুর যত নিজ-দাস ॥ ২১৫ ॥

nārada-prakṛti śrīvāsa kare parihāsa
śuni' hāse mahāprabhura yata nija-dāsa

SYNONYMS

nārada-prakṛti—with the nature of Nārada Muni; *śrīvāsa*—Śrīvāsa Ṭhākura; *kare*—does; *parihāsa*—joking; *śuni'*—hearing; *hāse*—smile; *mahāprabhura*—of Śrī Caitanya Mahāprabhu; *yata*—all; *nija-dāsa*—personal servants.

TRANSLATION

Śrīvāsa Ṭhākura, who was enjoying the mood of Nārada Muni, thus made jokes. Hearing him, all the personal servants of Śrī Caitanya Mahāprabhu began to smile.

TEXT 216

প্রভু কহে,—শ্রীবাস, তোমাতে নারদ-স্বভাব ।
ঐশ্বর্যভাবে তোমাতে, ঈশ্বর-প্রভাব ॥ ২১৬ ॥

prabhu kahe,——śrīvāsa, tomāte nārada-svabhāva
aiśvarya-bhāve tomāte, īśvara-prabhāva

SYNONYMS

prabhu kahe—Śrī Caitanya Mahāprabhu says; *śrīvāsa*—My dear Śrīvāsa; *tomāte*—in you; *nārada-svabhāva*—the nature of Nārada; *aiśvarya-bhāve*—the mood of full opulence; *tomāte*—in you; *īśvara-prabhāva*—the power of the Lord.

TRANSLATION

Śrī Caitanya Mahāprabhu then told Śrīvāsa Ṭhākura, "My dear Śrīvāsa, your nature is exactly like that of Nārada Muni. The Supreme Personality of Godhead's opulence is having a direct influence upon you.

TEXT 217

ইঁহো দামোদর-স্বরূপ—শুদ্ধ-ব্রজবাসী ।
ঐশ্বর্য না জানে ইঁহো শুদ্ধপ্রেমে ভাসি' ॥ ২১৭ ॥

iṅho dāmodara-svarūpa——śuddha-vrajavāsī
aiśvarya nā jāne iṅho śuddha-preme bhāsi'

SYNONYMS

iṅho—here; *dāmodara-svarūpa*—Svarūpa Dāmodara Gosvāmī; *śuddha-vraja-vāsī*—a pure inhabitant of Vṛndāvana; *aiśvarya nā jāne*—he does not know opulence; *iṅho*—he; *śuddha-preme*—in pure devotional service; *bhāsi'*—floating.

TRANSLATION

"Svarūpa Dāmodara is a pure devotee of Vṛndāvana. He does not even know what opulence is, for he is simply absorbed in pure devotional service."

TEXT 218

স্বরূপ কহে,—শ্রীবাস, শুন সাবধানে ।
বৃন্দাবনসম্পদ্ তোমার নাহি পড়ে মনে ? ২১৮ ॥

svarūpa kahe,——śrīvāsa, śuna sāvadhāne
vṛndāvana-sampad tomāra nāhi paḍe mane?

SYNONYMS

svarūpa kahe—Svarūpa Dāmodara said; *śrīvāsa*—my dear Śrīvāsa; *śuna sāvadhāne*—carefully please hear; *vṛndāvana-sampad*—the opulence of Vṛndāvana; *tomāra*—your; *nāhi*—not; *paḍe*—falls; *mane*—in the mind.

TRANSLATION

Svarūpa Dāmodara then retorted, "My dear Śrīvāsa, please hear me with attention. You have forgotten the transcendental opulence of Vṛndāvana.

TEXT 219

বৃন্দাবনে সাহজিক যে সম্পৎসিন্ধু ।
দ্বারকা-বৈকুণ্ঠ-সম্পৎ—তার এক বিন্দু ॥ ২১৯ ॥

vṛndāvane sāhajika ye sampat-sindhu
dvārakā-vaikuṇṭha-sampat——tāra eka bindu

SYNONYMS

vṛndāvane—at Vṛndāvana; *sāhajika*—natural; *ye*—whatever; *sampat-sindhu*—ocean of opulence; *dvārakā*—of Dvārakā; *vaikuṇṭha-sampat*—all the opulence of the spiritual world; *tāra*—of that; *eka bindu*—one drop.

TRANSLATION

"The natural opulence of Vṛndāvana is just like an ocean. The opulence of Dvārakā and Vaikuṇṭha is not even to be compared to a drop.

TEXT 220

পরম পুরুষোত্তম স্বয়ং ভগবান্ ।
কৃষ্ণ যাহাঁ ধনী তাহাঁ বৃন্দাবন-ধাম ॥ ২২০ ॥

parama puroṣattama svayaṁ bhagavān
kṛṣṇa yāhāṅ dhanī tāhāṅ vṛndāvana-dhāma

SYNONYMS

parama puruṣa-uttama—the Supreme Personality of Godhead; *svayam bhagavān*—personally the Lord; *kṛṣṇa*—Lord Kṛṣṇa; *yāhāṅ*—where; *dhanī*—actually opulent; *tāhāṅ*—there; *vṛndāvana-dhāma*—Vṛndāvana-dhāma.

TRANSLATION

"Śrī Kṛṣṇa is the Supreme Personality of Godhead full of all opulences, and His complete opulences are exhibited only in Vṛndāvana-dhāma.

TEXT 221

চিন্তামণিময় ভূমি রত্নের ভবন ।
চিন্তামণিগণ দাসী-চরণ-ভূষণ ॥ ২২১ ॥

cintāmaṇi-maya bhūmi ratnera bhavana
cintāmaṇi-gaṇa dāsī-caraṇa-bhūṣaṇa

SYNONYMS

cintāmaṇi-maya—made of transcendental touchstone; *bhūmi*—the ground; *ratnera*—of gems; *bhavana*—the original source; *cintāmaṇi-gaṇa*—such touchstones; *dāsī-caraṇa-bhūṣaṇa*—foot decorations of the maidservants of Vṛndāvana.

TRANSLATION

"Vṛndāvana-dhāma is made of transcendental touchstone. Its entire surface is the source of all valuable jewels, and the cintāmaṇi stone is used to decorate the lotus feet of the maidservants of Vṛndāvana.

TEXT 222

কল্পবৃক্ষ-লতার—যাহাঁ সাহজিক-বন ।
পুষ্প-ফল বিনা কেহ না মাগে অন্য ধন ॥ ২২২ ॥

kalpavṛkṣa-latāra——yāhāṅ sāhajika-vana
puṣpa-phala vinā keha nā māge anya dhana

SYNONYMS

kalpa-vṛkṣa-latāra—of creepers and *kalpa-vṛkṣa,* or desire trees; *yāhāṅ*—where; *sāhajika-vana*—natural forest; *puṣpa-phala vinā*—except for fruits and flowers; *keha*—anyone; *nā māge*—does not want; *anya*—any other; *dhana*—riches.

TRANSLATION

"Vṛndāvana is a natural forest of desire trees and creepers, and the inhabitants do not want anything but the fruits and flowers of those desire trees.

TEXT 223

অনন্ত কামধেনু তাহাঁ ফিরে বনে বনে ।
দুগ্ধমাত্র দেন, কেহ না মাগে অন্য ধনে ॥ ২২৩ ॥

ananta kāma-dhenu tāhāṅ phire vane vane
dugdha-mātra dena, keha nā māge anya dhane

SYNONYMS

ananta—unlimited; *kāma-dhenu*—cows that can fulfill all desires; *tāhāṅ*—there; *phire*—graze; *vane vane*—from forest to forest; *dugdha-mātra dena*—

deliver milk only; *keha*—anyone; *nā*—not; *māge*—wants; *anya dhane*—any other riches.

TRANSLATION

"In Vṛndāvana there are cows that fulfill all desires [kāma-dhenus], and their number is unlimited. They graze from forest to forest and deliver only milk. The people want nothing else.

TEXT 224

সহজ লোকের কথা—যাহাঁ দিব্য-গীত ।
সহজ গমন করে,—যৈছে নৃত্য-প্রতীত ॥ ২২৪ ॥

sahaja lokera kathā——yāhāṅ divya-gīta
sahaja gamana kare,——yaiche nṛtya-pratīta

SYNONYMS

sahaja lokera kathā—the talks of all the plain people; *yāhāṅ*—where; *divya-gīta*—transcendental music; *sahaja gamana*—natural walking; *kare*—they do; *yaiche*—like; *nṛtya-pratīta*—appearing like dancing.

TRANSLATION

"In Vṛndāvana, the natural speech of the people sounds like music, and their natural motion resembles a dance.

TEXT 225

সর্বত্র জল—যাহাঁ অমৃত-সমান ।
চিদানন্দ জ্যোতিঃ স্বাদ্য—যাহাঁ মূর্তিমান্ ॥ ২২৫ ॥

sarvatra jala——yāhāṅ amṛta-samāna
cid-ānanda jyotiḥ svādya——yāhāṅ mūrtimān

SYNONYMS

sarvatra—everywhere; *jala*—the water; *yāhāṅ*—where; *amṛta-samāna*—equal to nectar; *cit-ānanda*—transcendental bliss; *jyotiḥ*—effulgence; *svādya*—perceived; *yāhāṅ*—where; *mūrtimān*—assuming a form.

TRANSLATION

"The water in Vṛndāvana is nectar, and the brahmajyoti effulgence, which is full of transcendental bliss, is directly perceived there in its form.

TEXT 226

লক্ষ্মী জিনি' গুণ যাহাঁ লক্ষ্মীর সমাজ ।
কৃষ্ণ-বংশী করে যাহাঁ প্রিয়সখী-কায ॥ ২২৬ ॥

lakṣmī jini' guṇa yāhāṅ lakṣmīra samāja
kṛṣṇa-vaṁśī kare yāhāṅ priya-sakhī-kāya

SYNONYMS

lakṣmī—the goddess of fortune; *jini'*—conquering; *guṇa*—qualities; *yāhāṅ*—where; *lakṣmīra samāja*—the society of the *gopīs; kṛṣṇa-vaṁśī*—Lord Śrī Kṛṣṇa's flute; *kare*—in His hand; *yāhāṅ*—where; *priya-sakhī-kāya*—a dear companion.

TRANSLATION

"The gopīs there are also goddesses of fortune, and they surpass the goddess of fortune who abides in Vaikuṇṭha. In Vṛndāvana, Lord Kṛṣṇa is always playing His transcendental flute, which is His dear companion.

TEXT 227

শ্রিয়ঃ কান্তাঃ কান্তঃ পরমপুরুষঃ কল্পতরবো
দ্রুমা ভূমিশ্চিন্তামণিগণময়ী তোয়মমৃতম্ ।
কথা গানং নাট্যং গমনমপি বংশী প্রিয়সখী
চিদানন্দং জ্যোতিঃ পরমপি তদাস্বাদ্যমপি চ ॥ ২২৭ ॥

śriyaḥ kāntāḥ kāntaḥ parama-puruṣaḥ kalpa-taravo
drumā bhūmiś cintāmaṇi-gaṇa-mayī toyam amṛtam
kathā gānaṁ nāṭyaṁ gamanam api vaṁśī priya-sakhī
cid-ānandaṁ jyotiḥ param api tad āsvādyam api ca

SYNONYMS

śriyaḥ—the goddess of fortune; *kāntāḥ*—the damsels; *kāntaḥ*—the enjoyer; *parama-puruṣaḥ*—the Supreme Personality of Godhead; *kalpa-taravaḥ*—desire trees; *drumāḥ*—all the trees; *bhūmiḥ*—the land; *cintāmaṇi-gaṇa-mayī*—made of the transcendental touchstone jewel; *toyam*—the water; *amṛtam*—nectar; *kathā*—talking; *gānam*—song; *nāṭyam*—dancing; *gamanam*—walking; *api*—also; *vaṁśī*—the flute; *priya-sakhī*—constant companion; *cit-ānandam*—transcendental bliss; *jyotiḥ*—effulgence; *param*—the supreme; *api*—also; *tat*—that; *āsvādyam*—everywhere perceived; *api ca*—also.

TRANSLATION

" 'The damsels of Vṛndāvana, the gopīs, are super goddesses of fortune. The enjoyer in Vṛndāvana is the Supreme Personality of Godhead Kṛṣṇa. The trees there are all wish-fulfilling trees, and the land is made of transcendental touchstone. The water is all nectar, the talking is singing, the walking is dancing, and the constant companion of Kṛṣṇa is His flute. The effulgence of transcendental bliss is experienced everywhere. Therefore Vṛndāvana-dhāma is the only relishable abode.'

PURPORT

This is a quotation from *Brahma-saṁhitā* (5.56).

TEXT 228

চিন্তামণিশ্চরণভূষণমঙ্গনানাং
শৃঙ্গারপুষ্পতরবস্তরবঃ সুরাণাম্ ।
বৃন্দাবনে ব্রজধনং ননু কামধেনু-
বৃন্দানি চেতি সুখসিন্ধুরহো বিভূতিঃ ॥ ২২৮ ॥

cintāmaṇiś caraṇa-bhūṣaṇam aṅganānāṁ
śṛṅgāra-puṣpa-taravas taravaḥ surāṇām
vṛndāvane vraja-dhanaṁ nanu kāma-dhenu-
vṛndāni ceti sukha-sindhur aho vibhūtiḥ

SYNONYMS

cintāmaṇiḥ—transcendental touchstone; *caraṇa*—of the lotus feet; *bhūṣaṇam*—the ornament; *aṅganānām*—of all the women of Vṛndāvana; *śṛṅgāra*—for dressing; *puṣpa-taravaḥ*—the flower trees; *taravaḥ*—the trees; *surāṇām*—of the demigods (desire trees); *vṛndāvane*—at Vṛndāvana; *vraja-dhanam*—the special wealth of the inhabitants of Vraja; *nanu*—certainly; *kāma-dhenu*—of *kāma-dhenu* cows that can deliver unlimited milk; *vṛndāni*—groups; *ca*—and; *iti*—thus; *sukha-sindhuḥ*—the ocean of happiness; *aho*—oh, how much; *vibhūtiḥ*—opulence.

TRANSLATION

" 'The anklets on the damsels of Vraja-bhūmi are made of cintāmaṇi stone. The trees are wish-fulfilling trees, and they produce flowers with which the gopīs decorate themselves. There are also wish-fulfilling cows [kāma-dhenus], which deliver unlimited quantities of milk. These cows constitute the wealth of Vṛndāvana. Thus Vṛndāvana's opulence is blissfully exhibited.' "

PURPORT

This is a verse written by Bilvamaṅgala Ṭhākura.

TEXT 229

শুনি' প্রেমাবেশে নৃত্য করে শ্রীনিবাস ।
কক্ষতালি বাজায়, করে অট্ট-অট্ট হাস ॥ ২২৯ ॥

śuni' premāveśe nṛtya kare śrīnivāsa
kakṣa-tāli bājāya, kare aṭṭa-aṭṭa hāsa

SYNONYMS

śuni'—hearing; *prema-āveśe*—in ecstatic love; *nṛtya*—dancing; *kare*—does; *śrīnivāsa*—Śrīvāsa Ṭhākura; *kakṣa-tāli*—his armpits with his palms; *bājāya*—sounds; *kare*—does; *aṭṭa-aṭṭa hāsa*—very loud laughing.

TRANSLATION

Śrīvāsa then began to dance in ecstatic love. He vibrated sounds by slapping his armpits with the palms of his hands, and he laughed very loudly.

TEXT 230

রাধার শুদ্ধরস প্রভু আবেশে শুনিল ।
সেই রসাবেশে প্রভু নৃত্য আরম্ভিল ॥ ২৩০ ॥

rādhāra śuddha-rasa prabhu āveśe śunila
sei rasāveśe prabhu nṛtya ārambhila

SYNONYMS

rādhāra—of Śrīmatī Rādhārāṇī; *śuddha-rasa*—pure transcendental mellows; *prabhu*—Śrī Caitanya Mahāprabhu; *āveśe śunila*—heard with great ecstasy; *sei*—that; *rasa-āveśe*—in absorption in ecstatic love; *prabhu*—Śrī Caitanya Mahāprabhu; *nṛtya ārambhila*—began dancing.

TRANSLATION

Thus Śrī Caitanya Mahāprabhu heard these discussions about the pure transcendental mellow of Śrīmatī Rādhārāṇī. Absorbed in transcendental ecstasy, the Lord began to dance.

TEXT 231

রসাবেশে প্রভুর নৃত্য, স্বরূপের গান ।
'বল' 'বল' বলি' প্রভু পাতে নিজ-কাণ ॥ ২৩১ ॥

rasāveśe prabhura nṛtya, svarūpera gāna
'bala' 'bala' bali' prabhu pāte nija-kāṇa

SYNONYMS

rasa-āveśe—in ecstatic mellows; *prabhura*—of Śrī Caitanya Mahāprabhu; *nṛtya*—the dancing; *svarūpera gāna*—and singing by Svarūpa Dāmodara; *bala bala*—go on speaking, go on speaking; *bali'*—saying; *prabhu*—Śrī Caitanya Mahāprabhu; *pāte*—extends; *nija-kāṇa*—own ear.

TRANSLATION

While Śrī Caitanya Mahāprabhu was dancing in ecstatic love and Svarūpa Dāmodara was singing, the Lord said, "Go on singing! Go on singing!" The Lord then extended His own ears.

TEXT 232

ব্রজরস-গীত শুনি' প্রেম উথলিল ।
পুরুষোত্তম-গ্রাম প্রভু প্রেমে ভাসাইল ॥ ২৩২ ॥

vraja-rasa-gīta śuni' prema uthalila
puruṣottama-grāma prabhu preme bhāsāila

SYNONYMS

vraja-rasa-gīta—songs about the mellows of Vṛndāvana-dhāma; *śuni'*—hearing; *prema*—transcendental bliss; *uthalila*—awakened; *puruṣottama-grāma*—the place known as Puruṣottama, Jagannātha Purī; *prabhu*—Śrī Caitanya Mahāprabhu; *preme*—with ecstatic love; *bhāsāila*—inundated.

TRANSLATION

Thus Śrī Caitanya Mahāprabhu's ecstatic love was awakened by hearing the songs of Vṛndāvana. In this way He inundated Puruṣottama, Jagannātha Purī, with love of Godhead.

TEXT 233

লক্ষ্মী-দেবী যথাকালে গেলা নিজ-ঘর ।
প্রভু নৃত্য করে, হৈল তৃতীয় প্রহর ॥ ২৩৩ ॥

lakṣmī-devī yathā-kāle gelā nija-ghara
prabhu nṛtya kare, haila tṛtīya prahara

SYNONYMS

lakṣmī-devī—the goddess of fortune; *yathā-kāle*—in due course of time; *gelā*—returned; *nija-ghara*—to her apartment; *prabhu*—Śrī Caitanya Mahāprabhu; *nṛtya kare*—dances; *haila*—there arrived; *tṛtīya prahara*—the third period of the day, the afternoon.

TRANSLATION

Finally the goddess of fortune returned to her apartment. In due course of time, as Śrī Caitanya Mahāprabhu was dancing, afternoon arrived.

TEXT 234

চারি সম্প্রদায় গান করি' বহু শ্রান্ত হৈল ।
মহাপ্রভুর প্রেমাবেশ দ্বিগুণ বাড়িল ॥ ২৩৪ ॥

cāri sampradāya gāna kari' bahu śrānta haila
mahāprabhura premāveśa dviguṇa bāḍila

SYNONYMS

cāri sampradāya—four groups of *saṅkīrtana* parties; *gāna kari'*—after singing; *bahu*—much; *śrānta haila*—were fatigued; *mahāprabhura*—of Śrī Caitanya Mahāprabhu; *prema-āveśa*—the ecstatic love; *dvi-guṇa*—twofold; *bāḍila*—increased.

TRANSLATION

After much singing, all four saṅkīrtana parties grew fatigued, but Śrī Caitanya Mahāprabhu's ecstatic love increased twofold.

TEXT 235

রাধা-প্রেমাবেশে প্রভু হৈলা সেই মূর্তি ।
নিত্যানন্দ দূরে দেখি' করিলেন স্তুতি ॥ ২৩৫ ॥

rādhā-premāveśe prabhu hailā sei mūrti
nityānanda dūre dekhi' karilena stuti

SYNONYMS

rādhā-prema-āveśe—in ecstatic love of Śrīmatī Rādhārāṇī; *prabhu*—Śrī Caitanya Mahāprabhu; *hailā*—became; *sei mūrti*—exactly that same form; *nityā-*

nanda—Lord Nityānanda; *dūre dekhi'*—seeing from a distant place; *karilena stuti*—offered prayers.

TRANSLATION

While dancing absorbed in Śrīmatī Rādhārāṇī's ecstatic love, Śrī Caitanya Mahāprabhu appeared in Her very form. Seeing this from a distant place, Nityānanda Prabhu offered prayers.

TEXT 236

নিত্যানন্দ দেখিয়া প্রভুর ভাবাবেশ ।
নিকটে না আইসে, রহে কিছু দূরদেশ ॥ ২৩৬ ॥

nityānanda dekhiyā prabhura bhāvāveśa
nikaṭe nā āise, rahe kichu dūra-deśa

SYNONYMS

nityānanda—Lord Nityānanda; *dekhiyā*—seeing; *prabhura*—of Śrī Caitanya Mahāprabhu; *bhāva-āveśa*—the ecstatic love; *nikaṭe*—nearby; *nā āise*—does not come; *rahe*—keeps; *kichu*—a little; *dūra-deśa*—far away.

TRANSLATION

Seeing the ecstatic love of Śrī Caitanya Mahāprabhu, Nityānanda Prabhu did not approach but remained a little distance away.

TEXT 237

নিত্যানন্দ বিনা প্রভুকে ধরে কোন্ জন ।
প্রভুর আবেশ না যায়, না রহে কীর্তন ॥ ২৩৭ ॥

nityānanda vinā prabhuke dhare kon jana
prabhura āveśa nā yāya, nā rahe kīrtana

SYNONYMS

nityānanda vinā—except for Nityānanda Prabhu; *prabhuke*—Śrī Caitanya Mahāprabhu; *dhare*—can catch; *kon jana*—what person; *prabhura*—of Śrī Caitanya Mahāprabhu; *āveśa*—the ecstasy; *nā yāya*—does not go away; *nā rahe*—could not be continued; *kīrtana*—*kīrtana.*

TRANSLATION

Only Nityānanda Prabhu could catch Śrī Caitanya Mahāprabhu, but the ecstatic mood of the Lord would not stop. At the same time, kīrtana could not be continued.

TEXT 238

**ভঙ্গি করি' স্বরূপ সবার শ্রম জানাইল।
ভক্তগণের শ্রম দেখি' প্রভুর বাহ্য হৈল ॥ ২৩৮ ॥**

bhaṅgi kari' svarūpa sabāra śrama jānāila
bhakta-gaṇera śrama dekhi' prabhura bāhya haila

SYNONYMS

bhaṅgi kari'—showing an indication; *svarūpa*—Svarūpa Dāmodara; *sabāra*—of everyone; *śrama*—the fatigue; *jānāila*—made known; *bhakta-gaṇera*—of the devotees; *śrama*—the fatigue; *dekhi'*—seeing; *prabhura*—Śrī Caitanya Mahāprabhu; *bāhya haila*—become externally conscious.

TRANSLATION

Svarūpa Dāmodara then informed the Lord that all the devotees were fatigued. Seeing this situation, Śrī Caitanya Mahāprabhu came to His external senses.

TEXT 239

**সব ভক্ত লঞা প্রভু গেলা পুষ্পোদ্যানে।
বিশ্রাম করিয়া কৈলা মাধ্যাহ্নিক স্নানে ॥ ২৩৯ ॥**

saba bhakta lañā prabhu gelā puṣpodyāne
viśrāma kariyā kailā mādhyāhnika snāne

SYNONYMS

saba bhakta lañā—with all the devotees; *prabhu*—Śrī Caitanya Mahāprabhu; *gelā*—went; *puṣpa-udyāne*—in the flower garden; *viśrāma kariyā*—resting; *kailā*—performed; *mādhyāhnika snāne*—bath in the afternoon.

TRANSLATION

Śrī Caitanya Mahāprabhu then entered the flower garden with all His devotees. After resting there for some time, He finished His afternoon bath.

TEXT 240

**জগন্নাথের প্রসাদ আইল বহু উপহার।
লক্ষ্মীর প্রসাদ আইল বিবিধ প্রকার ॥ ২৪০ ॥**

jagannāthera prasāda āila bahu upahāra
lakṣmīra prasāda āila vividha prakāra

SYNONYMS

jagannāthera prasāda—the *prasāda* offered to Jagannātha; *āila*—arrived; *bahu*—many; *upahāra*—offerings; *lakṣmīra prasāda*—food offered to Lakṣmīdevī; *āila*—arrived; *vividha prakāra*—all varieties.

TRANSLATION

Then there arrived in large quantities a variety of food that had been offered to Śrī Jagannātha and a variety that had been offered to the goddess of fortune.

TEXT 241

সবা লঞা নানা-রঙ্গে করিলা ভোজন।
সন্ধ্যা স্নান করি' কৈল জগন্নাথ দরশন॥ ২৪১ ॥

sabā lañā nānā-raṅge karilā bhojana
sandhyā snāna kari' kaila jagannātha daraśana

SYNONYMS

sabā lañā—with all the devotees; *nānā-raṅge*—in great jubilation; *karilā bhojana*—took the *prasāda; sandhyā snāna kari'*—after taking an evening bath; *kaila*—made; *jagannātha daraśana*—visit to Lord Jagannātha.

TRANSLATION

Śrī Caitanya Mahāprabhu finished His afternoon lunch, and after His evening bath, He went to see Lord Jagannātha.

TEXT 242

জগন্নাথ দেখি' করেন নর্তন-কীর্তন।
নরেন্দ্রে জলক্রীড়া করে লঞা ভক্তগণ॥ ২৪২ ॥

jagannātha dekhi' karena nartana-kīrtana
narendre jala-krīḍā kare lañā bhakta-gaṇa

SYNONYMS

jagannātha—Lord Jagannātha; *dekhi'*—after seeing; *karena*—performs; *nartana-kīrtana*—chanting and dancing; *narendre*—in the lake known as Narendra-sarovara; *jala-krīḍā*—sporting in the water; *kare*—performs; *lañā bhakta-gaṇa*—with the devotees.

TRANSLATION

As soon as He saw Lord Jagannātha, Śrī Caitanya Mahāprabhu began to chant and dance. Afterward, accompanied by His devotees, the Lord enjoyed sporting in the lake called Narendra-sarovara.

TEXT 243

উদ্যানে আসিয়া কৈল বন-ভোজন ।
এইমত ক্রীড়া কৈল প্রভু অষ্টদিন ॥ ২৪৩ ॥

udyāne āsiyā kaila vana-bhojana
ei-mata krīḍā kaila prabhu aṣṭa-dina

SYNONYMS

udyāne—to the garden; *āsiyā*—coming; *kaila*—performed; *vana-bhojana*—picnic in the forest; *ei-mata*—in this way; *krīḍā*—pastimes; *kaila*—performed; *prabhu*—Lord Śrī Caitanya Mahāprabhu; *aṣṭa-dina*—constantly for eight days.

TRANSLATION

Then, entering the flower garden, Śrī Caitanya Mahāprabhu took His meal. In this way He continuously performed all kinds of pastimes for eight days.

TEXT 244

আর দিনে জগন্নাথের ভিতর-বিজয় ।
রথে চড়ি' জগন্নাথ চলে নিজালয় ॥ ২৪৪ ॥

āra dine jagannāthera bhitara-vijaya
rathe caḍi' jagannātha cale nijālaya

SYNONYMS

āra dine—on the next day; *jagannāthera*—of Lord Jagannātha; *bhitara-vijaya*—coming out from inside the temple; *rathe caḍi'*—riding on the car; *jagannātha*—Lord Jagannātha; *cale*—returns; *nija-ālaya*—to His own home.

TRANSLATION

The next day Lord Jagannātha came out from the temple and, riding on the car, returned to His own abode.

TEXT 245

পূর্ব্ববৎ কৈল প্রভু লঞা ভক্তগণ ।
পরম আনন্দে করেন নর্তন-কীর্তন ॥ ২৪৫ ॥

pūrvavat kaila prabhu lañā bhakta-gaṇa
parama ānande karena nartana-kīrtana

SYNONYMS

pūrva-vat—as previously; *kaila*—did; *prabhu*—Śrī Caitanya Mahāprabhu; *lañā*—taking; *bhakta-gaṇa*—all the devotees; *parama ānande*—in great pleasure; *karena*—performs; *nartana-kīrtana*—chanting and dancing.

TRANSLATION

As previously, Śrī Caitanya Mahāprabhu and His devotees again chanted and danced with great pleasure.

TEXT 246

জগন্নাথের পুনঃ পাণ্ডু-বিজয় হইল ।
এক গুটি পট্টডোরী তাঁহা টুটি' গেল ॥ ২৪৬ ॥

jagannāthera punaḥ pāṇḍu-vijaya ha-ila
eka guṭi paṭṭa-ḍorī tāṅhā ṭuṭi' gela

SYNONYMS

jagannāthera—of Lord Jagannātha; *punaḥ*—again; *pāṇḍu-vijaya*—the function of carrying the Lord; *ha-ila*—there was; *eka guṭi*—one bunch; *paṭṭa-ḍorī*—ropes of silk; *tāṅhā*—there; *ṭuṭi' gela*—broke.

TRANSLATION

During the Pāṇḍu-vijaya, Lord Jagannātha was carried, and while He was being carried, a bunch of silken ropes broke.

TEXT 247

পাণ্ডু-বিজয়ের তুলি ফাটি-ফুটি যায় ।
জগন্নাথের ভরে তুলা উড়িয়া পলায় ॥ ২৪৭ ॥

pāṇḍu-vijayera tuli phāṭi-phuṭi yāya
jagannāthera bhare tulā uḍiyā palāya

SYNONYMS

pāṇḍu-vijayera—of the ceremony of Pāṇḍu-vijaya; *tuli*—batches of cotton; *phāṭi-phuṭi yāya*—become broken; *jagannāthera bhare*—by the weight of Lord Jagannātha; *tulā*—the cotton; *uḍiyā palāya*—floats in the air.

TRANSLATION

When the Jagannātha Deity is carried, at intervals He is placed on cotton pads. When the ropes broke, the cotton pads also broke due to the weight of Lord Jagannātha, and the cotton floated in the air.

TEXT 248

কুলীনগ্রামী রামানন্দ, সত্যরাজ খাঁন।
তাঁরে আজ্ঞা দিল প্রভু করিয়া সন্মান॥ ২৪৮ ॥

kulīna-grāmī rāmānanda, satyarāja khāṅna
tāṅre ājñā dila prabhu kariyā sammāna

SYNONYMS

kulīna-grāmī—the inhabitants of the village known as Kulīna-grāma; *rāmānanda*—Rāmānanda; *satyarāja khāṅna*—Satyarāja Khān; *tāṅre*—to them; *ājñā dila*—gave an order; *prabhu*—Śrī Caitanya Mahāprabhu; *kariyā sammāna*—showing great respect.

TRANSLATION

Rāmānanda and Satyarāja Khān were present from Kulīna-grāma, and Śrī Caitanya Mahāprabhu, with great respect, gave them the following orders.

TEXT 249

এই পট্টডোরীর তুমি হও যজমান।
প্রতিবৎসর আনিবে 'ডোরী' করিয়া নির্মাণ॥ ২৪৯ ॥

ei paṭṭa-ḍorīra tumi hao yajamāna
prati-vatsara ānibe 'ḍorī' kariyā nirmāṇa

SYNONYMS

ei paṭṭa-ḍorīra—of these *paṭṭa-ḍorīs,* silken ropes; *tumi*—you; *hao*—become; *yajamāna*—the worshipers; *prati-vatsara*—every year; *ānibe*—you must bring; *ḍorī*—ropes; *kariyā nirmāṇa*—manufacturing.

TRANSLATION

Śrī Caitanya Mahāprabhu ordered Rāmānanda and Satyarāja Khān to become the worshipers of these ropes and every year bring silken ropes from their village.

PURPORT

It is understood that silken rope was being manufactured by the local inhabitants of Kulīna-grāma; therefore Śrī Caitanya Mahāprabhu asked Rāmānanda Vasu and Satyarāja Khān to get ropes every year for Lord Jagannātha's service.

TEXT 250

এত বলি' দিল তাঁরে ছিণ্ডা পট্টডোরী।
ইহা দেখি' করিবে ডোরী অতি দৃঢ় করি' ॥ ২৫০ ॥

eta bali' dila tāṅre chiṇḍā paṭṭa-ḍorī
ihā dekhi' karibe ḍorī ati dṛḍha kari'

SYNONYMS

eta bali'—saying this; *dila*—delivered; *tāṅre*—to them; *chiṇḍā*—broken; *paṭṭa-ḍorī*—silken ropes; *ihā dekhi'*—seeing this; *karibe*—you must make; *ḍorī*—the ropes; *ati*—very much; *dṛḍha kari'*—making strong.

TRANSLATION

After telling them this, Śrī Caitanya Mahāprabhu showed them the broken silken ropes, saying, "Just look at this sample. You must make ropes that are much stronger."

TEXT 251

এই পট্টডোরীতে হয় 'শেষ'-অধিষ্ঠান।
দশ-মূর্তি হঞা যেঁহো সেবে ভগবান্ ॥ ২৫১ ॥

ei paṭṭa-ḍorīte haya 'śeṣa'-adhiṣṭhāna
daśa-mūrti hañā yeṅho seve bhagavān

SYNONYMS

ei paṭṭa-ḍorīte—in this rope; *haya*—there is; *śeṣa-adhiṣṭhāna*—the abode of Śeṣa Nāga; *daśa-mūrti hañā*—expanding into ten forms; *yeṅho*—who; *seve*—worships; *bhagavān*—the Supreme Personality of Godhead.

TRANSLATION

Śrī Caitanya Mahāprabhu then informed Rāmānanda and Satyarāja Khān that this rope was the abode of Lord Śeṣa, who expands Himself into ten forms and serves the Supreme Personality of Godhead.

PURPORT

For a description of Śeṣa Nāga, refer to *Ādi-līlā* (5.123-124).

TEXT 252

ভাগ্যবান্ সত্যরাজ বসু রামানন্দ ।
সেবা-আজ্ঞা পাঞা হৈল পরম-আনন্দ ॥ ২৫২ ॥

bhāgyavān satyarāja vasu rāmānanda
sevā-ājñā pāñā haila parama-ānanda

SYNONYMS

bhāgyavān—very fortunate; *satyarāja*—Satyarāja; *vasu rāmānanda*—Rāmānanda Vasu; *sevā-ājñā*—order for service; *pāñā*—getting; *haila*—became; *parama*—supremely; *ānanda*—happy.

TRANSLATION

After receiving orders from the Lord for the rendering of service, the fortunate Satyarāja and Rāmānanda Vasu were highly pleased.

TEXT 253

প্রতি বৎসর গুণ্ডিচাতে ভক্তগণ-সঙ্গে ।
পট্টডোরী লঞা আইসে অতি বড রঙ্গে ॥ ২৫৩ ॥

prati vatsara guṇḍicāte bhakta-gaṇa-saṅge
paṭṭa-ḍorī lañā āise ati baḍa raṅge

SYNONYMS

prati vatsara—every year; *guṇḍicāte*—to the Guṇḍicā temple cleansing ceremony; *bhakta-gaṇa-saṅge*—with other devotees; *paṭṭa-ḍorī*—silken rope; *lañā*—taking; *āise*—came; *ati*—extremely; *baḍa*—great; *raṅge*—with pleasure.

TRANSLATION

Every year thereafter, when the Guṇḍicā temple was being cleansed, Satyarāja and Rāmānanda Vasu would come with other devotees and with great pleasure bring silken rope.

TEXT 254

তবে জগন্নাথ যাই' বসিলা সিংহাসনে ।
মহাপ্রভু ঘরে আইলা লঞা ভক্তগণে ॥ ২৫৪ ॥

tabe jagannātha yāi' vasilā siṁhāsane
mahāprabhu ghare āilā lañā bhakta-gaṇe

SYNONYMS

tabe—thereafter; *jagannātha*—Lord Jagannātha; *yāi'*—going; *vasilā*—sat; *siṁhāsane*—on His throne; *mahāprabhu*—Śrī Caitanya Mahāprabhu; *ghare*—to His residence; *āilā*—went back; *lañā*—taking; *bhakta-gaṇe*—the devotees.

TRANSLATION

Thus Lord Jagannātha returned to His temple and sat on His throne while Śrī Caitanya Mahāprabhu returned to His residence with His devotees.

TEXT 255

এইমত ভক্তগণে যাত্রা দেখাইল ।
ভক্তগণ লঞা বৃন্দাবন-কেলি কৈল ॥ ২৫৫ ॥

ei-mata bhakta-gaṇe yātrā dekhāila
bhakta-gaṇa lañā vṛndāvana-keli kaila

SYNONYMS

ei-mata—in this way; *bhakta-gaṇe*—to all the devotees; *yātrā*—the Ratha-yātrā festival; *dekhāila*—showed; *bhakta-gaṇa*—the devotees; *lañā*—with; *vṛndāvana-keli*—pastimes of Vṛndāvana; *kaila*—performed.

TRANSLATION

Thus Śrī Caitanya Mahāprabhu showed the Ratha-yātrā ceremony to His devotees and performed the Vṛndāvana pastimes with them.

TEXT 256

চৈতন্য-গোসাঞির লীলা—অনন্ত, অপার ।
'সহস্র-বদন' যার নাহি পায় পার ॥ ২৫৬ ॥

caitanya-gosāñira līlā——ananta, apāra
'sahasra-vadana' yāra nāhi pāya pāra

SYNONYMS

caitanya-gosāñira—of Lord Śrī Caitanya Mahāprabhu; *līlā*—the pastimes; *ananta*—unlimited; *apāra*—without end; *sahasra-vadana*—Lord Śeṣa, who has thousands of hoods; *yāra*—of which; *nāhi*—not; *pāya*—gets; *pāra*—the limit.

TRANSLATION

The pastimes of Lord Caitanya are unlimited and endless. Even Sahasra-vadana, Lord Śeṣa, cannot reach the limits of His pastimes.

TEXT 257

শ্রীরূপ-রঘুনাথ-পদে যার আশ ।
চৈতন্যচরিতামৃত কহে কৃষ্ণদাস ॥ ২৫৭ ॥

śrī-rūpa-raghunātha-pade yāra āśa
caitanya-caritāmṛta kahe kṛṣṇadāsa

SYNONYMS

śrī-rūpa—Śrīla Rūpa Gosvāmī; *raghunātha*—Śrīla Raghunātha dāsa Gosvāmī; *pade*—at the lotus feet; *yāra*—whose; *āśa*—expectation; *caitanya-caritāmṛta*—the book named *Caitanya-caritāmṛta; kahe*—describes; *kṛṣṇadāsa*—Śrīla Kṛṣṇadāsa Kavirāja Gosvāmī.

TRANSLATION

Praying at the lotus feet of Śrī Rūpa and Śrī Raghunātha, always desiring their mercy, I, Kṛṣṇadāsa, narrate Śrī Caitanya-caritāmṛta, following in their footsteps.

Thus end the Bhaktivedanta purports to the Śrī Caitanya-caritāmṛta, Madhya-līlā, *Fourteenth Chapter, describing the Herā-pañcamī-yātrā.*

References

The statements of *Śrī Caitanya-caritāmṛta* are all confirmed by standard Vedic authorities. The following authentic scriptures are quoted in this book on the pages listed. Numerals in bold type refer the reader to *Śrī Caitanya-caritāmṛta's* translations. Numerals in regular type are references to its purports.

Amṛta-pravāha-bhāṣya (Bhaktivinoda Ṭhākura), 1, 113

Anubhāṣya (Bhaktisiddhānta Sarasvatī), 31

Bhagavad-gītā, 31, 66, 96, 97, 196, 231, 247

Bhakti-rasāmṛta-sindhu (Rūpa Gosvāmī), 184, 296

Brahma-saṁhitā, 196, **332**

Caitanya-candrāmṛta (Prabodhānanda Sarasvatī), 185, 232

Caitanyāṣṭaka (Rūpa Gosvāmī), **221**

Chāndogya Upaniṣad, 95

Govinda-līlāmṛta (Kṛṣṇadāsa Kavirāja), **310, 314, 317**

Gurv-aṣṭaka (Viśvanātha Cakravartī), 242

Kalyāṇa-kalpataru (Bhaktivinoda Ṭhākura), 32

Kaṭha Upaniṣad, 32

Laghu-bhāgavatāmṛta (Rūpa Gosvāmī), 107

Mukunda-mālā-stotra (Kulaśekhara), 152

Muṇḍaka Upaniṣad, 32

Padma Purāṇa, 20

Padyāvalī (Rūpa Gosvāmī), 154, 173

Śikṣāṣṭaka (Caitanya Mahāprabhu), 64

Glossary

A

Ābhāsa—a shadow.

Advaita-siddhānta—conclusion of the monists that God and the devotee are separate in the material state, but that when they are spiritually situated there is no difference between them.

Aiśvarya-līlā—the Lord's pastimes of opulence.

Ālasya—laziness, a *vyabhicārī-bhāva*.

Amarṣa—anger, a *vyabhicārī-bhāva*.

Amṛta-guṭikā—thick *purī* (fried cakes) mixed with condensed milk.

Anartha-nivṛtti—cleansing the heart of all unwanted things.

Anavasara—period of retirement of Lord Jagannātha after Snāna-yātrā.

Aṅga-rāga—repainting of the body of Lord Jagannātha.

Anurasa—second-class type of *rasābhāsa* occurring when something is derived from the original mellow.

Aparasa—third-class type of *rasābhāsa* occurring when something is appreciated which is far removed from the original mellow.

Apasmāra—forgetfulness, a *vyabhicārī-bhāva*.

Aprakaṭa—unmanifest presence of Kṛṣṇa.

Arcā-vigraha—an incarnation of the Supreme Lord in the form of a material manifestation (brass, stone or wood).

Asūyā—jealousy, a *vyabhicārī-bhāva*.

Augrya—violence, a *vyabhicārī-bhāva*.

Autsukya—eagerness, a *vyabhicārī-bhāva*.

Avahitthā—concealment, a *vyabhicārī-bhāva*.

Avatāra—incarnation.

Āvega—intense emotion, a *vyabhicārī-bhāva*.

B

Balagaṇḍi festival—the festival when everyone offers various opulent foodstuffs to Lord Jagannātha at Balagaṇḍi during the Ratha-yātrā parade.

Balarāma—the elder brother of Kṛṣṇa, present as one of the three Jagannātha Deities.

Bhāvas—ecstatic emotional ornaments.

Bhoga-mandira—the place where the Deity's food is kept.

Brāhmaṇas—the intelligent class of men.

C

Cakita—a position in which the heroine appears very afraid although she is not at all afraid.

Cāpalya—impudence, a *vyabhicārī-bhāva*.

Cintā—contemplation, a *vyabhicārī-bhāva*.

D

Dainya—meekness, a *vyabhicārī-bhāva.*
Dakṣiṇā—right-wing group of *gopīs,* who cannot tolerate womanly anger.
Dayitās—servants who carry the Deity of Lord Jagannātha to His car.
Dayitā-patis—leaders of the *dayitās* coming from *brāhmaṇa* caste.
Devakī-nandana—name for Kṛṣṇa indicating that He is the son of Devakī.
Dhṛti—forbearance, a *vyabhicārī-bhāva.*

G

Garva—pride, a *vyabhicārī-bhāva.*
Gauḍas—pullers of Lord Jagannātha's car.
Gaurāṅga-nāgarīs—the name of a particular *sahajiyā sampradāya.*
Glāni—a feeling that one is in a faulty position, a *vyabhicārī-bhāva.*
Govinda—Kṛṣṇa in His original form as pleaser of the cows and the senses.
Guṇa-māyā—the material world.
Guru—Spiritual master.

H

"Hari bol"—"Chant the holy name."
Harṣa—jubilation, a *vyabhicārī-bhāva.*
Herā-pañcamī festival—celebration of the coming of the goddess of fortune to the Guṇḍicā temple.

J

Jāḍya—invalidity, a *vyabhicārī-bhāva.*
Jagamohana—area in front of the temple.
Jagannātha—a Deity form of Kṛṣṇa.
Jana-nivāsa—name for Kṛṣṇa indicating that He is the ultimate resort of all living entities.
Jīva-hiṁsa—envy of other living entities.
Jīva-māyā—the living entities.

K

Kāma—desire for material gain.
Kāma-dhenus—desire-fulfilling cows in Vṛndāvana.
Kāṇaphāṭā yogīs—beggars similar to gypsies who wear ivory earrings.
Karaṅga—waterpot carried by *sannyāsīs.*
Kila-kiñcita—type of ecstatic symptom manifested at the time of seeing Kṛṣṇa.
Kuti-nāṭi—duplicity or fault-finding.
Kuṭṭamita—happy within the heart, but externally angry and offended.

L

Lakṣmī-vijayotsava festival—pastime of Lakṣmī during the Ratha-yātrā festival.
Lalita-alaṅkāra—charm.
Lāphrā-vyañjana—combination of green vegetables, often mixed with rice.
Līlā-śakti—Kṛṣṇa's various subordinate potencies which assist Him in His pastimes.

M

Mada—madness, a *vyabhicārī-bhāva.*
Madana-mohana—Kṛṣṇa, the enchanter of Cupid.
Madana-mohana-mohinī—Rādhārāṇī, the enchanter of the enchanter of Cupid.
Mādhurya-līlā—Kṛṣṇa's pastimes of conjugal love.
Mahābhāva—topmost transcendental ecstatic symptom.
Mahā-mantra—the great chanting for deliverance: Hare Kṛṣṇa, Hare Kṛṣṇa, Kṛṣṇa Kṛṣṇa, Hare Hare/ Hare Rāma, Hare Rāma, Rāma Rāma, Hare Hare.
Mallikā—a sweet-scented flower of Vṛndāvana.
Maṇimā—an address used for respectable persons in Orissa.
Maryādā-laṅghana—a violation of the regulative principles.
Mathurā—the city near Vṛndāvana where Kṛṣṇa exhibited many pastimes.
Mati—attention, a *vyabhicārī-bhāva.*
Maugdhya—assuming the position of not knowing things although everything is known.
Māyā—illusion; an energy of Kṛṣṇa's which deludes the living entity into forgetfulness of the Supreme Lord.
Moha—bewilderment, a *vyabhicārī-bhāva.*
Moṭṭāyita—awakening of lusty desires by the remembrance and words of the hero.
Mṛdanga—two-headed drum used in *kīrtana* performances.
Mṛti—death, a *vyabhicārī-bhāva.*

N

Nagna-mātṛkā-nyāya—theory stating that one cannot become an exalted devotee overnight.
Nava-yauvana day—the day on which Lord Jagannātha, Subhadrā and Lord Balarāma enter seclusion for fifteen days before Ratha-yātrā.
Netrotsava festival—the festival of painting the eyes of Lord Jagannātha during the *Nava-yauvana* ceremony.
Nidrā—sleep, a *vyabhicārī-bhāva.*
Nirveda—indifference, a *vyabhicārī-bhāva.*
Niṣiddhācāra—accepting things forbidden in the *śāstra.*
Nṛsiṁha-caturdaśī festival—the appearance day of Lord Nṛsiṁha.

P

Paḍichā—superintendent of a temple.
Pāṇḍu-vijaya—the function of carrying Lord Jagannātha to His car.

Parakīya-rasa—the Lord's conjugal love with the *gopīs.*
Prabodha—awakening, a *vyabhicārī-bhāva.*
Pradhāna—ingredients of material nature.
Prakaṭa—manifest presence of Kṛṣṇa.
Prakṛti—material nature.
Pratiṣṭhāśā—desire for name and fame or high position.
Pūjā—hankering for popularity.

R

Rasa—mellow; relationship with Kṛṣṇa.
Rasābhāsa—adulterated relationship with Kṛṣṇa.
Ratha-yātrā—the festival celebrating Kṛṣṇa's return to Vṛndāvana, in which the Deity of Lord Jagannātha is pulled in a car.

S

Sac-cid-ānanda-vigraha—the transcendental form of the Lord, which is eternal, full of knowledge and full of bliss.
Śāstra-cakṣuḥ—seeing everything through the medium of the Vedic literature.
Sahasra-vadana—the thousand-mouthed snake incarnation, called Śeṣa Nāga.
Śaṅkā—doubt, a *vyabhicārī-bhāva.*
Saṅkīrtana—congregational chanting of the holy names of the Lord.
Sāttvikas—transcendental symptoms.
Siṁhāsana—sitting place.
Śimulī—silk cotton tree.
Smārta-brāhmaṇa—one who strictly follows the Vedic principles on the mundane platform.
Smṛti—remembrance, a *vyabhicārī-bhāva.*
Snāna-yātrā—the bathing ceremony of Lord Jagannātha.
Śrama—fatigue, a *vyabhicārī-bhāva.*
Subhadrā—the younger sister of Kṛṣṇa, one of the three Jagannātha Deities.
Supti—deep sleep, a *vyabhicārī-bhāva.*
Svakīya-rasa—the Lord's conjugal love according to the regulative principles observed in Dvārakā.

T

Tadīyānam—worship of everything belonging to the Lord.
Trāsa—shock, a *vyabhicārī-bhāva.*

U

Unmāda—craziness, a *vyabhicārī-bhāva.*
Uparasa—first-class type of *rasābhāsa* occurring when one tastes one kind of mellow and something extra is imposed.

V

Vāmā—left-wing group of *gopīs,* who are eager to be jealously angered.
Vilāsa—symptoms manifested in a woman's body when she meets her lover.
Viṣāda—moroseness, a *vyabhicārī-bhāva.*
Vitarka—argument, a *vyabhicārī-bhāva.*
Vivvoka—neglecting the presentation given by the hero.
Vrīḍā—shame, a *vyabhicārī-bhāva.*
Vṛndāvana-vihāra—pastimes of Vṛndāvana.
Vyabhicārī-bhāvas—the thirty-three bodily symptoms manifest in ecstatic love.
Vyādhi—disease, a *vyabhicārī-bhāva.*

Y

Yajña—sacrifice.
Yamunā—sacred river at which Kṛṣṇa performed many pastimes.
Yaśodā-nandana—name for Kṛṣṇa indicating that He is the son of Yaśodā.

Bengali Pronunciation Guide

BENGALI DIACRITICAL EQUIVALENTS AND PRONUNCIATION

Vowels

অ a   আ ā   ই i   ঈ ī   উ u   ঊ ū   ঋ ṛ

ৠ ṝ   এ e   ঐ ai   ও o   ঔ au

ং ṁ *(anusvāra)*   ঁ ṅ *(candra-bindu)*   ঃ ḥ *(visarga)*

Consonants

Gutterals:	ক ka	খ kha	গ ga	ঘ gha	ঙ ṅa
Palatals:	চ ca	ছ cha	জ ja	ঝ jha	ঞ ña
Cerebrals:	ট ṭa	ঠ ṭha	ড ḍa	ঢ ḍha	ণ ṇa
Dentals:	ত ta	থ tha	দ da	ধ dha	ন na
Labials:	প pa	ফ pha	ব ba	ভ bha	ম ma
Semivowels:	য ya	র ra	ল la	ব va	
Sibilants:	শ śa	ষ ṣa	স sa	হ ha	

Vowel Symbols

The vowels are written as follows after a consonant:

া ā   ি i   ী ī   ু u   ূ ū   ৃ ṛ   ৄ ṝ   ে e   ৈ ai   ো o   ৌ au

For example: কা kā   কি ki   কী kī   কু ku   কূ kū   কৃ kṛ

কৄ kṝ   কে ke   কৈ kai   কো ko   কৌ kau

The letter *a* is implied after a consonant with no vowel symbol.

The symbol *virāma* (্) indicates that there is no final vowel. ক্ k

The letters above should be pronounced as follows:

a –like the *o* in h*o*t; sometimes like the *o* in go; final *a* is usually silent.
ā –like the *a* in f*a*r.
i, ī –like the *ee* in m*ee*t.
u, ū –like the *u* in r*u*le.
ṛ –like the *ri* in *ri*m.
ṝ –like the *ree* in *ree*d.
e –like the *ai* in p*ai*n; rarely like *e* in b*e*t.
ai –like the *oi* in b*oi*l.
o –like the *o* in g*o*.
au –like the *ow* in *ow*l.
ṁ –*(anusvāra)* like the *ng* in so*ng*.
ḥ –*(visarga)* a final *h* sound like in Ah.
ṅ –*(candra-bindu)* a nasal *n* sound. like in the French word *bon*.
k –like the *k* in *k*ite.
kh –like the *kh* in Ec*kh*art.
g –like the *g* in *g*ot.
gh –like the *gh* in bi*g-h*ouse.
ṅ –like the *n* in ba*n*k.
c –like the *ch* in *ch*alk.
ch –like the *chh* in mu*ch-h*aste.
j –like the *j* in *j*oy.
jh –like the *geh* in colle*ge-h*all.
ñ –like the *n* in bu*n*ch.
ṭ –like the *t* in *t*alk.
ṭh –like the *th* in ho*t-h*ouse.
ḍ –like the *d* in *d*awn.
ḍh –like the *dh* in goo*d-h*ouse.
ṇ –like the *n* in g*n*aw.
t–as in *t*alk but with the tongue against the the teeth.
th–as in ho*t-h*ouse but with the tongue against the teeth.
d–as in *d*awn but with the tongue against the teeth.
dh–as in goo*d-h*ouse but with the tongue against the teeth.
n–as in *n*or but with the tongue against the teeth.
p –like the *p* in *p*ine.
ph –like the *ph* in *ph*ilosopher.
b –like the *b* in *b*ird.
bh –like the *bh* in ru*b-h*ard.
m –like the *m* in *m*other.
y –like the *j* in *j*aw. য
y –like the *y* in *y*ear. য়
r –like the *r* in *r*un.
l –like the *l* in *l*aw.
v –like the *b* in *b*ird or like the *w* in d*w*arf.
ś, ṣ –like the *sh* in *sh*op.
s –like the *s* in *s*un.
h–like the *h* in *h*ome.

This is a general guide to Bengali pronunciation. The Bengali transliterations in this book accurately show the original Bengali spelling of the text. One should note, however, that in Bengali, as in English, spelling is not always a true indication of how a word is pronounced. Tape recordings of His Divine Grace A. C. Bhaktivedanta Swami Prabhupāda chanting the original Bengali verses are available from the International Society for Krishna Consciousness, 3764 Watseka Ave., Los Angeles, California 90034.

Index of Bengali and Sanskrit Verses

This index constitutes a complete alphabetical listing of the first and third line of each four-line verse and both lines of each two-line verse in *Śrī Caitanya-caritāmṛta*. In the first column the transliteration is given, and in the second and third columns respectively the chapter-verse references and page number for each verse are to be found.

A

C

D

E

G

H

K

U

V

Y

General Index

Numerals in bold type indicate references to *Śrī Caitanya-caritāmṛta's* verses. Numerals in regular type are references to its purports.

A

Absolute Truth
as the Supreme Lord, 20
See also: Kṛṣṇa, Supreme Lord
Ācārya
one should not repeat writing of previous, 74
See also: Spiritual master
Activities
Caitanya can't engage in material, **184**
of conditioned souls, 187
Acyutānanda
as *saṅkīrtana* dancer, **136**
Adānta-gobhir viśatāṁ
quoted, 187
Advaita Ācārya
as prominent devotee of Caitanya, **116**
as *saṅkīrtana* dancer, **131**
chants "Hari bol", **157**
dances in first *kīrtana* group, **132**
engaged in mock fight with Nityānanda, **92-98**
feels Caitanya's touch, **129**
formed Śāntipura *saṅkīrtana* party, **136**
Advaita-siddhānta
explained, 95
Āiṭoṭā
Caitanya took rest at, **256**
Amṛta-pravāha-bhāṣya
Thirteenth Chapter summarized in, 113
Twelfth Chapter summarized in, 1
Anger
experienced by three types of women, **290-292**
of Śrīvāsa Ṭhākura and Haricandana, **160-161**
two types of, **300**
Anubhāṣya
quoted on materialists, 31
Anyābhilāṣitā-śūnyaṁ
quoted, 65, 184
Ārādhanānāṁ sarveṣāṁ
quoted, 20
Arcā-avatāra
See: Arcā-vigraha
Asahyā māna-nirbandhe
quoted, 299
Asamānordhva-mādhurya
quoted, 107
Association
of *guru* achieved by the Lord's mercy, 123
Athāpi te deva padāmbuja
quoted, 122
Atmā vai putra utpanna
quoted, 29
Austerity
as material enjoyment, 65

B

Balagaṇḍi
Jagannātha car stops at, **215**
Balarāma
ascends Ratha car, **125**
as Nityānanda, **158**
watches Caitanya dancing, **163**
Bhagavad-gītā
cited on perfect vision, 31
quoted on consciousness, 97
quoted on destination of envious, 66
quoted on escaping *māyā,* 247
quoted on fruit of devotional service, 231
quoted on Kṛṣṇa's superiority, 96
quoted on returning back to Godhead, 196
Bhagavān
as part of absolute knowledge, 95

H

I

J

N

Nṛsiṁha temple
cleansed by Caitanya, **68**

O

Opulences
of Kṛṣṇa maintained to please Yadus, **198**

P

Padma Purāṇa
quoted on worship, 20
Padyāvalī
quoted on Caitanya as servant of the servant, 154
quoted on Rādhārāṇī's remembrance of Kṛṣṇa, 173
Paṇḍitāḥ sama-darśinaḥ
quoted, 31
Pāṇḍu-vijaya
ropes broke during, **341**
seen by Caitanya and associates, **115**
Parama karuṇa, pahuṅ dui jana
quoted, 232
Paramānanda Purī
receives garland and sandalwood, **129**
Paramātmā
as part of absolute knowledge, 95
See also: Supersoul
Paramparā
system strictly observed by Gauḍīya Vaiṣṇavas, 60-61
Parāsya śaktir vividhaiva śrūyate
quoted, 145
Pastimes of Caitanya
as uncommon, **146**
Kṛṣṇa consciousness awakened by seeing, **110**
Sahasra-vadana cannot reach limits of, **345**
the Lord forgets Himself in course of, **145**
variegatedness of exhibited, 142
Pastimes of Kṛṣṇa
as unlimited, **320**
Pastimes of Kṛṣṇa
Caitanya always thinking of, **260**
compared with Caitanya's, **146**
no fault in, **282**
remembered by Caitanya, **80-81**
with wives of *brāhmaṇas* mentioned, 16-17
Pleasure
in *parakīya-rasa* superior to that in *svakīya-rasa,* 126
Lord Jagannātha's mind filled with, **127**
Potencies
līlā-śakti as one of Caitanya's, **145**
pure devotees understand the Lord's inconceivable, **139**
Prabodhānanda Sarasvatī
as author of *Caitanya-candrāmṛta,* 232
quoted on immediate elevation, 35
Prahlāda Mahārāja
as advanced devotee, 96
prayed to become servant of the servant, 233
quoted on materialists, 90
Prakaṭeha ānibe satvara
quoted, 197
Prasāda
distributed to beggars, **246-247**
offered to Lord Jagannātha, **237-241**
offering and distribution of encourages spiritual master, 242
serving of, **243-247**
taken with Kṛṣṇa, 196
Pratāparudra Mahārāja
allows Pāṇḍu-vijaya to be seen by Caitanya, **116**
anxious to meet Caitanya, **3**
appeals to devotees, **4-5**
as King of Orissa, **3**
Caitanya picked up by, **209-210**
cleanses road, **120-**122, 232
converted to ecstatic love, **140**
could see Caitanya's tricks, **141-**142
decides to become mendicant, **6, 10**
ecstatic symptoms exhibited by, **229, 254**
embraced by Caitanya, **228**
entered garden in dress of Vaiṣṇava, **225**

R

T

U

Y

The Author

His Divine Grace A. C. Bhaktivedanta Swami Prabhupāda appeared in this world in 1896 in Calcutta, India. He first met his spiritual master, Śrīla Bhaktisiddhānta Sarasvatī Gosvāmī, in Calcutta in 1922. Bhaktisiddhānta Sarasvatī, a prominent devotional scholar and the founder of sixty-four Gauḍīya Maṭhas (Vedic Institutes), liked this educated young man and convinced him to dedicate his life to teaching Vedic knowledge. Śrīla Prabhupāda became his student, and eleven years later (1933) at Allahabad he became his formally initiated disciple.

At their first meeting, in 1922, Śrīla Bhaktisiddhānta Sarasvatī Ṭhākura requested Śrīla Prabhupāda to broadcast Vedic knowledge through the English language. In the years that followed, Śrīla Prabhupāda wrote a commentary on the *Bhagavad-gītā,* assisted the Gauḍīya Maṭha in its work and, in 1944, without assistance, started an English fortnightly magazine, edited it, typed the manuscripts and checked the galley proofs. He even distributed the individual copies freely and struggled to maintain the publication. Once begun, the magazine never stopped; it is now being continued by his disciples in the West.

Recognizing Śrīla Prabhupāda's philosophical learning and devotion, the Gauḍīya Vaiṣṇava Society honored him in 1947 with the title "Bhaktivedanta." In 1950, at the age of fifty-four, Śrīla Prabhupāda retired from married life, and four years later he adopted the *vānaprastha* (retired) order to devote more time to his studies and writing. Śrīla Prabhupāda traveled to the holy city of Vṛndāvana, where he lived in very humble circumstances in the historic medieval temple of Rādhā-Dāmodara. There he engaged for several years in deep study and writing. He accepted the renounced order of life (*sannyāsa*) in 1959. At Rādhā-Dāmodara, Śrīla Prabhupāda began work on his life's masterpiece: a multivolume translation and commentary on the eighteen thousand verse *Śrīmad-Bhāgavatam* (*Bhāgavata Purāṇa*). He also wrote *Easy Journey to Other Planets.*

After publishing three volumes of *Bhāgavatam,* Śrīla Prabhupāda came to the United States, in 1965, to fulfill the mission of his spiritual master. Since that time, His Divine Grace has written over forty volumes of authoritative translations, commentaries and summary studies of the philosophical and religious classics of India.

In 1965, when he first arrived by freighter in New York City, Śrīla Prabhupāda was practically penniless. It was after almost a year of great difficulty that he established the International Society for Krishna Consciousness in July of 1966. Under his careful guidance, the Society has grown within a decade to a worldwide confederation of almost one hundred *āśramas,* schools, temples, institutes and farm communities.

In 1968, Śrīla Prabhupāda created New Vṛndāvana, an experimental Vedic community in the hills of West Virginia. Inspired by the success of New Vṛndāvana, now a thriving farm community of more than one thousand acres, his students have since founded several similar communities in the United States and abroad.

In 1972, His Divine Grace introduced the Vedic system of primary and secondary education in the West by founding the *Gurukula* school in Dallas, Texas. The school began with 3 children in 1972, and by the beginning of 1975 the enrollment had grown to 150.

Śrīla Prabhupāda has also inspired the construction of a large international center at Śrīdhāma Māyāpur in West Bengal, India, which is also the site for a planned Institute of Vedic Studies. A similar project is the magnificent Kṛṣṇa-Balarāma Temple and International Guest House in Vṛndāvana, India. These are centers where Westerners can live to gain firsthand experience of Vedic culture.

Śrīla Prabhupāda's most significant contribution, however, is his books. Highly respected by the academic community for their authoritativeness, depth and clarity, they are used as standard textbooks in numerous college courses. His writings have been translated into eleven languages. The Bhaktivedanta Book Trust, established in 1972 exclusively to publish the works of His Divine Grace, has thus become the world's largest publisher of books in the field of Indian religion and philosophy. Its latest project is the publishing of Śrīla Prabhupāda's most recent work: a seventeen-volume translation and commentary—completed by Śrīla Prabhupāda in only eighteen months—on the Bengali religious classic *Śrī Caitanya-caritāmṛta.*

In the past ten years, in spite of his advanced age, Śrīla Prabhupāda has circled the globe twelve times on lecture tours that have taken him to six continents. In spite of such a vigorous schedule, Śrīla Prabhupāda continues to write prolifically. His writings constitute a veritable library of Vedic philosophy, religion, literature and culture.